THE ADVENTURES OF CAPTAIN JACK JOHNSON

High Seas and Romance

As told by Captain Jack V. Johnson

WRITTEN AND COMPILED BY
Pamela L. Doerr
With Iris Beresford Johnson

© 2013 by Pamela L. Doerr.

All rights reserved.
This book may not be reproduced in whole or in part by any means (with the exception of short quotes for the purpose of review) without the permission of the publisher.

Printed & Published in the United States of America.
Published by Pamela L. Doerr.
Second printing, 2014.

Every effort has been made to give full credit for materials reproduced in this book. If anything has been inadvertently overlooked, the author extends her full apology. Ship names have been researched to verify spelling and pertinent details. With the passage of time, it is possible that some details are incorrect. Our apologies if there are any errors. Please send additional information to Pamela L. Doerr for inclusion in second printing.

Front Cover Photograph:
Captain Jack V. Johnson at helm of 42′ ketch *Mahina Tiara* off Cape Horn bound for Antarctica via the Falklands.
February 5, 1995.

ISBN 978-0-9790169-8-1
Library of Congress Number Pending

Printed by Econoprint
Billings, Montana

For additional information, contact:
Pamela L. Doerr
Women Making a Difference LLC
953 S Rebecca Drive
Palmer, Alaska 99645

ak.2109_productions@yahoo.com

Words to Live By

I followed my father's advice all my life:

"BE THE FIRST UP,

THE FIRST ON DECK,

THE FIRST ALOFT,

THE FIRST ON THE YARDARM,

AND ALWAYS SAY 'SIR.'"
~Jacob H. Johnson, né Skriffvaars~

I found you could apply it
to 'most anything
you do.
~Jack V. Johnson~

Knowing Jack made you realize that life was meant to be lived.
CAPTAIN ROBERT "BOB" CROWLEY, AMHS RETIRED

In Beagle Channel, Chile, South America. February 1995.

Tributes to Jack

*I must admit that Jack is indeed larger than life.
I worked for a number of years as an Able Bodied seaman
while he was the Chief Mate on the AMHS ferry MV* Tustumena.
*We spent many hours on watch sailing
across the Gulf of Alaska from Seward to Kodiak.
One of his nicknames was "Black Jack from Kodiak"
after some of his escapades in the Kodiak area.
Jack has a knack for finding adventure and the ability
to recall it in detail. I was always thoroughly entertained
by his stories and reminisces of his "many" lives that included
his time in French Indochina, his narrow escape from mainland
China when the communists took over,
his time in the British Army as an under-aged recruit,
spending time in Russia after his ship was sunk,
and then sailing to Palestine
on the* Exodus *at the beginnings of the Israeli state.
One of Jack's other nicknames was "Square-rigger Johnson"
after his stories of sailing on some
of the last square-rigged sailing ships.
I, of course, took this with a grain of salt
until we were in shipyard in Victoria, B.C.,
and, lo and behold, we were at the Maritime Museum
and there was a photo from the* Pamir
*with Jack sitting amongst the crew.
Knowing Jack made you realize that life was meant to be lived.
Thank God for his memory to be able to recall it in such detail
and having the gift to be able to relate it
to those of us who got such pleasure from his stories.
He is larger than life, literally and figuratively,
such that he was always mistaken for being the Captain
when sailing as Chief Mate.
I can't wait to read his book as I struggle to recall all the stories
I was told all those many years ago.*

CAPTAIN ROBERT "BOB" CROWLEY, AMHS RETIRED

Tributes to Jack

*Jack Johnson is one of the greatest men I ever knew,
I looked up to him like a real-life Super Hero,
even when he took it upon himself to straighten me out.*
JON STETSON

*Jack was our hero, a tall, husky man,
with a handlebar moustache, stiffly waxed to sharp tips,
eating a hearty breakfast every morning
in the officer's mess room telling wonderful sea stories—
the kind of seaman we can never forget.
Our chief mate was a salty figure, easy-going, friendly,
helpful, and talkative with a calm voice, a cheerful aspect,
and a warm smile that swept through the crew.*
CAPTAIN BILL HOPKINS, AMHS RETIRED

*The first time into Cold Bay is etched in my brain.
Captain Hofstad docking.
Black Jack on the stern to position the loading ramp,
and the wind blowing a gale on the starboard quarter
and the dark of night.
Everyone is shouting and the wind sucking your voice out.
I'm being told to take up on the quarter spring line,
which was tight as a piano wire.
Get tied up with the ramp over the bull rail and something
like a Dodge Valiant that had to be pushed up the ramp.
I can still picture it and the tension.
I know we kept adding ports and going further west.*
CAPTAIN ROBERT "BOB" CROWLEY, AMHS RETIRED

Tributes to Jack

SUBJECT: JACKMAGIC

*So, Jack, two or three of the crew,
and myself were in the wheelhouse.
Jack noticed one of the men (a guy new to the crew)
was wearing a sheath knife.
Jack mentioned to the man,
"That knife was probably too large to be allowed."
The crewman pulled the knife from its sheath
and mumbled something like,
"Nobody could take my knife away from me!"
Jack was casually slipping off his old work jacket
during all this and, with no fanfare,
did something magical and super-fast,
resulting with the knife ending up in Jack's hand
and the crewman howling about the horrible pain in his hand.
I've been proud to be friends with Jack for over 30 years
and it's always been great to witness
Jack pulling rabbits out of hats,
even with the use of an old work jacket.
All me best,*
CAPTAIN CAL CARY

Table of Contents

Acknowledgements XII
Author's Note XIV
Introduction XVI
Prologue—Hurled into History XVII

PART I   1926 – 1942   1

  1   The Captain Jack Club 1
  2   One Year in the Iron Lung 10
  3   Out to Sea at 13 16
  4   Crossing the Equator 32
  5   Stranded in Alexandria at 14 38
  6   Gordon Highlander at 16 40

PART II   1942 - 1945   50

  7   Him or Me 50
  8   Kathy 52
  9   Malaria & Tanker-Shankers 60
  10 Martinis with Hemingway 64
  11 Camels & Pukka Knives 68
  12 Sergeant in Russian Army at 18 76

PART III   1945 – 1947   89

  13 Off to Okinawa 89
  14 Nothing Like a Brother 95
  15 Designer, Embalmer & Diver 101
  16 Jumping Ship 107

PART IV   1947   109

  17 Crewmember on the Exodus at 21 109

| PART V | 1947 – 1949 | 120 |

18 French Foreign Legion 120

19 Margherita 132

| PART VI | 1949 - 1953 | 142 |

20 Coming to Terms with Life 142

21 Thelma 165

22 Jailed in Saudi Arabia 178

23 Florette 180

| PART VII | 1953 - 1960 | 186 |

24 Back Home in Alaska 186

25 Laura Belle 192

| PART VIII | 1960 - 1964 | 204 |

26 Mischievous Ways 204

27 More Hijinks 213

28 Fishing, But Catching Bears 219

| PART IX | 1964 - 1972 | 223 |

29 Connie 223

30 Fishing Partners 233

31 Serving in the Six Day War 237

32 Flying for a Change 240

| PART X | 1972 - 1980 | 248 |

33 Iris 248

34 Honeymoon, Alaska Style 259

35 Settling in Seward 265

36 The Hanging Judge of Seward 272

| PART XI | 1980 - 1992 | 280 |

37 Tustumena 280

38 Pilot for Southwest 287

	39	The Exxon Valdez Oil Spill	305
	40	The KGB	309

Part XII   1992 – 2006   319

	41	Telling Stories to Michener	319
	42	Around Cape Horn—Again	327
	43	Hard Sailing at 75	337

PART XIII   2006 - 2010   339

	44	Captain Ike & Me	339

PART XIV   2006 - 2013   359

	45	Poor Old Retired Pilot	359

PART XV   Appendices   365

	46	Brother Bucko Tramps at Sea	365
	47	Scourge of the Bering Sea	366
	48	Affidavit from Oscar G. Callow	369
	49	Foc'sle Chatter	370
	50	Sailed Under 18 Different Flags	372

About the Author 374

Acknowledgements

This project has had many turns, and I have a lot of people to thank for all their contributions. *The Adventures of Captain Jack Johnson* would not have come to fruition if it weren't for Captain Jack's eidetic memory and his wife Iris' additional prodding and editing, as well as a host of others. My sincere thanks go to:

- Ruthann Crosby Cleeves, my business partner, for her constant support and continual encouragement. It was her emphatic urging, "that I must meet Captain Jack!" that perpetuated this entire journey. It was *bashert*—meant to be.
- Rabbi Yosef Greenberg, for recognizing the importance of this project from its beginning, and for, not only being part of the process, but also part of the story.
- Alex Bortnick, for providing a platform for Captain Jack to share his stories with the East High History classes.
- Dave Stroh, for filming a short documentary with Captain Jack in our makeshift studio.
- Scott Cleeves, for spending an afternoon filming.
- Clarence Goward, for spending hours in production and editing the documentary.
- Deborah Stone, for that first interview with Captain Jack.
- My aunt, Carolyn McKennan, for proofreading and editing.
- My mother, Barbara Carr, for countless hours traveling with me to sit with Captain Jack and Iris, even during some of the worst Alaska weather imaginable, and encouragement.
- My father, George Carr, for encouraging me to follow my instincts, and instilled my love for a good story.
- My running partner, Cindy Charlton, who trained and accompanied me on 10Ks and half-marathons, Dirty Dashes, Spartan Runs, which allowed me time away from this project when I was discouraged that it would never come to an end.

- My producers, Rob Moran and Zen Gesner, for patiently waiting for this book to be completed so they can take the Captain Jack story to the next level! It's all yours boys!
- My children, spouses included; Jesse and Linnzi, Chelsea and Dave, Aimee and Ray, David and Teah, and Andrew, who provided me vehicles as I bounced back and forth across the Canadian borders, and coast to coast, gave me a place to rest my head, kept the home fires burning and animals cared for in my absence, covered my fitness classes, and gave me rides at 4:30 a.m. to catch early morning flights in and out of Montana, Alaska, and Philadelphia.
- My husband Mitch, who put up with all the craziness it takes to write and publish a book. And financed this project from the very beginning. I couldn't have done it without you!
- Iris Johnson, for her additional editing and prodding for stories and accuracy. You are valuable to this project.
- And the man himself, Captain Jack, for entrusting me to tell his wonderful story for him.

The book *The Adventures of Captain Jack Johnson* isn't my story—it is Captain Jack's story. I took those wonderful sea tales and wove them into a tapestry for all the world to share. I am confident that readers of all ages will feel a kinship with him since it is essentially a love story above all else. Captain Jack, in fact, was just in love with life.

May you be encouraged and motivated to embrace your life in pure Captain Jack fashion, just as I was upon hearing that first sea story. Let's grab hands, and one, two, three…jump! Man overboard!

Pamela L. Doerr

December 1, 2013

Author's Note

I am an Alaskan, and it was the Alaskan spirit that drew me to the incredible story of Captain Jack Johnson. Having been raised in the harshness, ruggedness, and beauty of the Last Frontier, and having continued the tradition with all five of my children, it is my hope to bring readers into the romance of Captain Jack's adventures because they, too, portrayed harshness, ruggedness, and beauty. And though his personal adventures extend well beyond the 49th state's perimeters, Jack's Alaskan spirit permeates each page.

Brought up in Alaska in the heart of the Matanuska Valley, I am what Captain Jack would call a landlubber. My husband, Mitch, was an Alaska State Fish and Wildlife Trooper. His work moved us around the great land, often from fishing village to fishing village. Our family lived in various coastal communities such as Dillingham, Cordova, Juneau, and even as far reaching as Dutch Harbor in the Aleutian Islands; yet all this coastal living had not prepared me for Captain Jack Johnson's amazing adventures.

Pursuing a documentary about Alaska Airlines, Operation Magic Carpet, the 1949 rescue of Yemen Jews, I found myself caught up in the 1947 Haganah ship *Exodus* story, an event that helped launch the nation Israel. In April 2009, I was introduced to a tall, handsome, charismatic fellow, impeccably tailored, with a handlebar moustache, a small Israeli flag pinned to his lapel, and a glint of mischief in his eye! Captain Jack Johnson's reputation had preceded him, and it wasn't long before we had a camera rolling and capturing this sailor's remarkable story on film.

Never having been one to back away from a challenge, I immediately followed up our interview with another conversation, and before too long we had scheduled our first taping session to gather information for a book. Logistically, this wasn't easy since my husband had purchased a retirement home in Montana—where he forgot to retire! Soon, we were bouncing back and forth between the Big Sky Country and *Alakshak*, which means *great lands* or *peninsula*. With my husband working in Alaska and me spending time at our Montana refuge, I had time to devote to the Captain Jack Project. I spent several years going back and forth from Montana to Alaska to sit with Captain Jack recording his sea stories. I'd gather the information and scurry back to my Western retreat. We arranged a weekly phone interview that I recorded with my trusty Blackberry, transferred to my computer, and later transcribed. Drafts were passed between Captain Jack, his wife, Iris, and me.

I had originally planned to write a book about a sailor's involvement with *Exodus*, but the work took on a life of its own and became *The Adventures of Captain Jack Johnson*—a love story depicting Captain Jack Johnson's passion for the sea, passion for survival, passion for women, and passion for Johnny Walker Red Scotch whisky. One chapter of Jack's life encompasses more adventures than most of us experience in a lifetime. Yes, there is a chapter regarding the 1947 Haganah ship *Exodus*, but that was just one port of call in *The Adventures of Captain Jack Johnson*.

I am thankful for my husband's patience and encouragement, since this four-year project took on a life of its own; with me bouncing back and forth from Alaska and Montana. I spent hours at my computer transcribing, editing, proofing, and reworking each taped session until I felt we had exhausted every angle.

My recording sessions with Captain Jack were always insightful; yet in typical Captain Jack fashion, I would be gathering up my belongings after a several hour taping session, only for him to nonchalantly throw out a randomly bizarre statement like, "Did I ever tell you that I met Hemingway?"

To which I'd reply, "No! Hemingway, as in Ernest?" And before you know it, I'd be hastily trying to record the answer and take notes and inevitably discover, not only did he meet Ernest Hemingway, but also they were drinking buddies and had developed a close friendship of many years, numerous letters, and frequent visits. He would recount it all in typical Captain Jack detail, complete with dates, humor, and intrigue. It has been a fascinating voyage with the Captain, as he piloted the story in vivid recall.

Introduction

Captain Jack V. Johnson went to sea at the age of 13. He has visited practically every port around the world and in Alaska, and he has sailed around Cape Horn twice in a square-rigger. He has survived German air raids and torpedo attacks, served in the British Army and the French Foreign Legion, liberated a German concentration camp in Poland while serving in the Russian Army, and shook hands with the Americans across the River Elbe at the end of World War II while in Russian uniform. He spent 12 days in the Haganah ship *Exodus*, the ship that launched the nation Israel, and he was in the Second Armored Brigade of the Israeli Defense Force during the Six Day War.

He has made friends all over the world, fallen in love all over the world, and drunk Johnnie Walker Red Label Scotch Whisky all over the world. Jack shared a weekend with Bette Davis, martinis with Ernest Hemingway, and vodka with Vladimir Putin. He has danced the Viennese Waltz with Imelda Marcos and shared stories with James Michener—just to name a few of his adventures. Recognized in ports far and away, Jack was regularly told, "Jack, if you went to the moon, there'd be someone who knew you!"

He was raised in Kodiak, Alaska, until polio threatened his health at the age of seven, and his father moved the family to Seattle, Washington. He spent two years in the Children's Orthopedic Hospital, with one year in an iron lung.

At the age of 87, Jack's reputation is worldwide. He has been featured in various newspapers, magazines, media sites, and news broadcasts from Alaska to Israel. He resides in Seward, Alaska, with his wife Iris. They have been married 39 years.

This is Captain Jack Johnson's life story.

Prologue—Hurled into History

By the time we got to Marseille, I made the decision. I had had enough of J. Preston Thomas, chief mate of the *James Ford Rhodes*. More than enough! I wasn't going to take any more of his shit! I was bosun, Johnny Fogle was carpenter, and we decided to jump ship. It would be a decision that would hurl us into history. It might not have been our finest hour, but we broke into the paint locker, took several gallons of paint, sold them over the side to the bumboats, and got a few francs for them. Then we sold some mooring lines and got a lot of francs for them. We managed to pilfer some linen and what not, until we had a pretty good bankroll. We fetched up staying in a small hotel on the waterfront. Of course, as soon as the ship left port, it was no time at all before we were in the arms of some lovely ladies. The girl on my arm was Michelle Aragonne or "Mickey."

"Ah, you crazy, Jack, you crazy!" was her running response to my many shenanigans.

We were dancing at a nightclub when three sinister-looking guys approached our table, complete with trench coats, looking something like Gestapo agents right out of WW II. This was June of 1947. I was 21 years old. Stopping at our table, one of them asked in very good English, "You guys are sailors?"

"Yeah," we responded, a little cocky, still taken aback at their unusual dress, "we're sailors."

Their line of questioning continued, "You're not working?"

"No, we're not working. We're enjoying ourselves on the beach. Why all the questions? Can we do something for you?" I shot back smugly.

"We're looking for a couple sailors. Would you like a job?"

Both Johnny and I knew it would be a good strategy to get out of town, considering some of our previous shady dealings. "What is it?" I asked.

"We're taking Jewish refugees into Palestine," they said, "and we need experienced sailors and crew because we are building up a little fleet here. We're out recruiting. Would you be interested? We've had our eye on you for several days."

Johnny and I looked at each other, grinning. Then our most important question. "What does it pay?" I asked. They named a price that was about $1,000 round trip, which in 1947 were *very* good wages! The plan was to make it into Palestine with a shipload of refugees and then make it on back to France and load up another one, and so forth. "Yeah, that sounds good. Where's the action?" I questioned.

"Well, we'd like you to stay here in Marseille and work some of these vessels getting them ready."

I was disappointed, "I don't want to do that."

Johnny said, "I'm not interested either. If you don't have anything going out right now, we're not interested."

They looked at each other, and the tall one said, "We have a ship going out right now. The SS *President Warfield* is docked at Port Sète. We renamed her *Exodus*."

This got my interest—a ship ready to go! "When's she sailing?"

"As soon as they get loaded."

"Okay, that sounds good. Let's go. That's where the action is." (I had no idea *Exodus* would become known as *The Ship that Launched a Nation*, as written by Ruth Gruber.) I'd just as soon be up and going than sitting around waiting. "I'll take that job," I said, pushing my chair back ready to get up, "as long as the pay's the same."

They seemed pleased. I extended my hand and shook on it. Johnny felt the nudge on his arm and the influence of a new love. He struck a deal to stay in port after all, getting things ready on the home front. The Gestapo-looking guys said they would send someone over to get me the next morning. Well, that didn't have to cut into the night's celebration, so we partied... and just like that, I became part of the historic *Exodus* crew.

Part I   1926 - 1942

The Captain Jack Club

*The world is teeming with Captain Jacks
as well as Jack Johnsons, both real and fictional.
I hope history will be kind to my contribution
to the Captain Jack Club.
~Captain Jack V. Johnson~*

My given name is Jack. Jack V. Johnson. Some have referred to me as Jacque, Slim, Big Jack, Jock (Scottish for "Jack"), Ivan Ivanovich (Russian for "Jack Johnson"), Gianni (Italian for "Jack"), Black Jack from Kodiak, Square-rigger Johnson, Hurricane Johnson, Bull Moose Johnson, and even Death Johnson. I'm sure a few have even labeled me jackass, pain-in-the-ass, or son-of-a-bitch, and god knows I earned and deserved them all. These days, most people refer to me simply as Captain Jack.

The world is teeming with Captain Jacks as well as Jack Johnsons, both real and fictional. I hope history will be kind to my contribution to the Captain Jack Club. To be certain, it is a privilege to be among those bearing the name Captain Jack and just as honorable to bear the name Jack Johnson.

Johnson is a common name today. Over 80 years ago, Jack was also fairly common. So, naming your son Jack with the last name of Johnson would have been an ordinary event except, like most things in my life, nothing is what it seems. And nothing is ordinary. There's an interesting story of how I got my name. How, you might say, I won the honor. It was my father who initiated my induction into this elite club, by declaring my name even before I was conceived.

The story goes something like this. Father was a bit of a gambler, which included a fancy for professional boxing. While at

Part I The Early Years   1926-1942

a boxing match featuring the champion prizefighter, Jack Johnson,[1] Father wagered a bet and a decree! Whether it was the prizefighter's "golden smile," as he had several gold teeth, or his amazing reputation in the ring, or maybe the coincidence of both of them having the same surname Johnson—something prompted Father to make a wager. He placed a bet on Jack Johnson and added a personal vow. He announced, "If he wins this bout and I have another boy, I'm going to name him Jack."

Well, Jack won, and Father kept his promise. It took a few years before another son came into the Johnson family, but in 1926, Father made good on his bet. That's how I got my name.

I guess you could say my life started on a gamble and ended with a fight. It's true. I've never backed down from either of them. Being named after a champion prizefighter was apropos. I have had to scrap and fight myself out of many situations. My survival might be considered luck, possibly destiny, or maybe fate. Kismet, you might say. But I like to think of it as just one hell of a ride!

I was born April 12, 1926, in Kodiak, Alaska. Well, kind of. I still call Kodiak my birthplace and Alaska my home, though technically it might not be accurate. It boils down to this: my parents conceived me in Kodiak. A few months before I was born, my mother was having some difficulty with her pregnancy. Father made the decision to put her on a steamship bound for Seattle. So, officially, I was born in Seattle, Washington, in the Swedish Hospital. Within a couple of months, we returned to Kodiak. Mother insisted I be christened and baptized into the Russian Orthodox Church. Baptisms, weddings, and funerals were a good excuse for the priest to get his nose stuck in a bottle of brandy or, in this case, a small cask of brandy furnished by my father. Who knows if it was the brandy or just oversight, but when Father Kashaveroff wrote out my birth certificate in Russian, it translated that I was born in Kodiak. At one time, I had two birth certificates: one from Seattle, Washington, King County, and the other from Kodiak, Territory of Alaska. It took some doing, but eventually I got it all straightened out. I have used the Seattle birth certificate

---

[1] The first African-American to hold the heavyweight title, and whom some critics have labeled the "greatest of them all."

Part I   The Early Years   1926-1942

for convenience, but I have always claimed Kodiak as my birthplace. After all, who am I to argue with a Russian Orthodox priest?

My parents arrived in Kodiak by unique circumstances. My father was a Russian Finn. He came from a long line of sea captains. He wound up on the west coast of the United States back at the turn of the century as a sea captain of one of his father's ships. While loading lumber in Port Blakely, Washington, on Bainbridge Island across Puget Sound from Seattle, he heard that the Klondike Gold Rush was going on Up North. Of course, as all young men at that time, he had visions of immense wealth and adventure, but unfortunately, he didn't have enough money to bankroll him to the Klondike. Being a ship's captain gave him prestige. He was sort of like a god. So, he cashed in on that prestige and sold his father's ship.

Along with the grubstake he obtained to head north for the Klondike, he also got a death warrant from his father for selling the ship. In an attempt to avoid the wrath of his father, he changed his name from Skriffvaars[2] to Johnson. Skriffvaars was the name given to my father's family by the monks when they came and Christianized that part of the world. My cousin, Runar Koping, maintains that my grandmother was of Russian Jewish descent. In any case, my father changed his name to Jacob Johnson. Jacob H. Johnson to be precise. The "H" in his name stood for absolutely nothing! Someone suggested he needed a middle initial, so he took one, and from that time forth, he was known as Jacob H. Johnson. He wanted something common to avoid being found, but my uncles still managed to locate him.

From the stories I heard when I was young, my father often did quite well financially. This was one of those times. He did well in his quest for Klondike gold and fetched up in San Francisco, living the good life. There his brothers, my uncle Oskar and my uncle Einar, found him enjoying his success. They came from Finland with one mandate from their father: to find their brother Jacob and persuade him to return home and face the

---

[2] Skriffvaars means "the scribes," those who write.

Part I The Early Years   1926-1942

consequences. They did their best to convince him to return to Finland, but my father refused. He knew if he returned, he'd face the wrath of his father, Johannas Skriffvaars, for selling the ship. In my grandfather's strict disciplinarian manner, there would be no mincing of words, and punishment would be swift. Father was certain if he returned, his father would kill him. He was not far from the truth.

My grandfather did come to the West Coast with the intent to find his ship and mete out the harsh consequences. It was the code of the sea. In the West, a man could be hung for stealing a man's horse, and for a Finnish sailor, it was the same for his ship. You don't mess with a man's ship! Fortunately for me, my father's father never found him, and Father never returned to Finland. And to add to his good fortune, his brothers joined him in his quest for fortune. Upon observing my father's success, it wasn't long before my uncles had gold dust in their eyes. They, too, never returned to Finland. I guess I owe it to gold fever that I exist today. After my uncles realized they couldn't talk my father into going back to Finland, they shifted focus. As the old saying goes, "if you can't beat 'em, join 'em." That's just what they did. The Gold Rush in Alaska was going full bore in Nome. It wasn't long before they all were heading north to Alaska. The rush was on!

Once the brothers arrived in Nome, they discovered the choicest claims were taken. They had to go east to stake their claims, over by Elim. Father always said the mother lode was some place around Elim. The mother lode was never found, but the brothers did quite well. Cashing in, they sold their claims and headed for Seattle. All three of them invested in downtown Seattle real estate, which proved just as lucrative.

They made quite a team. My uncle Oskar was considered one of the more levelheaded ones. He invested well and kept his wits about him. My uncle Einar was another story. He fancied himself a dandy, a real ladies' man, and was referred to as "somewhat of a playboy." He was a giant of a man, standing more than seven feet tall. With pockets full of cash and an eye for the ladies, he was living large and free. Father was kind of carefree, too. With their investments tied up in real estate, it was the perfect opportunity to

Part I   The Early Years   1926-1942

revert back to their first love, the sea. Father wound up with the Grace Line Company and remained with it until he eventually retired as Senior Captain, with the honorary title of Commodore.

L to R: My great-grandfather, my maternal grandfather Marcus Jonssen, and two uncles. Despite my best efforts,
I still haven't discovered many details about my family's history.

When Father and his brothers returned to Seattle, they discovered the big fishing companies needed masters to take their fully loaded sailing ships north with cannery supplies and workers. They accepted the challenge. They all headed north to Alaska to the salmon canneries in Kodiak and other locations with cannery supplies; they would return to Seattle loaded down with canned salmon. Father and his brothers became masters of several of those sailing ships, taking them Up North for Libby, McNeill and Libby,[3] and Alaska Packers, as well as other big fishing companies.

---

[3] One of the world's leading producers of canned foods.

Part I   The Early Years   1926-1942

In 1906, another piece of good fortune came Father's way. During one of those trips Up North, while his ship was anchored at Karluk,[4] he met and became engaged to my mother, Thea Marie Jonssen. My mother's father was a Cossack. He changed their name to Jonssen to escape the Russian Tsar. (I have always suspected contonism in my family lineage, the forcible conscription of under age boys from the Jewish population.) The church records state: *"The Russian taking the name of Jonssen, Marcus."* I was once in Fredrikstad, Norway, and saw the record with my own eyes.

When Father met Mother in 1906, Father was the master of both *Star of Greenland* and *Star of Alaska*. In 1909, three years after my mother and my father met, they sailed south to Seattle and wed. Out of that marriage came three boys and three girls: my brothers Theodore "Ted" and George, and my sisters Ethel, Thelma, and Ida Virginia "Ivy." Then there was me. The baby, and totally spoiled rotten!

Jackie Boy. Age 17 months.

Up until I was seven years old, we lived in Kodiak, except for the year when I was five that we spent out on the Aleutian Chain, in Unalaska, Dutch Harbor. The sea and the coastal regions of Alaska were my stomping grounds—the place I called home. Out of all my voyages to and from exotic ports all around the world, I have spent most of my life trying to get back to the coastal regions of Alaska.

---

[4] Karluk was a little village on the southwestern point of Kodiak. The Karluk River was once one of the biggest red salmon runs in the world.

Part I   The Early Years   1926-1942

Father continued sailing with Grace Line, but he was involved in fish canneries, gold mines, and timber in Alaska, as well. Each job posed a new adventure for a young lad like me.

Growing up in a Russian family in Kodiak in the late 1920s involved me in many traditions. One was the celebration of the Russian Orthodox Christmas. The tradition celebrated Christmas for 13 days beginning on January 7 (as noted on the Julian[5] calendar) instead of December 25.

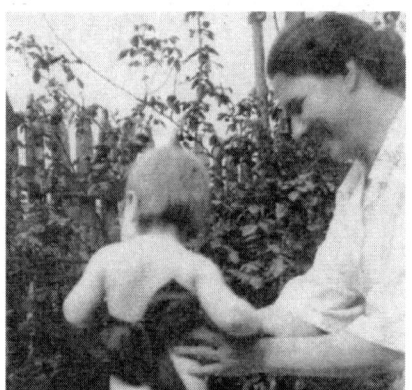

My mother Thea and me. Christmas, 1926.

We practiced the tradition of "starring," going from house to house carrying a large, twirling, brightly lit star on a long shaft. Now days, batteries light the star, but it used to be lit with candles, so you had to be careful. We would go from house to house singing Russian Christmas carols and lighting candles at the Holy Resurrection Russian Orthodox Church. Often more celebrated than Christmas is the Russian New Year, when Father Frost, the Russian Santa Claus, brought gifts to the children. Candy is a fond memory of the New Year's celebration. It was common to greet everyone with a "*S novim godom!*" meaning "Happy New Year!" and "*Spraznikom!*" meaning "Christ has risen!" My favorite event was "masking." Everyone would get decked out in costumes, and prizes would be given for the best. I won the honor three times: as a child and later as an adult dressed

---

[5] The Julian calendar year is, on average, 365.25 days long, instead of having 365 days plus a leap year every four years, and it is 13 days behind the Gregorian calendar.

Part I   The Early Years   1926-1942

as the mad monk Rasputin and as an adult as a Russian Cossack. Since my grandfather was a Cossack, I must have looked the part!

In our family, we had our own holiday traditions involving a lot of eating, singing, dancing, and drinking. My father would mix up a punch with lots of vodka and lots of rum. My grandmother's eggnog was also quite a hit, made with brandy, eggs, and of course, lots of rum. I fondly remember singing those wonderful Russian folk songs.

September 1927.

One Alaskan tradition I was particularly fond of as a child was making "squaw candy" or dried salmon jerky. The salmon is cut in long strips, soaked in 100% brine for 15 to 20 minutes, and then hung up to dry. Voila! It's candy! Another family favorite was the canned meat, Spam. It has been around since 1937. Deriving its name from spiced ham, I thought it was a real treat. I probably was in the minority on that score!

My sister Ida and me with Mother. Circa 1929.

Part I   The Early Years   1926-1942

Unseen forces have always been at work in my life, holding on to me tightly and granting me wellbeing. My carefree childhood was about to take a turn for the worse, but none of us could foresee it.

Part I   The Early Years   1926-1942

One Year in the Iron Lung

*I would be known all my life for my singing
and for bursting into song during my many travels.
It was part of the fabric Mother wove in me
and has remained with me to this day.
~Captain Jack V. Johnson~*

At the age of seven, I was stricken with polio—infantile paralysis. Polio wasn't as easily managed then as it is today. Intense medical attention was needed to ward off any chance of mild to severe permanent disabilities. Father took the diagnosis seriously and decided to move us closer to a medical facility. He packed us up and moved his family to Seattle, Washington. He bought a home on Queen Anne Hill from Hildar Sherman, whose husband had owned a big foundry. Hildar's husband had lost everything in the stock market crash of 1929, and tragically ended up taking his own life, leaving his widow with only the house. Father bought the house with the stipulation that Hildar would remain living there in the south wing. Hildar became part of the family, as well as our family cook. Believe me when I tell you: she was one hell of a fine cook! She remained with my mother for the rest of her life. Many years later, the sad news of Hildar's passing would come when I was at sea.

I spent the next two years in Seattle's Children's Orthopedic Hospital being treated for and recovering from polio. I was in an iron lung for one year during my hospital stay. After I was discharged, Father moved the family across Lake Washington to an area called Medina. Bellevue encompasses all that area now. Today, it is known for its most prominent resident, Bill Gates. Our home was just south of where the Evergreen Point Bridge crosses Lake Washington today, on a little lane called Kyer Lane. Father bought this estate from the Kyer family, a beautiful home with park-like grounds, but more importantly it had a dock with a nice spot to go swimming. The waterfront home was ideal. Father continued to work for Grace Line and was gone a lot.

Part I   The Early Years   1926-1942

Mother always kept busy. She fell into the restaurant business. I say "fell" because it came about when some people owed her a lot of money. To square up, a large building and restaurant on Rainier Avenue and Genesee Street were deeded over to her and my father. The people who had owned the restaurant helped my mother run it. My sisters were also working there. The restaurant called "Mom's Diner" was going full *fhart* (that's full speed ahead in Norwegian). It suited her well because Mother was an excellent cook and had worked off and on in many of the finer restaurants in Seattle. She sold it when the daily commute across Lake Washington got too much for her.

Kenneth "Andy" Anderson came to live with us when his parents were killed in a train wreck. He was a little older than me and became my adopted brother.

During my rehabilitation from polio, Father did all he could to build me up physically. He rigged up a whirlpool bath contraption by using a big copper tub with garden hoses. The worst and the best of it was that it came with a big Swedish lady, who would toss me around in it. At one point, Father got a big dory and taught me to stand up and row dory-man style. He even hired an old bosun,[6] Lars Larsen, who had sailed with Father. Lars personally mentored me in the fine art of sailing and seamanship. A bosun's position on a ship is to supervise the unskilled or unlicensed members of the deck crew. These sailors hold an Able Bodied Seaman's Certificate, as well as many years of sailing. Lars was such a man. He became part of our family, teaching me seamanship and how to rig a little *leg of mutton sail*[7] out on Lake Washington. Lars' style of education was hands on. He let me sail the dory, taught me how to row, tie knots, splice, mend nets, and so forth. I didn't realize it foreshadowed days to come.

Once when I was a young lad nine years old, I found myself in a bad situation. One highlight for Andy and me was when Father would take us on his ship. The cook would feed us pilot bread and sausage. It was July 1935 and I had just gotten out of

---

[6] Also bos'n or bo's'n—for boatswain.

[7] Triangular sail.

Part I   The Early Years   1926-1942

the Children's Orthopedic Hospital where I had spent two years recovering from polio. Father invited me to join him that day. It was a short hop to Tacoma from Seattle for the discharge of copper ore at the smelter. The quartermaster even let me take the helm, and it was always my delight. I liked to run around the ship. The sea was a boy's play land aboard ship.

On this particular day, I was playing out on the deck by the #3 hatch, just aft of the bridge on *Santa Eleana*, a Hog Islander.[8] Father was busy taking care of whatever he had to do. I was out of sight fighting pirates, chasing waves, and conquering the vast seas. Deep in my own adventure, I looked up and noticed this guy wearing a funny-looking hat. He was wearing a long topcoat with a velvet collar. He looked just like what you would expect a "pimp" to look like. I guess that was what he was, a pimp, and a real shady character. Evidently, he worked out of one of the boarding houses in Tacoma. Before I realized what was going on, he grabbed me. The next thing I knew, he cornered me and began yanking off my trousers. I struggled to get away. He grabbed my crotch. I yelled at the top of my lungs. That's when I noticed he had dropped his trousers. What happened next was a blur. All I knew was someone grabbed the guy from behind and threw him up against the edge of #3 hatch. I realized it was my father. Father was a strong, hefty man. Though the smallest of his brothers—the runt you might say—he was merely 6'8" tall and 250 pounds, like I said—the runt—but solid. I heard a big crack, and the guy let out a scream. Father tossed him overboard. He looked at me and roared, "Boy, go to my room!"

I obeyed immediately. I waited for my father. He walked in and, pointing to the bedroom, he snapped, "Get in there!" I was shaking. I had never seen my father that upset. He went over to his desk, opened the side drawer, and pulled out a bottle of whisky. The room was loudly quiet, only the sound of whisky going down fast and hard. He was about to pour himself another

---

[8] Hog Islanders is the slang for ships built at Hog Island shipyard just outside Philadelphia, Pennsylvania, built under government direction and subsidy due to a shortage of ships in the United States Merchant Marine during World War I.

Part I   The Early Years   1926-1942

one, when a couple of uniformed police officers came in. They knew my father.

"Hi, Captain, guess there was a mishap."

"Mishap, my ass. I threw the son-of-a-bitch overboard!" retorted my father.

Apparently satisfied by Father's response, the officers replied as they looked down at their notes, "Yes, we have it all down right here. He fell off the gangway."

"Fell! Nothing! I told you, I threw the son-of-a-bitch overboard!" Father insisted again.

"Yes, we have it all down right here. He fell off the gangway," persisted the officers.

Father poured another drink but not before offering a drink to the officers. Handing them each a glass half-filled with whisky, he said, "Here, have a drink."

Accepting his offer, they said, "Don't mind if we do while we finish out this report. Let's see, the victim fell overboard off the gangway. Such a pity."

"I told you, I threw the son-of-a-bitch overboard," Father muttered.

"Yes, we have it all down right here. He fell off the gangway," the officers kept insisting. That was the end of it.

Father instilled a love for the sea in both Andy and me. We would drift in and out of ports throughout our boyhood. We were 11 years old and determined to go to sea. The two of us, being about the same age, were trouble times two. Andy was a bit older, but I was a bit taller. We got involved in all sorts of mischief, all of which we instigated. There were many consequences, which we deserved!

Our passion was demonstrated when Andy and I tried to sail back to Kodiak. We had the perfect means of doing it with this big 22-foot dory. So, we thought, "Why not?" We both had spent many a day on the water, so we thought we knew what to do. We made a plan. We started with the most important thing. Food. We needed provisions. According to our calculations, Kodiak was a few days away. Actually, it was about 1,210 nautical miles from Seattle to Kodiak, but in our minds, it was a hop, skip, and a

Part I   The Early Years   1926-1942

jump. We talked Hildar into fixing some food for us. She was only too delighted to get rid of us since we were constantly causing her grief with our tomfoolery. She went along with our shenanigans, probably not giving it much thought, and fixed us some peanut butter and jelly sandwiches, as well as supplying us with couple of quarts of milk and dog food since we were taking Nero, our big Newfoundland dog, with us.

The three of us, Nero, Andy, and I, set sail across Lake Washington. We had a well-thought out plan and only forgot to do one small thing—tell Mother! Why should we tell her? We were old enough to make our own decisions. Setting off from the dock, we headed for Kodiak, which is all well and good, but we hadn't planned on going through the Ballard locks into Puget Sound. That's where friends of our family saw us and couldn't figure out what we were doing heading out to the Sound. We must have been quite a sight, with Nero up on the bow barking and leading the way, while we were back in the stern sheets, unaware our expedition would soon be cut short.

We must have been hungry shortly into the adventure because we weren't even up to Whidbey Island and had already eaten up our food. Pulling into Friday Harbor in the San Juans, our plan was to stock up on provisions. In the meantime, our mother had been informed. She got all upset and called the Coast Guard, the "U.S. Lighthouse Service," as it was still referred to at that time. Captain Ledbetter, a family friend and CO[9] of the lighthouse tender[10] *Cedar*, responded, telling her that the *Cedar* was in Friday Harbor that day, and they would find us and bring us home. Here we were, only hours into our Kodiak voyage, pulling into Friday Harbor, unaware of the events that were taking place around us and because of us. Before we knew it, a boarding party surrounded us! Here came all those big Coast Guard sailors! We couldn't repel them no matter how hard we tried or how much Nero barked. They took us, with our loaded dory, aboard the *Cedar* and back to Seattle. That ended our

---

[9] Commanding officer.

[10] The boat assigned to the lighthouse.

Part I   The Early Years   1926-1942

adventure of heading north to Kodiak in a 22' dory. We would have made it, I'm sure of it, because we were rigged with a little leg of mutton sail. From our reckoning, it wouldn't have been anything to make the 1,210 nautical mile trip, with smooth sailing.

Mother kept a logbook of all the mischief we ever did, and this was one big entry. Typically, when Father would come home, he would look the logbook over and mete out what he figured was proper punishment. It was no less the case for this little escapade. Father informed us that he wasn't punishing us because we took off in the dory, but for the grief we caused our mother by making her worry. Deep down, I think we made him a little proud, and I imagine he figured we would have made it, too!

No matter what we did, when Father punished us, he would always tell us what we were being punished for, so there was no mistaking our consequences. He was fair, determined, and very much a disciplinarian—which I am sure he learned from his father.

Mother was also concerned with my health. I was just skin and bones after the polio. Mother's choice of therapy was to have me build up my lungs by playing the baritone horn in the school's band. Mother was quite a musician and singer. She was always singing us tearjerker ballads like "Break the News to Mother," "In the Baggage Coach Ahead," "Utah Trail," and "The Spanish Cavalier." She would sing these songs about men on the battlefield, people dying, and babies without their mother, and we kids would cry. One of her favorites was "The Old Spinning Wheel" by Ray Noble. In the 1930s, there was a children's radio show with kids singing and performing. I was 12 years old when Mother had me go on and sing, "The Old Spinning Wheel." I can still remember the lyrics:

> *There's an old spinning wheel in the parlor.*
> *Spinning dreams of the long, long ago.*
> *Spinning dreams of an old-fashioned garden,*
> *and a maid with her old-fashioned beau.*

I did pretty good that day. I came out on top. I would be known all my life for my singing and bursting into song during my many travels. It was part of the fabric Mother wove in me.

Part I　The Early Years　　1926-1942

Out to Sea at 13

I was scared, seasick, and homesick. Everything had happened so fast.
I was quite frightened, but as soon as I got my sea legs,
I became a salty guy and developed my love for the sea.
~Captain Jack V. Johnson~

All their efforts to build me up must have worked because, in April of 1939, when I was 13, my father shipped me out to sea! According to Father, I was big enough (standing well over six feet tall), old enough, and more importantly, strong and healthy enough! After all, Father and his brothers were only nine years old when they went to sea. (If they were not captains by age 19, their father would have disowned them!) I was enrolled at Kirkland Junior High and made it through the 8th grade. Father took me over to the Lake Union dry dock where the three-masted schooner *Charles R. Wilson* was outfitting for cod fishing with the Pacific Coast Codfish Company.

Cod fishing was grueling and dangerous work in the North Pacific seas. Storms and rough weather were common in the shallow cod-fishing waters. The cod were caught on baited lines and hauled by hand aboard small dories. Cod could weigh up to 10 pounds. The dories worked from schooners, which were anchored along the coast or shallow banks in the deeper waters. The dory fishermen normally launched their boats early in the morning around 4:30. They would complete two shifts of fishing by evening before returning to the schooner for the night.

Father took me aboard. He introduced me to the Captain, Knute Pearson. Apparently, they knew each other quite well. Father took me around the ship with the chief mate.[11] The chief mate took Father and me for a walk around the ship. We went down to the foc'sle.[12] My bunk was up forward, two high.

---

[11] The chief mate is second in command under the captain. He is responsible for the safety and security of the ship and to look after the crew.
[12] An abbreviation of forecastle. Also fo'c'sle or focsle. The spelling indicates the common pronunciation. Refers to farthest forward portion of the ship.

Part I   The Early Years   1926-1942

As we came out of the foc'sle and out on deck again, Father stopped, laid his hand on my shoulder, and said, "Poy, (Finns can't say the letter B—they say P for B) when you're called, you be the first up, be the first on deck, the first aloft, and the first on the yardarm, and always say 'Sir.'"

I've followed my father's advice all my life. I tried to be the first one up, the first on deck, the first aloft, and the first on the yardarm, and I always said, "Sir." I found you could apply that to 'most anything you do. It became my motto and the words to live by.

Here's a side story about how Finns can't say Bs. Several years after Father died, Mother remarried and was living in Renton, Washington. I always visited her when I came in off a ship and would spend a day or two before going on a running drunk (as sailors are always wont to do). One of these visits still in my memory is a Saturday night dance. The highlight in Renton on a Saturday night was the dance at the Swedish-American Club, the Vasa Order of America, which is a fraternal society for Swedish immigrants. Everyone would go there to dance. There was this young lady, Ethel Swanson, who was born and raised in Finland. Her parents, Swedish Finns, had recently come over from Finland. Of course, Ethel was the belle of the ball. Everybody wanted to dance with her. She was a very beautiful blonde and a hell of an accordion player, too. After the dance, everyone crowded around her.

I strutted up to her and said, "Ethel, I'm Jack Johnson, Thea Danielson's son."

"Oh, yah," she replied. "I heard about you. Velcome."

I continued, "I'd like to meet you in Seattle one evening and have dinner. You can tell me all about Finland and teach me the Swedish Waltz."

"I vould like that," she said. "This is Saturday. How about after I get off vork in Seattle on Tuesday night?"

"Better yet," I replied, "I'll meet you here in Renton, and we will go to this restaurant in Tukwila that's very nice."

"Okay," she responded. "Vell, do you know vhere my house is?" she said with her Swedish-Finn accent.

"Yes," I answered. "I know where your parents' house is."

Part I   The Early Years   1926-1942

She went on, "You can't miss it because in the front yard is a 'pig pile of pricks'" (big pile of bricks)! Everyone burst out laughing. To this day we still tease Ethel about that. I ran into her in Seattle with her husband a few years back and reminded her.

She shook her head and smiled, "You'll never let me get over that will you!"

My father was well known and respected around the Seattle area. Once, in the 1930s, an important dignitary came looking for an opportunity to go fishing. It was President Franklin D. Roosevelt! Nick Bez and my father took him out on Elliot Bay to troll for salmon. He caught a 32-pounder! Nick Bez was quite a colorful character. He was the first processor to can dog salmon (chum salmon, often referred to as white salmon). There's a story about the label he used on his cans, which stated, "Alaska white salmon, guaranteed not to turn red in the can"—which fairly tricked the consumer into thinking red salmon was red because of the canning process and got consumers to eat hitherto unpopular white salmon.

Incidentally, I never called my father anything but Father or Sir. I never called him Dad, Daddy, Pa, Pop, or anything like that; it was always "Father" or "Yes, Sir." "No, Sir." "Yes, Father." "No, Father." It was the same with my mother. That was the way I was brought up. My father was a man of few words and much action. He was esteemed and well liked around the community. He was also my protector. Maybe my being the youngest or my bout with polio made him keep a closer eye on me than my siblings. Possibly he was worried that I would be soft in a fight because I had had people fawn over me as I was nursed back to health. Whatever it was, I was always aware of his presence.

I missed my father during my teenage years, while I was out at sea. I suppose his absence made me the man I am today. I grew up fast and strong. Father died of cancer shortly after my return from the first time at sea. We were still living in Medina,

Part I   The Early Years   1926-1942

Washington. I returned in October 1939. He died in January. He went on to *Fiddler's Green*[13] January 12, 1940.

I would never see him again, but for one eerie encounter aboard a vessel during WW II. I was in a T-2 Tanker coming out of the Persian Gulf, loaded full and down with aviation gas, when a figure appeared with a peculiar warning that saved me and Andy. It's an incident I will never forget—but that's another story.

Now back to my first time aboard ship. It was April 1939, just after my 13th birthday. Father had managed to get me a berth as a deck boy on a fishing schooner. He escorted me onto the cod fishing vessel *Charles R. Wilson.* She left the shipyard and shifted to the Seattle waterfront to load stores and provisions, along with the fishermen. We were set to head north to the Straights of Juan de Fuca. We were under tow quite a ways up the Strait when the wind picked up out of the southeast. Once we had a fair wind, we dropped the tug and away we went, keeping her full and bye.[14] I was scared, seasick, and homesick. Everything had happened so fast, but as soon as I got my sea legs, I became a salty guy and developed my love for the sea.

The crew and fishermen took me under their wing and taught me how to tie knots, splice, reef, and steer. I was very good at most of these skills already, thanks to the lessons from the old bosun, Lars. The mates were called splitters. Their job was to split the codfish when it came aboard. The guys were quite amazed that I was so adept at splicing, tying knots, and boxing the compass.[15] I explained to them that Lars Larson had taught me all that. (Incidentally, Lars died just about that time from cirrhosis of the liver.) My duties were to do anything I could on deck. I spent the summer bait cutting and pulling tongues, cutting out the

---

[13] A legendary imagined afterlife, where there is perpetual mirth, a fiddle that never stops playing, and dancers who never tire.

[14] A nautical expression which means sailing by the wind or close hauled, yet at the same time keeping all the sails full so that they do not shake through being too close to wind. Generally a vessel does better to windward when kept a 'good full and bye' than when nipped or starved of wind.

[15] All exchanging of directions to give orientation to an object or happening away from the ship are given in standard compass terms.

Part I   The Early Years   1926-1942

sounds (fish cheeks), and salting the split fish down in the hatch. I would clean up and wash down whatever was needed. One of my duties was to take the food from the galley aft to the splitters and the captain.

I recall an incident when a "highline fisherman" came back alongside with only a few fish in his dory. He was drunk! Booze was prohibited in the ship, but this "highliner"[16] must have kept a bottle hidden. That particular day was beautiful and sunny. We were just off the slime bank north of Unimak Island. The fisherman had gone out in his dory, but instead of fishing, he got drunk. The trouble began when he was back aboard.

The *Charles R. Wilson.*

Our captain in the *Charles R. Wilson,* Captain Pearson, was known to have a quick temper. In fact, he had the nickname "Dempsey," after the American prizefighter Jack Dempsey. Instead of talking, he'd punch you out. That's exactly what he did to this guy. It took him just moments to size up the situation and, before the guy knew what was coming, *wham!* Pearson belted him one. The guy went down, rolling over and over. Then, *boom!*

---

[16] A term given to fisherman in the commercial fishing industry.

Part I   The Early Years   1926-1942

Down he went into the open hatch. He tumbled head over heels, landing with his head and shoulders on the keelson.[17] The guy was lying there unconscious. The captain looked at me and said, "Boy, go down and rig a bowline on him. We've got to haul him up."

I went down and rigged a running bowline. We got him back up through the open hatch and laid him on the deck. Captain Pearson was kicking him, screaming, "Get up!"

The guy couldn't get up. He just lay there moaning and groaning. It was then we realized this guy was hurt. We dragged him aft to the dining saloon. The captain didn't know what to do. We had an old Northern radio onboard, the kind you had to warm up using a little old Wisconsin gas engine to power the battery. Captain Pearson got through to the Coast Guard cutter *Haida* that was on Bering Sea patrol about 24 hours away from us. The captain was telling them he was lying there and trying to explain the misshapen look of the fisherman's arm.

The doctor in *Haida* began talking back and forth with the captain relaying medical procedures, "Take his arm and hold it out straight, and see how that is." The captain did. The poor fisherman moaned, signifying his great pain.

The captain said to the Coast Guard doctor, "Yah, it's out straight."

The Coast Guard doctor said, "I think you have a dislocated shoulder by the sounds of it. Try pushing it in."

By this time, we were all watching what was going on and thinking, "Boy, this isn't good."

I remember hearing the American-sounding doctor say, "Pull it out a little bit, pull it way out."

Then the captain asked, "Like this?"

After much screams from the fisherman, the doctor said, "I think you're doing it right. Now shove it in!"

The captain tried it and told the doctor, "That won't work either."

---

[17] A longitudinal structure running above and fastened to the keel of a ship in order to stiffen and strengthen its framework.

Part I   The Early Years   1926-1942

Trying to get the arm back in the place, he rigged a "handy billy"[18] and, taking hold, pulled on his arm, and held it out.

"Let go and haul! Belay!" That didn't work either.

Then the doctor reported the *Haida* had changed course and should be at our vessel at about 0900 hours. "Good," said the captain, "we'll be waiting for you." In the meantime, he was trying to figure out what to do with the guy.

Captain Pearson nodded towards me, "Boy, hold him down." I got on his chest and held him down. The captain reckoned, "We'd better give him something to ease the pain."

Captain Pearson left a minute and returned, breaking out a bottle of whisky. Then he ordered, "Give 'im some of this."

I poured some whisky down his throat, thinking, "This is what got this guy in trouble to begin with." The whisky eased his pain a little. Seeing that it seemed to help, I took a swig myself. In fact, I took several swigs.

The captain was still twisting and pulling, pushing and turning the poor guy's arm. Rolling him over, the captain started pumping him on his back and saying, "Maybe this will do. It'll make room."

No amount of twisting, turning, pushing, or pulling did the trick. We ended up leaving him lying out there on the deck. I helped him up when he had to go to the head and back down again on the deck.

The *Haida* arrived with the doctor the next morning. He took one look at the patient and said, "My god, we've got to get him over to the *Haida*!"

The *Haida* had an x-ray machine aboard. They discovered he not only had a dislocated shoulder, but also he had three broken ribs, a broken arm, broken scapula, broken collar bone, and a punctured lung. He was pretty well beat up. No one ever knew which injuries came from the blow, from the fall, or from all the twisting and turning. No one dared to say a thing. I didn't see him in the ship again, but I did run into him a couple of times later on

---

[18] A handy billy is made with two blocks and tackle, and can be used to give mechanical advantage wherever needed.

Part I   The Early Years   1926-1942

the waterfront or in Belltown in Seattle. I never forgot his face or the taste of that whisky.

Eventually we pulled into Dutch Harbor out on the Aleutian Chain of Alaska. We were getting coal for the galley stove and foc'sle stove and some provisions. As a growing lad of 13 summers, the memories of living in Unalaska as a little boy were dim but familiar. In Unalaska, another schooner caught my eye, a four-masted schooner. This was late August in 1939, and it was quite an experience to see a big four-masted schooner. There she was, the *C.S. Holmes*. Her captain was Captain Beckman from Bainbridge Island. Andy and I had been friends with his son, Earl. She was a fur-trading schooner bound north. Captain Beckman would go all the way to Mackenzie River to trade. Don't ask me how I did it, but I convinced Captain Pearson I should get off the *Charles R. Wilson* and join the *C.S. Holmes*.

The *C.S. Holmes* headed north, while the *Charles R. Wilson* continued cod fishing. It was a thrill to be aboard the big four-master. We sailed north through the Bering Strait and into the Northwest Passage. This was the first time I was in the Northwest Passage. I would return there eight more times in my life—seven eastbound and one westbound. This was one of my finest moments, going through the Northwest Passage on a sailing ship with no engines! All that ice and fog—and yet—there we were. I can't describe the hallowed occasion of silently sailing through the ice. It would be my favorite spot on earth. Captain Beckman had the *C.S. Holmes* rigged so she had a dory under each stern quarter and three dories forward towing through the ice, each powered with a 10-horse power Johnson outboard. Out in the open water, he headed for the Mackenzie River where he traded with the Eskimos and Indians at Aklavik. We didn't stay long, just long enough to get all the furs traded. We kept some of the trade goods because we intended to hit Siberia on the way out. We were breaking out stores of supplies down below. The captain always threw a pint of whisky in when the deal was completed. Earl, the captain's son, and I thought we should sample it. I can still remember that whisky in pint bottles, *Old Quaker Rye Whisky*. Boy, did we catch hell. The captain logged us three days' pay as one,

Part I   The Early Years   1926-1942

which really didn't amount to much in those days. We were getting $16 a month, but the memory of the *Old Quaker Rye Whisky* has stuck with me all these years, so I'd say it was worth it!

After the trading in Aklavik, we headed out to the Bering Strait and into a river in Siberia. We got in over the bar, and a little steam tug came and hooked onto us, towing us up river, stern first! They had mooring lines ready for us, and we made fast. There we were laying stern first in the river, against the gentle current. We were the last of the trading schooners allowed into Siberia. At that time the commissars of the communist government were putting a stop to all the commercial trade. I was in the last trading schooner in the Soviet in 1939.

Returning to Port Blakely, Washington, we discovered the *Charles R. Wilson* was also there. That evening, the crew off both ships met up at a nice restaurant in Port Angeles. Seated at a long table, I wanted to sit up close to the captain of the *Charles R. Wilson*, Knute Pearson, since his ship was my first ship. Everyone looked over the menu to decide what to eat for this special dinner occasion.

Captain Pearson studied the selection for a minute. Then he proclaimed eagerly, "Oh, look, they have codfish! I'll have the codfish." Everybody in the crew ordered codfish! That might not have been so remarkable, except this was after a summer of fishing codfish and eating codfish *three times a day*! At the end of the meal, we parted ways. The *C.S. Holmes* went on to Bainbridge Island. I paid off and returned home.

At that time, Father had been working ashore just a few months before his passing. He had retired from the sea. They gave him a desk job in Seattle at the office of General Steam. He had the title of West Coast Superintendent. The desk job didn't agree with him. He died shortly afterward. He never was a landlubber.[19] Sitting behind a desk just squeezed the life right out of him. After a large Masonic funeral, Mother had a visit from Captain Arvid Peterson, the captain of the steam schooner *Cricket*. He had sailed with my father as mate. His ship was being loaded with lumber at

---

[19] A name given in contempt by sailors to a person who lives on land.

Part I   The Early Years   1926-1942

Everett, and he had come to offer his condolences to my mother. It was the 26th of January 1940. Mother was happy to see him. After a short visit, I convinced him to let me go with him. I was too young for American ships, but Mother agreed it might be the best thing because I was filled with so much grief due to my father's death. I was with Captain Peterson in the *Cricket* for 39 days. We sailed down the coast, fully loaded, for Mexico and into the Sea of Cortez. We dropped the deck load of piling and big timber at the port of Guaymas and then headed across to Santa Rosalia. That was where I first got my taste of tequila and a lovely senorita! After my 39 days, I paid off in Aberdeen, Washington, and was discharged as an ordinary seaman!

It was hard for me with Father gone. It was even harder trying to go back to things other 13-year-old boys were doing. I met back up with Andy, who had also been out to sea. Everything seemed different. Everything was small. Everybody seemed so kid-like. They weren't as sophisticated as Andy and I. We were even smoking in those days, though everyone thought that was awful. I enrolled in South Kitsap Union High in Port Orchard, near where we were living after Father died. They put me through some testing and immediately advanced me to the 11th grade.

I decided to take the easy way out and enrolled in an agriculture class and automobile shop. Automobile shop served me well. All I ever knew before was how to turn on the engine, fill the tank with gas, check the oil, and if the damn thing didn't work, I said "the hell with it." My cousin, Bill Forsmark, was in shop class with me. We had a grand time, constantly full of mischief.

Our neighbor, who we called Ol' Man Olund, had a 1930 Star truck similar to a small flatbed pickup. He was so proud of his Star truck. That year, he parked it safely in his barn and took his family to Sweden. Bill and I figured out how to play a trick on Ol' Man Olund. With our knowledge gained through working in the auto shop and with five other guys' expertise, we stripped the Star truck down, hoisted it up in the hayloft over the milking parlor of his barn, and then put it all back together again. Here was the Star truck, Ol' Man Olund's pride and joy, perched up above the

Part I   The Early Years   1926-1942

milking parlor in the pigeon loft of his barn. This was no easy task! We left it there and went about our business.

About a month later he returned from Sweden with his family. News spread fast. His Star truck was gone! He went wild! "My Star truck, where is it?"

He called the local marshal, state patrol, and the city police of Port Orchard. He had everybody but the National Guard looking for it. Boy, he was upset! Where was his Star truck? Someone had stolen his Star truck! I'd like to have been there when he was milking his cows and solved the mystery. Evidently, he saw some oil on the deck of his milking parlor. He looked up, and a spot of oil was coming down from the overhead. He must have wondered, "What the hell is going on here now?" He climbed up to the pigeon loft, and there was his Star truck! I could only imagine his shock and bewilderment! He called his two sons, Eric and Ludwig. The three of them got it down by removing the side of the barn and rigging a ramp. He kept asking, "Who could have done this? How could they have gotten my Star truck up there?"

The story of Ol' Man Olund's Star truck fetching up in his pigeon loft went all around the country. It was quite a humorous tale! Bill, I, and the other five never breathed a word about it.

Bill and I got into mischief another time. Mother always insisted I go to church, no matter which church it was, no matter where we were. We didn't have a Russian Orthodox Church in the area, so I'd go to the little Lutheran Church in Waterman, Washington. We were members of the young people's Luther League. We gathered once weekly and after Sunday services. One of our duties was to clean the church every Saturday. Two of us

Part I   The Early Years   1926-1942

would be scheduled for the task of sweeping, swabbing, and cleaning up in general. This one Saturday, the duties fell upon Bill and me. We were busy cleaning the church and polishing the brass. There was a big pipe organ, and of course we pumped it up and played a few chords. We looked behind the altar and discovered that's where all the pipes and tubes were located. We dusted around them with little foxtail brushes. We got to thinking, what if we took the tubes and switched them to different pipes? Another one of my distant cousins, Kermit Johnson, a funny little guy, was the organ player at the church.[20] That Sunday we were all sitting waiting for the service to begin. Pastor Selstrom came out and nodded to Kermit to begin playing the opening processional. Kermit put his hands on the keys and then, "*Raroww.*"

The organ started producing all these horrible noises! Kermit leaned back in a state of shock. Then he grabbed the keys again. "*Raroww.*"

The strange sounds continued. He began to panic, not knowing what to do or how to fix it. He started pounding on the keys as if he could change the sound by playing harder and louder. Bill and I were sitting there trying to hide our outbursts of giggles and chuckles. It was hilarious!

Pastor Selstrom was trying to get Kermit to stop. He shouted, "Somebody help him," but Kermit wasn't going to stop. He continued to play. All that was coming out was this ghastly roar.

A couple of the deacons came up and grabbed Kermit, dragging him away from the organ. He sounded like a gibbering idiot pleading with them, "Let me play! Let me play! I can play!"

They pulled him down the aisle and outside. It didn't take them long to guess who the perpetrators were. I can only imagine it was our inability to contain our delight that gave us away. Amazingly, we never heard any more about it. They brought in an expert to refit the piping and the tubes to get the organ ready for the following Sunday. To this day, I don't think Kermit has ever forgiven us. My boredom with the mundane got the best of me,

---

[20] Kermit later ended up being one of the greatest concert pianists in the United States.

Part I   The Early Years   1926-1942

and it wouldn't be long before I'd drop out of school and head for Seattle and another ship.

Living in Waterman, I had several relatives there, and the highlight of a day would be walking down the road and passing my aunt with Kermit. We'd say, "Hello, Kermit."

His mother would shake him and say, "Say, 'Hello,' Kermit."

Kermit would reply in a low voice, "Hello, Kermit."

We always got a kick out of it. During the war, Kermit got into the Army Military Band and later became a concert pianist.

Another boyhood memory of our neighborhood was the American Indian lady, who used to push her cart around the neighborhood. She had it mounted on big bicycle wheels. Sometime during the evening she would catch fish and peddle them down the road the next day. People came out and bought fresh fish from her. She would push the cart down the road yelling, "Fresh fish. Fresh fish. Fresh fish."

Her daughter would come along with another cart, similar to her mother's, shouting, "Me too. Me too. Me too."

Since I wasn't doing too well in school and wanted to go back to sea, making the decision to leave wasn't too hard. Andy had returned from Wisconsin after making several attempts to live with relatives. Both of us were struggling. Finally, in the spring of 1940, we had had enough. But at 13, we were still too young to be in American ships. Mother took us down to Father's office at General Steam. They were able to ship us out as ordinary seamen in a Swedish ship MS *Mirrabooka*. She was a Swedish American Australian Direct Line vessel. The crew was primarily Scandinavians, with a few Australians, and us. We sailed down the West Coast to San Pedro, California. We remained there several days, getting the ship topped off for Australia.

Part I The Early Years   1926-1942

The MS *Mirrabooka*.

While the ship was getting ready, so was I. Getting ready in my case meant I would take the plunge to fashion myself after my salty, old shipmates. You know how kids like to look like the people they hang around. I guess I was no different. Only it wasn't a fashion statement I wanted to copy. It was tattoos!

I, of course, still have all those tattoos, plus a few more. San Pedro will forever remind me of two things: my first tattoos and my first barroom brawl. The tattoo parlor was next to a gin mill on the corner of 5th and Beacon Street and was called Shanghai Reds.

Shanghai Reds was a waterfront bar. Its infamous reputation was being the roughest waterfront bar in the world—or at least in L.A. On the waterfront, the men were tough, and the women were tougher. Up and down the street you could see nothing but flophouses, laundry shops, chop suey joints, greasy spoons, and pawnshops, as well as any other unsavory act you wanted to partake in. It was rumored there was a brick-lined tunnel from Shanghai Reds to the harbor where drugged seamen were hustled off to ships heading for the Orient and elsewhere.

Part I   The Early Years   1926-1942

The infamous Shanghai Reds.

To Andy and me, San Pedro was a playground of delights! The crew assembled across the street from Shanghai Reds at the Good Fellows Bar. After a few drinks, Andy and I headed to the tattoo parlor next door to Shanghai Reds. After some excruciatingly painful minutes, I got a sailing ship on my left arm and anchors between my thumb and forefinger. Andy got a sailing ship on his left arm, and on each nipple he had them tat "sweet" and "sour."

It hurt like hell, but we thought we were really salty. I was pretty big for 13, standing just over 6 feet tall. I had recovered well from polio and was now quite husky, easily passing for 18. When we were done, the two of us headed back over to the Good Fellows to join the crew and show off our new tattoos.

Just as I came through the door of the bar, *kapow!*—I got belted right in the jaw. There was a big, drunk Norwegian standing by the door looking to hit anybody who came through. I, unfortunately, happened to be available. Before I could catch my breath, he nailed me again! I went tumbling across the room and landed flat on my ass. I sat there stunned. He kept looking at me, swaying back and forth, clutching his hands as if egging me to come back for more. I didn't know what to do.

Part I   The Early Years   1926-1942

As I sat there, trying to get my bearings, he spat on me! I was shaken, humiliated, and just plain pissed... not to mention wet from his spit. I had enough. I might have only been 13, but I had never walked away from a good fight. I got up, straightened my back, readjusted my jaw, and started walking towards him. He said, "You want another one?"

I mustered up all of my strength and came in hard, but instead of throwing a solid punch, I kicked him right in the balls! Down he went to his knees. This would become my signature move and the beginning of my many barroom brawls. I graduated with a BA—a Bad Ass—majoring in a "whopping good time."

Knowing there were no second chances in a fight like this, I nailed him down on the deck. Once he'd doubled over, up came my knee again and, *pow*! Boy, I really put the boots to him! I began stomping all over him and kicking him in the head. I didn't dare stop until he'd quit moving for fear he'd kill me. Finally, the big drunk Norwegian lay there unconscious, like a spawned out dog salmon. And like a cocky rooster, I walked over to the bar.

The bartender yelled out, "Hey kid, you done pretty good. Here, have one on me." I might have only been 13, but that didn't stop me. I had a big belt of whisky. Andy had come in behind me. He had a belt of whisky, too.

The crew was pretty proud of me that day, patting me on the back and saying, "Well done." They admired our newly acquired tattoos.

After that, I seemed to have a weakness for barroom brawls. Every time I got into one, no matter what happened or who started it, there'd be eyes blackened and kicks well placed. I usually didn't come out on top because I would end up laughing

Later, I got the nickname "Hurricane Johnson," and later on in Kodiak, I was dubbed "Death Johnson," after I hit a guy with one punch and he ended up deader than a mackerel.

I've been in barroom brawls from Port Said, Egypt, to Cape Town, South Africa, to Rio de Janeiro, Brazil, and many ports all over the world. Being 6'4" and kind of a big guy at an early age, it seemed everyone wanted a piece of me, and I never failed to accommodate a worthy opponent.

Part I The Early Years   1926-1942

Crossing the Equator

*We were just in time for school to start. We gave it our best shot.
Once again, we couldn't hack it, even though I was getting good grades.
We had to ship out.
~Captain Jack V. Johnson~*

Shortly after leaving San Pedro, we crossed the equator on my 14th birthday, April 12, 1940. I never did return home for more than a day or two after that. It would mark the beginning of my long voyage home, returning not only to Washington, but also north to my beloved Alaska. We were bound toward Brisbane, Australia, by way of Tahiti, Fiji, and New Caledonia.

That's me, Jack Johnson, Ordinary Seaman. MS *Mirrabooka*.
Crossing the Equator on my 14th birthday, April 12, 1940.
Bound towards Australia...
the beginning of the *long voyage home*.

Part I   The Early Years   1926-1942

We got to Sydney on a Saturday morning and tied up at Circular Key. We were a neutral ship in peacetime colors—a Swedish ship flying the blue and yellow flag, a stark contrast to the other ships in the harbor painted gray. The war was going on in that part of the world. After we got tied up and squared away and after doing a little deck work, the bosun knocked us off at 5:00 p.m. instead of our regular time of 6:00 p.m. Andy and I didn't have to work the next day, Sunday. We got all cleaned up and ready to head ashore.

Neither Andy nor I had ever been ashore in Sydney, but most of the crew had. They headed for the Woolloomooloo district, located just east of Sydney's business district. Their destination was a brothel, the Frenchman's House. The Frenchman poured a good shot of whisky for a few pence. I can remember seeing that whisky on the table—Old Court Whisky. There was Victoria Gin there, too. But Old Court Whisky has stuck with me all these years. Of course, everyone was interested in the Frenchman's "daughters," the painted ladies of the evening. Andy and I joined the crew at the Frenchman's House. We got ourselves a taste of the Frenchman's whisky and came close to getting a taste of his daughters. As we were drinking, some of the men made their choices and took off with one of the daughters. The bosun was a tough old Finn, meaner than hell, but a good bosun and a good sailor. He set me up with one of the Frenchman's daughters. She took me to her room and looked me over. "Yank, how old *are* you?"

"Oh, I'm 21," I boasted, standing up good and tall, tattoos and all.

"Aye, you're not 21. How old are you?" she asked again, giving me a good once over.

"I'm 21," I kept insisting.

Noticing the lack of hair on my face, she tugged at my drawers and, noticing the lack of hair elsewhere on my body, she screamed, "You're only a baby! You son-of-a-bitch, you're only a baby! Out! Out! Sending a baby in to me. I can't crack him! He's only a baby!" She grabbed me and threw me out the door.

She then went over to the bosun and started slapping him, "Aye, you got your nerve, you bastard, sending a baby in to me."

33

Part I   The Early Years   1926-1942

Andy and I were kicked out of the Frenchman's that evening. Disappointed, we wondered what to do next since everyone we knew was inside.

Standing on the street in Sydney, we began wandering back to the ship, hands in our pocket, disgusted, and sorry for ourselves. We walked around, hoping we would find a bar to sneak in and have another drink. We stopped when we heard music. It sounded like church music. We followed the sound to the Salvation Army. Looking in, we noticed all these tables set with food. Everyone was standing up and singing songs. We listened for a while. When they were done singing, they sat down, getting ready to start eating. We decided this was as good a place as any to stop, and we were hungry. We straightened up our hair, tucked in our shirts, and walked in. Immediately we were approached by two little Salvation Army lassies that came up to us and said, "Welcome, welcome. Come in and eat. And where are you from?"

We said, "We're off the Swedish ship."

"Oh, you're off the Swedish ship," they echoed in their strong Aussie accent. From our accents they determined, "You're American."

"Yes," we said, "we're from the United States."

"Well, welcome. Come in, sit down, and eat." We sat down. From the brothel to the buffet—now this was heaven to two 14-year-old lads. They said a little prayer, and we started eating. It was great! Did I mention we were quite hungry?

After eating, they started singing again. As I said before, I had always liked to sing songs, especially if they were in Russian. I joined right in, belting away at the top of my lungs in my fine tenor voice. I thought they were all impressed with my singing, but it might have just been my ego! The two lassies seemed impressed anyway and invited us to return the next day. "Tomorrow is Sunday. Would you come to our service?" they asked smiling and giggling.

"Yes," we said, "why not?" We kept our word and joined them the next day at the church service.

Part I   The Early Years   1926-1942

After church, these two little Salvation Army lassies said, "We'd like to show you around." Playing our little tour guides, they informed us everyone that comes to Sydney had to see the bridge. We were game. They took us to the Sydney Harbor Bridge. Up on the bridge, and looking out over the harbor at all the gray painted war ships, they asked, "Where's your ship?"

"The one down there," we said. "The pretty one." We explained we were painted in peacetime colors, since Sweden was a neutral country. Oh, they thought that was great. The ship was so pretty.

We continued walking across the bridge to Bronte Beach and sat down on the sand. These two little lassies turned out to be rather interesting. They were not what we were expecting, but everything we could hope for. The first thing they asked was, "Do you have any cigarettes?"

Well, it just so happened, we did. Andy and I would get sea store cigarettes for six cents a package of Dominos, an American brand. We would smoke what we wanted and use the rest ashore for trading stock. We took out four cigarettes, offering two to them. Before we knew it, the lassies lit up. We thought that was great. "There's some real potential here," I thought. The next thing you know, we were making out with the Salvation Army lassies. Our time ashore wasn't a total bust. We were getting some action when we couldn't get any at the Frenchman's. You know how sailors are—a girl in every port. We saw those girls several times over the years whenever we were in Australia. Andy and I just added two notches to our long list of heartbreaks!

We finished loading the ship and headed down to Melbourne and Adelaide, where we turned around. We eventually ended back in San Pedro, California. Andy and I paid off and took a greyhound bus back to Seattle. We were just in time for school to start. We gave it our best shot. Once again, we couldn't hack it, even though I was getting good grades. We had to ship out. The year was 1940. We were still too young for American ships, so we shipped again in a foreign vessel.

Part I   The Early Years   1926-1942

We were elated to be aboard another Swedish ship, the MS *Kanangoora*. She was sort of a sister to the MS *Mirrabooka*—a little bigger, but built by the same company.

As I grew up, Andy was my closest friend, and truly a brother, and often a mate. I am grateful to have him come into our little family, because he brought adventure, laughter, and mischief! The two of us were unstoppable and quite incorrigible. I dare to think how my life would have turned out without his influence. Though I know it couldn't have been easy for him, loosing his parents, and all, I hope he also felt our brotherhood was unique.

Since there were a lot of years between my older brothers and myself, I only vaguely remember them. Ironically, I would be the only one to follow in my father's footsteps and become a sailor. I was pretty much raised by my sisters, Ethel, Thelma, and Ivy. Me, being the youngest and all, was babied by all the females in my family, my mother included. My brother Ted died at the age of 16 from pneumonia. George was an activist. He was what you called a political right-winger. He left home when he was quite young. The last time I saw him was during his brief trip home for Father's funeral. His reputation preceded him. In the '30s, there was a rumor about him going to Spain to fight in its civil war.

Part I   The Early Years   1926-1942

Maybe you've heard of the Abraham Lincoln Brigade,[21] American volunteers who served in the Spanish Civil War in the International Brigades. Many of the people who went over there to fight were members of the Communist Party U.S.A. or affiliated with other socialist groups who fought on the Left.

Well, that wasn't my brother. He didn't go over there to fight on the Left. He went over there to fight against them. George joined Franco's[22] forces. He became a general and never returned home. The only person he kept in touch with was Mother. And she never ever breathed a word about George to anyone.

---

[21] http://en.wikipedia.org/wiki/Abraham_Lincoln_Brigade

[22] Francisco Franco y Bahamonde, 1892 –1975, was a Spanish military leader, who ruled as the dictator of Spain from 1939 until his death. He came to power during the Spanish Civil War while serving as the Generalissimo of the Nationalist faction.

Part I   The Early Years   1926-1942

Stranded in Alexandria at 14

*It all happened swiftly. Bombs rained down, and the ship set sail.
In all the confusion, I was left ashore. Fourteen years old,
a sailor without a ship, stranded in the middle of World War II
with Hitler's army invading Egypt.
~Captain Jack V. Johnson~*

When we got to Sydney, we looked up our Salvation Army lassies. Why not? From there we sailed to Brisbane and then on to Darwin. We were slated to go to Dutch East Indies ports to pick up diplomats and embassy people because the Japanese had invaded their country. We had Batavia[23] on our schedule, as well as Surabaya and several other ports along the way. Leaving our last port loaded down with diplomats, we sailed through the Red Sea to Alexandria, Egypt.

The Swedish ship MS *Kanangoora*, sister ship to MS *Mirrabooka*.

It was now 1941. The United States hadn't entered it officially, but Europe was at war. Our ship was tied up at the dock in Alexandria when the Jerries[24] flew over. *Damn me eyes*! Alexandria was being bombed and I was ashore! The *Kanangoora* had no recourse but to quickly set out to sea. It all happened swiftly. Bombs rained down, and the ship set sail. Andy was still aboard.

---

[23] In those days Jakarta was Batavia.
[24] Jerries was slang for Germans.

Part I   The Early Years   1926-1942

In all the confusion, I was left ashore. Fourteen years old, a sailor without a ship, stranded in the middle of World War II with Hitler's army invading Egypt!

I had very little cash in my pocket and only about a half a pack of cigarettes to my name. Standing on the dock, frightened, confused and literally lost, my ship was nowhere to be seen. I knew, if I could find the American Consulate, they would help me. I began wandering the streets of Alexandria, hoping to stumble onto some kind of sailors' home. Though Egypt had been under English rule, the people in the neighborhoods I was groping around didn't speak a word of English. In fact, it was all "Greek" to me. Just when I was beginning to lose hope, I heard some guys talking English. I went up to them and pulled on their coats. I told them who I was. They said, "We'll take care of you."

That's when I first met Stan Lee, who would become a frequent character throughout my voyages. I must have looked a sight, a young American lad alone and far from home.

They took me to the American Consulate. I got signed on in the American-Hawaiian Steamship Company ship called the M/S *Minnesotan*. Stan Lee was an AB[25] in her. She was a neutral ship, homeward bound, westward towards San Francisco. I signed on as a "consulate work-away"[26] for a whopping salary of one penny a month. Once in San Francisco, I paid off. The crew took up "tarpaulin muster."[27] They mustered up about $90 for me, making sure I didn't depart empty handed. That's what kind of people sailors are! Taking the money, I caught a Greyhound bus to Seattle. Andy was already waiting there. It was good to see him. He was glad I made it out of Egypt, none the worse for wear. We were back home again and just in time for the upcoming school year. We really tried our best and had every intention of making it this time, but the sea kept calling to us. We just couldn't hack it. We hounded Mother until she relented, again.

---

[25] An able seaman is an unlicensed member of the deck department of a merchant ship.

[26] Consulate-authorized man to work on ship for fare home.

[27] Tarpaulin muster is the pooling of cash by seamen by throwing money on the tarp to muster up some cash.

Part I   The Early Years   1926-1942

Gordon Highlander at 16

As I was sitting on the beach waiting to go back aboard with my booze,
the damn Jerries attacked **again** *with another air raid!*
Everyone ran to take cover. I thought, "Oh, shit! Not again!"
Of course, the only recourse for the **Empire City** *was to up anchor.*
So, they did! Away they went! For the second time in my life,
thanks to those damn Jerries,
I was stuck on the beach without a ship.
~Captain Jack V. Johnson~

The country was changing since the attack at Pearl Harbor, December 7, 1941. During WW II it was easy to find berths on merchant ships, especially out of New York. So Andy and I headed for New York. At 15 years old, we still were too young for the American ships in Washington, but we heard if you went to New York you could get a ship there. Determined, Andy and I rode Greyhound buses, hitchhiked, and even rode a train for a short time, until we finally fetched up in New York. It was definitely a cultural shock to come to New York City after traveling across country—especially compared to our surroundings in Seattle. We didn't know where to go or who to see. Somehow we located the Seamen's Church Institute[28] (SCI) and checked in with them. They were extremely helpful and guided us in the direction to locate a ship. We were disappointed to find out we were still too young to be in an American ship, even in New York. The people at the SCI assured us we could probably ship in a foreign ship—Greek, British, Swedish, or possibly Norwegian. "We'll get you out," they said.

In the meantime, they put us up in nice quarters, and the food was great. After about a week, we had the opportunity to meet with the British Consulate. He was duly impressed by our experience aboard other ships.

"Yes," we were told, "we can get you in a ship." They informed us there were openings on several ships.

---

[28] SCI was founded in 1834 as a mariners' service agency in North America.

Part I The Early Years   1926-1942

April 9, 1942, three days before my 16th birthday, I shipped in *Empire City*[29] as an EDH. That's a fancy British term for an "efficient deck hand." It's one or two jumps below an ordinary seaman. Andy shipped out in a Castle Liner bound for South Africa. We found ourselves separated on foreign vessels. We wouldn't see each other again for a couple of years.

An American Liberty Ship.

It was well into 1942. The world was changing fast. The *Empire City* was loaded with provisions, supplies, and other wartime cargo. During the war, you didn't know exactly where your orders would take you. Everything was pretty hush-hush. I found out the *Empire City* was destined to attempt to get supplies to the British Army garrison besieged at Tobruk.[30] Since April 10, 1941, the Germans had Tobruk surrounded and besieged.

After 240 days, a company of the Australian 9th Division took the city after heavy fighting against the Italian-German force. To get supplies to the Brits, we didn't go through the Mediterranean; we took an indirect route. We went down around South Africa

---

[29] American Liberty Ships were cargo ships built between 1941 and 1945 used in World War II.
[30] Tobruk was a seaport on the northern Mediterranean coast.

Part I The Early Years 1926-1942

and the Cape of Good Hope and up through the Red Sea. We got to Tobruk, anchored up, and started unloading. As usual with sailors who have been at sea for some time, where liquor is not allowed, everyone was very thirsty. With the ship anchored off shore, the crew was looking for booze. Hearing there was some ashore, we talked to the locals around Tobruk and found out where to go. We took up a tarpaulin muster and came up with enough money to negotiate with the locals and get us what we wanted.

As I was the youngest and considered (ha!) trustworthy, they sent me ashore. I boarded an amphibious landing craft that was equipped to go from sea to dry land. The work crews were already in the process of unloading our cargo and shuttling it ashore. The cargo consisted mainly of food and nonperishable provisions, ammunition, armaments, and other wartime material.

I got on shore and fell in with a British sergeant. I noticed this sergeant looked kind of funny. His physique wasn't what made me stare. I was intrigued at what he was wearing. He had on a skirt! It was a Scottish kilt. (I had no idea that, in the very near future, I'd be wearing one me-self.) There he was, in his kilt—his battle kilt! That's when I first met Oscar G. Callow. He was a company sergeant in Dog Company, First Gordon Highlanders. (I would meet Oscar again, and again, *and again*! Each time, we would meet under different circumstances throughout my life.)

Oscar took it upon himself to help me find all the booze I needed. I had the money, and he had the connections. We rounded up some Johnnie Walker Red Label Scotch Whisky, some gin, and a few cases of beer. As I was sitting on the beach waiting to go back aboard with my booze, the damn Jerries attacked *again* with another air raid! Everyone ran to take cover. I thought, "Oh, shit! Not again!"

Of course, the only recourse for the *Empire City* was to up anchor. So, they did! Away they went! For the second time in my life, thanks to those damn Jerries, I was stuck on the beach without a ship. Except this time, I had a few more bargaining chips, not just a few bucks and a half pack of cigarettes. This time I was stuck on that godforsaken beach with a stack of Scotch

Part I   The Early Years   1926-1942

whisky, beer, and gin! And guess who came to my rescue? The guy in the skirt, Oscar Callow! I told him my story. He said, "Come with me, and we'll take care of you."

I don't think he was looking at me, but eyeballing the stack of booze and beer. Well, he took care of me all right. Evidently, he took care of the booze, too, because I never saw it again. I went with him to the British headquarters. I was agreeable at this point to almost anything. Right there on the spot, I enlisted in the British 8th Army as the lowest private possible. A guy's got to do what a guy's got to do. It seemed like a good idea at the time. I became part of Oscar Callow's regiment, the 1st Gordon Highlanders, D Company, 51st Highland Division, British 8th Army on the 4th of May, 1942.

There's an old Gaelic saying, *"Là á bhlàir's math, na càirdean"* (on the day of battle, friends are good). It is inscribed on many Highland War Memorials. It wasn't long before I became familiar with their traditions and routine. We were directed by reveille. Each call was an old well-known bagpipe tune. I had to learn the sounds of the call for "Fall In," "Dinner," and "Lights Out." We learned to identify artillery fire, and occasionally there was the trading of shots. It was two weeks after I enlisted that Dog Company, the 1st Gordons, was able to break through the enemy lines with help from a Gurkha Company—Nepalese soldiers who were part of the British Indian Army. They were famous for their ever-present kukris, a heavy knife with a curved blade. They were fierce and brave. The Jerries had us surrounded, and we couldn't get out.

By the way, there are two versions as to why the British called Germans "Jerries." One claims it's a short version of German, but another says it was the term for the "chamber pot" used under the bed as a toilet. Well, whatever the reason, I learned to call them Jerries, and they had us surrounded. Even though we couldn't get out, we made damn sure they weren't getting in. The 1st Gordons and the Gurkha managed to break out through the enemy lines and take off. We were preparing to do everything we could. When they discovered us, all hell broke loose. Bullets were flying everywhere. I remember running like a

Part I   The Early Years   1926-1942

gut-shot cougar, in my kilt no less! I was thinking I could outrun the bullets, but I was wrong. They got me right in my ass, right in the starboard stern quarter! The damn bullet is still in there. We finally broke out of Tobruk; only our company and a Gurkha company made it out.

We continued east and got down the road to El Alamein, a town in northern Egypt on the Mediterranean, west of Alexandria. I was not too thrilled to be so close to Alexandria again. Oscar volunteered himself, me, as well as three others who had made it out for "Popski's Private Army" (PPA).

Vladimir "Popski" Peniakoff.

Vladimir Peniakoff commanded a small unit, which became known as the PPA. The PPA was named after Major (and later commissioned Lieutenant Colonel) Vladimir Peniakoff. He had worked as an engineer for a sugar manufacturer. Born in Belgium of Russian Jewish descent, he was intelligent, articulate, and highly cultured in literature and the arts. He was a businessman in Cairo and Fellow of the Geographical Society. His vast knowledge of the Egyptian and North African desert made him an asset to the British intelligence gathering. He spoke English, Russian, Italian, French, and Arabic.

Part I The Early Years 1926-1942

British radio operators had trouble pronouncing the name Peniakoff over the airwaves. One of his commanding officers, Pendergrass, dubbed him Popski. Pendergrass deliberately did this in Peniakoff's presence while addressing a radio operator. At that time, there was a character named Popski in the *London Daily Mirror* comic strip. It was a name familiar to the Brits. So, Peniakoff became Popski and, thus, Popski's Private Army.

The PPA was one of the several raiding units in the Western Desert during WW II. It was made up of almost two hundred men making raids from Africa to Italy. It was responsible for a lot of devastation behind enemy lines. I was with him only until November 23, 1942.

The PPA was officially known as No. 1 Demolition Squadron, an irregular unit of the British Special Forces. They were a long range, desert reconnaissance group. You might remember, back in the '50s and '60s, a television series known as Rat Patrol, the Desert Rats. The show was loosely based on the PPA. We weren't quite that illustrious or glorified as those blokes. We described ourselves as kind of snakes in the grass, slithering in and out, hopefully unnoticed. We were granted our own uniform and cap. It originally had a patch with PPA in red letters on a field of blue. Popski immediately changed it to PPA with white letters on a background of black. We did everything we could to get behind the enemies' line. (The British term is to *"turn the lines."*) The purpose of this group was to turn the lines and create all the mischief we could.

It was our job to infiltrate and commit sabotage against the Germans' rear supply points. Our mission was to harass and destroy fuel depots, ammo depots, or everything and anything we could. We wanted to capture anyone we could, but concentrated on the most sought out items: transportation, trucks, cars, jeeps, or pretty much anything else we could get back to our lines. Oscar had been promoted in the field to Lieutenant, and I was promoted to Lance Corporal.

 One time we hit a German motor depot. There wasn't too much of a firefight. They didn't know how many there were of us, and we didn't know how many there were of them. We soon

Part I   The Early Years   1926-1942

discovered it was pretty much a skeleton crew. Here were all these big German lorries sitting around for the taking. Even though there were just a few of us, we managed to liberate some rolling stock. Five of us jumped into the lorries, me being one of them. I got in this big truck. I didn't know how to drive it, but I resolved to get her going. There was enough adrenaline running through my veins to keep me moving. A key was left in the ignition, making her ripe for the taking. Everything seemed to be in order, everything that is except the grinding of the gears. I was trying to get that sucker out of there. After what seemed like forever, I finally got her going, and away I went.

There was a lot of spinning wheels and wild steering, but I managed to get her back to our company. The rest of our skeleton crew came along with the four other lorries. When they found out what was in my truck, I was instantly nominated for the Victoria Cross! The highest order of the British Army! I was the hero of the day! What did I do, you ask, to deserve such a prestigious recommendation? The truck that I had stolen was loaded full and down with Beck's Beer! Being a non-British subject, I couldn't really receive the British Victoria Medal, but it was a nice gesture. Nonetheless, in the eyes of my company, that day I was a hero.

Life with the PPA didn't allow for much rest and relaxation. Maneuvers were planned religiously. We were all too eager to accept the next challenge—one of which found us hitting a headquarters unit. After a brief firefight, we captured three officers (two Italian generals and one German general) as well as a couple of lesser officers (a colonel and a major). We ended up getting seven of them and loaded them into a truck we had "commandeered."

Away we went, loaded down with Jerries. I was sitting in the back holding a gun, a German Schmitzer machine pistol, on them. I purposely had it pointed at the German general. He was really angry. I don't know if he was more upset about being detained by someone so young, or that I had one of his pistols. Whichever it was, he was pissed! I can't say that I blamed him. He asked me who I was, and when I told him I was an American, Boy! He got even angrier. When we got back, we turned him over as ordered.

Part I The Early Years   1926-1942

Our group had been out on missions working behind the lines for quite a while. It was early November. Things were pretty well in hand as missions went. Some of us went back to Cairo for a little R&R, and that was when I first drank a powerful cocktail known as the "Suffering Bastard."

You take a tall highball glass filled with ice, add one ounce Haig & Haig Scotch whisky, one ounce of Hennessey brandy, two ounces of Victoria gin, one ounce sweetened lime juice, three generous dashes of bitters, and fill it to the top with Ginger Ale. Stir. Drink. And wow! Whee!

The Shepheard's Hotel, in the heart of Cairo, Egypt, and home of the "Suffering Bastard."

As the name indicated, in the morning you'd be a "Suffering Bastard." Joe Scialom, the bartender at the Shepheard's Hotel where we were staying, created it. I managed to drink five of those "Suffering Bastards" and ended up with a tri-color hangover!

Oscar Callow's only comment was, "I say, rather good. Not too bad." (Which translates to "superb" in British jargon.) His drink of choice was whisky without a mixer—neat—which also explains why all that whisky I had acquired when I first came ashore from *Empire City* had mysteriously disappeared.

Part I   The Early Years   1926-1942

After a little rest and much relaxation at the expense of the British Army, they held a parade. When the British discovered how old I was, and given the fact I was an American, I was given an Honorable Discharge signed by King George.

I was also given the Military Medal for Bravery in capturing the enemy and the Star of Africa for serving in Africa. This ended my time with the British Army. Oscar was kind enough to vouch for me in an affidavit on May 4, 1971, in King County, State of Washington.[31]

Star of Africa Military Medal

It wasn't long before I was flown to England. We crossed the Mediterranean, landed in Portugal to refuel, and finally made it to London. In a pub in Liverpool, I found myself sitting next to a little lady. I admit—I was looking for a good time. I was unaware that she was the girlfriend of a British soldier, who happened to walk in the pub about the time she leaned over and kissed me on the cheek. Her kiss packed one hell of a punch, because the next thing I knew, her boyfriend pulled back and punched me square

---

[31] See Part XV.

Part I   The Early Years   1926-1942

in the face, knocking out my front teeth. I had the damnedest time trying to locate a dentist to get roots pulled out! It wasn't too long after that I got on a plane to Gander, Newfoundland, then on to Tacoma, Washington, and back home.

Once back home, I tried to attend school for one last spurt. It was my senior year. I was due to graduate the next spring in May of 1943, but by mid-winter I dropped out and shipped out again. December of 1942 was when I left school for the final time. I would never go back. Eventually, I would get what is equivalent today of a G.E.D.

By this time I was pretty sure I could find a ship—an American ship. And I did. I wasted no time before I shipped out. This would be my life for decades to come, traveling port to port, harbor to harbor, and navigating across the oceans until I would finally toss up on dry land back home in Alaska.

PART II   1942 - 1945

Him or Me

There really was no other option. It was either him or me.
~Captain Jack V. Johnson~

After leaving school in the middle of my senior year, I joined the Army Transport Service. We were the civilian crewmembers of Army vessels. (At that time, the Army had more ships than the Navy.) We met every morning at 0800 hours, standing by in a cadre. We would work in a rigging loft until given other orders. When a ship needed crewmembers, they would come and get the crew out of the cadre. One day when the call came, they needed an AB in the SS *Anne Hanify*. I answered the call and shipped out. I was 16.

The *Anne Hanify* was a wooden hull steam schooner with a load of lumber bound for Alaska. Unfortunately, we went aground the third day out. The second day out, I was just getting off the four to eight watch at 2000 hours, when this low life character of a crewmate, known as Tiny, grabbed me as I was coming out of the mess room and heading forward. At first I was baffled, but soon had a clear understanding of his not-so-worthy intentions. He intended to rape me!

For the most part, the crews I sailed with were good, decent men, but as in any crowd, there are always rotten apples. Life at sea is rough, and rapes were sometimes part of it. With crews of men too long at sea, you may find yourself in a situation where you had to make yourself *unavailable*. Having already had a run in of a similar nature when I was a lad, I remembered how my father took care of the situation—throw him overboard. I was prepared to do the same if necessary. Once I gathered my senses, I fought the bastard with all my strength. We struggled, and somehow, I managed to pull away.

Part II   The Sea and the Russian Army   1942 - 1945

I had an 18-inch marlinspike stuck in my belt over my back right side pocket lodged in the small of my back. As the son-of-a-bitch came at me again, I pulled out the marlinspike and stabbed him with it. It took him completely off guard. I will never forget the way he looked at me with eyes wide open in shock and then anger. He uttered a guttural curse as that marlinspike bore deep in his chest. Down he went, deader than a mackerel.

I was in shock. I quickly pulled the marlinspike out of his chest and cleaned it off with his shirt. He was laying there, dead, face up, eyes open! It was just after the watch change. We were loaded down with lumber. No one was around to witness the attack. No one was around to witness what I did next. took all my strength to drag him over to the portside.

We were just forward of the deck load, at the foc'sle where the crew's quarters were. I pulled him under the ladder leading up to the foc'sle head. I managed to get him over the rail and gave him a burial at sea. I looked around, noticing the trail of blood. I didn't have time to do anything about that. I went directly to the shower and scrubbed the blood and the filth off me. I cleaned the marlinspike and put it away in the toolbox before quietly turning in. It was close to midnight. I don't know when I fell asleep or if I even slept that night. My mind was racing. I couldn't get the picture of the dead man out of my head. Every time I closed my eyes, there he was. I played the scenario over and over again in my head with the same conclusion. I had little choice in the matter. It was either him or me.

The twelve to four watch came down the next morning and gave us the call. In the galley over breakfast, everyone wondered what had happened to Tiny. Nobody had seen him. He didn't come to relieve the wheel. Everyone was murmuring. Someone asked me about it, and I just shrugged my shoulders. It didn't take long before everyone's focus shifted when the ship ran aground. A Canadian Coast Guard cutter came out and rescued us. In Prince Rupert, the crew paid off. While the ship was being repaired. We were sent to Seattle, and back to the cadre, waiting for another ship.

Part II   The Sea and the Russian Army   1942 - 1945

Kathy

*To think back about it now, it does seem a little wild,
but youth has a way of making you think that everything is forever.
After all, in my eyes, I was every much of a man, having already
encountered what seemed like a lifetime of circumstances.*
~Captain Jack V. Johnson~

I found a way to numb my senses by becoming a frequent patron of the bars. Drinking seemed to steady my nerves and fade the images. Though I was underage, Seattle was no different than most places back then; if you looked the part, they didn't ask your age. At 16 years old, 6'2" and solid muscle, I easily passed for 21. It was in one of those bar establishments that I met Della Roland. Della, in turn, introduced me to Kathy Jameson. Kathy's father was big in real estate holdings in Seattle. Kathy and I hit it off. Before long we were in love. We decided to get married. We also decided not to let anyone know. We were both underage, and I knew they wouldn't let us get married in Seattle. Rumor had it, if you went to Idaho, you could get married there. We two lovebirds got a train to Spokane and from Spokane to Idaho.

To think back about it now, it does seem a little wild, but youth has a way of making you think that everything is forever. After all, in my eyes, I was very much of a man, having already encountered what seemed like a lifetime of circumstances. We were married in Idaho. When we returned to Seattle, Kathy's mother immediately had the marriage annulled!

Though the marriage didn't make it, we did create something wonderful. I was 17 by the time the marriage was officially null and void, but occasionally I saw Kathy, and Geoffrey was conceived sometime during the process. Kathy chose to keep the pregnancy a secret, so I was somewhere overseas doing my thing in the battle of the Atlantic when Geoffrey was born. He came into this world, ironically, on my 18th birthday, April 12, 1944. I had no knowledge of the child and wouldn't have any contact with him

Part II   The Sea and the Russian Army   1942 - 1945

until sometime later. (Once I found out, I sent Kathy money as often as possible.)

After the war, Kathy contacted me to see if it would be okay for her fiancé to adopt him. After they were married, I agreed. Geoffrey Johnson became Geoffrey Patton. It would be years later, on Geoffrey's 21st birthday and my 39th birthday, that our paths would cross for the first time.

To mend my disappointment and broken heart, I shipped out in the SS *Morlen*. She was another Army Transport ship, a four-hatched freighter, small compared to today's vessels. She was built during WW I. Two of the sailors on this ship were Stan Lee and a man I knew only as Lance that I had met earlier in Alexandria, Egypt, when I had been left at the dock while in the *Kanangoora* in 1941. Stan became my best friend. Later he would introduce me to his girlfriend, who would later become one of my ex-wives, but that's another story.

The *Morlen* went north after a lengthy stay in dry dock[32] in Seattle for repairs. The first stop was Unalaska/Dutch Harbor. The Aleutians always felt like being back home. Unalaska, even more so. It is a beautiful island with breathtaking sights. Dutch Harbor was hopping with activity since it was the site of two military bases operating in the Aleutians: Dutch Harbor Naval Operating Base and Fort Mears, U.S. Army. Construction had begun earlier in July of 1940. Army troops occupied the island. The Aleutian Islands would be the only portion of North America invaded by the Japanese. It was a thriving little town with bunkers, Quonset huts,[33] and barracks—many of which are still there—scattered amid the green volcanic hillside of Unalaska. From there we went on to the next island, Atka, where an Air Force base still exists. We unloaded the supplies and set sail west for the next Army and Naval-operating base, Adak. Adak was the most populated island

---

[32] A large dock from which water can be pumped out; used for building ships or for repairing a ship below its waterline.

[33] A Quonset hut is a lightweight, prefabricated structure of corrugated galvanized steel having a semicircular cross-section. The design was based on the Nissen hut developed by the British during World War I.

Part II   The Sea and the Russian Army   1942 - 1945

in the Aleutian Chain. We finished discharging our cargo and turned around. I paid off in Seattle.

In January 1943, I did a quick stretch in a salvage tug, the *Slocum* as an AB/diver. I had taken a diving class, and was excited about getting into the salvage crew and testing my new skill. The *Slocum* was a big two-stack coal-burning salvage tug. We had left Dutch Harbor and were headed to Cold Bay. That's when the captain erred! Instead of going into Cold Bay, he went in west of Round Point. And put the ship hard and fast aground![34] We credited him with not having much sense. But what did I know? I was only an AB and a mere 16 years of age. We ran aground just outside of Cold Bay; *Slocum's* bones lay there today. We took what personal possessions we had and left her. The crew consisted of a captain, a mate, four ABs, two ordinaries, two engineers, two firemen, two oilers, and a cook. We were hiking toward Cold Bay when we ran into an Army patrol. The soldiers thought we were the invading Japanese. It was quite a tense moment, but we managed to convince them we were on their side. They took us into Cold Bay. A week later we were repatriated back to Seattle in an old United Fruit Company ship, the SS *Taloa*. She was a 6,494-ton banana reefer[35] built in 1917. Now, the Army Transport Service operated her.

The SS *River Raisin*.

Off the ship and lying around the cadre, again, I heard all I had to do was go to the Union Hall and ship out as a union sailor.

---

[34] The nautical term "hard and fast" refers to a ship firmly aground.
[35] Slang for refrigerated.

Part II The Sea and the Russian Army   1942 - 1945

Andy had just come in off another Army Transport ship. We both joined the National Maritime Union. They put us right to work. We shipped out in the tanker SS *River Raisin*, a brand-new T-2 tanker built by the Kaiser Company right out of the yard in Portland, Oregon, in 1943. The SS *River Raisin* could haul about 10,000 tons and was used to carry oil and gasoline.

During WW II, these ships supplied the fuel used by bombers, naval ships, and other ships. The SS *River Raisin* pulled into San Pedro and was greeted by the United Seaman Service (USS), the counterparts of the United Service Organizations[36] (USO), made famous by Bob Hope for entertaining the troops. These beautiful ladies did their best to make us feel welcome and raise our spirits. Just being around those beautiful ladies as they entertained us with a star-studded production of song and dance, as well as gifts and cookies, was enough to raise this 16-year-old's spirit. I was lucky enough to be singled out by one of the most beautiful of these ladies. She took me home for the weekend. And you know how we sailors are! Oh, did I mention the star-studded beauty's name? She was none other than Bette Davis! And *wow*! What a weekend! Complete with martinis, etc., and etc.!

While in the *River Raisin*, I had my 17th birthday someplace in the South Pacific. We shuttled back and forth, picking up petroleum products in Peru and taking them to the Southwest Pacific to Australia and New Guinea. One trip, we loaded at Talara, located in northwest Peru.

---

[36] A nonprofit organization that provides programs, services, and live entertainment to United States troops and their families.

Part II   The Sea and the Russian Army   1942 - 1945

Kitty-Kat just grew and grew and grew.

While ashore, I saw a little spotted cat. I thought it was an ocelot. I've always been very fond of cats, and I thought, *"Damn me eyes!"* I couldn't believe my luck. I could get an ocelot! I considered it a belated birthday present. I paid the price for the cat and brought her aboard ship. She was a tame kitten with a very loud purr and loved to play—really an exquisite creature. She fit right in and took over, becoming the ship's mascot. We called her "Kitty-Kat."

After our ship was loaded with blending stock[37] in Talara, away we went, Kat and all. Since the war was now worldwide, we often sailed without knowing where we were going. The captain got his orders sealed. It was anyone's guess where we'd end up. This trip took us to Bahrain, Arabia. They routed us way down along the ice, the high latitudes of the South Pacific, the Indian Ocean, and on up to the Persian Gulf to Bahrain. After discharging the blending stock from Talara, we back loaded full and down with aviation gas and bunkers. We left Bahrain. An amazing thing about the ocelot was that she grew, and grew, and grew until it was evident she was *not* an ocelot. She was a jaguar! Andy and I could handle her just fine, but the ordinary[38] that bunked with us was quite frightened by her. He moved into the day man's room.

---

[37] Any substance used for compounding gasoline, including natural gasoline, catalytically reformed products, and additives.

[38] Ordinary seaman.

Part II The Sea and the Russian Army   1942 - 1945

We were heading out of the Persian Gulf. Andy and I had just gotten off watch. It was pushing 2100 hours, and we were turning in. I was lying in my bunk ready to go to sleep. Andy was already sawing logs. Kat was lying peaceful on the deck, alongside of me. All of a sudden, Kat jumped up and snarled. She dashed away, banging into the corner under the washbasin. It was the oddest thing. She sat there, snarling and hissing. I looked up, trying to figure out what had startled her.

That's when I made out the outline of a figure. To this day, I will always say it was my father standing there. As I held my breath, the outline got clearer. I could now see him plain as the nose on my face. It *was* Father! He was leaning on the top bunk looking down at me. He said, "Poy, you better get up! Get on deck. You're in a bit of trouble. Better get up! *Up now!*"

I sat up on the edge of the bunk. I looked over at Andy. He was staring at me like he'd just seen a ghost. He must have heard the same thing I did because he asked, "Was that the Ol' Man?"

I said, "I don't know, but we'd better do what he said!"

We grabbed our lifejackets. We even had a lifejacket for Kat. We put her leash on and went up to the mess room. Everyone looked at us, wondering what we were doing with our lifejackets on. All of sudden, the general alarm bell rang! The after-gunners had seen a torpedo go past our stern. With the general alarm ringing in our ears, we headed for our battle stations. Andy and I carefully tethered Kat beneath the rail near lifeboat number two on the port side midship. Andy relieved the guy at the wheel. I relieved the guy on standby. It was a calm night, but there was a big sea rolling in. Big swells. We were taking water over the bow. The gunners and the lookout had left the bow and were on the flying bridge. I was on the starboard wing of the bridge. All of a sudden there was a blinding yellow flash! An explosion! We took a torpedo from a Japanese I-boat, forward at number one and two tanks on the starboard side. The ship was shuddering from the loud explosion and rolled to port. We were showered with aviation gas. Miracle upon miracle, it didn't ignite.

At some point in those fleeting moments, I remember thanking my father for waking us up. That was probably my

Part II The Sea and the Russian Army   1942 - 1945

eeriest experience with the supernatural. Supernatural or not, both Andy and I recognized it was the Ol' Man who had woke us up and prepared us for the coming disaster. I don't think you could convince either of us he didn't have something to do with sparing our lives that day.

As I said, we took the torpedo forward at number one and two tanks on the starboard side. We were able to keep going because the tanks were compartmentalized. The captain put the ship on a zigzag course. We made it into Fremantle, Australia, where we pumped out as much aviation gas as they could receive. Then we sailed up to Broome and pumped out some more fuel. Still carrying gas, we went down to Albany, on the southwest tip of Australia, and pumped out the rest. We then went around to Sydney, cleaning tanks as we went. We got into Sydney. We lay there in dry dock seven weeks, getting repaired. Andy and I filled our days working and our nights chasing girls! The girls just happened to be our little Salvation Army lassies! "Why not?"

We were dry-docked in Sydney, across the bridge lying at the foot of Harris Street. It was a bad place for a bunch of sailors looking for a drink. Halfway up the hill on the left was a small hotel and a pub; on the right was a sugar refinery where they made some fine rum. To get into town, we had to walk up the hill to get a tram or a taxi. It was easier to get gassed up at this pub, because then we didn't need to worry about going any place else. This one night we were having a fine time. That's the good news. The bad news is that the pubs in Australia always closed about nine o'clock at night. We managed to get a jug from a sly-grogger—that's a bootlegger in Australia. We were headed back to the ship, and Andy started getting sick. He stopped and was leaning against the light pole trying to puke. I watched as he continued to gag. Always helpful, I chimed in with some words of wisdom. I told him, "Andy, tickle the back of your throat; maybe that will help."

So while leaning with one hand on the light pole, Andy took his other hand and began tickling the back of his neck. He looked at me all pale and sweaty, and without missing a beat, he flatly stated, "It doesn't work."

Part II   The Sea and the Russian Army   1942 - 1945

I'm not sure where I learned those words of wisdom, but that night, like other nights, I was just "full of shit!"

We left Australia and sailed back to Peru. We loaded up and headed back west to Australia. At the Sydney Zoological Gardens, we found a home for Kat. Traveling light, we crossed the Pacific again.

By the time we reached Panama, I had become quite ill. I paid off the ship while Andy stayed aboard. We didn't see each other again for a couple of years. I had malaria, but that wasn't the thing bothering me most. I thought I had appendicitis. I was able to get in to the army hospital in Panama. There my ailment was diagnosed—malaria. I didn't have appendicitis after all. As for malaria, once you get it, it just never seems to fully leave your system. I had some treatments and was soon feeling better. I was repatriated in a Liberty troop ship SS *William M. Evarts*.[39] She went to New Orleans where I paid off. Then back to New York, the union hall, and another ship.

---

[39] There were over 1,600 Liberty ships built by 18 shipbuilders and 20 engine makers, under 18 U.S. Navy classifications. These classifications included cargo, troop-carrying, hospital, general stores, technical and scientific research, aircraft repair and supply, aircraft ferry, radar station ship, miscellaneous auxiliary ships, experimental minesweepers, radar picket ships, and distilling ships.

Part II The Sea and the Russian Army   1942 - 1945

Malaria & Tanker-Shankers

*When I awoke, my leg was under a linen sheet covering
with what looked like a wicker basket. I thought, "Damn me eyes!
They cut off my leg." I panicked and looked under the sheet.
I was relieved to find my leg was still there. Looking closer,
I saw what was under the wicker basket.
A mass of maggots! They had put them on the wound
to eat at the decay and rotten flesh.
~Captain Jack V. Johnson~*

In 1943, I shipped AB in the Liberty Ship SS *Hugh Williamson* with Captain Poletti. She was an American-South African Line ship. We sailed around Africa, hitting ports like Dakar in Senegal and Takoradi. Takoradi was an important staging point for British aircraft destined for Egypt. It is located on the Gold Coast. We then went on to Matadi, the chief seaport in the Congo. Matadi's official name was Ville de Matadi or The Stone City. It is located 86 miles up on the left bank of the Congo River. We loaded mahogany logs for a mill in Cape Town. We had laid over in Takoradi for a while. That's when I hit my shin on the hatch combing of the door on the ship. The hatch combing is always a hazard to sailors. Hitting your shin happened so often that we had a name for the injury, calling it *"tanker-shanker."* You would hit your shin coming or going through the hatch. If you managed to hit your shin hard enough, it produced a big gash, and you ran the risk of it getting infected. That was my case. My cut became very infected. In fact, I still have a hole in my shin from my *"tanker-shanker."*

I was taken to the hospital at Matadi where I was treated. While I was limping around on my swollen leg, I needed a drink. The only place one could find a drink in Matadi was at a bar which catered to the European sawmill personnel. (The sawmill produced big mahogany logs.) They were a mixture of English and Belgian workers, more Belgian than English. A very British gentleman ran the drinking establishment. He was kind of a

Part II The Sea and the Russian Army   1942 - 1945

Colonel Blimp-type[40] character with a curly white mustache and snow-white hair, ruddy cheeks, and a bit on the heavy side with his sleeves held up with elastic sleeve holders. He poured rather generous drinks. I thought I would do a little self-medicating. After a few of these stout drinks, I could no longer feel the pain in my leg. The next thing I knew, I woke up in a double bed. Lying beside me was one of my shipmates, Hank Koltinak. I wondered, "What the hell is going on and how did I get here?"

There was a big mosquito netting over us. We were both lying on the bed fully clothed. I do, however, remember the hangover. It was in Technicolor. I swung my feet over the side of the bed and tried to hold up my aching head. I looked down between my legs and "Holy shit!" There was a snake! It looked to be about 50 feet long as it stretched across the room! In actuality, the snake was about 12 to 14 feet. It was coming through the window and slithering across the floor. The head of the snake was just under the bed. Man, I jumped up and pushed the door, attempting to get out of the room. The door wouldn't budge. Now in a full panic, I tried again. I finally realized I had to pull the door and not push it to open. Once I figured that out, I pulled the door open wide and ran down the hallway into the main area of the bar. The old gentleman bartender was cleaning up. Looking up from wiping down the bar, he noticed my frightened state, saying, "I say there, ol' chap, what's going on?"

Catching my breath, I responded frantically, "Snake! Snake! There's a snake in there!"

"Tut, tut, my boy, have some gin. There's no snake in there. It's all in your head," he said teasingly, thinking it was just part of a hangover. Shaking his head, he poured me a generous glass of gin.

I quickly inhaled it and argued, "I swear to you, there's a snake in there!"

"That's just nonsense," he insisted, "here, have another drink." He handed me another glass. I took a big gulp! I was starting to feel a little better. I took another drink, then another, and then another. The gin began to calm my nerves. "Now, now,

---

[40] Irascible British cartoon character.

Part II The Sea and the Russian Army   1942 - 1945

my boy," the gentleman said, still thinking I was seeing things, "you just go back and have a bit of a lie down, a bit of a lie down, I say. There's no snake. Go get you some more rest. You'll be all right."

He patted me on the back. By this time, he had *me* convinced I was hallucinating. He walked me back to my room so I could sleep it off. When he opened the door, wouldn't you know it, I was right! There it was—the *snake*! "Colonel Blimp" saw it and let out a whoop, backing down the passageway. He scrambled over to the bar where a couple of big elephant guns were hanging. He grabbed the first one he laid his hands on. It looked like an anti-aircraft gun 88 millimeters or something, but it was a 600 double barrel nitro express. There he was coming back down the passage way and trying to cram shells down the gun's magazine. As he got to the room, he opened the door and began shouting, "Stand back, stand back, everybody. I say, stand back!"

I looked around and noticed there was no one there but me. But that didn't stop him. He kept shouting, "Everyone, stand back!" He held his arm up high in a backward wave.

He brought the gun up on his shoulder, took aim, and *kaboom*! The blast reverberated throughout the room and hallway. He hit the snake and blew its flipping head off. The body of the snake continued to flop around. Hank was jarred awake by the sound of the gun firing. Seeing the snake flopping around on the floor, he jumped up out of bed, hitting his head up against the wall. He was totally disoriented, trying to claw his way against the wall while covered in mosquito netting. In his fright, he relieved himself and made quite a mess of an already messy situation, and I just about peed *my* pants! The drinks flowed freely after that. "Colonel Blimp" was considered the hero of the day!

All that activity didn't help my infection go away. After much deliberation, the hospital staff at Matadi decided my injury was serious enough to need more medical attention. They transferred me up the Congo River to Leopoldville (Leopoldstad, as the Belgians called it), the capitol of the Belgian Congo at that time. I was in a lot of pain, and the infection was getting worse. The entire ordeal was becoming very unpleasant. The infection stank.

Part II The Sea and the Russian Army   1942 - 1945

Gangrene was setting in. The medical team assessed the situation and prepared me ready for surgery. The last thing I remember was a sweet smell and someone putting a mask laced with chloroform over my face. When I awoke, my leg was under a linen sheet covering with what looked like a wicker basket. I thought, *"Damn me eyes*! They cut off my leg."

I panicked and looked under the sheet. I was relieved to find my leg was still there. Looking closer, I saw what was under the wicker basket. A mass of maggots! They had put them on the wound to eat at the decay and rotten flesh. That's how they did things in those days, especially if you were in need of medical attention up the Congo River of West Africa.

When the maggots had finished their job and the staff thought I was well enough to sail again, I shipped aboard another ship. She was going south. I sailed as a supernumerary[41] and had nothing to do. I got off at Cape Town. My ship, the *Hugh Williamson*, was still there. In those days it was break bulk.[42] Ships could lie at a dock as long as a week or two. I rejoined her just two days before they sailed.

---

[41] Individuals who join a vessel but have no crew contract, passenger ticket, or onboard responsibilities, often as a courtesy from the ship captain.

[42] In shipping, break bulk cargo or general cargo is a term that can be described as goods that must be loaded individually, and not in containers nor in bulk as with oil or grain. Ships that carry this sort of cargo are often called general cargo ships.

Part II The Sea and the Russian Army 1942 - 1945

Martinis with Hemingway

Hemingway is quoted as saying: "The world breaks everyone, and afterward, some are strong at the broken places."

We exchanged a sundry of sea stories. I finally had to sober up and get on with my job. I said, "So long," and that I'd see him down the pike. The truth is I never did see him again.
~Captain Jack V. Johnson~

We journeyed from Cape Town to Durbin and East London, and then up to Lourenco Marques in neutral Portuguese East Africa. There was also a big German raider lying in Lourenco Marques. The German crew would hit the bars and the casinos and experience the delights of Madame Olga's and Madame Yvonne's lovely *ladies of the evening*. We were in the middle of WW II in East Africa at a neutral port with German sailors rubbing shoulders, drinking, and fraternizing with our ship's crew. Lying right outside the harbor were South African ships, waiting for them to try and slip out. I never did find out what happened to the German ship.

In Lourenco Marques, Mozambique, we loaded a cargo of coal, plus six Italians, who had been confined in the neutral port. (Italy had joined the Allied forces on October 13, 1943.) The Italians were waiting to be repatriated back home. We had a little cargo left for Mombasa and Zanzibar. Our port for the coal was Catania, Sicily. Before going on to Catania, we stopped at Port Said on the northern end of the Suez Canal. *The gateway to hell…*

Captain Poletti was always finding us things to do. He took some of us up to Nairobi while the ship was in Mombasa. While we were in a hotel in Nairobi having dinner, a guy in his mid-40s was sitting there having a martini. It was Ernest Hemingway! His wife, Martha Gellhorn, was covering the war as a correspondent for *Collier* magazine. Hemingway had already covered the Japanese war in China and had followed his wife, working as a wartime correspondent. We introduced ourselves. He jotted down

Part II   The Sea and the Russian Army   1942 - 1945

our names. Hemingway and I got talking about my life at sea. He was curious about me being 17-year-old sailor and listened to my stories. The next day we went back to the ship.

A few years later, I had the opportunity to run into Hemingway a second time. This time it was in Florida. I was in a ship on a Caribbean cruise and had just left her, when I ran into Hemingway at a local bar in Key West. We had a few drinks (okay, a lot of martinis) and conversations about the sea. He said he remembered meeting me in Nairobi. Hemingway liked to listen; in fact, he was quoted saying, "I like to listen; I have learned a great deal from listening carefully. Most people never listen."

I can attest to the accuracy of this statement because he always was interested in where I had been and what I was doing. I often wondered if my answer to all his questions didn't end up in one of his books. After a well-rounded evening of drinking and talking and drinking some more, we said our farewells.

The next time I bumped into him was in late December 1949. I had gotten off the pilot Schooner *Columbia* and was in the Seattle area. I was in the Olympic Hotel having a drink in the old Marine Room, and there was Ernest Hemingway with his usual retinue of followers. By this time, Hemingway had several books published; better known were "The Sun Also Rises," "Farewell to Arms," and his more recent one, "For Whom the Bell Tolls." We gathered there, partaking of his favorite drink, the martini! I admit the memory is a little vague after that.

A few years after in 1952, I was on the East Coast, sailing in *Mormac* ships and had some time off. I wanted to go down to Key West to visit my now old friend, Hemingway. We had kept in touch over the years, a few letters here and there. (I lost those letters in a fire a while back.) Hemingway was now known worldwide as a literary success. He had just published "The Old Man and the Sea," an enormous sensation that invigorated Hemingway's literary reputation. (In 1958, that story became a hit movie, starring Spencer Tracy, and is still required reading in many high schools.) When I got to Key West and arrived at Hemingway's home, I was given a big welcome. He and Mary

Part II   The Sea and the Russian Army   1942 - 1945

were quite the hosts! Immediately we started on his famous martinis, even though I preferred rum. Sometime by the third or fourth evening, someone, maybe me, said, "We've got to get some more rum."

A couple of us volunteered to take the speedboat to go get some. We sped away across the water to Havana, Cuba, and bought a couple of cases of rum, some gin, and cigars. Then back again to Key West. The party continued for quite a while, about 10 days, if I recall (and I don't recall much). This was the last time I was able to spend any length of time with Hemingway, although I would run into him once more.

I was working out of Seattle for the famous salvage diver, Leiter Hochett. There was a fish tender in Vancouver that collided with the Lion's Gate Bridge. Down she went. They wanted to raise her. I was in the diving crew. It required tunneling under the vessel and pass lifting slings around her. We were successful in getting her up. But that was the first and only time I ever got the bends or decompression sickness (DCS), caused when divers surface too quickly. We were working in about 170 feet of water, and my tender told me my bottom time was running out. I said, "Okay, you can pull me up in a few minutes."

I started backing out, but I guess he misunderstood me because he pulled me right up, without any decompression stops! I told him, "I gotta get back down."

I could feel the bends starting. This was a diver's worst nightmare. They flew me over at water level to Victoria to the big tug *Sudbury* II and put me in their decompression chamber. There I got *"unbent."*

They flew me back to Vancouver to the Vancouver Hotel, where I was staying. I went in to pick up my key, and who happened to be at the counter but Ernest Hemingway! He was fit to be tied! They weren't going to give him a room because he wasn't dressed properly. Hemingway was kind of a big deal by then and world famous. He had settled in Ketchum, Idaho, leaving Cuba after the revolution broke out. He had earned celebrity status and had won the Nobel Prize in Literature, the Pulitzer Prize for Fiction, and had published a slew of books. But

Part II   The Sea and the Russian Army   1942 - 1945

because he had on an old blue chambray shirt and jeans, his hair was kind of mussed up, and added to that, he was about half in the bag (full of martinis), the hotel manager was not going to give him a room. Hemingway had his entourage of followers there with him. He yelled at the clerk, saying, "The hell with it! I'll buy my own hotel!"

I tapped him on the back, and he greeted me with a hearty handshake, inviting me to join him. Off we went to North Vancouver in typical Hemingway style. He didn't buy the hotel, but he might as well have, because he booked the whole place. We had quite a get together—an all-night party.

Instead of going back to go to work, I decided to use the bends as an excuse to take a few more days off. I stayed drinking his martinis—called Hemingways—comprised of three shots of straight gin on the rocks with a whisper of vermouth. We exchanged a sundry of sea stories. I finally had to sober up and get on with my job. I said, "So long," and that I'd see him down the pike. The truth is I never saw him again. Hemingway is quoted as saying: "The world breaks everyone, and afterward, some are strong at the broken places."

It would appear that the world finally broke him in a place he couldn't come back from. He was diagnosed with inoperative cancer. The demons he had fought for so many years finally got the best of him. He took matters into his own hands by taking his own life in 1961. I talked to his wife, Miss Mary, shortly after it happened and offered my condolences. As for me, all I can say is he was one hell of a man!

Part II   The Sea and the Russian Army   1942 - 1945

Camels & Pukka Knives

*Evidently, he didn't like my response,
because the next thing I knew, he pulled a knife on me.
Well, that wasn't a good thing, since my Russian Finn blood
takes poorly to having a knife pulled on me.
~Captain Jack V. Johnson~*

Back to 1943, and the *Hugh Williamson*. While we were in Port Said, Egypt, Captain Poletti took some of the crew to the Pyramids in Giza outside of Cairo. We got to ride on camels. It seemed I had gotten the worst one of the bunch. Mine was horrible! The creature's name was "Ginger Beer." Once we got to the pyramids, I asked, "How do I get to the top?"

**At the pyramids in 1943 with Captain Poletti.
Third from right in back row, I am on "Ginger Beer,"
and Captain Poletti is in front on his camel.**

The guide replied, "It costs one Egyptian pound to take you to the top of the pyramid." I was excited! I could brag I had climbed one of the Egyptian pyramids. I paid him the one pound and followed him as we climbed to the top.

Part II The Sea and the Russian Army   1942 - 1945

When I began my descent, the guide stopped me, "To go down, you must pay me five Egyptian pounds!"

"What do you mean?"

"You can try, but you won't make it," he grinned. I ended up paying the five pounds and followed him down the pyramid. In all fairness, it *was* a tough climb down!

While we were in Port Said, we visited a bar full of the local characters, as well as some Greek sailors, including one who made some smartass comment to me. Of course, I responded with equal enthusiasm. Evidently, he didn't like my response, because the next thing I knew, he pulled a knife on me. Well, that wasn't a good thing, since my Russian Finn blood takes poorly to having a knife pulled on me. I, in turn, pulled out my pukka, the knife my father gave me at birth. (It is a Finnish tradition to give your son or daughter a knife at birth.) The type of pukka I had was a tool rather than weapon, but it proved to be good in close combat.

The Greek sailor lunged for me and made a swipe at my right arm. I still have a scar from his failed attempt. I, on the other hand, didn't miss. I grabbed his left arm, pulled him close, and rammed the pukka knife in his armpit. Blood spurted everywhere, and he fell to the floor of the bar. I wiped off my knife on his shirt and returned it to my belt, and we quickly left. I lost that knife some years later when the *Sam Suva* was torpedoed. Down went the ship, along with my pukka knife. I have had other pukka knives, but none dearer to me than the one my father gave me.

While we were still in port, moneychangers came aboard, as they often did, exchanging South African pounds for Egyptian pounds or other currency. One of the moneychangers tried to pull a fast one on my good friend, Hank Koltinak. Hank realized he was getting shortchanged. He grabbed the moneychanger, roughed him up a bit, took his moneybag, and tossed his sorry ass overboard. The guy made it out of the water all right, and Hank made out all right, too, keeping the moneybag and all. I met up with Hank a few years later, when I joined the French Foreign Legion. He was a good shipmate and a good friend.

Our orders finally came through, and we set sail for Catania, Italy. When we got there, we discharged our coal and the six

Part II The Sea and the Russian Army   1942 - 1945

Italians. It took us over two weeks to unload the coal. It wasn't too bad staying in Catania. They have a lot of fine people there. It is the home of Vino Nero (the finest wine the world has ever known) and the loveliest of lovely ladies. It's no wonder that I fell in love! The romance ended as soon as we were done off-loading the coal. The *Hugh Williamson* set sail for New York. I paid off and looked for another ship. I ran into a couple of guys I knew from Seattle. We had drinks in a nightclub with some ladies from the United Seaman Service. I had acquired a taste for martinis and pretty girls. A club photographer took a picture of us.

Drinking martinis in a New York night club at 17
with Lloyd Halsather and two hostesses from the USS,
an organization similar to the USO, but for merchant seamen.
No IDs were checked—there was a war on. December 6, 1943.

The SS *Penelope Barker* departed New York and sailed to Iceland. There we joined a convoy heading for Murmansk, Russia. Off North Cape, Norway, German bombers found us and started bombing. This began what I have called "the 24 hours of terror." The convoy split up, hoping to evade the German bombers. The maneuver didn't work. Our ship was hit at the number two hatch. We managed to stay afloat. There were all sorts of shrapnel and scrap iron flying around. The bomb created a lot of mischief. My battle station was at a 20 mm gun on the port wing of the flying

Part II The Sea and the Russian Army   1942 - 1945

bridge. One of the loaders was George, a Navy sailor in the Armed Guard and someone I considered my best ship mate. When the bomb hit, I was knocked off my feet. As my head began to clear, I found I was sitting in the bottom of the gun tub. I looked down. George was lying there with his head in my lap. I took another look and realized it was only his head! It gets pretty fuzzy after that, and I was probably in shock—not just from the ordeal, but also the loss of a close friend.

The convoy was scattered, and we proceeded on alone with bomb damage to the port side of the ship at the number two hatch. As we were limping along, we took a torpedo. Down we went! We lost 10 men that day. We were flung overboard, wearing survival "zoot" suits. These suits were made of thin rubber with attached sea boot bottom feet. We had to wear Kapok lifejackets for flotation.

If you forgot your life jacket, you were dead in the water, and would sink like a rock and drown. Even with your life jacket, you were at risk. It is claimed that a man without proper protection will die of hyperthermia in those northern waters in less than 10 minutes. And that water was cold! Our watch made it off the ship and into the water safely. We were hanging on to a donut raft when, through the smoke and waves a British frigate HMS *Savage*, came to our rescue. They shouted, "You have one chance, lads. We have a net overboard for you; grab it if you can!"

They came really close to us. We managed to grab the cargo net. They parbuckled[43] us right up on deck—literally rolling us aboard. Once we were brought to safety the search for more surviving crewmembers continued. They managed to find 33 more, including the fireman and a wiper, who were hanging on the donut raft with us. The ship sailed on.

The ghostly details of this experience often show up in my dreams. I carried the image of George's head in my lap for many years, until one day sailing out of Kodiak I decided to put them both, the image and George, to rest. I wrote a letter expressing my

---

[43] Parbuckle salvage, or parbuckling, is the righting of a sunken vessel using rotational leverage.

Part II   The Sea and the Russian Army   1942 - 1945

fear, pain, and regret for George. Then, with a prayer, I gave the letter and the memory a decent burial at sea.

The ordeal was far from over as the "24 hours of terror" continued. That night the HMS *Savage*,[44] the frigate that had rescued us, took a torpedo, and down she went. They lost about 200 of their crew, including the wiper that had been rescued off our ship. We were picked up by a salvage tug and taken to Greenock, Scotland. Some of the American seamen, including me, who were waiting to be repatriated, finally made it back to New York. I swore I would never make that Marmansk run again. Being torpedoed and dumped twice in 24 hours was enough to make me want to stay far, far away from that part of the world.

Since captain's orders were sealed, it was hard to know where you were shipping out to, but we had a way of finding out through the grapevine where ships were going. All the cargo was stamped with the port of destination in codes and numbers. You could figure out where they were headed and determine the port of destination.

Using this strategy, I shipped in the SS *William Gaston*. She was bound south on what we called the Romance Run. I wanted to get as far away from the war as possible. We headed south towards South America and down to southern Brazil to Porto Alegro, which means "joyous port." Indeed it was joyous! Then back up the coast and the Port of Santos, Brazil. There we loaded full and down with grain and headed for the U.K. We left Santos and were running alone.

We were off of Recife, Brazil, which is located where the Amazon flows into the Atlantic Ocean. It is considered the mouth of the Amazon River. Wouldn't you know it? On July 25, we took a torpedo. I was on the four to eight watch. My watch partner was Joe Bodner. It wasn't a usual hit. We heard a kind of muffled explosion. The ship rolled to port. The ordinary seaman on the eight to twelve watch came down and said, "We've been torpedoed!"

---

[44] January 25, 1944, HMS *Savage* picked up 56 survivors from the American merchant *Penelope Barker* that was torpedoed and sunk by German U-boat U-278.

Part II The Sea and the Russian Army   1942 - 1945

No general alarm bell had gone off or anything. Then all of a sudden, all hell let loose. The general alarm bell started blaring. I had just done some laundry and was hanging it in the fiddley, which is the partially raised deck over the engine room. This was a great place to dry your clothes. As the alarms were sounding, we scrambled into our life jackets. I was in the number three boat on the starboard side. We got three boats and one raft away.

Our captain was kind of a dingy guy. He jumped overboard, but somebody dragged him into a boat. We did not lose a single man. We were lying out there watching the ship go down. It took about 20 minutes. All of a sudden, out of the gloom, we heard a high-speed diesel engine. It was a German U-boat, the submarines operated by the Germans during both World Wars. At that time, they didn't have their name or number on the boat. The German U-boat came within hailing distance and stopped short of running us over. Then, in perfect English, someone from the U-boat hollered, "What was the name of your ship?"

Nobody answered. To this day, it seemed I could hear the cocking of a machine gun. It is a sound to remember! The third mate must have heard it too, because he shouted out, "The *William Gaston*! The *William Gaston*!"

"Very well, thank you for the confirmation," came the very English reply. Then the German said, "Stand by."

They threw us a heaving line.[45] The Germans sent over two packets of Danish cigarettes and a first aid kit. Motioning with his hand, he shouted out, "Brazil's that way!"

They never did find the boat that the captain and the chief engineer were in. The Germans would have taken those men as prisoners since they would have detailed information regarding their vessel.

Decades after the war, I was piloting a cruise ship through the Northwest Passage, and one of the passengers was an ex-U-boat commander, Reinhardt Hardigan. He was the commodore of a

---

[45] A lightweight line that can be used on board a ship to make a connection with people, either in another ship, on shore, or for shipmates who have gone overboard.

Part II The Sea and the Russian Army   1942 - 1945

small flotilla that created a lot of hell on the East Coast. Hardigan had the U-123 that came into New York Harbor during the war.

That's how I learned the identity of the U-boat that torpedoed us. It was U-861. The U-boat captain's name was Jürgen Oesten. Amazingly, I was able to look him up, and we became friends! I kept in touch with him over the years, but I got wind that he finally went on to the big U-boat in the sky. It is difficult to confirm because surviving U-boat commanders have a kind of clique of their own, and they don't reveal much about themselves.

Another passenger in the cruise ship was Mason Grey, an old shipmate of mine. He had been torpedoed on the East Coast off a tanker. The sub that sank him was the U-123 with Commander Reinhardt Hardigan. Mason looked at the guy who had torpedoed him and said, "You're forgiven—but not forgotten!"

After the sinking of the *William Gaston*, we spent four days sloshing around the Atlantic Ocean in our well-stocked lifeboat. We might have avoided the misery of thirst and hunger, but there was no escaping the sun. The hot rays beat down on the sea and burnt any exposed skin. Finally, on the fifth day, a U.S. Navy seaplane tender picked us up. They took us into Jacksonville, Florida.

I eventually made it back to New York. It would take some doing, but after a few days of getting all the kinks shook out of my sunburned body and when I could handle a shot of whisky without shaking and spilling it, I went back to the hall and another ship.

The next ship was the SS *Elisha Graves Otis*.[46] We loaded full and down and in convoy headed toward the United Kingdom. Our first port of discharge was Glasgow, Scotland, on the River Clyde. Again, I fell ill. I guess the bouts of malaria were getting to me. I went to the hospital. When I got out, the ship had sailed. Finding my way back to Greenock, I checked into the sailors' home and waited to be repatriated.

---

[46] The ship was named after the inventor of the elevator.

Part II   The Sea and the Russian Army   1942 - 1945

The SS *Elisha Graves Otis*.

I spent pleasant days in Greenock, playing chess and drinking in the pubs in the evening. I was referred to as a "lucky Yank." Then one afternoon, on a beautiful day, the tides turned in my favor again. We had been out on a walkabout. When we came back to the home, I heard someone say, "Hey Yank! There's a ship bound for New York. Why don't you take her?"

Part II   The Sea and the Russian Army   1942 - 1945

Sergeant in Russian Army at 18

*At the close of all of her lectures, Tatianna urged very strongly that we should join forces with Russia in their battles and help them to victory. Being dazzled by her beauty, eight of us thought it sounded like a good idea.
We convinced ourselves it would give us something to do—mainly, getting us out of there and eventually home.
I volunteered, with several others, and joined the Russian Army.
~Captain Jack V. Johnson~*

Going back to New York sounded great, so I looked into it and found they needed an AB on the British ship SS *Samsuva*.[47] Though my days in Greenock were very enjoyable, I was glad to find another ship. Ready for work, I approached the lady at the sailors' home, telling her I'd like that AB job.

The lady said, "Oh, there's a good Yank." She got everything ready for me and sent me down to the shipping office. I went down and signed on as AB. The purser and one of the mates were doing paperwork with the shipping master. I was eager to get back to work and went straight back to the sailors' home and got my kit. As I approached the vessel, I recognized her cargo. She was loaded down to her marks with tanks and airplanes bound for Murmansk, Russia! It ended up we didn't go to Murmansk after all. Instead, we went on to Archangel, Russia, in the White Sea, which was just as bad.

We made it into Archangel and discharged our cargo. We back loaded some kind of clay or mud that was used to make ceramic tile. We headed out, joining a convoy off Murmansk. We were heavily laden with all that clay. That's when the nightmare happened all over again. We took a torpedo! Down she went. The ship behind us in the convoy came right over the top of us. We lost 17 men off that ship, including the captain. The surviving

---

[47] She was built on the same hull lines as our Liberty Ships, but had a different house configuration with the number three hatch between the bridge and the stack. The number three hatch in American ships is just forward of the bridge.

Part II   The Sea and the Russian Army   1942 - 1945

crew and I were floundering around in the water like a bunch of spawned-out dog salmon. Luckily we had our lifejackets and zoot suits on.

Out of nowhere came a big Russian icebreaker. A coal burning ship! I can still see the smoke coming out of her stacks to this day. Black! I could read the Russian name *Inia*. They picked us up, at least all of us who were still alive. Not many people in those days were speaking Russian, but having learned Russian as a child in Kodiak, I could speak it pretty good so I understood what was going on. The Russians thought I was pretty exceptional. Because the ship I was in was a British ship, they took us in to Murmansk and turned us over to some British officials. I was the only American aboard.

That's how I met up with Lt. Percy Janes, a hell of a nice guy, though a little old to be in the Navy, about mid-40s. I guess that's why they had him operating as the American Liaison Officer. He supplied me with Camel cigarettes, safety matches, chewing gum, and anything I needed—even clean clothes. He fitted me out pretty good. He said, "When you are allowed ashore, you can fetch up over there" (nodding to the barracks across the way). "It's kind of a gathering spot," he continued, "where you can get whatever you want, some soft drinks, a few drinks of vodka. Lemonade is the big thing here. But where they get the lemons, I don't know. Anyway, you'll only be allowed just a couple drinks, and then you can wander around. There will be no restrictions where you can go, but you have to be back in those barracks by 1700 every day. They will give you all the instructions when you get there."

I thanked him and checked into the barracks. There were about 200 of us, various nationalities and survivors from other torpedoed ships. It wasn't too uncomfortable. He was right—we weren't locked in. We could come and go as we wanted, but we had to be in between 1700 hours in the evening until 0900 hours the next morning.

We were rousted out of bed at 0500 every morning. We had to get up, make our bunks, clean up, and shower—which we welcomed. We were given decent clothes. Percy had us gathering

Part II The Sea and the Russian Army   1942 - 1945

before breakfast each day in a big mess hall area, listening to a lecture by this very delightful, beautiful, young Russian lady, affectionately known as the "Commissar." When she spoke, she had a cute lilting Russian accent. Her name was Tatianna. Her lectures were on communism, Karl Marx, the Great Patriotic War, and the soon-to-be victory. I didn't pay much attention to what she was saying, but I could listen to her for hours and look at her even longer. It wasn't long before I took a real liking to her. (You know how we sailors are!) Soon, I fell head over heels in love! Being able to speak Russian was a huge advantage in getting to know her better.

We developed a set-up. I would get my ration of Camel cigarettes from Lt. Janes. Tatianna would take the cigarettes and trade them for a full liter of vodka. We had a real good thing going there. Of course, we drank the vodka. A full liter would last us a couple of nights. Tatianna was passionate about Russia. One of the things she stressed at the end of her communist lectures every morning was our joining forces with Russia and enlisting to fight against fascism.[48] She tried her best to convince us to be sympathetic to their fight in the Great Patriotic War, which was how the Russians referred to WW II.

She would go on about how the Russians were fighting against fascism and explained to us about the heroes of the Revolution: Lenin, Stalin, Trotsky, and others, and how it all started with Karl Marx. (I now know more than most people about Karl Marx.) At the close of all of her lectures, she urged very strongly that we should join forces with Russia in their battles and help them to victory. Being dazzled by her beauty, eight of us thought it sounded like a good idea. We convinced ourselves it would give us something to do—mainly, getting us out of there and eventually home. I volunteered, with several others, and joined the Russian Army.

My group was put on a train bound south. We were going to Moscow. We thought, "Whoopee!" It would be great to see

---

[48] Fascism is a way of organizing a society in which a government ruled by a dictator controls the lives of the people and in which people are not allowed to disagree with the government.

Part II The Sea and the Russian Army   1942 - 1945

Moscow. Well, we did go to Moscow. But the countryside we rode through told a grim story of what was in store. Everything was in turmoil, and buildings were burned to the ground. When we finally pulled into Moscow, it was truly an unbelievable sight. The city and station had been bombed. It was chaos—nothing like what we were expecting. It was beginning to sink in that a war was going on and we were in the middle of it. Most people are unaware that Russia lost over 20 million people in WW II!

We transferred trains in Moscow and went on to Kiev for some very rapid basic training and to be sworn into the Red Army. When they found out I had been in the British Army with some limited military training and could speak, read, and write Russian as well, I was immediately promoted to the rank of sergeant and given command of a T-34 tank. One day I am an 18-year-old distressed American seaman in Murmansk, and the next, a sergeant in the Russian Army! We moved forward to catch up with the advancing troops. I was attached to the 13th Tank Army 2nd Regiment B Company. I had a very rapid training period of about five days in order to learn about the T-34 tank that had been assigned to me. The speedy training came complete with learning how to drive it, load the guns, and pass the ammunition, as well as how to be in command of one. When we were finally deployed, we moved forward to catch up with our advancing troops. The battle was pretty well advanced on the Ukraine front. We were chasing German troops, who were in retreat, but they weren't about to give up. They were in full destruction mode every step of the way.

We were up against the German Panzer V, the Panther, the Panzer VI, and the Tiger I and II, known as the Königstiger—King Tiger. The Germans had tanks that made our T-34s look like Tonka toys. Their Panther and Tiger tanks had thick armor with enough firepower to knock out virtually any allied tank and enough armor to shrug off most allied firepower at the time. They had 88 mms, and some of their tanks had 105 mms! We were the underdog, fighting back with our 55 mms.

Shortly after we were deployed, our tank got hit. We all made it out with limited injuries and a few abrasions, except for the

Part II   The Sea and the Russian Army   1942 - 1945

loader, who was pretty well broken up. We continued without him. The driver, the gunner, and I got off safely. My jaw was broken with the addition of several pretty good lumps on my head. They took us back to the field hospital, patched us up, wired my jaw, and sent us back into battle. Several more tank carriers arrived, and we were given another tank. My crew was deployed once again. I said goodbye to the loader, who was recovering from his broken bones. A Norwegian guy took over for the loader, so he, the driver, the gunner, and I prepared for battle. We were back in action.

We took off and caught up with another outfit that was backed by an infantry regiment made up of Mongols from Siberia. This infantry was tough and mean. I won't go into the gory details of what happened after they followed up and took over. I will only tell you this, "They never took prisoners." We were engaged at another point about 280 miles south of Moscow, which ended up being the largest tank battle of WW II, the Battle of Kursk. It was the largest of armored clashes and the costliest single day of warfare. Kursk was Germany's last strategic offense in the east and a decisive victory for the Red Army. We (our tank crew) were credited with wiping out four German tanks with our little 55 mms. We did quite well, even with our handicap. We were backed up and followed by the Mongol Infantry. The whole infantry division spread out across the front, but in this one regiment, we had the best.

Sergei Panamariov headed our company. He wasn't a captain but a major! He was from Siberia and had suffered from the German invasion and seethed with revenge. It was understandable. He had lost his entire family—grandmother, grandfather, aunt, uncles, mother, father, sisters, and brothers—all killed by the Germans. The only reason he had been spared was because he was away in the army. His mother, wife, and daughters had all been raped before they were murdered. He was not alone in his suffering. In fact, no one in our outfit was spared from suffering. Each had experienced great loss of family members. What they described to me made me more sympathetic to their cause. It was mindboggling that over 20 million were

Part II The Sea and the Russian Army   1942 - 1945

killed in Russia due to the German invasion, which was stopped at Stalingrad. We were the last of the forces pushing the invaders back.

In March of '45, we were coming up to the German border on the Polish side and came upon a German concentration camp near Lubsko. Our company liberated the camp from under the German-Nazi control. When we arrived there, some of the prisoners, mostly Jews, were still alive. Seeing the emaciated bodies of the prisoners was appalling. It is almost impossible to describe the horrific state they were in. I remember the stacks of dead bodies. From what we could gather, it appeared the Germans were trying to bury them and vacate the premises. We arrived before they were able to leave and cover up their atrocities. We had to convince the prisoners in the camp we were there to help.

After the liberation of the camp, the Mongols helped bury the bodies with a degree of respect and tenderness. It was a kind of flip-flop from their usual duties. The Mongol troops communicated with the prisoners that they were there to take care of them and not to worry. Some of the liberated prisoners could apparently understand the Mongol Tatar language.

When we entered the camp, we immediately captured the commandant and all 12 guards, as well as any other Germans involved. Our company commander, Major Panamariov, took it on himself to execute swift justice for the war crimes that were evident in this death camp. The major ordered the captives to be taken into one of the officers' buildings and instructed them to be seated at a long conference table. There were the 12 prison guards as well as the commandant sitting around the table. Now the tables were turned, so to speak.

We were told to take our positions behind the Germans. Standing behind each of them was one of us. As the German guards were seated, I looked outside the window and saw the dead bodies piled up like cordwood. The sight of barbwire surrounding the camp left a sickening taste in my mouth. An armed Russian soldier stood behind each German guard. They were now our prisoners. I did what I was told and stood behind

Part II The Sea and the Russian Army   1942 - 1945

mine. Major Panamariov had his pistol on the table in front of him, facing the highest-ranking German officer. He asked the commandant through a German translator, "Are you (and he uttered some name)?"

The commandant nodded, "Yes."

Then our commander continued with his line of questioning. "You are responsible for all this? For the conditions of this camp?"

The commandant pleaded, "I was only doing my duty. I was following orders. This is what I was here for!"

Thereupon, Major Serge Panamariov said, "Well, *I* am just following orders," and then he shot him between the eyes.

He gave the nod to the rest of us, ordering us to do likewise — to shoot each German in the back of the head. This time it was us following orders. We did as commanded. Twelve of us stood behind the prison guards and shot them in the back of the head. Swift justice. It was gruesome and gut wrenching. The major stood up and exclaimed, "Well, that's it. It's complete."

As we were leaving, a woman came running up to the major and proceeded to hit him in the chest. The German translator said, "This is the German commandant's wife!"

The major responded, "I have met her already." Then he took out his pistol and shot her between the eyes.

Everything from that day has remained with me. Seeing the malnourished Jews, the piles of dead bodies, and the execution of the Germans caused me to turn a corner in my boyhood innocence — if there was any left by then. If all my time at sea had not made me into a man, that experience did. I had seen humanity at its worst.

We took care of the decimated prisoners as best we could before moving on. The troops coming up behind us got everyone settled and helped begin the prisoners' slow recuperation with food, clothing, shelter, and medical attention. We were not told where they took the survivors. Our orders were to move on. We said good-bye to the Mongols. Their assignment was to take care of everything, bury the dead, and help the ones that were still alive. There were about 18 Russian POWs liberated at the camp, which was very rare. The Germans usually did not take prisoners.

Part II   The Sea and the Russian Army   1942 - 1945

The Russian POWs wanted to join us, but our company commander said, "No." They had to go back to their own units, which I guess they did. That might seem like a good thing, but it was likely when they rejoined their outfits that they were executed for surrendering. If they surrendered to the enemy it was their death sentence, the same as being shot.

Life was hard in the Red Army. We left the camp, and to be truthful, none of us knew the atrocious events we had witnessed were viral throughout Europe. We had chalked it up to the by-products of war.

Marshal Georgy Konstantinovich Zhukov.

We moved right along and made it into Berlin. Our outfit was under Marshal Konev. We weren't the first into Berlin, but we were right behind Marshal Zhukov. Marshal Georgy Konstantinovich Zhukov was the most successful Russian general in WW II. He was known for liberating the Russian people and conquering Berlin, Germany's capitol, after Stalin agreed Zhukov could take his army in first. The Allies made the largest aerial bombardment ever. For two hours it was a constant rain of death

Part II The Sea and the Russian Army   1942 - 1945

and terror with bombs. We followed. Everything was in ruins. The Germans surrendered on the 25th of April, 1945.

After the surrender, we waited for the British and Americans to come as reported on the other side of the River Elbe. We parked our tanks. We were standing by to stand by. In the last week in April, orders came to get cleaned up because we were going to meet the Americans. We changed into the best uniforms we could muster up. Some were in mixed uniforms, evident by some of the pictures taken showing us in winter gear. I had to borrow a dress uniform. I even took a bath, a rare treat! Sure enough, on the 1st of May 1945, we met the Americans on the River Elbe. We greeted one another with the universal "V," arms held high in victory, as the two armies came together.

LIFE Magazine **photograph. May 1945.
Second on right, I am still in the Russian Army,
shaking hands with the Americans.**

We were featured in *LIFE Magazine*. If you have that particular issue, you will find me shaking hands with the Americans on the River Elbe. I'm the tall one, the second from the right. The journalists didn't know I was an American. Other magazines were also documenting the historic event. *LIFE, Time,*

Part II The Sea and the Russian Army   1942 - 1945

and *Look* magazines all took pictures of us toasting the Americans with whatever booze we could find. I had some kind of schnapps. I couldn't get it opened, so I broke the neck off on the edge of a table and drank right out of the jagged glass. Everyone was having a good time, singing and dancing.

The next day it was orders as usual, back to our tank and standing by to stand by. We were out of our uniforms and back into our fatigues. We hung out, trying to stay out of mischief. We didn't know what was going to happen to us. Some were expecting to get shipped back east or go into garrison as occupational troops. It wasn't long before we were confined to a certain area and couldn't leave. They provided us with a lot of beer, booze, and schnapps. Somehow we located musical instruments like accordions, guitars, violins, and flutes. There was a lot more singing and dancing. Of course, I was leading most of the singing and doing my share of drinking and dancing the Cossack dance!

Back on duty with nothing to do, we serviced our tanks, keeping them in top running order. I was listening every day to the American and British voices. While sitting down inside the tank one morning, I determined I had had enough. I said, "This is it. I'm leaving."

I jumped out of the tank. The Yanks and Brits were all around us. I went around to everyone in my crew—the Norwegian, the two Russians, and the Dutch gunner. I gave everyone a handshake and saluted my comrades good-bye, *"Do svidan'ya"* (until we meet again).

Off I went. I got to the American lines. They didn't believe I was an American. Still believing I was Russian, they were unwavering in their conclusion and determined to send me back. I would have been shot if they had sent me back. The Americans were convinced I was just another Russian trying to escape the U.S.S.R. I started to get a little worried and I said, "Look, I'm an American from Alaska."

They still didn't believe me. I argued, "Either send me to the American Army to enlist, or send me home. The war is over; I want to get out of this trap."

Part II The Sea and the Russian Army   1942 - 1945

One of the guys said, "You speak pretty good English for being a Russian."

I insisted, "I'm an American. Of course, I speak English. Here, look at my tattoos. I got these in San Pedro in 1940." I waved around all my credentials that I had kept in a waterproof bag in my inside pocket. "Look at these," I pleaded.

They still didn't believe me. They said they had been warned about situations like this and weren't going to help me.

"Hey look," I said, "I was in the British Army, and Gordon Highlanders. I'm a merchant seaman. I wound up in Murmansk and enlisted in the Russian Army. Here I am, and I want to go home!"

It was a good thing there was a British major standing by listening to the conversation. He piped in, "So, you were really in the Gordons?"

I rattled off about my experience with the Gordons in 1942.

"What was your commander's name?"

I told him I was with the PPA, and Oscar Callow was company sergeant. He finally believed me.

All the Americans could say was, "This is amazing. We'll take care of you," they assured me.

The British major arranged for me to be in a DP[49] camp in the British sector. A week later I was bound for England. I had a layover in England near Liverpool. Everyone was feeling pretty positive because of all the advancements made by the Allied Forces and all the areas of liberation. The war in Europe was mostly over, but was still going on with Japan. It was only a matter of time.

While awaiting transport out of England, I spent my time in the local pubs. You'd think I would have learned from my previous experience in Liverpool pubs. Everyone was celebrating with drinking and dancing. We were sitting at a table. It was common that, every time you'd order a drink, the barmaid would six-pack you—give you six at a time to drink—so she didn't have

---

[49] Displaced person.

Part II   The Sea and the Russian Army   1942 - 1945

to keep hustling back with more drinks. This little lady sitting beside me said, "Ah Yank, give me some gin."

I said, "I'm not going to buy you any gin. I just want to hit the sack with you!"

She angrily charged back, "You can't say that to me!"

Then she picked up a beer bottle and hit me right in the face, knocking out my front teeth! Again! Who'd have ever thought that, not once, but twice, I'd get my teeth knocked out in Liverpool, England? After getting new teeth a second time, I caught the next flight out of town. At least this time I had found a good dentist.

When I was able to leave Liverpool, I hitched a ride aboard a plane to Gander, Newfoundland, to make it back to New York. From New York City, I flew back to Tacoma, Washington, and on home to Seattle. Fresh out of the Russian Army, I was not the same guy who had left Seattle not that long before. Not much older—but a lot wiser.

My mother was glad to see me. She hadn't heard from my brother, Andy. After a short visit, it was back to the Union Hall for another ship.

PART III   1945 - 1947

Off to Okinawa

Captain Champion interviewed me. We had a nice chat, and I signed on as AB. December 22, 1945. We sailed, January 5, 1946, from Vancouver. This was the **Pamir** *voyage number seven bound toward New Zealand. How I loved those four-masted barques, "the likes the seas will never see again."*
~Captain Jack V. Johnson~

There was a desperate need for mates in 1945 on merchant ships. The war was still going on, although it was winding down. I decided to get a Second Mate's license. I enrolled in Captain Kildahl's Nautical School and studied navigation. After a couple of months, I was ready to sit for my Second Mate's license. I got a 100% on rules of the road. (You have to get 100%.) I was able to jump over Third Mate and received my Second Mate's license.[50]

Down to the Union Hall, I shipped out in a C-1 troop ship, the MS *Cape Canso*, C1-A. She was built for short routes and high speed and had a load of Women's Army Corps (WACs) as well as other troops aboard. We were bound out to the Pacific for Honolulu. We got to Hawaii, and in one of my drunken states, I missed the ship. There I was on the beach—but being stranded in Honolulu wasn't so bad. At least I could understand the language. There was plenty to drink and plenty of food. I had a few bucks in my kit and was having a good time. I couldn't stay long because the brass didn't take too kindly to sailors who missed their ships.

---

[50] I would continue to upgrade over the years until I finally made Unlimited Master's License, not only in steam and motor vessels, but also Unlimited Master's License in sailing ships.

Part III   As Sailors Are Wont To Do   1945 - 1947

I located the Union Hall in Honolulu. That's when I joined the Liberty Ship *Samuel G. Howe* as an AB. If the name Howe sounds familiar, *it should* for anyone who knows history or American literature. This ship was named for the husband[51] of Julia Ward Howe, the author and reformer. We had a lot of war material on board the *Samuel G. Howe*. We were off to Okinawa, Japan, on VJ Day,[52] when Japan surrendered—effectively ending WW II, August 15, 1945. There were several kamikaze-type[53] uprisings with Japanese soldiers determined to kill themselves rather than surrender to the Americans.

After Okinawa, we were ordered into Kure. We had a Japanese pilot aboard. He said, "Ah, all the shipping lanes, no more buoys because of war. I know channel."

Captain Reese said, "What about over here?" pointing to the place we were trying to go.

The pilot replied, "Oh, cannot go there, plenty water, plenty water. Not deep enough." The Japanese had a comical way of interpreting our language and often flipped the emphasis. The pilot successfully got us to the dock in Kure.

Once in Kure, we loaded and continued on to Yokosuka. We were the first American merchant ship into Yokosuka. It is now the home to a Naval Air base and military hospital. There had been plenty of Navy ships in there, but we held the status of the first merchant ship. We unloaded our goods and then proceeded down to the South Pacific, loading up material which had been left at Iwo Jima and other islands. We fetched up in Noumea, New Caledonia. The ship lay there nine weeks, loading miscellaneous cargo. I happened to have a friend of mine stationed there, Elmer Hatlestad. He was a lieutenant in the army, in charge of the motor pool. I was able to talk him out of a set of wheels, a nice little army sedan. I now had wheels and was able to get around.

---

[51] Samuel Gridley Howe was a 19th century United States physician, abolitionist, and an advocate of education for the blind.

[52] Victory in Japan Day.

[53] A Japanese pilot trained in World War II to make a suicidal crash attack, especially upon a ship.

Part III   As Sailors Are Wont To Do   1945 - 1947

As fate would have it, I met and fell in love with Renee Harbeaulet. She was the closest thing to a sailor's dream. (You know what a sailor's dream is? A widowed deaf mute, nymphomaniac, with a washing machine, that owns a bar and liquor store.) Renee was almost there. She was a widow and had a washing machine. *And* she owned Wendy's Bar. She was close enough to the dream. We had a whirlwind romance.

During my stay in Noumea, I spent my free time with Renee. I would help out at Wendy's. One Sunday afternoon as I stocked the bar, I had an occasion to go to the basement. As I was looking around, I came on an old, dusty crate. Dusting it off, I found six full bottles of pure absinthe! Absinthe is liqueur made from high-proof brandy, wormwood, and other aromatics. The product had been banned in most countries, due to its potential for addiction and other possible health problems. I was curious, so I opened a bottle and had a belt. It had quite a kick. I became more interested in drinking than working. All in all, I must have had about eight straight shots of absinthe. I lost count and passed out. I woke up. I didn't feel sick and didn't have a hangover. With a sigh of relief, I headed for the toilet. There I made an interesting discovery. I had an erection! I considered this a good omen and went to find Renee. All went as expected for quite some time. But after about five hours, I began experiencing pain. The pain worsened.

By Monday morning, I was doubled over in pain, barely able to walk. Renee drove us to the Navy sickbay. I was in great pain by this time and could barely open the car door. Renee assisted me into the building. A nurse met us. She asked the nature of the problem. I said I needed to speak with a corpsman. The nurse told me she was a R.N. and that there was nothing I could not tell her. The pain got the best of me, so I blurted out that I had had an erection for over 24 hours. She called for the *corpsman*! He and Renee helped me on to an examining table. A doctor was summoned.

The doctor took a look and pronounced, "You have gleet." He explained that the condition was rare and that blood vessels become engorged, preventing the blood from circulating normally. With that, he left the room. Soon he returned, bringing

Part III   As Sailors Are Wont To Do   1945 - 1947

the entire sickbay staff with him. With one dramatic gesture, he pulled back the sheet for all to view this rare sight. He held forth a counseling session for some time, explaining all the details of gleet to the rapt audience. The remedy was brought in. It was a cylinder of frozen ethylene gas, and my privates were sprayed with the foam. The pain was excruciating. Then I got a shot in the ass.

I woke up at home, feeling ready to go again! Renee was happy and relieved. Renee and I had a wonderful relationship. Marriage was talked about and even considered, but it never happened. Renee was going back to France. She said that, after she got back from France, which would be the following year, we would stay in touch and consider marriage. Well knowing how we sailors are, that ended our romance.

My ship finished loading up material left over from the war and was ready to sail. I left my sailor's dream girl behind in Noumea. We took the material to Guam. In Guam, the surplus scrap was loaded onto barges. Then it was dumped in the water to help form the breakwater at the main port. (People were not environmentally conscious in those days.)

I paid off the *Samuel G. Howe* in San Francisco, late-November of 1945. Making my way back to Seattle, I went down to the Union Hall in search of another ship.

I heard there was a big square-rigger in Vancouver, British Columbia, the *Pamir*. The four-masted barque *Pamir* was one of the famous Flying P-line sailing ships built for the German shipping company, F. Laeisz. She was a war prize and had made several voyages under the New Zealand ensign. I always had a thing for sailing ships. I headed up to Vancouver, and there she was loading general cargo for New Zealand and flying the New Zealand flag. I went aboard, hoping against hope to ship in her. This was December 20, 1945.

She was beautiful. Towering masts and all her sails in a harbor furl. I spoke to the first person I came to, "I'd like to talk to the chief mate or the captain."

The guy looked at me and said, "I'm the chief mate."

I asked, "Do you need anybody? I'm looking for a berth."

He asked, "Do you have any experience in sailing?"

Part III   As Sailors Are Wont To Do   1945 - 1947

"Oh, yeah! I have experience in sail," I replied.

He nodded, "Okay, I'll take you to the captain." He introduced me to Captain Champion. Captain Champion interviewed me. We had a nice chat, and I signed on as AB December 22, 1945. We sailed January 5, 1946, from Vancouver. This was the *Pamir* voyage number seven bound toward New Zealand. How I loved those four-masted barques, *"the likes the seas will never see again."*

This picture of the *Pamir* crew is in the Maritime Museum of British Columbia, in Victoria, B.C.

I paid off in Wellington, New Zealand, March 18, 1946. Captain Champion also noted on my discharge, that I was not only an able seaman, but also a "chantyman"[54] I gained this title because I was always the one singing and leading the songs as we carried out our daily tasks. Whenever they needed someone to lead in the singing, the mate would call on me. I became known as

---

[54] Commonly spelled chantey. Sailor songs, from "chant."

Part III   As Sailors Are Wont To Do   1945 - 1947

the "chantyman." I think I am the only able sailor with a discharge paper that says, "chantyman."

From there I went to Sydney. I joined the C-1 freighter *American Press* as AB and found my brother, Andy, aboard her! He was AB on the twelve to four watch. I was his new watch partner. We left Sydney and paid off in San Francisco. There I fell in love. Again.

Discharge Papers from the *Pamir*, 1946.
Note the "chantyman" designation, middle right.

Part III   As Sailors Are Wont To Do   1945 - 1947

Nothing Like a Brother

*Andy never could hold his alcohol. At my suggestion,
we'd take his ID and money and put him on an outbound train.
We'd send him to Tacoma. Andy would wake up
when the conductor told him to get off the train,
that his ticket was up. Andy would try to get his bearings,
not knowing where he was or what had happened.
He'd eventually wind up back in Seattle, madder than hell.
~Captain Jack V. Johnson~*

It was good to be back with Andy. Not only did we work well together, but we also behaved just like brothers. My most favorite memories with Andy were fighting or just being mischievous. Andy and I got into our share of barroom brawls together, and often with each other. Andy usually ended up throwing the first punch, because—truthfully—most of the time I deserved it. When we were older and drinking in Seattle, I'd pull this trick on him. Someone would yell out, "Hey, he's passed out." Andy never could hold his alcohol. At my suggestion, we'd take his ID and money and put him on an outbound train to Tacoma. Andy would wake up when the conductor told him to get off the train—his ticket was up. Andy would try to get his bearings, not knowing where he was or what had happened. He'd eventually wind up back in Seattle, madder than hell. We'd get into a big fistfight and after we'd knock the hell out of each other, we'd laugh about it until the next time.

Andy and I were notorious when it came to drinking and carousing. We would hit Seattle or Tacoma with a bunch of other sailors who had just paid off ship. We'd always head for the gin mills, dance halls, or brothels. Our preferred topside bar was called the Seven Seas at 1315 First Avenue. It was right above the National Maritime Union Hall, which was 1313 First Avenue. The Seven Seas was a seamen's bar. While drinking at the Seven Seas and thinking about girls, we would decide to go visit our friend, Anne Thompson. She had this world famous sporting house in Tacoma. She was always entertaining international crews,

Part III   As Sailors Are Wont To Do   1945 - 1947

particularly Scandinavian crews, that pulled into Tacoma and Seattle, along with the likes of us.

This one time, Andy and I decided to go down to Anne Thompson's. Anne poured one hell of a shot, double of whatever you could get at any other bar. It wasn't good whisky, but it wasn't rotgut, usually Three Feathers or Four Roses. Sometimes she'd splurge, and we'd get Seagram's Seven. After we'd get loaded on the whisky and if we were still capable and not too drunk, we'd retire to the upper regions of her very humble abode and wind up topside with one of the ladies of the evening. If you got too gassed up, she had a couple of rooms on the top floor with twin beds, so you could sober up in comfort.

This one night I woke up and found myself lying on a bunk, fully clothed. I must have been tanked. I looked over, and in the other bunk was Andy. "It figures," I thought, but wait, he didn't have a stitch of clothing on! He must have gotten really drunk. I remember he had taken off with one of Anne's ladies. As I was taking in the god-awful scene of Andy naked, he woke up and looked over at me. I said, "Where's your clothes, Andy?"

He said, "I don't know." Looking across the room, he said, "There's one of my shoes." As he tried to sit up, he blurted, "Oh, god, I'm sick." Then he ran to the window and started puking his guts out. It was the dead of winter. He had an upper partial plate of false teeth. As he threw up, the plate fell out of his mouth onto the icy roof. Quickly, Andy stretched out, but it slipped farther away. He had to climb farther and farther out the window until finally he got too far out, and "whoosh" slid down over the icy sloping roof and onto a big snow bank!

I thought, "Good grief!" and ran downstairs. Anne Thompson was holding court with some Norwegian sailors and all of the girls, sitting around downstairs drinking. Even the "hostess," the big black lady that took care of the door, was there. I screamed, "Andy just fell out of the window!"

"Oh, my god, what happened?" the hostess yelled, scurrying toward the stairs.

"He's not up topside," I shouted, "He fell out of the window. He's outside. We've got to get him."

Part III   As Sailors Are Wont To Do   1945 - 1947

About that time we heard this loud banging on the door. The big hostess opened the door, "Why, Andy!"

"Yeah, okay," he mumbled as he came busting in the door without a stitch of clothes on, wearing nothing but his teeth, which he had successfully retrieved on the way down. The Norwegian sailors laughed, and the girls shrieked.

Andy stopped and looked at them, and without skipping a beat, he assured them, "Don't worry girls, don't worry, you'll all have a chance. I'll be right back." And he hurried up topside. He was quite the character and a hell of a sailor.

Another time, Andy and I were staying at the Frye Hotel in Seattle. It was handy to the waterfront and handy to where our ship was docked. We were walking up Third Avenue, looking for a watering hole. When we came to the first bar, I looked around and no Andy. I looked for him and found him lying on the sidewalk. He had put his topcoat down on the ground, put a dime in the parking meter, and proceeded to lie down to take a nap. He was always pulling stunts like that.

Andy and I were in the *Melrose*, a coal carrier, running coal from Norfolk, Virginia, to Fall River, Massachusetts. The chief mate was named Edward. He thought he was pretty hot stuff, always rather verbal and abusive, throwing his weight around and giving everybody a pretty tough time. After listening to him spout off and boss everyone around for a while, he tried it with me. I was fed up and told him, "You can have your way out here in the ship, but if I see you on the beach, we'll see what happens."

His smart mouth shot back, "Anytime, lad, anytime."

Andy and I paid off in Fall River and went our merry way. Sometime later, we were in Baltimore down on South Broadway in one of our favorite bars, when who shows up but this mate, Edward! "There's the bucko[55] mate," I called to him.

He laughed and said, "What are you doing here?"

I replied, "I'm having a drink; have one on me."

He said, "I'll never drink with you."

---

[55] A mate whose brutality made life a hell on board for the crew.

Part III   As Sailors Are Wont To Do   1945 - 1947

I said, "Well good, that'll save me a couple of bucks." I then said, "Well, how about this to finalize everything?" With my right fist from somewhere way back deep, I laid a Sunday punch on his jaw. He fell to the floor.

When he got up, he said, "Now, here's one for you!" Boy, he belted me one. I didn't see it coming. He got me good on the left side of my jaw, and down I went! We had quite a battle. I finally got him down. He was lying there, shaking his head.

I said, "Well, what do you think?"

He said, rubbing his jaw, "Aye, it was more than I expected," and he held out his hand. I pulled him up, we shook hands, and we've been friends ever since!

Baltimore became a regular homeport for Andy and me. One time after we paid off, we went down to South Broadway. We were drinking heavily and got pretty oiled up. When we sobered up, Andy said he had lost his wallet. I asked, "What did you do?"

He said, "The last thing I remember I laid it on the bar."

I looked at him in disbelief! "Your whole payday was in there?"

He said, "Yeah!"

I said, "Okay, let's go down and get it." We went back to the bar where he had been drinking the night before.

We sat down, and the bartender said, "What'll you have?"

We said, "We'll have straight shots of rum; make 'em doubles, both of them." The bartender set them up. I said, "Hey, my mate, Andy, left his wallet here last night with quite a bit of money in it."

The bartender continued to wipe down the bar and said, "So, what? I don't know anything about it."

I looked at him, "Let's have it."

"What do you mean, 'Let's have it'?" He was still acting like he didn't know what I was talking about.

I was carrying a piece in my hip pocket, a Colt .45 automatic. I pulled it out and pointed it right between his eyes, "I think you'll remember *now*!"

He pulled back abruptly and shouted, "What are you doing?"

Still aiming the gun right at him, I said, "Put his money and wallet on the bar."

Part III   As Sailors Are Wont To Do   1945 - 1947

"I don't have it," he kept insisting.

Pow! I shot right by his right ear, shattering the mirror behind him, and knocking a couple of bottles off the shelf. I said, "Let's have it!" and boy, he started piling up money and wallets on the bar. There were seven wallets along with Andy's laying on the bar. I picked up Andy's and took all the money out of it before handing it back to him. After all, it was my ass on the line! Then I took all the money from all the other wallets. I said, "Okay, set 'em up for the house."

The bartender was running up and down the bar pouring drinks hither and yon. He came back and said, "That comes to $30."

I looked at him, laughed, and said, "It's on you, bartender. Any more remarks and it's right between the eyes."

I pulled out the pistol and pointed it at him, and he said, "Okay, okay. It's on me." And away we went.

When Andy and I were in Baltimore, we always stayed with Daisy Samara. Daisy was a very wonderful lady. She was a little heavy set and heavily tattooed. She used to appear in carnivals. When we met her, she was married to a Filipino named Freddie Samara. Daisy ran a flophouse and was very particular about her girls. Andy and I somehow fell into her good graces. We had met her one night in a bar, and one thing led to another. Pretty soon she took us under her wing. She told us we could stay at her place, but we couldn't touch the girls. We agreed—fair enough. We ended up staying in the two rooms on the top floor of Daisy's house. We'd take an offshore or coastwise ship as mates or ABs, but when we were in Baltimore, it was back to Daisy's house. It became our headquarters.

One time we came in after drinking all night down on South Broadway and went up topside to sleep off the drunk. Daisy came up and said, "Hey, I need some help!"

I woke up and said, "Okay." She handed me a bottle of whisky. I said, "What do you need?" pouring a generous shot of whisky. I downed it and asked, "Daisy, what can we do for you?"

She said, "I just shot my old man."

"You did *what*?" I became more awake!

Part III   As Sailors Are Wont To Do   1945 - 1947

"Yeah, the little son-of-a-bitch. I went down to the basement and laid it on the line. I told him this was it. He didn't see it my way, so I shot him right between the eyes." She looked around and said, "Where's Andy?" I nodded to the room across the hall. She went next door said, "Andy, wake up. You got to help your brother here; he's gonna do something for me."

Andy got up and sat on the side of his bunk. Rubbing his eyes he said, "What do you need?"

She answered, "I want you to come down to the basement and take my ol' man out of here."

"What do you mean, 'take him out of here'?" Andy was now a little more awake.

"Well, come on down and see," she insisted. We got dressed and combed our hair. This was going to take both of us a few more shots of whisky. Down the hatch, and then down we went to the first floor where some of the ladies blew us kisses. We followed Daisy to the basement, and sure enough, there was her ol' man lying face up in a pool of blood. She had shot him right between the eyes, as well as three or four times in the chest. It wasn't a very big pistol, a palm-sized .25 automatic. The shot between the eyes must have done him in. She said, "I don't want this gun." I put it in my pocket. She said, "Get him out of here."

I looked at her husband lying on the cellar floor, and I said, "I hope you haven't called the cops! What are we going to do?"

She said, "No cops! I don't care what you do with him—just get him out of here." It was about midnight. Andy and I were having a tough time trying to pick him up. Daisy brought in a blanket and said, "Here, carry him in this." We rolled him up and I took one end and Andy, the other and moved him about six blocks away to a convenient garbage can and stuffed his dead body in it! The next day, Andy and I shipped out.

When we got back to Baltimore the next hitch, we went straight to Daisy's. She broke out a bottle of Bushmills Irish Whisky. We polished it off. I had never had Bushmills Irish Whisky before, but now it remains one of my favorites. After some time on shore, it was back to the Union Hall and another ship.

Part III As Sailors Are Wont To Do 1945 - 1947

Designer, Embalmer & Diver

The menu this evening included some rather tasty meat. After several bites, I asked, "This is very good. What is it?" Le Ah Pah responded, "Dog."
~Captain Jack V. Johnson~

In 1946, Andy and I fetched up in San Francisco after our Sydney reunion in *American Press*. I fell in with June Durdigian. She was a fashion designer, and I tried my hand at it for a while. I was pretty good and even contemplated taking up the profession. I did some sketches. I do have a little artistic touch—one of my many hidden talents! June took me on. I was studying to become a fashion designer.[56] June and I had a falling out.

It was then I met Cheri Elliot and, of course, fell in love. She was a beautiful girl, doing postgraduate work at the San Francisco College of Mortuary Science. I let her talk me into going to school with her. She thought it would be a good idea since we were planning a life together. I enrolled and started classes at the San Francisco College of Mortuary Science. Cheri imagined us going happily through life embalming cadavers. I studied intensely and did quite well. About then, we fell in with an old friend and shipmate, Bill Morrison, and Andy.

It was like old times. I had a pocket full of money, and it wasn't long before all of us were living the good life. I bought a luxury car, a 1941 Lincoln Continental Cabriolet. New, the car sold for $2,390 (a mere $40,000 in today's prices). I had a snow white Carson top put on her and 18 coats of lavender paint. Not deep purple, but lavender. She was a beauty!

Cheri and I decided to take a week off. We ended up going to Reno, Nevada. Las Vegas wasn't the big gambling attraction that it is today. Reno was the place to go. We were playing the casinos

---

[56] I designed some dresses for my sister Ivy's 80th birthday. I designed, created, and sewed them. I also designed and created some ballroom dance exhibition gowns for my daughter Laurel.

Part III   As Sailors Are Wont To Do   1945 - 1947

when a telegram arrived from my Andy. The telegram was straight to the point. It said: *Get back to the city <stop> Dump the broad <stop> Sell your car <stop> We bought a schooner and heading for Tahiti <stop>.*

I told Cheri, "We're going back to town." I didn't actually dump her. In my most charming way, I said, "This is the end, my friend, of our friendship and love," or some other bullshit. She understood. We embraced and kissed. It was a tearful farewell...

I sold the car, making a thousand dollars profit, which was pretty good money in those days. Andy had arranged for the three of us, Andy, me, and Bill, to ship in a Norwegian ship MS *Thor Isle* II. She was bound for Australia via Tahiti. We told the captain we were going to pay off in Tahiti. There were lots of sailors on the beach in Tahiti waiting to get out.

We arrived in Papeete,[57] Tahiti. We looked for the schooner we had bought (sight unseen) from a Chinese man. He directed us to this beautiful two-masted 95-foot schooner. We kept her under the French flag. We were bound and determined to make our fortune pearl fishing. We named her *Les Ami Trois*—The Three Friends. It was the happiest six months of my life. Every night was Saturday night, and Saturday night was New Year's Eve! We dove for pearls but only found a few. We did stack up lots of shell. We worked from the Taumatoas, east, then west to Tongass.

There was a big market for shell in those days before plastic took over. You couldn't sell things on your own, so the man who sold us the schooner hooked us up with a broker, Fred Long, an Englishman. To find a buyer for the shell, you had to have a middleman. In our case, the middleman was Fred Long. Fred found a buyer for the large amount of shell we had stockpiled. A Chilean ship came through, loaded the shell, and took it on to Japan. We had quite a celebration, thinking we were in the money. The next morning we set off to find Fred Long to pick up the check to pay off the Chinese who had sold us the schooner. We planned to "burn the mortgage!" When we got to the office, there was no Fred Long! I asked the Chinese guy, "Where's Fred Long?"

---

[57] Papeete means: water from a basket.

Part III   As Sailors Are Wont To Do   1945 - 1947

"Oh, Mr. Long," he said, flapping his arms, "He fly bye and bye. Go Suva side." In other words, he got a plane out of Tahiti (which was rare in those days), bound for Suva in the Fiji Islands. That's Chinese for Fred Long had skipped town with our money!

I looked at the Chinese, finding it hard to understand what happened, saying, "I guess you know we can't pay you off."

He looked sincere and seemed concerned, shaking his head and mumbling, "Ah, too bad, too bad." He was, however, less than sympathetic and wouldn't extend the mortgage. He took back his ship. No telling how many times he had sold that boat, or if he and Fred were in on the scheme together. We will always say we lost our beautiful little schooner on the "reefs of finance."

Andy, Bill, and I agreed that, because of my past encounters and reputation, I'd be the best to find Fred Long, mete out quick justice, and get what money I could from him. The planes were few and far between in 1946 out of Tahiti. I got in a little inter-island ship and headed for Suva. By the time I arrived, Fred Long had been there and left. They said he was bound for Australia. I continued on to Australia, looking for him. I went to Brisbane, Townsville, Cairns, and down the line. In Sydney, I heard Fred was down in Melbourne, so I went to Melbourne. In Melbourne, the word was, "Fred Long was here, but he headed back north."

I heard he was in Port Moresby, New Guinea. I headed to Port Moresby. I had just missed him in Port Moresby. I heard he had gone onto Hong Kong, so I went to Hong Kong. "He's around here," someone said, "but I think he's on the Kowloon side." I went over to the Kowloon side. I missed him again! *Damn me eyes!* I returned to Hong Kong. I was running out of money. In fact, I was completely broke. I could only hope Fred Long would die a miserable death. He should have died in his mother's womb and saved us all this trouble.

Being broke, I went to the American Consulate. I was told there wasn't much they could do for me. If I wanted a ship, they advised me to check in with the other consulates, the British, in particular. They said to check with Jardine Matheson, "You'd probably have a chance to work for them."

Part III   As Sailors Are Wont To Do   1945 - 1947

I had my Second Mate's license. After checking with the Jardine Matheson office, I got a berth in the coastwise passenger freighter *Poh Hai*. I shipped third officer in her. In spite of the name, she was a British ship. Hong Kong served as an entry port of the British Empire. I turned down the food in the officers' mess. I didn't like the boiled mutton, boiled beets, and blah English cooking. My eating solution was I'd go down to the crew's mess and sit with a Chinese named Le Chong Chu. He was the *sha rang*—the bosun. American missionaries raised Le Chong Chu in an orphanage. They gave him the name Le Ah Pah. There were very few of us who knew him well enough to be privileged to call him that. Everyone else called him Le Chong Chu. I would meet up with Le Chong Chu again in Seattle in 1952.

The other officers got a kick out of me eating down in the crew's mess. One day, when we were leaving Tsingtao or Port Author, Manchuria, either way, I was on the eight to twelve watch. Sitting down to an evening meal in the crew's mess, I was in for some great food, eating with chopsticks. The menu this evening included some rather tasty meat. After several bites I commented on how good the meal was and asked, "This is very good. What is it?"

Le Ah Pah responded, "Dog." The bite almost fell out of my mouth. Needless to say, I lost my appetite. I would never have knowingly eaten dog meat. That was my first and *only* time. Not that I didn't have several opportunities later on, but I couldn't bring myself to touch it again. All I could think about was my dog, Nero. Those Chinese are clever. Watch out if you ever hear them say something about, "Wokking the dog!"

I was aboard *Poh Hai* for quite a while—long enough to fall in love with the Jardine Matheson personnel manager Mary Fong. Mary was beautiful. Her delicate oriental features complemented her olive skin and almond eyes. I was smitten. She was a very sophisticated lady in her 40s and looked flawless. On one visit to her elegant penthouse apartment, she offered me a small brown block of what looked like tar. It was opium! Opium is a narcotic made from the white liquid of the poppy plant. It supposedly makes you feel euphoric with a sense of wellbeing, but that wasn't

Part III   As Sailors Are Wont To Do   1945 - 1947

my case. It made me deathly ill. I was nauseated and confused. On another visit, I decided to try it again. The second time, I experienced a feeling of weightlessness. It seemed as though I was bouncing off the ceiling. Euphoria at last! That was the last time I smoked opium. The euphoria frightened me. I was afraid I could easily become hooked. I may have ended my opium experimentation, but not the romance. It continued full fhart ahead. I moved in and made my home with Mary.

The *Poh Hai* would depart Hong Kong, heading south to Haiphong, Indochine Française—French Indochina. Then we'd sail back up the coast to Canton, and return to Hong Kong. From there, to Macao, Shanghai, Amoy, Foo Chow, Tsingtao, Tin-Sen, Port Arthur, Gen Sing (Inchon), Korea, and back down. One night as the ship was south bound from Tsingtao pirates boarded us. I had just got off watch at midnight. After a bit of a wash and getting ready for a lie down, the door burst open.

Captain McKenzie yelled, "Aye, Jock," and tossed me a loaded pistol. "Arm yourself, Mr. Johnson—pirates on the bridge!"

He headed up the passageway to the bridge. I grabbed the gun and was behind him in lock step. When we got to the bridge, there were three armed pirates in the process of taking over the ship. Someone had turned on the overhead lights, and in the dim glow, I could make them out. Captain McKenzie fired three shots, killing one of them. I saw one of the other pirates raise his gun. I shot him! Right between the eyes! I fired another shot, missing the third pirate. He quickly surrendered.

At that moment, the bosun, Le Chong Chu, appeared and reported the crew had overwhelmed two other pirates down below. All three of the remaining captured pirates, as well as the two dead ones, appeared to be quite young, and not too well organized. Usually pirates are successful in taking over a ship and getting to their secret ports on Formosa, now Taiwan, or the island of Hainan, or any one of the numerous dog holes anywhere along the coast. It is likely we prevented them from picking up reinforcements. Upon radioing the company office of the situation, we were ordered to proceed directly to Foo Chow, now Fuzitu. When we arrived at Foo Chow, we were boarded by a

Part III   As Sailors Are Wont To Do   1945 - 1947

contingent of six policemen, headed up by the tallest Chinese I had ever seen. He was about 6'5"! They promptly took charge of our three captives, literally dragging them down to the dock.

This was after much hollering, shouting, and pleading from the pirates. Captain McKenzie made a hasty statement to the police. On the dock, about 30 feet from the gangway, the tall officer shouted for about two minutes. Then the other officers forced the three pirates to their knees. The tall officer in charge pulled out his pistol and shot all three in the back of their heads. Then he looked down at them, kicked each lifeless body, and once again put another shot in their head. Holstering his pistol, he and the other five officers walked away to their waiting cars. This happened as the usual activities on the dock continued with passengers boarding and disembarking. The cargo continued loading and unloading as if to say, "What the hell!"

A rickety truck showed up a short time later. Two guys jumped out. They threw the three dead bodies in the truck and took off. Life was cheap on the China coast.

I liked sailing the China coast. Our southern-most port was Hanoi, "French Indochina," now Vietnam. It was a nice port of call, a regular sailor's paradise. Our northern-most ports were Tsina Tao, Tiin Seng, Taku Bar, Port Arthur, Manchuria, and Geng Seng, now Inchon, Korea. My most favorite port was Hong Kong or—more to the point—Mary Fong at Hong Kong. I shall always remember Mary Fong! On one of these trips upon arriving in Shanghai, I noticed a small American ship. I made a point to visit the crew. We got to talking. They told me there were openings aboard their ship. I went back to Captain McKenzie. "Captain," I said, "I have an opportunity on an American ship that could get me home, and I think I'll do it."

He said, "Aye, that's good on you, Jack. We're going to miss you. Good sailing to you and good fortune always."

We parted ways. I paid off in Shanghai, got my discharge papers, and immediately went over and joined the American ship. The year was early 1947. I was 21 years old and soon to be stateside again.

Part III   As Sailors Are Wont To Do   1945 - 1947

Jumping Ship

*The Congressman seemed to make a career out of giving people hell.
The same could be said for his brother, the chief mate.
Let me just say, we did not make happy shipmates.
Even so, it was good to get out on the open sea again.*
~Captain Jack V. Johnson~

In 1947, shipping was tough. The war was over. You would go down and register at the Masters, Mates, and Pilots Hall. *Damn me eyes!* You'd have to sit around for days or even months before you got a chance to ship out. Jobs were scarce all around. I had retired my book out of the Sailors' Union and National Maritime Union (NMU), but people still knew me as I wandered in and out of every hall.

One day in the NMU Hall, I was greeted by a couple of guys. One of them gave me a cigar and opened up a place in a chess game. While we were engaged in a serious game of chess, a job call came up for several jobs, including a bosun job in the SS *James Ford Rhodes*. I was half listening, putting my concentration into the chess game. The bosun job went on the open board. I was oblivious and continued to play. One of the guys said, "Jack, that bosun job went on the open board."

I looked up from the game, and sure enough it was on the open board. "How about holding this game; I'm going to go up and see about getting that job." I went up to the union agent, and asked, "Is that bosun job still open?"

He replied, "It sure is."

"You know I'm not registered here anymore," I admitted.

He said, "Well, do you want it?"

"Do I want it? Sure, I want it!" I shipped bosun, even though I had my Second Mate's license.[58]

I have often wondered why that job went to the open board. There were plenty of bosuns sitting around, and work was hard to come by. The only thing that might lend some clarity was the chief

---

[58] The second mate is considered third in command and the ship's navigator.

Part III   As Sailors Are Wont To Do   1945 - 1947

mate had a reputation for being a hard ass. Of course, nobody bothered to reveal that bit of information to me. I joined the *James Ford Rhodes*, and down the coast we went.

It wasn't too bad of a ship, but Chief Mate J. Preston Thomas was a piece of work. He lived up to his reputation as being a son-of-a-bitch. He was the brother of the highly publicized Congressman of New Jersey, J. Parnell Thomas.[59] The elder brother was hell bent on rounding up and convicting anyone he suspected was communist. This was a big deal in our nation at the time. The Congressman seemed to make a career out of giving people hell. The same could be said for his brother, the chief mate. Let me just say that we did not make happy shipmates! Even so, it was good to be on the open sea again.

We sailed down the coast, keeping the lower hatches open, and through the Panama Canal. We anchored off Tunas de Zaza, Cuba, and loaded a cargo of sugar bound for Marseille, France. We made a stop in between, at Bizerte, Tunisia. By the time we got to Marseille, I made the decision.

I had had enough of J. Preston Thomas—more than enough! I wasn't going to take any more of his shit. Johnny Fogle, the carpenter, decided to join me and jump ship. It would be a decision that would hurl us into history. It might not have been our finest hour, but we broke into the paint locker and took several gallons of paint and sold it over the side to waiting bumboats. We got a lot of francs for that paint. Then we sold some mooring lines and got lots more francs for that. We pilfered some linen and what not, until we had a pretty good bankroll.

We fetched up, staying in a small hotel on the waterfront. Of course, as soon as the ship left port, it was no time at all before we were in the arms of some lovely ladies. The girl on my arm was Michelle Aragonne or "Mickey."

"Ah, you crazy, Jack, you crazy!" was her running response to my many shenanigans.

---

[59] Parnell rounded up screenwriters, actors, directors, and anyone he suspected of having communistic slants. He convicted the "Hollywood Ten."

PART IV   1947

Crewmember on the *Exodus* at 21

> *"We're taking Jewish refugees into Palestine," they said,*
> *"and we need experienced sailors and crew*
> *because we are building up a little fleet here.*
> *We're out recruiting. Would you be interested?"*
> *Johnny and I looked at each other, grinning.*
> *Then our most important question, "What does it pay?"*
> *~Captain Jack V. Johnson~*

One night not long after we jumped ship, we were dancing at a nightclub when three sinister looking guys approached our table. They were complete with trench coats, looking something like Gestapo agents right out of WW II. The war had been over for a couple of years. This was June of 1947. I was 21 years old. Stopping at our table, one of them asked in very good English, "You guys sailors?"

"Yeah," we responded a little cocky, still taken back at their unusual dress. "We're sailors."

Their line of questioning continued, "You're not working?"

"No, we're not working. We're enjoying ourselves on the beach. Why all the questions? Can we do something for you?" I shot back smugly.

"We're looking for a couple of sailors. Would you like a job?"

Both Johnny and I knew it would be a good strategy to get out of town, considering some of our previous shady dealings. "What is it?" I asked.

"We're taking Jewish refugees into Palestine," they said, "and we need experienced sailors and crew because we are building up a little fleet here. We're out recruiting. Would you be interested? We've had our eye on you for several days."

Johnny and I looked at each other grinning. Then our most important question, "What does it pay?" I asked.

Part IV   The *Exodus*   1947

They named a price that was about $1,000 round trip, which in 1947 were *very good wages*. The plan was to make it into Palestine with a shipload of refugees and then make it on back to France and load up another one, and so forth.

"Yeah, that sounds good; where's the action?" I questioned.

"Well, we'd like you to stay here in Marseille and work some of these vessels getting them ready."

I was disappointed. "I don't want to do that."

Johnny said, "I'm not interested either. If you don't have anything going out right now, we're not interested."

They looked at each other, and the tall one said, "We have a ship going out right now. The SS *President Warfield* is docked at Port Sète. We renamed her *Exodus*."

This got my interest, a ship ready to go! "When's she sailing?"

"As soon as they get loaded."

"Okay, that sounds good. Let's go. That's where the action is." (I had no idea *Exodus* would become known as *The Ship that Launched a Nation,* as written by Ruth Gruber.[60]) I'd just as soon be up and going than sitting around waiting.

"I'll take that job," pushing my chair back ready to get up, "as long as the pay's the same." They seemed pleased. I extended my hand and shook on it. Johnny felt the nudge on his arm and the influence of a new love. He struck a deal to stay in port after all, getting things ready on the home front. The Gestapo-looking guys said they would send someone over to get me the next morning. Well, that didn't have to cut into tonight's celebration, so we continued to party.

The next morning, just as they said, two guys showed up to drive me over to Sète, which is about half way between Port de Bouc and Marseille. It was about an hour's drive. During the drive, my escort revealed the recruiters were with Haganah (which means defense in Hebrew), an underground Jewish Zionist military organization. Friends of the Jewish Army Resistance had purchased the old SS *President Warfield* through an

---

[60] Ruth Gruber, an American journalist, photographer, writer, humanitarian, and a former United States government official, saw the nearly destroyed *Exodus* and its 4,500 Holocaust survivors in Haifa.

Part IV   The *Exodus*   1947

intermediary for $40,000.[61] One of the promising things about the *Warfield* was she had a draught of only 7'8" which would allow her to sail close up the Palestine coast to disembark the refugees without other ships being able to follow her.

The crew had been assembled by the Haganah connections. When we arrived, I looked, and there she was. I could hardly believe it. There seemed to be thousands of people swarming around everywhere. Bill Bernstein, the second mate, met us at the gangway and took us to the bridge. He introduced me to the chief mate, Bernie Marks. Marks couldn't figure out why they were bringing me aboard because they already had a full crew. That's when the captain walked in. He was a short fellow with a fiery look in his eyes. He looked like a young kid in his teens, but I found out later he was 23 years old. He introduced himself as "Captain Ike." His real name was Yitzhak Aronowicz, and this was his first command.

He waved his hand as if shooing me away. Shaking his head, he flatly said, "We don't need anybody. We've got a full crew." Looking at the men who brought me, he stated bluntly, "I don't know why you brought him here."

They began talking and telling the captain, "This is a guy we recruited and he wants to go right to work."

Again, the captain said, "No," shaking his head, "we've got a full crew."

I tried not to feel let down, but always having an ace up my sleeve, I replied, "Well, that's too bad; maybe there's something else I can do." I reached my right hand into my left inside jacket pocket and pulled out my waterproof wallet, which was standard issue during the war. I opened the wallet and said, "I have this Second Mate's license."

"Second mate! Oh, of course, we'll take you." the captain exclaimed. "When we leave Palestine, you can be one of the mates for our next trip. Oh, this is wonderful, a Second Mate's license, too. Oh, great!"

---

[61] http://www.insideout.org/documentaries/exodus47 (December 19, 2007)

Part IV   The *Exodus*   1947

The chief mate's eyes lit up like a tilt on a pinball machine. "Yeah, great!" He introduced himself again, "I'm Bernie Marks." He was an alumnus of the class of 1944 out of King's Point, the U.S. Merchant Marine Academy in New York. "The more licenses we can get with people who have experience like you, the better it is going to be for this ship and any other ship we're going to run people in."

I didn't know at the time that sailing experience was limited with this crew, but what these men lacked in sailing skills, they made up with *chutzpah*—audacity! And just like that, I became part of the historic *Exodus* crew.

The SS *President Warfield* aka the Haganah Ship *Exodus*.

It was July 11, 1947. The ship set sail from France. We finally got the Haganah ship *Exodus* loaded. She had originally been the SS *President Warfield*, a packet steamer for the Baltimore Steam Packet Company, carrying passengers and freight from Norfolk, Virginia, to Maryland, and designed to carry about 400 passengers. She was flying a Honduras flag. Refugees traveled from the displaced person camps to Marseille. It took 160 trucks to transport the passengers. This once luxury liner was fully gutted and now loaded down with 4,554 passengers: 1,600 men, 1,282 women (six pregnant), 1,017 young people, 655 children, a full crew of 31 counting me, and supplies. Lifejackets and water were assigned. This illegal ship wasn't the first attempt of trying to get

Part IV   The *Exodus*   1947

Jewish refugees away from the DP camps and into Palestine.[62] In the SS *Exodus*, sleeping racks had been installed, some 4,500 or more. I was a supernumerary, noted in the manifest as Chief Steward, U.S.A., and one of the two non-Jewish crewmembers.[63] My job was providing services, maintenance, or work as needed. Once in the ship, I was standing by to be officially logged in as crewmember once we left Sète. At Sète, we needed a tugboat to turn us around and get us pointed in the direction for Palestine. The pilot didn't show up; nor did the tug to assist us out. There we were waiting. Finally, Captain Ike said, "I'll take her out. I have to. We've got to go."

It is difficult to get a 330' ship to turn without a tug, but they managed with some fancy turns to get the ship through the narrow channels and into the open waters. Once they got her squared away, they let the lines go. Unfortunately, the stern line got fouled in the propeller. We were hanging on with one line forward and trying to get the stern line clear of the propeller. I told the captain, "I have a lot of experience diving."

"Oh, no, you're the new guy," he said, dismissing my worthy gesture. Then, the captain himself, with Bill Bernstein, went down in the water. They had to hold their breath and cut the line in order to clear the propeller. Eventually, they got it clear. We let go of the last line, finally got turned around and headed to sea, and then promptly ran aground on the mud bank across from the dock. Once we got off the mud bank and made it out to sea, we were aware the British warships were watching and waiting.

The mandate to control Palestine was awarded to England at the end of WW I. Immigration was strictly controlled. As the British first approached, there were five British warships, and then there were six, bird-dogging us. We were on the slow bell, no faster than six or eight knots. We were capable of going a lot faster, but purposely proceeded with caution due to being followed by those British warships.

---

[62] They were classified illegal immigrants, displaced people, or Jewish DPs by the British.
[63] John Grauer, a Methodist minister, was also part of the *Exodus* crew.

Part IV   The *Exodus*   1947

The dog and pony show began. The British would come alongside the ship, announcing, "We understand you are heading for Palestine. This is forbidden—you know you can't do that!"

We ignored them and kept on sailing. The attitude of the people aboard was incredible, despite the abhorrent conditions in the ship—many of which were hard to fathom. It was a cattle ship with people stacked on top of each other. The latrines below deck were backed up. The smell was atrocious. One young man[64] begged for any job that would take him up on the deck and away from the smell of feces, urine, and god knows what. I gave him some paint and a canvas to paint Haganah Ship *Exodus 1947*.

We experienced an unforeseen tragedy. A woman died trying to give birth to a child. Her body was cast overboard. The infant later died in Haifa. There was a radio broadcasting in several languages transmitted throughout the ship. The crew spoke mostly in Yiddish (combining Jewish culture with the Hebrew language). In light of the destination, the refugees' spirits remained high, as most of them had survived concentration camps. Next to the camps, these conditions were bearable.

Soon we were swinging east just off the North African coast toward Egypt, intending to move up towards Palestine later, hoping to shake off the British. Upon changing our route towards Palestine, we figured we could run her ashore and get the people off. With our ship having a shallow draft, we could get in a lot closer than the British ships could. We were up for about 24 hours preparing our defense if the British tried to board. Barbwire was put around the ship. We had plans to place nets around the deck to repel the British if they tried to board, but never got a chance. No firearms. We were armed with potatoes and cans of kosher meat on deck for ammunition. We were getting close. The banner was lowered over side, and the blue and white flag of Zion with the Star of David now flew from the mast.

Originally we were supposed to land in Tel Aviv, but changed landing sites. It was a fitful night that July 18. No one

---

[64] Sixty years later in 2007, I would have an opportunity to meet this young lad again in Israel, who was known then as Professor Gutenberg.

Part IV The *Exodus* 1947

slept. Out of the darkness about 25 miles away from land, loud sirens were blaring, "You're in territorial waters. You are under arrest. Stop your ship!" Bill Bernstein alerted the sleeping passengers by sounding the ship's whistle. It was apparent very quickly that the odds were not in our favor. The raid happened at midnight. About 17 miles off the beach, two of the British destroyers came in and rammed us. One ship came along side of us on the starboard side, and one on the port side. It made it all the easier to board us. They held us in place liked canned sardines.

Once the British Navy boarded us, we did our best to repel them. It was a lopsided fight. We were no match for the British with their machine guns, pistols, rifles, and bayonets. We countered their blows with our canned kosher meat and potatoes, which we flung with great force—anything we could find to throw became our weapon of defense. We actually wrestled two of the Brits overboard. The British managed to drag them aboard before they were crushed between the ships. It was quite a melee, which lasted for about four hours.

Bill Bernstein rushed the wheelhouse and had locked it in hopes of preventing the British from taking the ship. Captain Ike and a few others disconnected the steering gear. The AB Bill Millman and I were on the bridge. All of a sudden, one of the British personnel shot Bill right in the face. He fell to the deck. I got down, trying to help him. Next thing I knew, the same guy was pointing the gun right between my eyes. About that time, Bill Bernstein engaged in a scuffle as the Brits were trying to take the bridge. He had been clubbed brutally with the butt of a rifle. Some of the crew dragged his unconscious body to the captain's bunk, where he later died. Bill Millman was bleeding in the face where he had been shot. We managed to get him patched up and on a stretcher. We found out later that he suffered a compound fracture of the jaw. A 16-year-old boy was shot in the face, as well as another casualty. About 150 people were wounded by the unequal battle with the British Navy.

When the ship was all-fast at the dock, the British began boarding—fully armed with tear gas and guns. They began rounding up the refugees. The passengers had been sprayed with

Part IV The *Exodus* 1947

tear gas, clubbed, shot at, and for now were defeated. In the early morning hours of July 18, 1947, we surrendered. The *Exodus*, pinned in on all sides by the British fleet, was towed to the port of Haifa.[65] As the crippled ship approached Haifa, the people sang the *Hatikvah*, "The Hope," now the national anthem of Israel.

They were taken ashore and told they were going to Cyprus, but they were put on three prison ships, the *Ocean Vigor*, the *Empire Rival*, and the *Runnymede Park*, bound back to France to the DP camps. Amazingly, many of these same passengers would later make other attempts to make Palestine their homeland. And many of them would eventually succeed. The passengers were unforgettable. The first person I noticed getting off the ship was a lady with a tattered oversized grey coat. She turned around and looked up at me with the saddest eyes. Those eyes spoke a thousand words, tired and defeated. She turned back and continued going down the gangway with the long parade of refugees, whose hopes were destroyed after being so close to their dream of getting to Palestine.

Now, after our failed attempt to get the refugees to Palestine, we were sitting in Haifa Harbor. Bill Millman was lying on a stretcher, waiting to be taken ashore to a hospital. Bill Bernstein and two others were dead. Hundreds were wounded. In my mind, we had failed. I was sad and disillusioned. Others would try and fail also in their attempt to get to Palestine, but eventually progress would be made.[66]

I was unaware that our determination to go to Palestine became a beacon for others, who would also attempt and succeed. In Israeli history, our trip was monumental. At some point, someone began to listen. Thanks to the efforts of journalists like Ruth Gruber, voices would be heard, and decisions would prevail to attain a Jewish homeland in Palestine. Somewhere on this journey, their battle became my battle. It was no longer just a job and a paycheck. I blended in with their purpose. I united with

---

[65] The SS *Exodus* remained damaged at Haifa harbor until it was burned August 26, 1952. An Italian firm bought it in 1962 and scrapped it.

[66] See http://exodus1947.org/eindex.html for full roster of passengers and crew.

Part IV The *Exodus* 1947

their cause. This would prove to be a milepost in my character and it would shape my alliance with these unwavering people.

Ruth Gruber was in Palestine with the United Nations Special Committee on Palestine for *The New York Tribune*. Being the only journalist allowed on board, she documented everything she could. Her camera captured photos of refugees being forced to disembark, being sprayed with DDT as all their possessions were taken and they boarded the British ships. She sent the images to thousands of newspapers and magazines internationally, including *LIFE Magazine*. I left unaware, but people were beginning to take notice of the Holocaust survivors' plight, and *Exodus* took her rightful place in history.

On shore, Bernie Marks was arrested. The rest of us who were American tried to blend in with the refugees as to not be taken into custody. Some of us clamored with the British to take Bill Bernstein ashore and give him a decent burial. It took some doing to convince the little cocky bantam rooster of a British major who was in charge to let us take Bill ashore. He finally consented.

Carrying Bill Bernstein's body.

I waited around with the others until they took Bill Millman off the ship to get medical attention. We put him into an ambulance, and they took him to the Haifa Hospital. We were given permission to use a pickup to take Bill Bernstein's body ashore. We took him to Martyrs' Cemetery in Haifa where they laid him in a casket, wrapping him in an American flag and burying him. That day he had demonstrated the best of King's Point virtues, "*Acto Non Verbo*," Deeds not Words, for his selfless act of valor. The other two bodies of the young men were buried close to Bernstein's burial site.

Part IV   The *Exodus*   1947

After the funeral, I slipped away with the help of a couple of the Haganah guys. They had their escape planned out. David Lifschitz, who had been with Haganah for quite some time, was an American from New York who helped me slip away. That's when I joined the beginning of the Israeli army.

Once, while I was with David, we were in three jeeps bound out to a kibbutz (little community farm). We were driving down the road, and some Arabs (that's what they called the Palestinians in those days) ambushed us and started shooting. We pulled off the road and positioned ourselves behind the rocks. I was unarmed. David had a pistol and started firing back at them. I was a little confused, figuring the war was over. Why were we being shot at? After all we had already been through, now we were being shot at again. I looked at David and asked, "Good god, David, how long has this been going on?"

David looked at his wristwatch and then looked at me. He fired another shot. He looked at his wristwatch again, and exclaimed loudly without missing a beat, "For 5,000 years!"

Portrait of Jack Johnson - crew member Exodus...He was recruited in Marseilles with John Fogle - June, 1947. Jack Johnson remained in Israel joining Haganah. In August he and several other Americans were rounded up and forced to leave Israel, returning to Marseilles. He continued his sea-going and lives today in Seward, Alaska, working as a marine pilot... He has returned to Israel many times and in particular, in 1967. [Photograph # 16843]

In September 1947, several other Americans and I were rounded up and forced to leave Israel. I met up with Johnny back in Marseille, France. He had worked for the Zionist cause in Marseille. Not much had changed. Marseille was still Marseille, and Johnny was still Johnny, and still in love. I was soon back in the arms of Mickey. We had a grand reunion and got a little carried away as sailors are wont to do. Johnny and I had quite a

Part IV   The *Exodus*   1947

few bucks between us and soon were living the good life again, dancing, prancing, and romancing.

This began my fondness for Israel and their plight and struggle for independence and recognition. Ironically years later, I returned to Israel just by happenstance at the beginnings of the Six Day War. I pulled a nose dive, faked an illness, and stayed ashore. I reenlisted my services. It wasn't long before I was assigned as a tank sergeant in the Golan Heights.

Part V   1947 - 1949

French Foreign Legion

"I stopped in at the recruiting office for the French Foreign Legion. You want to join the French Foreign Legion with me?" I asked.
"Ah hell! Not today," Johnny muttered.
~Captain Jack V. Johnson~

There is no place finer than Marseille, France. It's vibrant, dirty, and a little wild. Marseille was full of immigrants of various nationalities from all over. There was chemistry in the air. We were having a grand time. One morning as I was walking up Rue de la Paix, trying to bounce back from a horrible hangover with my usual routine of stopping here and there for shots of cognac and coffee (I'm a true believer in what is referred to as having a little *bit of the hair of the dog that bit you*), I stumbled onto a new twist in the road. My custom of hitting about three or four coffee shops down Rue de la Paix always seemed to straighten out my hangover—enabling me to get back to the hotel room and Mickey, of course. Then the four of us, Johnny and his girl and Mickey and I, would usually spend the day on the beach swimming and never letting the party end. This particular morning as I was walking along, I noticed a sign on a building, which I had seen several times in the past, *La Légion Étrangère Françoise*, the French Foreign Legion.

The *La Légion Étrangère Françoise* was made up primarily of foreign nationals who wanted to serve in the French Armed Forces. Mostly, it was made of ex-military personnel from various countries that still wanted to stay in the fight. By the age of 21, I had already been in the British Army Special Forces, the Gordon Highlanders; a Lance Corporal in Popski's Private Army; a Sergeant in the Russian Army; and in the Israeli paramilitary—so why was the idea of joining the French Foreign Legion so

Part V   The French Foreign Legion   1947 - 1949

attractive to me? Beats me! But the thought wouldn't leave me, and I figured I was well qualified. I wandered into the building, and sure enough, it was just as the banner advertised, a recruiting office for *La Légion Étrangère*.

After introducing myself, I asked, "What does a guy have to do to join the Foreign Legion?"

The French recruiting officer gladly explained what was needed. An interview. A physical. Not to mention a slew of hoops to jump through. It wasn't like the other military operations I had been involved where you go and just sign up. They were a little stricter. It was 1947. The war was over. France had a ready-made army of German Prisoners of War (POWs) and Displaced Persons (DPs)—a collection of people who had nowhere else to go. They were joining the Legion.

The recruiter said, "Sit down, and we will have an interview."

I declined at that moment, only because I wanted to soften Johnny up to the idea. I went back to the room to recruit him. Johnny was barely moving, trying to get his bearings from the night before, and contending with a whopper of a hangover. We went to get some sweet rolls and more "potent" coffee filled with the good stuff (cognac).

The ladies were already decked out, ready to go to the beach. I told Johnny, "I stopped in at the recruiting office for the French Foreign Legion. You want to join the French Foreign Legion with me?"

"Ah, hell! Not today," he muttered, still combating a hangover.

I said, "Well, why don't you get feeling better and think it over." That evening we were all out dancing and talking more about it. There were some other sailors from other ships, and we got talking to them. Telling them about our adventures, and having a good time, I told them about being in the *Exodus*.

They asked, "What are you doing here?"

I said, "Well, we've been here for quite a while and I guess it's time to get out of here. We were hoping to get a ship, but I think we are going to join the Foreign Legion."

Part V   The French Foreign Legion   1947 - 1949

They got a big laugh out of that. "A lot of us have often thought about that," they admitted. We kicked the conversation around a little bit more. The next morning, I got up feeling pretty good. I didn't get too inebriated the night before, but it wasn't for the lack of trying.

Johnny got up in a pretty spry mood, too. He looked at me and said, "Jack, let's go! Why not? Let's go join the Foreign Legion."

I said, "Okay. Let's go." And away we went to join the La Légion Étrangère.

We went down to the recruiting office. The same recruiting officer was there. I found out he was a Belgian sergeant. We sat down, and he said, "So, you want to join the Legion?"

We answered nodding, "Yes."

He interviewed us, asking a lot of questions like where we were born and how old we were. We gave him our real names, which for us was a big deal. We told him of our background and what we had been doing. I told him about my stint in the British Army, the PPA, and the Russian Army. I talked about the *Exodus*.

He said it all sounded pretty good, and things looked favorable, but he wanted us to think about this overnight. If we were still inclined, come on back and we would continue from there.

We went back to the hotel and met with the girls. They were beside themselves. They couldn't understand why we were doing this. Why we would volunteer to fight when there was no war?

Mickey kept saying, "You crazy, Jack. You crazy. Why you want to do that? You die!"

I disregarded her concerns, laughing at her frantic distress. "We'll be all right. We will only be in Africa," I assured her.

"No," she said, "we'll never see you again." By now both girls were chiming in. We tried to calm them down as best we could, telling them things would work out fine. The girls were relentless. They kept objecting to us joining *La Légion Étrangère*. They almost had us talked out of it.

I looked at Johnny and said, "Come on, Johnny; let's take care of this business once and for all."

Part V   The French Foreign Legion   1947 - 1949

We went back to the recruiting office. The same Belgian sergeant greeted us. "So, I see you're back," he said, nodding his head. "You want to join the *La Légion Étrangère*?"

We told him, "Yes!"

"Okay, well, before you go any further, there is small thing we have to get out of the way before we can begin the paperwork."

"What's that?" we asked suspiciously.

"Oh, it is really nothing," sensing our wariness. "We must first give each of you a physical to make sure you are physically fit for the task at hand. You look like fine men; I am sure it is no problem."

Johnny and I looked at each other and thought, oh, well what the hell. He sent us off to another part of the building where we met a doctor who administered the physical. The doctor checked us over, noticing my tattoos right off the bat. (Mind you, I didn't have near as many then as I do now.) For some reason, this caused uneasiness. Evidently, they were not taking people with tattoos into the Legion. I am not sure of their *raison d'être* (reasoning). I figured at that moment, this was the turning point, and maybe we wouldn't get in. The examination seemed to stop. An official-looking officer walked in. He didn't identify himself, but we figured he was working with the recruiting sergeant. Whatever he said cleared us at that point with the doctor, giving him the okay to continue with the physical. He stated, "No, that's okay; let them go. It will be fine. We are taking anyone we can at this point in time."

The doctor consented and continued with the physical. He held up two fingers and asked, "How many fingers am I holding up?"

We said, "Two."

"Okay," he said, signing the paperwork. "You passed the physical."

Everything must have been up to snuff because the next thing we knew the sergeant was sitting us down and handing us an application to fill out. It was in French. "You will need to fill out this application. It is in French, and I will translate for you. It

Part V   The French Foreign Legion   1947 - 1949

states exactly what we require to be part of the *La Légion Étrangère*," he said, rattling off other things here and there.

So the process began. The application called for our name, birth date, and any military experience. Johnny had spent three years in the Navy. Once we were finished filling out the application, the sergeant looked it over favorably. All that was needed was our signature to complete the process. Johnny and I signed on the dotted line. We were officially sworn into the *La Légion Étrangère Francaise*.

The *Légion Étrangère* was formed in 1813 to take care of troublemakers and foreign mercenaries who caused trouble for French. The new *Légion Étrangère* was based at Sidi Bel Abbès in Algeria, and that's where they'd be taking us. The *Légion* were known for their toughness with brutal conditions and ways. They were often on the front lines throughout the French colonial expansion, as well as the Franco-Prussian War and both World Wars. Their assignments varied to wherever the uprisings arose. They are still considered one of the most elite military units in the world.

Once we were sworn in, the honeymoon was over. The parts about the brutal conditions were not overrated. In fact, they were downplayed. Our recruiting sergeant, who moments before had been such a polite, nice guy, did a 180 and turned into a snarly beast. We were quickly hustled off to Fort St. Jeans waiting for a transport to Oran and Sidi Bel Abbès, Algeria—the headquarters for the *Légion Étrangère*. This was a little worrisome, and we were wondering if we had made a grave mistake. We crossed the Mediterranean. We fell in, marching down the dock to the railroad train that would take us to Sidi Bel Abbès, about 75 kilometers or roughly 46 miles away. It was the headquarters and training quarters for 1st Foreign Regiment. Located on the Wadi Mékerra River, it was considered "the holy city" or spiritual home of the *La Légion*.

Shortly after a few weeks of basic training, we were able to go into town for a brief R&R. It was then I fell in love with the way the Arabs served coffee: *"hot as hell, thick as blood, black as death, and sweet as love."* (I still like my coffee that way.) In Sidi Bel Abbès,

Part V   The French Foreign Legion   1947 - 1949

we were too poor to afford a glass of wine, but for the equivalent of a half-cent, we could get a couple of drops of dark brown hashish oil in the coffee. Consider that a drop or two of this liquid on a cigarette is equal to a single "joint" of marijuana—three in our coffee meant we were well on our way.

After a few cups of coffee, the Arab belly dancers began looking like Marilyn Monroe and Brigitte Bardot. This was the first time I ever saw belly dancers. They would dance, and then we'd throw coins on the floor. They'd pick them up. We were informed that for another moderate amount we could experience their pleasures, but I never had sufficient funds for that. *Damn me eyes!* Our pay was only about $16 a month.

We went through quite a rigorous basic training. Our company was referred to as a strike force. Our company sergeant was Fritz Kruger. He was a mean son-of-a-bitch—a good soldier—but one mean son-of-a-bitch. He had been an Oberst[67] in the German army in the Afrika Korps and an aide to Marshall Rommel. And he wasn't going to let us forget it. One night we were late getting back and didn't make reveille. He punished us by having us clean the decks in the latrine—with our tongues! We licked the deck (or in this case, the floor) clean. That was how they kept mental control over the men. One man from our company committed murder and was punished with the guillotine. It was the one and only time I had ever seen someone put to the guillotine, as well as the devastative results. It changed your morale right quick.

There were quite a number of Germans who had nowhere to go after the war, so France had a ready-made army. In our outfit were just a few Americans including Johnny and me. There were some Poles, some Greeks, some Brits, one Albanian, and a whole mixture of people, but the majority of them were Germans—really nice guys, and I had become friends with a few of them whom I had met in 1942, under different circumstances, when they were in the Afrika Korps. There were also sailors I knew, like Hank Koltinak.

---

[67] *Oberst* is a German noun and defines military rank of colonel or group captain.

Part V   The French Foreign Legion   1947 - 1949

We were 90 men of the 13e DBLE *(13e Demi-Brigade de Légion Étrangère)* 2ⁿᵈ RMLE *(Le régiment de marche de la légion étrangère)* Company Groupe Mobile. The 13e DBLE was headed up by a French captain, Fritz our sergeant, and some other German NCOs[68] (corporals). We were considered "mean sons-o'-bitches" and I fell right in with the bunch.

Our first deployment was to Douala, in the French Cameroons. Douala was the largest port in West Africa. There was a little difficulty going on down there. That was the time when all of the colonies of France, particularly in Africa, wanted to nationalize and become independent nations. The Cameroons wanted to become a separate state, and France had no intentions of relinquishing any of her colonies.

As a strike force, our job was taking care of any difficulties and to quell any of the uprisings. I guess we did a good job of it. We headed back north to Fort-Lamy, which is now N'Djamena.[69] In Fort-Lamy we reorganized, and from there we were sent to a little troubled spot up in the upper Niger and fetched up in Timbuktu, of all places—so I can always say I was in Timbuktu (Two Buck Tim from Timbuktu).

We were in garrison there, standing by for little over a month. Then we were sent from there all across Africa to Djibouti on the Red Sea nestled in between Somali and Ethiopia. Later in life I returned there again as bosun in the *Extavia,* an American Export Line ship. It was always fun to go to Djibouti. You could get everything duty free. I'd pick up a couple of cases of Haig & Haig Pinch Scotch for a dollar a bottle, 12 dollars for a case!

Back at Fort-Lamy, we were in garrison duty, keeping everything spic and span. From there we went to Fez, French Morocco, and then to Marrakesh. That was good duty. We were in barracks, but if we could afford it, we could live off base. Johnny and I ended up with a little apartment. I can still smell the jasmine flowers blooming outside the window. While we were in

---

[68] Non-commissioned officers.

[69] Fort-Lamy was named after Amédée-François Lamy, an army officer, who had been killed in the Battle of Kousséri.

Part V   The French Foreign Legion   1947 - 1949

Marrakesh, our company got orders to board a troop ship for French Indochina. After WW II, Indochina was re-occupied by the French, but Chinese communists joined forces with the Viet Minh and resisted the French occupation. Indochina consisted of Vietnam, Cambodia, and Laos. The United States and Great Britain supplied military assistance and modern weaponry to the French sides as war broke out. Russia and China supplied support to the rebels. It was penned "the dirty war." The war had started in 1946, so it was well in the trenches by the time we were set to arrive in '47.

A little R&R in Marrakesh, Morocco, with Hank Koltinak "The Pole," out of uniform and playing like a couple of tourists. January 1948.

Part V   The French Foreign Legion   1947 - 1949

The Legionnaires formed the bulk of the volunteer relief force and lost large numbers of men in the defense of Dien Bien Phu during the First Indochina War. It wouldn't end until France's defeat in 1954. The result would be losing 75,000 soldiers, with over a 100,000 wounded or captured. This would lead to the Second Indochina War breaking out in 1959, which the world will remember as Viet Nam.

As the news circled round that we were bound for Indochina, none of us were thrilled. Reports were coming back of lots of casualties, particularly in the units that the Foreign Legion had sent there. Now, here *we* were being ordered to board a ship bound for Indochina. Johnny and I were thinking seriously about this and trying to figure out what to do. We approached Fritz Kruger and told him we wanted out. He named a price. If we could come up with it, he'd see we would get a transfer. It was pretty pricey. Johnny and I had a few bucks left over from our departure from Marseille. We pooled our funds and managed to come up with what Fritz Kruger wanted with a bit left over. We were transferred out of our outfit and into a military police unit in Oran.

When we got there, lo and behold, who was our Sergeant? Oscar Callow! Major Oscar Callow, my friend from the Gordon Highlanders. I couldn't believe my eyes—Oscar Callow. Oscar's father had been a silversmith for the Royal family of England and an art dealer. Sometime after the war, Oscar had gotten himself in a wee bit of trouble with antiques. The details are fuzzy, but he was the Commandant of the misplaced Jewish people in the aristocratic part of Italy. I asked him how he came to be in the *La Légion Étrangère.*

He said, "Oh, tut, tut, my boy. I got into a bit of difficulty. We won't go into that, but I was handling some objects of art that I was obtaining for my father and fell into the wrong hands. Beat a hasty retreat, and here I am safe and sound!"

I said, "Well, you're no longer a Major?"

"Oh, I'll always be a Major," he stated, "but right now I have to take the position of Sergeant." Then he said very loudly in French, "*Une attention!*"

Part V   The French Foreign Legion   1947 - 1949

Johnny and I stood up, and he kind of laughed and said, "You're at ease. You're with me now, and you're going to be on patrol every day. Sometimes we will switch off, and you will be on night patrol, but right now you will be on day patrol. Your day will start at 0500. You will actively be on patrol from 0600 until 1700. You will be relieved at 1800."

He continued giving us all the rules and regulations. He gave us little pads to write up any infractions we encountered, to document people we might put under arrest, or to issue them a citation to report to the authorities. This went on for some time. It was good duty and went pretty well. We fetched up with a couple young ladies, who were there for the strict purpose of keeping company with the *La Légion Étrangère*. Even though it was good duty, Johnny and I decided we had made a mistake along the way and needed to get out. Our time with the *Légion* would end soon.

One day on patrol down on the waterfront there was a familiar sight, an export liner the *Extavia*. I had shipped in the *Extavia* before. Johnny and I looked it over pretty carefully, and decided this was it. The first part of our plan meant we had to get out of our uniforms. There were a couple of longshoremen on the dock—we got them aside and hastily arranged a change of clothing. Of course, it wasn't too easy (they weren't inclined to cooperate), but after they were knocked on the head, we didn't have much difficulty convincing them to see it our way. We managed to get them out of their clothing. We quickly dressed in the flowing, lice-infested robes and rag heads (turbans) and went aboard.

The gangway guard looked at us and was about to stop us to ask *"what"* and *"who"* were we.

Johnny looked him in the eye and motioned with one index finger a slit across his throat.

The guy put up his hands and said, "Entré, entré, come aboard."

I immediately found the bosun and told him who I was and what we were doing. He was an American and said, "Okay, come into my room."

Part V   The French Foreign Legion   1947 - 1949

When I went into his room, I said, "This looks familiar. This used to be my room!"

We laughed about it and talked a bit. "It was a couple of years ago," I admitted.

He smiled knowingly, "Yeah, I heard about you."

Then they let go of the lines, and off through the Straits of Gibraltar we went. We stopped in Lisbon and then went on up to Oporto where we loaded fine Portuguese wine. We had to stop in the Azores and then on to Hoboken, New Jersey, the homeport of the export line. We got off the ship with no passports. We were apprehended by the immigration and customs. We were interned for a while.

Not knowing what to do, I got hold of my brother-in-law, Dr. Albert "Bert" E. Bailey, (married to my sister Thelma). He was the head statistician for the United States, one jump under the Surgeon General. With me being from Seattle and Johnny from Tacoma, he was able to help us by getting hold of the Senator of the State of Washington, Warren G. "Maggie" Magnuson. "Maggie" used his seniority and persuasive skills to work things out for us so we were able to get back and obtain our American citizenship. You can say that I became an "act of Congress."

The year was 1948. It was nice to be back in the good old U.S.A., back on familiar ground. I went down to the Union Hall to see how shipping was. After getting settled in, I was ready to go to work. I took a coal ship out of Newport, Virginia, as an AB in the SS *William H. Edwards* and fetched up in Trieste, Italy. At that time Trieste was a free territory, governed by three different nations, the United States, the British, and Yugoslavia. It was 1952 before Trieste was returned to Italy. When I was there in 1948, the Allied military government ran it, and the governor at that time was a Major Brown, U.S. Army, a real nice bloke.

While in the SS *William H. Edwards*, and after our first trip into Trieste, we went back to Newport, Virginia, for another load of coal. We stopped at Ceuta, Spanish Morocco, for bunkers. While there, we noticed a big whale factory ship and five small chaser ships used to go after the whales. The small chaser ships were all numbered. We tied up at the dock not very far away.

Part V   The French Foreign Legion   1947 - 1949

After wandering around, we decided to go aboard one of the ships. A friendly Norwegian greeted us. He was real hospitable and broke out a bottle of Scotch. After we had several drinks, he showed us around his ship. He took us up on the bridge and onto the catwalk, forward to the gun. He showed us how they shot whales. He took us back down to the engine room and into the galley, back up on the bridge, and then back to the galley again. She was a beautiful ship, yacht-like in her style and appearance. I was sitting there admiring the beautiful little ship over another shot of Scotch.

I had previously gone whaling for a very short time, though personally it was not my cup of tea. I couldn't find the stomach to kill such magnificent creatures, especially with their connection to the sea. My short stint as a whaler ended as quickly as it had begun when I caught the dispatch vessel that ran between Cape Town and the fleet that carried messages and mail, and that aborted my whaling prospects.

Soon it was time to leave the Norwegian and move on. I thanked the Norwegian captain for the Scotch and said, "Thanks for showing us around; it's a very interesting ship." I asked, "Where are you going from here?" thinking he was going to the northeast Atlantic such as Iceland or even as far south as Antarctica.

He looked at me with a stern, steady look in his eye that I will always remember, glaring at me he stated in a loud resonating voice, "Going? Where are we going? We're going whale fishing!"

Part V   The French Foreign Legion   1947 - 1949

Margherita

*I will always remember the song she was singing
and can remember her singing it to this day.
I fell in love with her. She was sensationally beautiful.*
~Captain Jack V. Johnson~

The first night ashore in Trieste, Italy, I was holding court in the Yankee Doodle Bar, getting drunk, when out on the stage came the love of my life, Margherita. I still remember the little sign posted outside at the Yankee Doodle Bar: *"We specialize in American food. Come in and try our hotdogs and hamburgers."*

Who could resist a marketing strategy like that? The Yankee Doodle had a nice bar and poured a pretty good drink. That's all it took for us to go in and give her a try. I was enjoying myself out on the dance floor when Margherita came out on the stage to sing.

I will always remember the song she was singing and can remember her singing it to this day. I fell in love with her. She was sensationally beautiful. She had raven black hair, just like my mother. She was "five foot two, eyes of blue,"[70] with deep blue Elizabeth Taylor eyes and olive skin.

After she sang, I called her over to my table and asked her to sit down. I bought her a drink—rose-red wine—which was the watered-down version they would serve to the girls working the bar to keep them sober to charge up the patron's tab. She became my muse. I was truly smitten. We quickly became an item. I saw her every time I was in Trieste. I continued to sail from Trieste and back to Virginia for cargos of coal. After several months, I proposed.

While I was in Trieste, I stumbled on a lucrative means of gaining a little wealth—well, to be honest, a lot of wealth. I was taking floral fragrances from Bulgaria and selling them to a buyer from New York for a tidy profit. I would bring in attar of roses[71] and oil of Taboo, a Moroccan oil, and various other fragrances like

---

[70] Song by Sam Lewis, Young, and Henderson, California Ramblers 1925.
[71] Attar of roses is actually rose oil and is used in perfume.

Part V   The French Foreign Legion   1947 - 1949

lilac. After the war, there was a big demand for these luxury items and businesses were trying to get fragrances back on the market. We would buy the little vials in Trieste for $1,000 each and sell them in the United States for up to $10,000. As I said, it was quite a lucrative business.

Margherita. 1948.

I'd also get a case or two of rationed cigarettes when sailing. They went over big in Trieste. Little bumboats would come along side. We'd sell to them right after we'd pick up the pilot at Ancona, located in central Italy, on our way into Trieste. Captain William Sleek was aware of what was going on. Hell, in fact, he was into peddling cigarettes as much as the rest of the crew. That's just how it was in those days. You pulled every trick out of the bag to gain a nickel or a dime—whatever it took to get by.

Part V   The French Foreign Legion   1947 - 1949

Dazzling Margherita and me. 1948.

It was our third trip into Trieste, when I had paid off the ship, that Margherita and I were officially married. That was an ordeal. Margherita had been married before but never divorced. She knew it would be a little difficult to find someone to grant her a divorce, considering the traditions of the time and the country we were in. The main obstacle that stood in our way was the Pope. Italy was pretty subjugated by the Catholic Church. Neither Italy nor the Catholic Church would grant or recognize divorces. I got desperate. In one harebrained scheme, I decided it might help if I become a devout Roman Catholic, so I quickly took instructions from a priest. That didn't help any.

Part V   The French Foreign Legion   1947 - 1949

We had to resort to other means to obtain the divorce. Instead of letting this drag on any longer, we determined to take matters into our own hands. We went over into Zagreb, which is in the Croatian part of Yugoslavia, and saw the right people for the right price. Presto! Margherita was able to get a divorce! A couple of days later, we were married.

Life was never boring with Margherita. On our wedding night, we heard a knock at the door. When I opened it, I was taken aback to see policemen standing there. After much arguing and confusion, they arrested me on charges of being a spy. It's almost laughable. A big whoopee! I've never been at a loss for words or a lack of charm. The next day at my hearing, I was able to weasel my way out of the charges.

Leaving the short arm of the law, we meandered on down to Belgrade on what Margherita thought was a honeymoon. I might have referred to it as a business trip, if you catch my drift! We did a quick turn around and came back into Trieste with treasures in hand. We established our home there. I was into all sorts of mischief in those days and gained a bit of a financial foothold.

I had a knack for sniffing out what folks needed most desperately, so I developed a specialized package delivery service. With Trieste being a free territory, it was a perfect location with lots of things coming through and going on to wherever. Trieste was a melting pot—a soup kitchen of sorts. The port was always buzzing. The business part of the package delivery service was simple: people needed someone or some way to get the objects or packages from Trieste to wherever they were going. I'd like to think I was an early version of a package delivery service. In my defense, I was just supplying a service. My motto was simple, "don't ask, don't tell," and for us it was strictly business. Some people might have had a different take on our profession and called it something less glamorous than a package delivering service—smuggling, perhaps.

Part V   The French Foreign Legion   1947 - 1949

The Piazza San Marco.

I would take packages of unknown contents to anywhere in the world for a set price. For instance, going to Tangiers would be so many thousands of dollars, or to Beirut, where I had an apartment. Establishing apartments throughout the region was a perfect setting for my trade. I set up a few of them. I had an apartment in Tangiers, also in Vienna. I had a way of getting through the border guards with these packages using different code words at various places and was always quick with a peace offering of some sort. It got to be a regular thing—I'd be nice to them, and they'd look the other way. My apartment in Venice was right near the Piazza San Marco—Venice's most famous piazza—and not too far from Harry's Bar and Grill where they served patrons like Ernest Hemingway and Sinclair Lewis. Italy was a hot spot after the war, and Venice was the jewel in Italy's crown. I took advantage of the opulent culture. I would go on little trips and come back with additional wealth. It all worked out. I ended up purchasing the Grande Ristorante Fortuna with a friend in Trieste.

The Grande Ristorante Fortuna was a very nice restaurant and nightclub with a long serpentine bar, which I advertised as the longest bar in Europe. Of course, there was no way of knowing whether it was or not, but it made for good advertising. Everyone believed me, so who cared? It had three regular dining

Part V   The French Foreign Legion   1947 - 1949

rooms, a bigger dining room, a dance area, another little secluded inter-sanctum dining room, and then a room called the "secret" room, which would accommodate a large table for exclusive "private" dinner parties with some *very private* guests. The Grande Ristorante Fortuna is located in the Piazza Goldoni near the center of town and is there to this day. We did quite well there, Margherita and me. Each Wednesday and Saturday, Margherita and I would entertain the patrons by performing dances like the *Tarantella* and singing. We became a novelty, and everyone got quite a kick watching me dance the Russian Cossack dance!

One of the best things to happen to our little family was on January 26, 1949. Our daughter Giannina Maria was born. She was a beautiful baby girl, and it was a wonderful occasion. We named her Giannina after me and Maria after Margherita's mother. We were one happy family. I can say I truly loved my life.

One of the best things about living in Europe was their market for fast cars with lots of pizzazz. As a gift for Margherita, I bought her a sexy rig. It was one of the first German-made Porsches, which had started production in 1949. With its 400 horsepower air cooled engine, it was quite a speed wagon. The color was silver grey with lots of chrome. Margherita really lit up when I gave it to her. She enjoyed driving around the hills of Trieste like a Hollywood movie star with the pedal to the metal. In early March, Margherita was out driving in the hills. She lost control of the car, and didn't make a turn. Over the cliff she went. I was in Rome at the time and quickly chartered a plane back to Trieste. I was grief stricken—devastated. Here I was newly married, with a two-month-old infant daughter, and now a widower.

It is an understatement to say I was a mess. My life was in complete chaos! It seemed to be unraveling too fast, and I couldn't get a handle on it. To add injury to insult, my partner at the Grande Ristorante Fortuna was robbing me blind. The package delivery service was at a standstill. I didn't know what to do. After much deliberation, I came to a difficult conclusion. I did not have the wherewithal to care for my daughter. I carefully considered my options and made some inquiries. Calling my good

Part V   The French Foreign Legion   1947 - 1949

friends in Switzerland, Luigi and Maria Gambozzi, an Italian-Swiss couple living in Basel, I asked if I could take my daughter to them. They cared for her and ended up adopting her. I made all the necessary arrangements, knowing it was the best I could do for my daughter—considering the circumstances.

Luigi was one of the greatest cellists the world has ever known. Maria was a diva and prima ballerina. I knew my daughter would grow up with much music and culture, exquisite food, and fine European schooling. Remember in 1949, I was only 23 years old, and my life was not such that I could care for a small infant. It was a very hard decision, but I felt it was best for everyone at the time. I would think of my daughter often with bittersweet memories. I reunited with her 33 years later in 1982.

Back in Trieste, I was in a real bad funk after Margherita's death. I was working night and day in the Grande Ristorante Fortuna. One of the customers had a two-masted schooner. He was trading in the Adriatic Sea and on down to Sicily. His cargo was good European goods south and casks of Vino Negro (black wine) north from Sicily. Real good wine! The captain was in one day. I said, "How about it, Captain, can I make a trip with you?"

He said, "Sure, come on. We need a good sailor." The whole crew would come in off and on, and I was friends with the whole bunch. The bosun, a big Sicilian and real mean looking, had a heart as big as the moon. He was a good sailor and a good *nostromo* (bosun in Italian).

We were on deck one day and had just left Durres, Albania. Something carried away on the main gaff. The bosun said, "We've got to take care of that." I started up the ratlines[72] on the windward side, and he came up behind me a little to my left and not far below me. About half way up, I broke wind, real loud! The bosun called to me, *"Hey Gianni, no parla me amore! Lavoro! Lavoro!"* (Don't speak to me of love. Get up and go to work!)

---

[72] Pronounced "ratlins," ratlines are lengths of thin line tied between the shrouds of a sailing ship to form a ladder. http://en.wikipedia.org/wiki/Ratlines

Part V   The French Foreign Legion   1947 - 1949

I continued to sail to keep busy after Margherita's death. I was third mate in SS *Jacob Luckenbach*.[73] We were running to the Mediterranean in a States Marine Line Charter. While we were in Barcelona for a few days, I tried to look up my brother George. I told Captain Leverock I had a brother in Spain somewhere, and I'd like to look him up. The captain said, "Sure, Mr. Johnson, go ahead. Just make sure you're back here by sailing time, a week from today."

I said, "Okay, Captain, thank you." I went to the other mates and clued them in to what was happening. I told the second mate, "I'll make it up to you, if you take my watches."

"That's fine, Jack, go ahead," he said. That's the way we were in those days.

I took a train from Barcelona to Madrid. I didn't know where I was going, but with my sailor's instinct, I headed for the proper offices, the War Department, and so forth. I informed the first person I met that I was looking for General George Johnson. He went away and came back very concerned. He said, "Would you please sit here and wait. We'll take care of you."

I sat down cooling my heels. Another guy came in and said, "Sir, will you come with me?"

I did, and again, I had to wait. This guy seemed to be a higher ranked officer. Next thing I knew, all sorts of people were running around, whispering and talking. The PA system came on with announcements in Spanish. I presumed the chatter was about my request. I was sitting there thinking, "What's going on?" All I wanted to do was see my brother. They didn't know that he hadn't seen me since I was a kid.

A very officious gentleman came out in a uniform similar to what you would see on a New York doorman. He had gold braid all over him and gold teeth. He walked up to me and said, "Ah, Mr. Johnson. We are sorry we are unable to help you. However, we want you to be our guest for as long as you like. We have a hotel room booked for you, and we will provide transportation for

---

[73] In 1944, the SS *Jacob Luckenbach* was the C3 cargo ship christened the *Sea Robin*.

Part V The French Foreign Legion 1947 - 1949

your return to Barcelona. We will make certain that you get down there."

I said, "Too bad you can't find my brother. Don't you know who he is?"

"We are unable to help you," was all he volunteered, motioning me to follow him. When we went outside, a long black limousine awaited. The officious guy opened the door, and I got in to the plush limousine. Within minutes, other people climbed in with me. There was a guy sitting beside the driver and two other guys who positioned themselves in the jump seats facing me. Once they were all in, we were off. We drove a piece and soon pulled up to the biggest and finest hotel in Madrid. We got out, and boy! They had the red carpet rolled out for somebody. Lo and behold, all this hoopla was for me!

I was escorted into the hotel with the same grand fuss as before. They said, "Anything you want, Mr. Johnson, whatever it is. The dining room is open at 1800 hours. If there is anything you want, we will provide you with it. There is champagne or whatever you want in your room. There is a choice of cigars there, too. We can even provide an escort for you if should desire, a young lady to help you out. She can translate for you; she speaks very good English."

This type of helpful service went on the entire time I was there. The food was great. The service was excellent. The young lady was delightful company. The next morning over breakfast, I was approached by more uniformed officers, who said anytime I wanted to return to Barcelona to let them know—this morning, this afternoon, tomorrow, tonight, anytime. I said, "Well, I think I better head back now."

After breakfast, I packed my little overnight bag, got squared away, and went down to say goodbye to everybody. Expecting some charge for all this hospitality, I checked out, and asked for my bill.

"Everything is taken care of," was their reply. Stepping out of the hotel, I was astonished to find another long, black limousine waiting for me. Ahead of it was another limousine, and behind it another. If that wasn't enough, mounted motorcycle escorts

Part V   The French Foreign Legion   1947 - 1949

flanked us on either side all the way to Barcelona from Madrid. The convoy of three limousines and motorcycle escorts arrived in Barcelona and pulled up to the dock.

You should have heard the crew when I arrived. The longshoremen were all saluting and waving with their hands, whispering amongst themselves, and shouting "Olé!"

The men on board were making quite a ruckus, too. I could see Captain Leverock on the bridge, watching what was going on. I can only imagine what he was thinking when his third mate got out of the limousine. He probably thought to himself, "Now what?" I said goodbye to everybody who had so graciously escorted me.

When I got aboard, the captain said, "What was all that?"

I replied, "Captain, I don't know. I never did find my brother, but they were very kind to me and brought me back." That was all that was ever said.

PART VI   1949 - 1953

Coming to Terms with Life

*It was too late. I was aboard and signed on.
I had a job to do, and I did it.
It was good that conditions were so bad.
I couldn't spend much time thinking
about how bad my life was at this time.
~Captain Jack V. Johnson~*

Once I was back into Trieste, I threw myself into drinking, living pretty fast and hard. All the good that did was to get me into a little mischief—so much mischief, in fact, that I had to leave town in a hurry—like yesterday—keeping one jump ahead of the law. Using my Italian passport, I joined a Greek ship the SS *Ioannis P. Goulandris*. We went from Trieste down the coast to Durres, Albania, on to the Black Sea, to Constanta, Romania, Varna, Bulgaria, Odessa, Russia, and on up to the Sea of Azov to Mariupol. We continued down the Black Sea to Batumi, tramping around from port to port. She was a tramp steamer, a modified American Liberty Ship. The Greeks are good sailors. It was a good crew. I liked the captain, Captain Alex Potamianos, but conditions were wanting in a lot of ways. It wasn't long before I got fed up with it, so at the first opportunity, when we were docked at Port Sudan, I said, "The hell with it." I told the old man, "I want to draw everything I can get!"

He said, "What are you doing?"

I said, "I'm leaving." Being a very fair person, he gave me all the money I had coming. I was on the beach in Port Sudan, and of all places in the world this was truly one of the worst places in the world. Us sailors referred to it as the "armpit of the world!" That's how bad it was.

I went to the American Consulate looking for a ship, and they had nothing. I went to the British Consulate and scored. He said,

Part VI   Life After Margherita   1949 - 1953

"We have a place in the engine room. A stoker on a Blue Funnel Liner."

It was a small step up from staying another night in Port Sudan, but I was desperate enough to take *any* job, even one in the engine room. It proved to be as bad as I imagined it would be. It was again my bit of hell on earth.

The SS *Adrastus*. Blue Funnel Liner. Built 1923. Coal burner.

As the newest crewmember aboard the SS *Adrastus*, I was in the stoke hold. It was a mad house down there. It was a pressurized stoke hold (pressurized 5# psi), 16 stokers on watch, four firing aisles, 16 trimmers (coal passers), eight water tenders, and three engineers. The engineer on our watch was a flaming redheaded Scotchman—a miserable bloke. The Chief Engineer wasn't much better. It was too late. I was aboard and signed on. I had a job to do, and I did it.

It was good that conditions were so bad. I couldn't spend much time thinking about how bad my life was at this time. But man, it was hot! How hot was it? It was so hot, that as Johnny Carson would say, "The hardware store is selling thermometers with readings on it of Fahrenheit, Celsius, and Holy Crap!" It was so hot in the stoke hold going down the Red Sea that we could only make it by working what was called "monkey watches," one hour on and two hours off. That was all the time we could take down there in the heat with temperatures rising to 120 degrees. Once we'd get up on deck, we'd drink iced tea, pop salt tablets, and flake out. Then, two hours later, we were back down the stoke hold! That lasted until we got to Aden where we took on more bunkers (coal) and went on about our business down the coast of India. We made stops at Rangoon, Pei Nang, Singapore, and finally, Darwin, Australia. That's where I left her.

Part VI   Life After Margherita   1949 - 1953

That was the thing about grabbing a pier head jump (a job you took at the last minute). You never knew what was in store for you. This was especially true if you were desperate. The minute you got aboard, the lines were let go. That's when you'd look around and find out you were in a ship from hell with a rough chief mate or an indifferent skipper. These runs were usually headed down to the hot latitudes of the southwest Pacific and into the Indian Ocean and East Indies. It's a bad run. Going the other direction in the Atlantic down the West African coast wasn't much better. The work was hard, and the conditions were usually miserable. The pay was probably one of the lowest on the scale, and all you could hope for was to jump ship when you got into port. Before and during the war, AB wages were $87.50 a month, and OS wages were $75.00 a month. This was an increase from the Swedish ship I started out in when I was 13—it paid $22.00 a month.

One of the best paying ships I sailed under the Honduras flag was the MS *Nitro*. We were paid well because we carried a cargo of liquefied nitroglycerin. We loaded in an out-of-the-way port, just south of New Orleans, north of the Venice Pilot Station. It was very slow loading. I joined her on the last day before they left port. We battened the tanks down and took off for Genoa, Italy. We were there over a week because it took a long time to pump out the nitroglycerin tanks. When they were empty, we cleaned and washed the tanks with a mixture of a neutralizer, similar to baking soda, and then load seawater back in the tanks. One trip was enough for me. I understand she made one more trip and was never heard of again. The one nice thing about carrying a cargo of liquefied nitroglycerin was an AB was paid $330 a month. Sailors were willing to risk their lives for money like that.

Other hellish ships we shipped in were called "death wagons." Bound for the hot latitudes, you were always hungry, and water was rationed. This meant you couldn't bathe. The weather was *Hot! Hot! Hot!* You also had to deal with bugs, rodents, and other unwanted passengers. Believe it or not, sometimes this became your path to survival.

Part VI   Life After Margherita   1949 - 1953

One of our cargos was copra, the dried meat of the coconut. There was a time copra was king. A ship carrying copra is highly susceptible to copra beetles, cockroaches, bacon beetles, merchant grain beetles, meal moths, and dried fruit moths. Copra beetles are the worst because these ¼" long, red-legged beetles multiply rapidly and will infest anything and everything. Your entire ship becomes infested with them. They are in the food, in your hair, in your clothes, and in your bunk. Each night before turning in, you would turn your top covers down, and there would be pint-size gatherings of copra bugs. You would just scrape them off and climb in. Before long, you would feel them crawling back into bed with you.

Even the finest, well-kept ships will harbor cockroaches aboard, and they were pretty bold. You would come on watch; say you are on the midnight to four watch. You get a call at 11:30 p.m., go into the mess room, grab a cup of coffee, and make yourself a quick sandwich, and here would be all these cockroaches. They would not only crawl over everything, they were also quite capable of flying. As you sat there, trying to scarf your sandwich down before going on your watch, *bing*! They would come sailing by. I was almost certain they would try and grab a bite right out of my sandwich.

Sailing on the West African Coast hauling cocoa beans, you'd get these big cocoa bugs. These cocoa bugs were very prevalent. They are like cockroaches, only *three times as big!* And they bite! After a while, you sort of accept the critters as part of the daily routine, no different than swatting a fly. You generally wipe them away with your hand or, if you have a chance, smash them. *Pow!* You hit 'em with your fist. Then to add to our warped sense of humor, we would capture these big cocoa bugs and have bug races. We would put a dab of paint on them to identify them, draw a big circle on the table, and put a line across for the finish. We'd put the bugs in a bowl and then capsize the bowl on the table. The bugs would take off in all directions, and the one to cross the line first wins! It's always more interesting with a small wager; it helps to pass the boredom at sea.

Part VI   Life After Margherita   1949 - 1953

If you were on the east coast and wanted to get on the west coast, you'd hop a banana boat. The banana boats were good for quick intercoastal runs. I've been in a few. Banana boats are interesting. The bananas would come on big stalks. You have overhead rails with hooks on them. The longshoremen would fling the stalks of bananas on these hooks and push them back among the rails they hang on. You'd frequently find huge tarantula spiders making their homes in the stalks. These large, furry spiders are virtually harmless; in fact, many of the sailors would make pets out of them. They did have a bite, but nothing deadly. We would turn them loose on the table and watch them go forth and back. I even took one home to my mother in Seattle. She had a fit and kicked us both out!

Another time, I was in a small ship, the MS *Mormac Wren*. We went up the Amazon to Iquitos, Peru, then back down to Manaus, and up the Rio Negro to load latex rubber. Rio Negro is known not only for rubber, but also for "jivaro" (tribes of headhunters). Once the jivaro would get the head off their victims, they would shrink them. We know them as "shrunken heads." I bought one of these "shrunken heads" for $10 and kept it in my sea bag. I took it home to my mother in Seattle. I didn't tell her. She had this big bay window with venetian blinds and a big valance over the top. I took the shrunken head and hung it up in the middle of the big bay window. Mother didn't notice it for a while. I usually stayed home for three or four days. It was on the fourth day I was home that Mother came across the "shrunken head." She had a little two-blade duster that she used to dust the venetian blinds. All of a sudden I heard a scream. I ran into the room to see Mother pointing and screaming, "That, that! *What is that*?"

"Mother, it's a shrunken head!"

"Out, get it out!" I grabbed it as she ran after me, yelling, "You, too!" I grabbed my gear, and away I went off to Seattle to find a ship. I took the shrunken head down to the famous "Ye Old Curiosity Shop" on the Central Waterfront of Seattle. I sold that chunk of head for $100. Not a bad profit. The last time I was in Seattle, there it was, as gruesome as the day I left it.

Part VI   Life After Margherita   1949 - 1953

Coral snakes are also commonly found in stalks of bananas. They are known for their red, yellow, white, and black bands. They inspired the folk rhyme, *"red on yellow, kill a fellow; red on black, friend of Jack."* Coral snakes don't bite; they grasp. They have raspy teeth, and if they get a hold of you, they grab your skin and won't let go. According to the first aid book on ship, under the section *"cure for a coral snake bite"* — there wasn't one. If they bit you, it took about three minutes, and you were dead, due to its powerful neurotoxin that paralyzes your breathing muscles. I was relief third mate in the SS *Fra Berlanga*. I was walking forward and looked down, and this guy was lying on deck with his eyes rolled back in his head. He had been bitten by a coral snake on his left hand. I immediately asked what was going on, and the crew was chattering in Spanish. They all stood up, shrugged their shoulders, and left. The guy was dead.

Not all critters are visible to the naked eye. Take for instance the behavior of sailors. Once we got to shore and took up with what was considered "a lady of the evening," it would only be a matter of time before you realized you got more than you gave and ended up with crabs. When a guy would bring them back aboard the ship, it was mayhem. They multiply quite rapidly, and pretty soon, everyone would be scratching himself as the crabs crawled all over you like fleas on a dog. The first-aid officer was usually the third mate and responsible for the health and well-being of the crew. He doled out this purplish-blue lotion. You'd smear it on and shower two or three times a day (if you had enough water on board). This was our only defense against crabs.

Maybe you would catch a job on a mule carrier, like I did once. We were loaded down with mules in the *William W. McKee*. We had been carrying a load of lumber from Vancouver, British Columbia. When we got rid of our cargo at Rotterdam, we loaded 300 mules. I guess something happened to their ship, because they were dry-docked. We took them aboard. They were bound for Gdynia, Poland. These mules were swarming with big, blue-tailed flies. They were all over the ship. They're from the blowfly family and grow about twice the size of a housefly, about a half-inch long. They feed on dead meat, open wounds, and animal poop.

Part VI   Life After Margherita   1949 - 1953

And we had a lot of that with the mules on board. The crew built temporary shacks out on the deck for the mule tenders, who took care of them. In this case, these mule tenders were from Poland. We got along pretty good with them—not the mules, and definitely *not* the flies.

The *Pamir* berthed ahead of her rival,
the *Passat,* at Penarth Wales, U.K., October 7, 1949.

After leaving the stoke hold in the SS *Adrastus* at Darwin, Australia, I got a job with an American salvage company, "the black horse of the sea," Merritt-Chapman and Scott. They were clearing the harbor of American ships that had been bombed and sunk. They needed a diver, and I needed a job. They already had a couple divers, but they could always use more. I was hired. It was a good job and paid well. It was the best I had felt in a long time. Australia was very therapeutic for me, helping me heal some deep wounds. The year was 1949, and the month was May. It had been six months since Margherita's death. Australia was on the other side of the world, which was good.

Part VI   Life After Margherita   1949 - 1953

In June I got word there were two big square-riggers laying in Port Victoria, Australia. I quit! I got my drag up check, and away I went, heading south. I heard one was a Flying P-Liner, the *Pamir*. I wanted to ship in her because I had been in the *Pamir* before. I did everything but roller-skate, getting from Darwin to Port Pirie, and then Port Pirie to Port Victoria. That's when I met up with guys from both the ships to get the scoop as to whether or not they were hiring. I went over to the *Pamir*, but the captain said they had a full crew. He told me to go over and check with the *Passat*, which was the sister ship to the *Pamir*. I went over to the *Passat*. Captain Ivar Hagerstrand heard my story and my experience. I was hired on the spot, as AB. The *Passat* was a short-handed hungry Finn with 14 in the deck crew, seven on each watch.

Aboard the *Passat*, we were watch and watch, and dog the watch! She was the last commercial square-rigger around Cape Horn. We were loaded with grain. The *Pamir* pulled out the first of June, and we sailed in the *Passat* four days later. We got into the roaring 40s (that's prevailing winds for you), out of the west and going along the latitudes of the 40s south, but that wasn't enough for the captain. He dropped down to the screaming 50s!

From there we were under a reduced sail and the spanker. At one time, we were logging a giddy 17 knots![74] Which was unbelievably fast for a sailing ship! We made it to Cape Horn. It's pretty treacherous because of strong westerly winds, large waves, strong currents, and icebergs. It's these conditions that have made it a sailors' graveyard. It was exciting going around Cape Horn. (I would be fortunate enough to do it not once but twice.) We managed to make it around the Cape and on up through the South Atlantic. In the Doldrums[75] we got becalmed. Sails flapping and with any little bit of wind that came up, we'd trim sheets and haul on the brace wenches, trying to catch every breath. There wasn't much. We knew we'd get out of there sooner or later, but it was probably going to be later rather than sooner.

---

[74] 17 knots would equal about 19.56 miles per hour.

[75] Doldrums refers to the area around the equator where the winds from the northern and southern hemispheres converge. It is believed to be the area between about five degrees north and five degrees south of the equator.

Part VI   Life After Margherita   1949 - 1953

Photo of the port watch on the main yard of the *Passat*, furling the mains'l. I am fourth from the end of the yard (see arrow).

When you find yourself in a situation and facing starvation, you start eating anything you can get your hands on. Sometimes you have different kinds of critters as stowaways on your ships. I am not referring to the two-legged kind. In this case, we were very grateful for the critters aboard this grain carrier, because they served a purpose. Our stowaways were rats. Lots of rats! We ground up grain in a mortar to make flour to dip our daily catch. We would catch them and skin them out, dip them in the flour, fry, and eat them. They're quite tasty, a lot like squirrel.

Part VI   Life After Margherita   1949 - 1953

Making fast the mains'l. Wind building up to a force 9-10.
A short-handed hungry Finn running her easting
down in the roaring 40s. Barque *Passat*, June 1949.

After lying there awhile on a diet of rats, we were happy to see a big Castle Liner bound out of the Caribbean on their regular run to South Africa. She came within hailing distance to us. We were a curiosity to all the passengers on board. Here they were a big liner, and we were a big square-rigger. *"The world shall not see such ships again..."* Square-riggers, that is. Coming closer, our captain hoisted the International Flags for chronometer time.[76] They signaled back the chronometer time. We struck our signal and hoisted the International Flag, thanking them. Our captain hollered across to them through a megaphone, "Do you have any provisions we could purchase?"

The British captain hailed back and said, "If you can get a boat alongside, we'll load you down." I had never rigged a three-purchase tackle faster in my life. Getting the boat ready, turned over, and into the water, down we went. There were five of us in our boat. I grabbed the sweep oar. We rowed over to the Castle Liner. They loaded us up with fresh fruit, vegetables, meat, chickens, and wonderful provisions. Back we went with the mother lode. I remember sitting on the hatch eating an onion just as you would eat an apple. My god, it was good! Better than rat!

---

[76] Chronometer is a marine clock used to determine longitude.

Part VI Life After Margherita 1949 - 1953

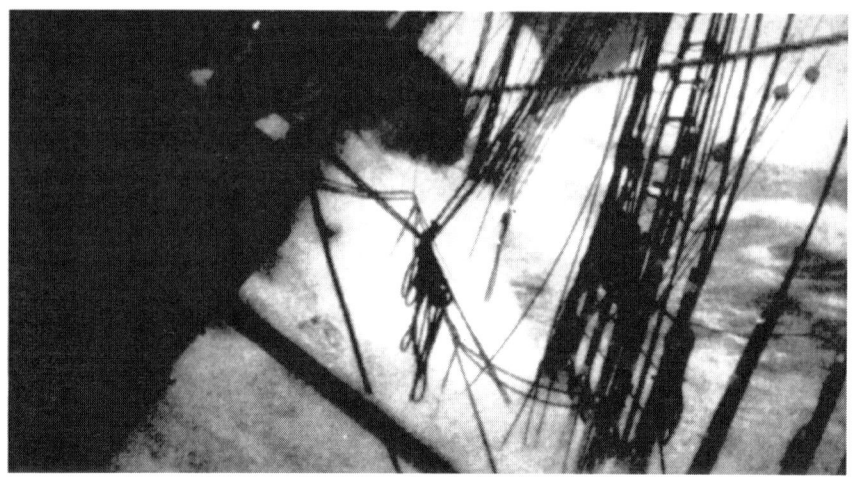

Taking a green one aboard the *Passat*.
Running her easting down. A whole watch was lost off
the *Parma* in conditions like this.

Shortly after that, we picked up a breeze and got out of the Doldrums. We set our course north. As we approached Falmouth, we got word we were to go on to Queenstown, Ireland, for orders, and then to Penarth, Wales, to discharge our cargo. We picked up our pilot and tugs. Incidentally, it took 111 days from Port Victoria, Australia, to Queenstown for orders, and a couple of days added, getting over to Penarth and alongside. The best satisfaction was we beat the *Pamir* into port by six days! I wanted to stay aboard, so I worked her for a week. The captain had orders to pay us off. Gustaf Erikson's son came down, representing the company, so everyone was paid off. (Frugal Finns, you know. They didn't want to pay anybody.)

In late 1949, I sailed in another four-masted barque, the *Sea Cloud*, as AB and foremast captain. Marjorie Merriweather Post, the daughter of C.W. Post and Ella Merriweather, and her husband, E.F. Hutton, owned the *Sea Cloud* (Hussar V). Marjorie became the wealthiest woman in America when her father passed away. She was an American socialite and the founder of General Foods, Inc. The *Sea Cloud* was the largest, privately-owned seagoing yacht in the world at the time. I was in charge of all the foremast and headsails. *Sea Cloud* had a big crew. But of course, money was no problem.

Part VI   Life After Margherita   1949 - 1953

Gustaf Erickson of Mariehamn, Oland Islands, Finland, whose ships, the four-masted barques *Pamir* and *Passat*, were the last commercial cargo-carrying square-riggers, Australia to Queenstown, Ireland, for orders. 1949.

In early 1950, I found myself in the Philippines. It was there I had my first command as a Master of an inter-island ship for the Pacific Far East Line. I had aimed to head back to Alaska, but things don't always go the way you plan. It wasn't long before I once again worked for the Salvage Company, Merritt-Chapman and Scott. I had been in New York and was anxious to get back to Kodiak. I had a little apartment in New York and was kicking around looking for work. It was slow. One day I was eating kosher food at the Second Avenue Deli. I decided to touch base with the Masters Mates and Pilots Hall. My card hadn't run out; it was nearing the top. I ran into the chief mate in a Mormac ship. He told me about an opportunity aboard the Merritt-Chapman and Scott ship. They had a salvage job in North Africa and needed a diver.

I checked it out, applied for and got the job, and then on to diving off Bizerte, Tunisia. There was a sunken American Liberty ship that had been carrying 10 million dollars in gold. The ship had been torpedoed in 1945. The gold had been bound for Malta to help them rebuild after the war. It was a partial shipment, and the second shipment arrived before the first, since the first was settled on the bottom, about 150 feet down in the Mediterranean

Part VI Life After Margherita 1949 - 1953

Sea. My tender was Anton Shields. There was another diver, Johnny Daves. Johnny and I worked well together. The gold in the sunken ship was stowed in the space above the engine room called the fiddley. It was lashed down on a pallet board covered with a canvas. I was the first diver down in the space where the gold was stored. Having been in many Liberty ships, I understood the structure of the fiddley. We got our charges set and blew the tops off. The next three days we took the gold bars topside. Eight days later, we headed back to New York and payday. The pay was good. Ten thousand dollars good, so I didn't have to worry about finding a ship for a while. I sent $1,000 to my sister in California and $1,000 to my mother in Washington.

The four-masted barque, *Sea Cloud*.

I ended up going back to Trieste, but the memories were a little much for me. I hung around a bit. At first, I got the impression I was no longer wanted there, but soon I fell back in

Part VI   Life After Margherita   1949 - 1953

good graces with the old gang. It didn't take long, though, before the memories caught up with me, and I had to get out of there. I went over to Genoa. There I moved in with Adrianna Giacabelli. She had a large contingent of "working girls." I kicked around with Adrianna for a while, but had to get back to reality and the real world. I decided again to try and get home to Alaska. In Naples, I ended up shipping in the old SS *Walter A. Luckenbach* (as a work-away for a penny a month). We went to Marcus Hook, known as "The Cornerstone of Pennsylvania." Everybody paid off. (I don't know where the old *Walter A.* went after that, but I joined her later on an intercoastal trip.) I fetched up in Baltimore and tried to return to Alaska. It didn't work out that way, so I grabbed another ship back to Italy.

Back in Trieste, again I thought I could handle it. I settled in and continued my part ownership of the Grande Ristorante Fortuna. I started up my little package delivery service again. I got myself into a bit of mischief. It wasn't anything serious, or so I thought. It was a regular morning, just like any other morning. I was up, getting shaved, dressed, and ready to go downtown when Mama Falgone (my cook and caretaker) and Luigi (her husband, the grounds keeper) came to me, speaking worriedly in Italian. It didn't make much sense. Mama Falgone kept saying there were two guys at the door looking for me. She described them as looking like a couple of Neapolitan[77] ruffians. That sparked my curiosity. I went downstairs to see what was going on. Sure enough, she was right. They looked like a couple of ruffiani Napolatani or Neapolitan pimps.

The men identified themselves as U.S. Army Criminal Investigation Command (CID). They said, "Major Brown wants to speak to you."

I replied, "Okay," trying not to sound nervous or guilty, "I'm just getting cleaned up to go downtown, so I'll drop in and see him."

"No," they insisted, "we want to take you down there now."

I finished getting cleaned up and put on my tie, as I did every day, and downtown I went with the two ufficio Italianos. They

---

[77] Italians, specifically from Naples, Italy.

Part VI   Life After Margherita   1949 - 1953

turned out to be a couple of nice American guys. They just looked the part straight out of an Italian melodrama.

Arriving at Major Brown's office, he stood up and shook hands with me. "It's good to see you again, Jack," he said. (I wasn't Captain Jack in those days. I was just plain Jack, or Jacque, or anyone else depending on which passport I was using.)

"Sit down," he said, motioning to the chair in front of his desk. I sat down, still trying to act like I couldn't imagine what I did to get such an official meeting.

I asked, "What's happening?"

He said, "Well, to tell you the truth, Jack, we're a little disappointed as to what is going on in your part of the world and what you're doing. We're not very happy with it."

I responded with a clueless remark, claiming, "I haven't done anything."

He sat back in his chair, clenched his hands on top of his desk, and went on to say, "We think you have, and what you're doing, we frown on. It's my responsibility to tell you that you have to leave Trieste."

"What do you mean?" I raised the question.

"Well, it's as plain as this," he said. "You're being deported."

"Where am I going?" I asked trying not to sound perturbed.

"Well," he answered, "anywhere outside of Trieste! It doesn't make any difference to us; we just want you out of our jurisdiction."

I shrugged indifferently, stating, "Well, okay, I was thinking of leaving anyway. I'll get things squared away and get out of here in about a month."

He looked at his watch, "The Oriental Express comes through here at 5:15 p.m., and you'll be on it."

I felt my mind racing, wondering if there was any way to get out of this. I responded, "Oh."

He said. "Yes, 5:15 p.m. today."

Thinking I could negotiate for a better deal, I asked, "Is that all the time I got?"

"Yes," he said. "Knowing you, I think that's plenty of time."

Part VI   Life After Margherita   1949 - 1953

I went back to the house and told everybody what happened; I had to get out of Trieste. I packed a couple of little suitcases. One was full of clothes and personal possession, and the other one was stuffed full with American money, over a quarter of a million dollars! I arrived at the train station early. Looking around and walking down the platform, I noticed nobody there to see me off. I expected a formal unwelcoming party, but seeing no one, I looked around and thought to myself, "What the hell, I don't think I'll go."

I started back down the ramp. All of a sudden, here came those same two guys, one on each side of me. They literally picked me up off the deck and turned me around. In unison they said, "You're not going anywhere, except on that train."

They meant business. They stuck with me, never missing a step—right beside me. They even followed me onto the train and into a compartment. I was starting to get nervous, especially with the suitcase of money. I threw the suitcase up on the rack above the seats. Trying to make light conversation, I teased, "What is this, you don't trust me? You thought I wouldn't leave?"

"It was very obvious that you weren't going," one of the escorts replied.

I said, "Look I'm leaving. What the heck? You don't have to stick around."

They wouldn't budge. "We're staying with you until Mestre," they said. "Then you're on your own after that. And don't try to come back."

When we got to the frontier at Monfalcone, here came the custom and immigration officers. They opened the door, "Passport?"

And I thought, "Oh, shit!" I pulled out my passport, hoping I had grabbed the right one with my official name on it. (I had many passports in those days: Italian, British, French, Romanian, and American.)

One of the officials said, "We have to look in your suitcase."

"*Damn me eyes!*" I thought, "This is probably the end of the road for me." I hesitated, not knowing what to do.

Part VI   Life After Margherita   1949 - 1953

The other immigration officer with him said, "No, you don't have to look in there. We know he's okay; he's with them," nodding toward the official escorts. I tried hard not to bring any attention to myself the rest of the trip, thanking the gods for smiling on me that day.

When we got to Mestre, I boarded a little motorboat to Venice. Mestre is the town where you get off to enter Venice either by motorboat, steamboat, or even gondola. In Venice, I went straight to the apartment that I still had there. I settled in—more like hunkered down—for a spell. It was late 1951. I took inventory of my situation and decided I was back to square one. My new goal was to get to the States and to Alaska. I had enough of being overseas for a while. I canceled the lease on my apartment and moved on, with my sights set on the *"home of the brave and the land of the free,"* as well as the *"land of the midnight sun."*

It didn't quite work out as quickly as I had anticipated, and before long I found myself back in Genoa. I fell back in with Adrianna—again. I kind of loved that girl in a lot of ways. She was rather a remarkable woman and easy to be around. You could say she was just what the doctor ordered.

Adrianna had never been to Paris. It had always been a dream for her. So, I took her to Paris. Then to put the icing on the cake, I took her on down to southern France, specifically Monaco. I can always say I gambled in Monte Carlo. I didn't break the bank, but that day I was lucky in love and lucky in winnings. I can't say the same for Adrianna. She lost almost everything she had. We carried on from Monte Carlo to San Remo, another big casino city in Italy. Again, I was lucky, and even Adrianna's luck changed, too. She got a few bucks ahead this time. We took the winnings and left San Remo. We went down to Rome so she could introduce me to her parents. From Rome back to Genoa, Adrianna was a nice distraction, but I couldn't get the *old red, white, and blue* out of mind.

I didn't wait to get in a ship back to New York. I just paid for a ticket second-class on an Italian passenger liner, the *Conte Biancamano*. There I met Countess Anna Maria de Savoy. She was a remarkable lady. She was going home to Columbus, Ohio,

Part VI   Life After Margherita   1949 - 1953

where a big part of her family lived. She made the trip pleasant. I mean very pleasant, if you get my drift.

When I arrived in New York, I got to figuring, I might as well ship out. Only trouble was, I had this suitcase full of money. I didn't want to be too obvious about it. I managed to "launder" it back to Seattle in good hands and in a safe place where I could get to it at any time. I decided to keep a low profile.

I went down to the Union Hall and shipped out with the Mormac company. I went out as chief mate in the SS *Mormac Cedar*. We picked up a big power generator for Hammerfest, Norway. It was war reparation for what Germany had done to Norway. We had huge machines on deck to take to Hammerfest.

While we were there, we went ashore to the one and only bar. They were serving the usual—Johnnie Walker Red! No matter where you went in the world, you would find Johnnie Walker Red. I've drunk Johnnie Walker Red from Cape Town to Sydney, Paris, Nome, Point Barrow, Hammerfest, Singapore, Rangoon, Tokyo, Shanghai, Hong Kong, Macau—all over the world. It translates the same in any language. Where there's a port, you can bet there is Johnnie Walker Red. We left Hammerfest and went back to Narvik, Norway, where we loaded iron ore. I got off her in Baltimore, returned to New York, and shipped as chief mate in the SS *Mormac Fir*, a WW II Victory Ship.

It was a short stint, just a summer run to the Baltic. When we got back to Baltimore, they only had one more ship going to the Baltic. I went Third Mate in the little *Mormac Wren*. The *Wren* was a 300' C-1 motor ship. She made the Amazon run. We picked up our pilots at the mouth of the Amazon and then went about 2,600 miles upriver, making stops along the way. The chief mate was Stan Lee. I had met Stan for the first time in 1941 in Alexandria, Egypt, when I had been left at dock by the *Kanangoora*. We'd met up again on a small stint up the Aleutian Islands in SS *Morlen* in '43 and again back home in Kodiak when he'd introduce me to one of my wives, Laura Belle. We had become good friends.

We'd pick up our pilots in Belem, Brazil, and go on up the river almost 3,000 miles to Iquitos, Peru. We called it, "Peru's Atlantic Seaport." The only way out of Iquitos by water was down

Part VI   Life After Margherita   1949 - 1953

the Amazon River to the Atlantic. Once in Peru, we dropped off our general cargo and back loaded whatever they had for the return. We hauled in a lot of material, pipes, and all sorts of stuff for the oil fields in Peru and Columbia. While we were lying there for several days, I wanted to see some of the sights. A few of us took a plane out of Iquitos to Lima. You wouldn't believe what kind of a plane we flew in—an old Ford tri-motor! We got lashed into our wicker chairs and flew up the valley. As we looked up, we could see the tops of the mountains. We were flying at almost ground level. We came out of the mountains. It was a long sloping ride down to the airfield at Lima. We spent a couple of nights in Lima and back to Iquitos, again in a Ford tri-motor.

When we were back, I entered my room and noticed a big hump in the middle of my bed. I couldn't figure out what the hell it was. I didn't remember leaving anything bunched up like that. I pulled the covers back only to come face to face with a large, ugly snake. Not just any snake, mind you, but a big boa constrictor or an anaconda, as they called them in South America. It had burrowed into my bunk with a little help from my friend Stan Lee. He was always a jokester. I was scared speechless at the sight of it. It must have been 500 feet long—well, it looked that long! I went screaming out of there, and Stan got a big chuckle out of the whole ordeal. He grabbed a stick and wrapped the snake around it to get it out of there. Fortunately, it wasn't a full-grown snake, but it still looked big to me. Stan, I still owe you one! Not for introducing me to an ex-wife—but come to think of it, maybe I owe you one for that, too—but for the snake in my bunk! This was the second time I came a foul with those awful creatures! The first time, if you recall, was in Matadi in Africa. Now I had the unpleasant experience in Peru.

We set sail from Iquitos down river to Manaus, and then up the Rio Negro to a turning basin where we loaded pure latex rubber. The Germans had dredged the turning basin out during WW I. And back again to New York. After we got rid of our cargo, we loaded up to go down the South America coastline to Argentina to Buenos Aires and up river to Rosario. While we were back-loading cargo for New York, we got word there was a British

Part VI   Life After Margherita   1949 - 1953

ship disabled out in the Falkland Islands. They had cargo aboard and desperately needed to get it to Antarctica where they were developing a station. Somehow, the British government managed to charter the *Mormac Wren*. We went to the Falklands, picked up their cargo, and took it to the British Antarctica Station. It was a memorable trip and the first time I was ever in the Antarctic. (I would go again decades later.) We managed to get them their cargo in a very quick manner by lashing two lifeboats together making a scow. Then we took the cargo ashore. They were so appreciative they gave us, not one, not two, but three cases of booze, Johnnie Walker Red Label Scotch. That lasted us until we got back to New York.

As I said, wherever you go in the world, you could always find Johnnie Walker Red Label Scotch. It's a good scotch by the way, not a great scotch, but a good scotch, and that's all that mattered. Hell, in those days I liked everything but the cheaper grades of shellac!

Back in Baltimore, I shipped in a Texaco tanker. Our northern port was Marcus Hook, Pennsylvania. We loaded in Port Arthur, Texas. Port Arthur was dubbed "Sin City." It was a Texas boomtown, 50 miles from the Louisiana border and known as a "Cajun town." It was also a merchant sailors' dream. Some of its famous citizens ranged from Tex Ritter to the Big Bopper[78] and from Janis Joplin to Jimmy Johnson.

But for my money, I headed up Proctor Street to see one of its more infamous citizens, Gracie Woodyard! Proctor Street was known for its gambling joints, brawling saloons, and brothels. Gracie poured a fine shot of whisky down off the main drag at the end of Proctor Street. She owned a string of brothels from Brownsville, Texas, to St. Petersburg, Florida. In the 1930s, Gracie and her husband Rusty controlled all the rackets, moonshine, and vices in Port Arthur. Mysteriously, one day Rusty vanished. It was all pretty hush-hush. I happened to overhear her once talking to one of the girls in Cajun-French. Since I was fluent in French, I

---

[78] Jiles Perry "J. P." Richardson, Jr., was an American musician and songwriter, whose big voice and exuberant personality made him an early rock and roll star.

Part VI   Life After Margherita   1949 - 1953

could follow their conversation. In the conversation, she indicated that she had a fight with her husband and she had wound up taking matters into her own hands. As she put it in Cajun-French, "I done him in." Gracie was quite a lady.

Whenever we'd come into port, we'd tie up for about 20-24 hours, and head for Gracie's place. Grace Woodyard's brothel was known all around the world. There was even some story about Steve McQueen working in the brothel. I didn't put it together until years later when I ran into him in Galveston, Texas, and I realized who he was.

Gracie's place was a frequent stop for many. She'd pour a pretty hefty drink the size of a water glass for 50 cents. Also on the menu were some delightful ladies of the evening. I took a real liking to a young girl, a Cajun lady, from the swamps of Louisiana. I called her Miss Red, because she had beautiful red hair. With long watches in a ship, you start thinking about what you are going to do when you get off. This one thought came to my mind when we got close to Port Arthur: I was going to get Big Red for nothing at Gracie's and ride in Gracie's baby blue Cadillac. That was practically impossible.

No, I take that back, *it was impossible*! You see, Gracie had this baby blue Cadillac that she enjoyed being driven around in. One of the ladies would be the chauffeur. Gracie held a tight fist on her money and girls. No one pulled one over on Gracie Woodyard. And as for the Cadillac, nobody, I mean nobody, but Gracie and her chauffeur rode in it. Nobody else.

One time we were sitting around drinking and dancing and having a good time. I looked at Gracie, and said, "Gracie, I'm gonna ride in your baby blue Cadillac!"

She said, "Mr. Jack, you ain't gonna ride in my baby blue Cadillac. Nobody rides in my baby blue Cadillac!"

We continued to talk, and I chided her, "Gracie, if I managed to get things done with Miss Red without paying, will you give me a ride in your baby blue Cadillac?"

She said, "What are you talking about? You gotta pay! You can't get around without paying."

Part VI   Life After Margherita   1949 - 1953

"But if I can," I teased, "will you give me a ride in your baby blue Cadillac?"

She looked at me and said, "Mr. Jack, if you could ever get something for nothing here, you *could* ride in my baby blue Cadillac!"

I went up topside for an encounter with Miss Red. When we got in the room, she held out her hand. She said, "Jack, you know the first thing you have to do is put the money down."

I looked at her and said, "Well, I don't have to pay. Gracie said I could have this for nothing."

She disagreed and said, "Oh, no, Mr. Jack. You're never gonna do that."

I kept looking at her with a straight face and insisted, "Well, yeah, Gracie said it was okay. I didn't have to pay."

"I don't believe you," and she went to the top of the stairs.

I went out with her and, seeing Gracie on the floor below, I said, "You wait here." And I went down the stairs to talk with Gracie.

"Gracie," I whined like I was tattling, "Red won't let me do anything. She says I'm sick."

"What are you talking about, Jack? Get in here." Gracie pulled me into the little bathroom, yanked down my pants, and said, "Let's see." She took full assessment of my assets and declared me fit as a fiddle. "You look okay; you're all right." We got to the bottom of the stairs, and she yelled up to Miss Red, "He's okay, he's okay. Let him go."

So I went up back up topside ready for action. Miss Red was a bit confused, muttering, "I do declare!" She was a delight as always.

Afterwards, when Gracie found out that I didn't pay, she blew a gasket. To make matters worse, when she remembered our little agreement about riding in her baby blue Cadillac, she hit the roof. I heard about it in every language you could imagine, but I can always say that I got to ride in Gracie Woodyard's baby blue Cadillac!

I used to hang out in the old Olympic Hotel in Seattle between 4th and 5th Avenue and University and Union. I always

Part VI   Life After Margherita   1949 - 1953

thought it was a fine place to drink. The Olympic Hotel had been known for hosting John F. Kennedy in its presidential suite back in '61. I would drink in the Marine Room. They'd pour a pretty generous drink there and had a nice dining room also. I'd take dates there often.

One night, sitting to the right of me at the corner of the bar was a rather attractive lady. Sitting next to me on the left was a young Navy Officer. He looked like he had just gotten out of the academy and had ensign bars on his shoulders—a real nice young fellow. The attractive lady and I started talking, and the young ensign kept looking at her. I'm sure he thought she must be someone famous, a celebrity of some kind.

Finally, the curiosity got the best of him, and he looked at her and asked, "Excuse me, miss, but just who are you?"

Without flinching, she looked right back at him and replied, "I'm the best damn lay in the 13th Naval District!"

I thought he was going to fall off his stool. He turned beet red and didn't say another word. We had a few more drinks. The lovely lady and I moved into the dining room and had a bite to eat. She took me to her room at the Benjamin Franklin Hotel. I was going to find out if her boasting was true or not.

We walked into her room, and lying across the chair was a uniform jacket. "Hey! There's a Rear Admiral's jacket. What's this doing here?" I asked.

She said, "Oh, that old man's passed out somewhere."

I don't know if it was her beauty or my heightened awareness of the previous occupant, but I would have to say, "She *was* the best in the 13th Naval District!"

Part VI Life After Margherita 1949 - 1953

Thelma

Settling down and being a househusband
didn't suit me for too long. Soon, I became restless.
Thelma's legs might have been great,
but mine were longing for the sea.
I was a young sailor, and the sea was calling.
~Captain Jack V. Johnson~

In the 1950s, I was in Seattle doing a bit of dating. Soon, I found myself married again. Her name was Thelma, a very beautiful blonde Norwegian. She was a tad bit older than I was and quite sophisticated. Also, she had great legs! (That was always my weakness!) She had looks and brains, a deadly combination. Thelma was a businesswoman. She had her own CPA firm in Seattle with about 20 people working for her. Her office was located on the 9th floor of a big Seattle building. Why she married me, I don't know. I guess it was love.

She always thought like a cash register. I tried to fit into her world. I got involved with the Lutheran Church—not in the way that led me to skipping town after my pipe organ days, but in a genuine fashion. I had already been a Russian Orthodox and a Roman Catholic, and now I was a Lutheran. Not that I became formally involved with anyone of them, but it seemed to be the thing to do at the time. Settling down and being a househusband didn't suit me for too long. Soon, I became restless. Thelma's legs might have been great, but mine were longing for the sea.

I tried everything I could think of to occupy myself. I heard I could get my high school diploma by going to Edison Old Broadway High, a vocational school in Seattle. I studied and passed with flying colors. I received what is similar to a G.E.D. At the same time, I took my entrance exam for the University of Washington. I aced that also and enrolled in the University of Washington, majoring in psychology with a minor in

Part VI   Life After Margherita   1949 - 1953

ornithology.[79] I made really good grades, and learning came easy for me.

I have always had an excellent memory. You might say it is photographic. It has served me well over the years. Once I was called as an expert witness on a court case. The judge looked at me once I was sworn in and asked what it was that made me an expert witness.

I thought a minute. "My memory," I said. Then I asked him if there was a phone book around anywhere.

He said, "Yes, but I don't see how that pertains to this case."

I said, "You want to know what makes me an expert witness. I'll show you."

So the judge asked the bailiff to bring me a phone book. I told the judge to open up to any page in the book. He opened it up and then handed me the phone book. I spent a few minutes looking over the names. I handed the book back to him.

He looked at me quizzically and asked, "What do you want me to do?"

I told him, "Ask me anything on the page!"

He hesitated, so I began listing the names, phone numbers, and addresses in order of their appearance on the phone book page. After I recalled about 50 names, addresses, and numbers, he held up his hand to stop me.

"Okay, okay! I get it. I guess that does makes you an expert witness."

College didn't seem to do it for me, I was a young sailor, and the sea was calling. I began to see what was available. They didn't have anything in the Masters, Mates, and Pilots Hall, so I wandered into the Sailors' Union of the Pacific (SUP) Hall. There was an AB job in a steam schooner, the old *Daisy Gray*. She was a wooden ship with steam power built in 1922, a small 750 horsepower reciprocating steam engine. I shipped in her, and she was loading at Newport, Oregon. She could carry one million board feet of lumber. There was a big demand for lumber in California. We took the Newport lumber to San Pedro and then

---

[79] There seemed to be nothing in the world that Jack wouldn't try.

Part VI   Life After Margherita   1949 - 1953

went back to Eureka and loaded up redwood. Carrying lumber was exclusively the *Daisy Gray* cargo, up and down the West Coast. We loaded up with Douglas fir and took it once again to San Pedro. I paid off in San Pedro. The SS *Daisy Gray* only made a couple of runs after that before she went off to the graveyard.

The SS *Daisy Gray*.

In 1950, after a short visit with Thelma, I shipped out of Seattle as JR Third Mate in the SS *Mary Luckenbach*. She was under an American Mail Line charter to the Philippines and to China. On my watch, there was also Earl Daly, AB, and Lyle McAlpine, AB. While at the port of Iloilo, the two ABs and I went ashore for a few "heaves ahead"—and then to the head and heave!

Coming back, we were feeling no pain and having a little difficulty walking. We bought some booze. Determined to get it aboard ship, we hired a guy with a little donkey cart to bring us back in style. Here we were, the three of us, riding back to the ship in a donkey cart. It was quite a sight, and we were quite a mess. When we got to the foot of the gangway, we came up with a harebrained scheme! *We wanted that donkey!*

We told the guy we wanted to buy the cart and donkey, "Oh, no," he couldn't sell them. After working out a deal with the

Part VI   Life After Margherita   1949 - 1953

owner of the donkey, we bought the monkey. I mean the donkey—the monkey is a different story! We made him an offer he couldn't refuse, paying him more pesos than he'd see in a month. He said goodbye to his little donkey, pushed his cart to the side of the dock, and wandered off. That left us with the donkey.

Now it was time to put our plan into action. We were going to put that donkey in the bosun's room. Earl Gard was the bosun. Years later I married his daughter, Connie. I'm not sure which he resented me more for, the donkey or marrying his daughter.

It took some time, but we proceeded to work the ass up the gangway or the ass worked us—one of the two. Anyone who has ever had any dealings with donkeys can attest this would be a difficult endeavor in the daylight, but it was night, and we were drunk. The three of us were trying to get that damn donkey up the gangway. Earl Daly was behind pushing, and Lyle McAlpine and I were up ahead pulling. The donkey was as stubborn as donkeys get and didn't want to go up the gangway. It was a regular push-me pull-me situation. We managed to get the hang of it, and it was all going pretty good for a while, until that donkey stopped in the middle of the gangway. Earl Daly yelled at the ass of the ass, as it was backing down into him, "Whoa, you scroungy maverick!"

The name stuck, and to this day, we still refer to Earl as "Scroungy Maverick!" We finally got the donkey aboard and in the bosun's room. The bosun was passed out on his bunk. That didn't stop us. We pushed the donkey in his room and closed the door. I would have paid good money to witness him waking up from his drunken state and seeing that donkey in his room. The guys and I waited for the commotion to start.

When it did, we tried to hold our laughter in check. The bosun came shouting and hollering out of his room in half Norwegian and half English. Rumor had it he was scared speechless, and we weren't 'fessing up to knowing what ass put the ass in his room. I am sure they all had a good idea who it was! He got the donkey out of his room, and it clambered down the passageway. The crew didn't know there was a donkey on board,

Part VI   Life After Margherita   1949 - 1953

so when they came running out of their rooms to see what all the commotion was about, they ran smack into this donkey. It created a bit of mischief, but we finally got the donkey tied up back aft.

We fed him rolled Quaker Oats from the galley and anything else he'd eat, like lettuce, carrots, and fresh vegetables. He fared pretty well. We kept that donkey aboard for a while. Lyle and I called him "Maverick," and Earl Daly called him "the son-of-a-bitch." I'm sure Earl Gard had other names picked out as well— one for the donkey and one for us! We sailed to Zamboanga City in the Philippines and then to Davao City, Mindanao. We ended back up in Iloilo, taking the donkey ashore where we had picked it up. We sold it back to his owner, at a hell of a loss. He was happy, and we were happy. We said goodbye to our little donkey.

At Mindanao, the chief mate, Mr. Smith, heard we were going ashore. He said, "Lads, when you go ashore, will you bring me back a case of beer? Here are some pesos to cover it."

This wasn't an unreasonable request. We said, "Sure, a case of beer. You got it, mate. We'll bring it back."

Earl, Lyle, and I went ashore. We got pretty gassed up, but managed to remember the beer. We were working our way back to the ship. I was packing the case of beer, and it was getting pretty heavy. I tossed the case over to Earl, "Here, you take it for a while."

Earl put the case over his shoulder and walked a bit, staggering around. Earl transferred it to Lyle, and Lyle gave it back to me. It was hot and humid! We were tired and thirsty. Finally I said, "Piss on it. Let's sit down. I don't think the mate will mind if we have one of these beers!" One beer led to two, two to four, four leads to eight, eight to sixteen. Before you know it, we had drunk up the entire case of beer. All 24 bottles were gone. We threw the empty bottles off to the side.

I looked at the guys, "What the hell are we going to do? We can't take this empty case back to the mate." I looked at the now empty case of beer and reckoned, "Geez, we had better bring something back to the chief mate."

One of the guys spoke up, "Well, we better go back and buy another one."

Part VI Life After Margherita 1949 - 1953

"No," I said, "Let's just tell him we dropped it."

"No, somebody stole it—tell him somebody stole it," another suggested.

I shook my head, "No, he won't believe that either."

"What do we do?" they asked. "He'll know we drank it."

I looked around, trying to think of what to put in the case to replace the bottles. "Ah! I have an idea." I noticed everywhere we looked, there were these toads about the size of your fist hopping around. "Let's catch these toads, and we'll bring him back 24 toads. He'll get a kick out of it!"

Well, it wasn't easy, but we managed to grab those slimy sons-o'-bitches. We caught 24 of them and stuck them into the empty spots where the bottles had been just a short while earlier. The damn toads would hop out, and we would push them back in. It took a little finagling, but we filled each slot, closed the lid, and carried the case of toads back to the chief mate.

We were still half gassed up, but feeling pretty savvy about solving our dilemma. We walked into the saloon where the chief mate, ship agent, immigration agent, port security officer, and other Filipino officials were drinking tea and coffee. The captain had just left the saloon. We walked in carrying the case and said to the chief mate, "There's your beer, Mister Mate!"

He answered, "Thanks a lot, lads. Why don't you set it there?" suggesting we put the case of beer on the table. We did and turned to go. The chief mate stopped us, "Don't run off. I got an opener, and we can all have a beer."

We declined, "No, no. We got to get going. We'll see you later," now clamoring for the door, but *not* before the chief mate opened up the case.

To everyone's surprise, all those toads started hopping out. The Filipinos let out a scream, and jumped up on the table in a panic. There was shouting and toads hopping all over the place. Come to find out, those toads were poisonous. The slimy mucus on them was deadly, and we were covered in it! I don't know what happened to the toads. I ended up taking a shower with all my clothes on trying to get all that mucus washed off. Mr. Smith, the chief mate, never saw the humor in the whole thing. I think he

Part VI   Life After Margherita   1949 - 1953

was more upset about not getting the case of beer, though, than about getting a case of toads!

I know you are wondering about the monkey I mentioned earlier... in Zamboanga, we picked up a little monkey. We got it into our drunken heads that we should buy a monkey and sell it to the bosun—yes, the same bosun Earl Gard—my future father-in-law! Lyle McAlpine talked me into buying the monkey for about $3 in pesos. When we got back to the ship, Earl Gard asked, "What do you have there?"

We sold him the monkey for 20 bucks! The monkey was quite active and crawled up on his shoulder. It then climbed on the top of his head and relieved himself! (How we tormented that poor guy!)

The voyage ended in San Francisco. We paid off. I elected to stay in the *Mary Luckenbach* as third mate. Captain Leverock had broken his leg. He got off, and Smitty went captain. The date was August 25, 1950, and we were leaving San Francisco on an intercoastal run.

The USS *Benevolence*.

Having just dropped the pilot off, we were on the slow bell, having encountered fog. It was dense fog, so thick you could cut it with a knife. We didn't have radar aboard. We were sounding the

Part VI   Life After Margherita   1949 - 1953

proper fog signals. It was a little after 1700 hours, and I had the eight to twelve watch. I was just going to relieve the chief mate for dinner. As I was going up port ladder leading up to the bridge, I looked, and there was a big ship coming out of the fog. *Pow*! We hit the starboard bow of the hospital ship, USS *Benevolence*.

We went down her port side just like opening a can of sardines. You could look right into the ship. She went limping off into the fog. We made a big circle around, and there were people in the water flopping around like a bunch of spawned-out dog salmon. We started picking them up and ended up rescuing 41 crewmembers. They lost 23 people. The Coast Guard showed up, and ordered us in. The *Benevolence* sank. She is still visible from the cliff house in San Francisco. They had two pilots aboard. They also had radar, and we didn't. Evidently, they saw us, but we didn't see them.

When we got back into port, I said, "Piss on it!" I didn't want to stick around any longer. After the hearing, I paid off and headed north.

It was 1951. I shipped JR third mate in a Navy tanker, the USNS *Tamalpais*. At the Bremerton Navy yard gate, the guard looked in my luggage as I was waiting to board. I had one small suitcase and my sea bag. He opened the suitcase, I didn't think too much about it. I stood there waiting for the go ahead to board the ship. The next thing I knew, the guard is shouting at the top of his lungs, "Spirits, spirits! This man has spirits!"

I looked at him, startled, trying to make sense of what was going on. I looked around, wondering where the "spirits" were.

"Corporal of the guard, this man has spirits!" he shouted.

The Corporal comes up, and then he shouts, "Sergeant of the guard, this man has spirits!"

I was beginning to get a little worried. It finally dawned on me what they were looking at. I had three bottles of Haig & Haig Pinch.

The sergeant came out and said, "Bring it to the office." They dragged me, the suitcase, and the sea bag into his office. He walked over to the suitcase that was sitting on a table, looked in it, and declared, "Yeah, you have spirits."

Part VI   Life After Margherita   1949 - 1953

I laughed and said, "Whew! I thought there was some ethereal thing hovering about me, but I can see now what your boys referred to as spirits! The Haig & Haig Pinch."

He smiled, "Yeah, that's what we call spirits." He took one bottle and put it in his desk. He then shoved the other two deep into my suitcase. Motioning to the guard, he vouched for me, "This man's okay. Get him to his ship."

Once I got aboard ship, I was surprised to see my old friend Johnny Fogle. I hadn't seen him since we parted ways in Washington after the French Foreign Legion stint. I knew Johnny would be glad I had two bottles of "spirits" tucked away in my suitcase!

The *Tamalpais* was an Escambia-class oiler.[80] She was used in WW II to provide fuel to ships in combat areas, but in 1948 she had been reacquired by Navy civilian contractors, and transferred to the Military Sea Transportation Service. We were running between the Persian Gulf and Japan. Once while in Kobe, Japan, an older Japanese pilot came aboard to take us out.

We were on our way back to the Persian Gulf. As JR third mate, I was handling the engine room telegraph, what we called "rabbit ears." I was taking the pilot's orders, repeating them, and then ringing them down to the engine room. We were coming out and ready to make a turn. The elderly Japanese pilot was sitting in a chair, giving orders. He said to the quartermaster, "Quartermaster, hard left!" (You don't say port or starboard in American ships.)

"Hard left, quartermaster."

"Hard left, sir," was the quartermaster's reply, repeating the command.

"Come to course," he said. Here we were going click, click, click, hard left, click, click, click.

The ship was swinging, and the pilot was rubbing his forehead, "Come to... course. Come to course."

Again, click, click, click. "Come to course."

---

[80] Named *Mt. Tamalpais* in Sausalito, California, it's the only oiler on display at the Defense Logistics Agency in Fort Belvoir, Virginia. In 1951, USNS *Tamalpais* visited major ports all over the world carrying fuel or petroleum for the Navy.

Part VI   Life After Margherita   1949 - 1953

I cried, "Pilot, what course, what course?"

"Ah Hai! Course 274," the Japanese pilot replied.

"Course 274?"

The Japanese pilot nodded in assurance, "Ah yes. Course 274. 274, quartermaster."

"Aye, Sir, 274," the quartermaster and I repeated. Whew! We steadied up on 274.

I had become quite ill, so I got off the ship in Ras Tanura, Arabia. Malaria never leaves your system, and every once in a while I would get a flare up. I went to the company hospital run by Arabian American Oil Company (ARAMCO).

I left the hospital and went to work for them as a loading mate on the dock. They had big tankers coming in. I worked the night shift because it was a little easier due to the heat. It would get up to 120 degrees at times. You would open the door to your cottage, and it was just like opening a firebox door and shoveling a bunch of hot sand in your face.

After about six weeks, I dragged up and went to Italy. I visited my close friends and my Italian family in Trieste. From there, I began working my way back to Seattle. I was still married to Thelma, though it was getting hard to remember what those legs looked like. I figured it was time to make my way back home for a quick visit. The year was 1952. I got back to New York and shipped out of the NMU Hall as an AB in the old SS *Walter A. Luckenbach* on an intercoastal run. The *Walter A. Luckenbach* was one of those intercoastal ships that had eight hatches and four booms on each hatch and was heavily rigged. She took me down the coast through the Panama Canal and then up the coast into Seattle. We tied up at the Luckenbach docks in Seattle.

In those days, the steward departments were almost all Filipinos. I always liked the Filipinos, especially the ones I sailed with. They had been a part of most all my ships even as far back as 1950 in the Philippines when I got my first command. They were a good bunch of people and wonderful cooks. We had great food. I was walking down the gangway and noticed some of the Filipinos in this car. I reckoned they were all part owners. It was a

Part VI   Life After Margherita   1949 - 1953

big beautiful sedan. They yelled at me, insisting, "Come on, Jack. We give you ride. Where you go?"

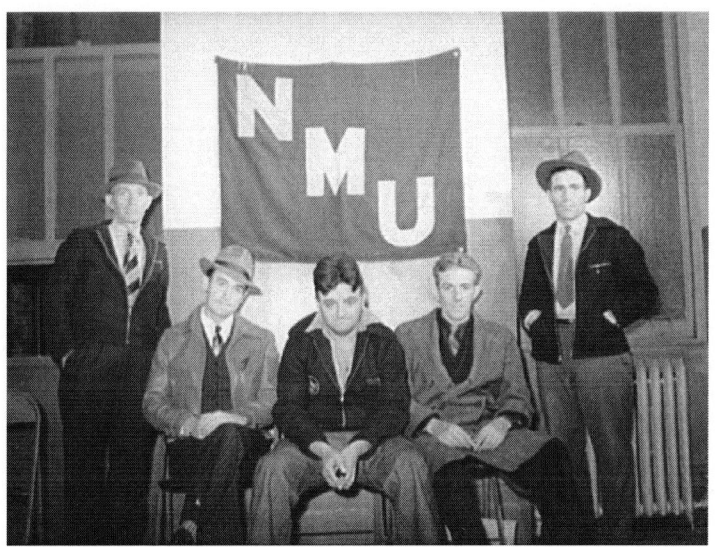

Men waiting in the NMU Hall, New York City. 1941.

I motioned to them I was fine and yelled politely I was going ashore and had things to do.

They said, "Jack, we give you ride." These were the type of guys who wouldn't take no for an answer, so I got in the back seat. I'm well over six feet tall, and had to scrunch to get my legs up under my chest to make room in the backseat. They were stuffed in there like sardines, with four in the front seat and four, plus me, in the back. I was trying to figure out what all the fuss was about, noticing they were all leaning over watching the driver.

One guy in the backseat yelled out, "Reverse. Reverse, I tell you! Reverse." The driver was grinding out gears, until he finally got her into reverse. He pressed on the gas and *bam*! He backed right into the warehouse. The air was immediately filled with cussing and screaming in Tagalog. A guy in the backseat yelled derogatory remarks at the driver, who tried to get his bearings.

"You son-of-a-bitch, you son-of-a-bitch, damn you! When I tell you reverse, I don't mean back up!" It was all very hilarious to me, but I didn't want to insult them by aborting. I remained steadfast until they got it all squared away, and they finally delivered me up town.

Part VI   Life After Margherita   1949 - 1953

Me and Thelma about 1952.

I got back to Thelma just in time to be served with divorce papers. Thelma was none too happy with my bouncing around the globe. Since she always thought like a cash register, she presented me with a check for $50,000, a 1950 Ford, and the deed to a condo we owned in Seattle. She was calm and calculated. That

Part VI   Life After Margherita   1949 - 1953

was the end of that! The thing for me to do was to find another ship and fall in love again. It didn't take me long to do either.

Work was work, and when waiting for sailing jobs I'd give anything a gander. Going north in the early '50s, I ran into a lady from Kodiak, Annie Chichenoff, a stewardess with the Flying Tigers. The Flying Tigers were the first American volunteer group of the Chinese Air Force in 1941–1942. They were regrouped during the Korean War with Trans Pacific Service, the Flying Tiger Line. They carried airfreight on contract. Annie told me I could probably go to work for them. I checked into it, and sure enough, they were hiring. I went to work as a navigator for the Trans Pacific Flying Tigers. I had never taken a sight out of an airplane in my life and the sextants were quite different from sextants aboard a ship. I made two trips, the first one to Manila and then to Hong Kong. We stopped in Tai Pei and back to Manila. We touched back down in the Pacific at Honolulu and then San Francisco. The pay wasn't all that good. I left them in San Francisco. That was my "long" extended career with the Flying Tigers Line. I ran into Annie sometime later in Anchorage. She stayed with the Flying Tigers Line until the 1960s.

The Flying Tiger Line.

Part VI   Life After Margherita   1949 - 1953

Jailed in Saudi Arabia

*I looked through the little barred window in the door
and saw they were dragging some poor guy down the hall
as another guy was chopping him to ribbons with a big machete.
I thought, "Oh, my god. I must be next."
~Captain Jack V. Johnson~*

I took a summer run out of New York in the *Mormac Cedar* in the Baltic. We'd stop at different ports: Gdynia, Poland, up into Leningrad (now St. Petersburg), then Finland, Sweden, and Norway and wind back up in Norfolk. I paid off the *Mormac Cedar* and headed back to New York. I met up with Lawrence Langner. He was uncle to my sister Ivy's husband, Robert "Bob" Camara. Bob used to tell me, "When you're on the east coast, look up Lawrence Langner. He is the head of the American Theater Guild and lives in Connecticut." I did.

I met him with his wife, Mara. Langner was known as "Lawrence Langner, the Great," a playwright, author, and producer, and now the head of the American Theater Guild. Born in the South of Wales, he was one of the founders of the Washington Square Players. He received a Tony in 1958 for one of his plays. I met him in Connecticut, and we hit it off splendidly. I enjoyed spending time with him and would visit from time to time.

I shipped in the export liner *Exporter*. We hit Port Said, Port Sudan, and Port Suez and then across to Jeddah. In Jeddah, you were warned of only a couple of places you could get a drink in Saudi Arabia, Muslim country. The agent would come aboard with the American Consulate, telling us to be very careful when we went to any hotel to get a drink. They encouraged us to keep a low profile and to travel in groups, not alone. We adhered to their warning. Some of us were sitting in a hotel, drinking.

I decided, "Enough of this, I'm going back on board." Nobody wanted to go back. I started wandering toward the waterfront and back to the ship. I could see the ship. Next thing I knew, here came a jeep. It pulled up and stopped next to me. Two

Part VI   Life After Margherita   1949 - 1953

guys in uniforms got out and grabbed me, placed cuffs around my hands, and threw me in the back of the jeep. Off to jail I went. I didn't understand a word they were saying. I got there and still didn't understand what was going on. They put me in a cell that had a big oaken door with bars across a small high opening. A strong stench was coming from the floor. You've seen those cartoons with the prisoners' arms hung up to the wall in shackles? Well, that's what they did to me! They chained my hands and hung my arms up to the wall. Then they left me there.

Sometime later, a guy came in with a bowl of something to eat. He took the chains off my hands, and I gagged down what I could. After the meal, they didn't chain me up again. Later in the day, I heard screaming in the passageway. I looked through the little barred window in the door and saw they were dragging some poor guy down the hall as another guy was chopping him to ribbons with a big machete. I thought, "Oh, my god. I must be next."

The Sudan Prison.

Fortunately, some of the guys saw me leave the hotel, and when I didn't arrive back at the ship, they called the American Consulate. Approximately 20 hours later, the consulate came and got me out. I can't stress this hard enough: *"Don't ever go to jail in Saudi Arabia!"* That cured me from going to shore in Saudi Arabia.

We stopped at Djibouti, Africa. I had been there before. You could buy all the whisky you wanted duty-free. I got a case of John Haig Scotch and took it back to the States for Lawrence. I paid off the *Exporter* and headed straight for Connecticut. That's where I met Flo.

Part VI   Life After Margherita   1949 - 1953

Florette

When I returned home, Flo had left.
She had gone back to Connecticut. That was that.
She didn't wait the six weeks. Not that I could really blame her,
but it was a big shock to arrive home to find your love nest empty.
~Captain Jack V. Johnson~

Flo was my shortest marriage. It was in the early '50s when I met Florette through my friend Lawrence Langner. He told me to get in touch with him if I was in town, so I gave him a call. Lawrence extended an invitation to stay at his place for a while, so I did. He and his wife ended up having a big party one night with dancing and singing and, of course, lots of drinking. That's where I met this very charming lady. She told me to call her Florette or Flo. I did, and we hit it off.

She was very pretty, a little bit older than I was. We spent every waking minute with each other, and in less than a week, we got married! Lawrence was the best man. It was a nice ceremony. For a honeymoon, we took a train ride across Canada to Vancouver. From Vancouver we went down to the condo and car in Seattle, compliments of my ex-wife.

I had a lot of change in my pocket from that very handsome check that ended the marriage with Thelma. Flo and I set up house. To be truthful, even I was concerned about the rapid marriage, but things were working out pretty nice.

Flo had lost two children in the Hartford's circus fire on July 6, 1944, in the worst circus fire in U.S. history. Started by a cigarette onto the dry grass, it ignited and consumed the main tent almost immediately, killing 168 circus fans. Flo was a very lovely lady, but due to past events and losing her children in such an awful way, she could be insecure.

After about a week of being married, I told her, "Look around. What we have is enough to get us started, but we can't live this way for long. Tomorrow, I need to find work."

She agreed. After another week of looking for work in Seattle, I came home and told Flo, "I have three options for work. I could

Part VI   Life After Margherita   1949 - 1953

either go to work as an ironworker or a boilermaker, or I could ship out."

Flo didn't act concerned and replied naively, "Well, do what you have to do; that's okay with me."

The Day The Clowns Cried, **Hartford's circus fire, July 6, 1944. The worst circus fire in U.S. history.**[81]

I knew I could make fast money by grabbing a quick trip, so that's what I opted for. I went down to the Union Hall, and on the 10 o'clock call that morning, I landed a second mate's job. It was a Pacific Rim run of the Asian ports, going from Japan and Korea to Cambodia and back to Seattle. The entire run would take less than two months. I went back to the house and told my new bride, "I got a job! I'll be leaving tomorrow."

"Leaving?" she questioned.

"Yeah," I replied, "I got a job."

"Oh, you got a job?" she seemed happy to hear the news. Still confused, she asked, "What do you mean leaving?"

---

[81] www.rarenewspapers.com
http://circusfire1944dotcom.weebly.com

Part VI   Life After Margherita   1949 - 1953

"Yeah, I'll be leaving tomorrow. I got a ship. I'll be coming back in about six weeks." I now realized she hadn't caught the full spectrum of my line of work.

Flo looked at me; she cocked her head and slowly repeated, "Ship. Six weeks?" I could hear the panic in her voice. I tried to calm her concerns and let her know everything was going to be fine.

"You're okay. You're good. I'll be back before you know it," I assured her. She got really quiet, on the verge of tears. "You've got this apartment. A little money still left and a car to get around. You'll be fine." She still didn't say anything. I went on, "You knew this is what I've done my entire life. I'm a sailor, my father was a sailor, and his father was a sailor."

She nodded, acknowledging she knew that, but she still wasn't grasping the meaning. She was miffed about me leaving her in Seattle while I traipsed around the world. I did all I could to calm her down and get her to understand the nature of the sailor. Thinking I did a pretty good job of explaining it to her, I shipped out.

I was second mate in the American Mail Line ship, the SS *Oregon Mail*. We went to Rangoon, then the capital of Burma. (Rangoon is called Yangon today.) Since I was in Burma, I decided to go to Mandalay. I always wanted to see Mandalay because *"the dawn comes up like thunder outer China 'crost the bay. On the road to Mandalay."*[82]

There we were laying in Rangoon. As second mate, I went up to the Captain Olsen and said, "Hey, Cap! I'd really like to go to Mandalay since we're going to be here for another eight to 10 days."

He said, "Johnson, if you arrange your watches, go ahead."

I arranged my watches and took off with a couple of other guys, taking the train to Mandalay. *"On the road to Mandalay, where the fly'n' fishes play. An' the dawn comes up like thunder outer China 'crost the Bay!"*

When we got there, we checked into a hotel. The next morning I got up bright and early at the crack of dawn. I wanted

---

[82] *Mandalay* is a poem by Rudyard Kipling. It was adapted into a song by Oley Speaks, and made popular by Peter Dawson and Frank Sinatra.

Part VI Life After Margherita 1949 - 1953

to see if *"the dawn comes up like thunder outer China 'crost the Bay"* like the song said.

Walking down along the canals in Mandalay, I saw everyone popping some little red berries in their mouths. I thought they were cherries or some kind of fruit. I went to a vendor, and he gave me a cone-shaped container of the beautiful little red things.

I started down the canal and popped one in my mouth. *"Damn me eyes!"* Sirens were going off in my head. "Hot! Hot!" I have never tasted a pepper as hot as they were. "Whooeee!" That evening at the consulate's office, we were having a few little "heaves ahead" and started talking about it. I told him what happened, and he laughed out loud. He said, "What you experienced was probably the hottest pepper in the world." If you're wondering if *"the dawn comes up like thunder outer China 'crost the Bay,"* it doesn't, but I can always say, "Yes, I have been to Mandalay by the old Moulmein Pagoda."

The Liberty Collier SS *Melrose*, EX *Mingo Seam*, off the U.S. East Coast.
I served as carpenter. Norfolk to Fall River. 1951. Over the years,
I served in 26 vessels of this type as AB, bosun, carpenter,
quartermaster, third mate, second mate, chief mate, and master.

We crossed the Pacific about six weeks later back to Seattle. I was looking forward to being with my bride. When I returned home, Flo was gone. She went back to Connecticut. That was that.

Part VI   Life After Margherita   1949 - 1953

She didn't wait the six weeks. Not that I could really blame her, but it was a big shock to arrive home to find your love nest empty. Our marriage lasted two months and then, *kaput*, it was over. I had no other recourse but to go out and find true love again.

In 1951 I shipped in a coal boat, the Liberty *Collier*, SS *Melrose* EX SS *Mingo Seam*, out of Norfolk, Virginia. It was just a short stint. I got off in Fall River, Massachusetts, and headed back to New York. The next day I shipped out AB in the SS *Penelope Barker*.

In 1953, I was back in Seattle. Shipping was tough with the Korean War winding down. I had my Master's license in my pocket, but wasn't having any luck finding work. I ran into Earl Mitchell at the NMU Hall. He mentioned there were a couple of AB jobs. He asked, "Do you want to ship out?"

I said, "I'm going to have to." I was pretty well down on my uppers. I needed work. We shipped in the *Creighton Victory*. It was just a quick trip, six weeks over to Korea with a load of lumber. We hit a couple of Japanese ports on the way back. There was an emergency, and we had to pull into Adak at the Naval base out on the Aleutians. We lay there for three days with no shore leave. After the second night, Earl and I snuck ashore and made it to the Chief's Club. We had a nice steak dinner and were able to buy a bottle of Seagram's Seven. We scored like a couple of tall dogs. We got back aboard ship, and, oh, did we catch hell.

The Old Man called us up and read us the riot act. He said, "When we get to Seattle, have your bags packed. You're going down the gangway. You're fired!"

Earl stood up, looked at the Old Man, and said, "Don't feel too bad about it, Captain. I've been fired off two stackers!" Then he turned around and left the room.

That might have been true for Earl, but I had *never* been fired off a ship. But instead of feeling gloomy, we passed the time finishing off the Seagram's Seven until we got back into Seattle.

Back in Seattle, I took a diving job with Leiter Hockett. We were laying big sewer pipe, ditching down through the sediment in the bay to bedrock. We couldn't lay the pipe in all that mud, so we had to high-pressure it with a big fire hose. We would spray it down, and the mud would dissipate into the water so we could

Part VI   Life After Margherita   1949 - 1953

lay the pipe. It worked well. I was doing a pretty good job up until down about eight feet where we hit bedrock. I was in my hardhat gear ditching down through the sediment until, all of a sudden, the mud caved in on me.

An old-time diving helmet.

I lay buried on my left side under a few feet of mud. I couldn't move a muscle except my hands a little bit. I lay there for an hour until another diver managed to get me out. He rigged a line under my arms, and I was pulled out. It really wasn't too uncomfortable, but it's a good thing I don't suffer from claustrophobia. I used my right hand to get to the belly valve. I had a nice nap while I was waiting. I was grateful to get back to the surface, taking into account I was almost buried alive! I had that old diving helmet up until recently. It served to remind me of those happy times.

Part VII   1953 - 1960

Back Home in Alaska

*I shipped in the **Bagaduce** and later in the **Eugenie Moran**,
then a small two-hatch freighter.
It was nice to be back sailing in the Aleutians.
I was home.
~Captain Jack V. Johnson~*

It took a while, but it finally happened. I came full circle, back home to Kodiak, Alaska. It was 1953. Alaska was still a territory. It would be five more years until she would take her place as the 49th state. At the time, I was sailing chief mate with Alaska Steam in the SS *Palasina*. On our first trip in to Kodiak, we tied up at the City Dock. Lots of people were there to greet us. I looked out among the onlookers, amazed I actually knew some of the folks gathered there. They nodded to me, asking, "Hey, Jack, what are you doing here?"

"I'm mate," tilting my head towards the fore deck.

"You chief mate?" they asked.

"I sure am." One thing led to another, and soon I was catching up with people I knew and remembered from my childhood. I told them, as soon as I paid off ship, I was going to establish a home in Kodiak.

The *Palasina* headed back to Seattle, where I paid off, much to the chagrin of Port Captain Andy Subcleff. (He later became one of the Southwest Alaska Pilots before I did.) Andy was quite a character. I had a cousin, Neil Larsen. We called him Nippy. He was chief mate in an Alaska Steam ship. For some reason Andy fired Neil. To this day, every time I see Andy, he apologizes for firing my cousin. I never found out why, and Nippy never told me what got him fired. Nippy went on to finish his career at sea with the American Mail Line.

Part VII   Full Circle—Back to Kodiak   1953 - 1960

In Alaska steam ships, the menu was the same every morning, salt codfish, salt herring, or salt salmon bellies. The cook would soak the fish in fresh water the night before. And woe to the twelve to four watch if they did not change the water at 0300 hours! We had salt fish for breakfast. That's where I discovered the salmon's tastiest part: the belly. Salmon belly is the fatty piece of the fish, but it is considered the best tasting of all! I found it very delicious.

When I paid off in Seattle, I packed a bag, and it was Pacific Northern Airlines (PNA) all the way back to Kodiak. We landed in Kodiak, and I went into town and checked into a hotel. That evening I had dinner and looked up a few friends, and the next day I found a place to live. It was a little house up above the school. I settled in and found a job with Military Sea Transport Service (MSTS), the Navy Civilian outfit that mans its ships with civilian crews.[83] It had a couple of ships working out of Kodiak. One of them was the big sea-going tug, the *Bagaduce*, which went westward to Adak, Attu, Kiska, and different military establishments. I shipped in the *Bagaduce* and later in the *Eugenie Moran*, then a small two-hatch freighter. It was nice to be back sailing in the Aleutians. I was home.

I was with the MSTS for several months. I then shipped in the *North Star*, the Alaska Native Service vessel. This really became my education around the coasts of Alaska. We'd run the coastline all the way from Seattle, up through Southeastern and Prince William Sound, and then out to the Aleutians, up to the Bering Sea, and to the top of the world at Barrow. It would total 91 villages along the way, bringing them fuel and groceries.

It wasn't long after that when I fell in with Bob Logan (or B.J. Logan, as we called him). He had three salvage vessels. They were large landing crafts tanks (LCTs)—not the huge ones. When I went to work for him, he was salvaging what he could out in the Aleutians because the military bases had closed down. Dutch Harbor was the last of the military establishments, other than

---

[83] Today it would be the Military Sea Command. In those days it was converted from the Army Transport Service to the Military Sea Transport Service.

Part VII Full Circle—Back to Kodiak 1953 - 1960

Adak. He had the *Kodiak Salvor*, the *Aleutian Salvor*, and the *Alaskan Salvor*.

I shipped in the *Kodiak Salvor*. I did everything in that little ship from being a sailor to being a diver—I even wound up being the captain. We would go out to the Aleutians. Our job was to pick up non-ferrous metals, copper in particular. We reeled aboard miles of underwater communication cable and stripped it down, getting the lead and the copper out. We picked up odds and ends and little generators sets from the survival camps that were located on almost every island out there. Once we found some machinery, two big old D-8 cats, that were still able to run. We managed to get them aboard. We headquartered out of Dutch Harbor and stockpiled all our stuff there. We ended up coming out with many tons of copper, lead, etc. We made some pretty good paydays.

Eventually, we made it back to Kodiak. I left Bob Logan for a life ashore, taking various jobs. I got in with Local 2520 Piledrivers, Bridge, Dock Builders and Divers Union. I started pile-bucking[84] and diving around Kodiak, working as an iron worker, longshoreman, or a rigger for boilermakers.

My uncle, Heiny Berger, had the mail run out to the Aleutians with a vessel called the *Garland*. I went to work with him for a while. They were based in Seattle. They would start to run westward out of Seattle and up to Seward and Kodiak and then westward to all the ports along the Southwest Alaska coastline. My uncle eventually lost the contract to Niels P. Thomsen, a famous Coast Guard Commandant in Alaska during WW II, who had the small ship called the *Expansion*. I went to work for him in 1954, first as an AB wench driver and then second mate, chief mate, and finally master of the vessel. We had some good guys: a lot of the old timers from Alaska Steam, Alaska Transportation, and Steam Schooner Skiffs. Guys like Ed Larsen, Ed Kimbrill, Slim Doyle, and Dick Lawrence (who was a baseball player for the Alaska Rainiers), along with some of the Soriano boys, Rupert and

---

[84] Another term for pile drivers. Drive wood and concrete pilings to hold up docks, wharves and bridges.

Part VII   Full Circle—Back to Kodiak   1953 - 1960

Amigo (who were also baseball players). I guess their first love was the sea—or they were in between seasons. I fell in with the Sorianos when I was with the Army Transport Service.

I had gotten my master's license and was second mate in the mail boat *Expansion* headed west. The *Expansion* was a 114' wooden Army surplus freight ship. Libby, McNeil, and Libby had purchased her. She was very sea worthy and had big skegs[85] on the bottom, which enabled her to sit on the mud.

One of the passengers was the Bureau of Indian Affairs nurse, who went out and took care of people in the villages. One mail boat's routine was to take the health nurse to the villages free of charge. The nurse was on the bridge. Jack Pym (a great guy) was captain. We were approaching Chignik, having left Kodiak and a couple of other ports along the peninsula. We overheard a conversation on the ship's radio as we were approaching Chignik between a guy named Sven on one of the fish tenders laying at Perryville, and his friend Lars in Chignik. The conversation went something like this...

> "Lars?"
>
> "Yah."
>
> *"This is Sven over here in Perryville. I want you to get the health nurse out here 'cause we got a bad case of gonorrhea. Seven people out here have gonorrhea."*
>
> *Lars came on and said, in a loud whisper, "Yah, you have a lot of diarrhea there in Perryville. I'll tell the health nurse that you have a lot of diarrhea there."*
>
> "Nay, nay. Not diarrhea, gonorrhea."
>
> *Sven shot back. "Yah, yah, I heard ya, diarrhea. I'll tell the nurse," replied Lars a little quieter, not to embarrass Sven.*
>
> *Sven was getting pretty frustrated and said slowly, "Lars, it's not diarrhea; it's gonorrhea!"*
>
> *As Sven got louder, Lars got quieter, "Yah, diarrhea, I hear ya. That's fine. Okay, I'll tell her it's diarrhea," saying it as slowly and loudly as Sven had said it.*

---

[85] A timber that connects the keel and sternpost of a ship.

Part VII   Full Circle—Back to Kodiak   1953 - 1960

Sven was becoming exasperated, "Yesus, Yesus, Yesus. It's not diarrhea. It's gonorrhea! Clap! Clap! Clap! Tell her we got a lot of clap here in Perryville. Yesus, are you such a stupid Norwegian that you can't understand English? We've got gonorrhea here!"

"Okay, okay," said Lars defensively, "I'll tell the nurse."

Another time in the *Expansion*, we were up on the north side of Unalaska, heading for Nikolski. The trip was easy to remember because the fog was so thick you could cut it with a knife. I remember you couldn't even see the foc'sle head from the bridge. The fog is one thing when you are out at sea and often times manageable, but when you add winds blowing about 80 knots, that's when the real fun begins!

Having come full circle, I was back in Seattle, coming down from Kodiak. I had a good payday fishing. I was kicking around with a friend of mine, Clifford Machado. We had been shipmates together years before. We were out on the town drinking. A lot. At one particular bar, Clifford announced that his girlfriend wanted me to meet a friend of hers for a dinner foursome. I agreed, and we planned to meet at a nice restaurant for dinner.

When we all arrived at the restaurant, in came this beautiful lady, Dorothy Lewis. She was going to be my date for the evening. I thought, "Wow! This is going to turn out great."

She came over to us and was introduced, but began apologizing right away saying, "I have a houseful of people, and I didn't realize this was going to happen. I am going to have to cancel the dinner date, or you can all come to my house."

Cliff looked at me and said, "What do you want to do?"

I shrugged my shoulders, "I don't know."

Then Dorothy turned to me and said, "Why don't you come with me? You'll enjoy meeting these people."

I said, "Okay." Cliff and his girlfriend stayed at the restaurant. Off I went with this beautiful lady. Dorothy drove up to her place on Lower Queen Anne Hill.

I said, "Oh, I know this area pretty well." We struck up conversation about the surroundings as we ventured toward her

Part VII   Full Circle—Back to Kodiak   1953 - 1960

place. She parked the car in the assigned parking place. It was just a short walk up the front steps.

As we walked up to her place I heard a very distinct laugh. I stopped and looked at her and said pointing my finger toward the laughter, "That's Oscar Callow!"

She looked at me with astonishment, "Yes, it is. How did you know that?"

"I know that laugh. That's Oscar Callow's laugh."

She said, "You know Oscar Callow?"

I said, "I sure do." Sure enough, there he was, my old friend Oscar Callow. It wasn't long before I caught up with him on who, what, when, and where life had taken him. Oscar had moved to Canada after the French Foreign Legion, and from there, to the United States where he had obtained citizenship. He was selling furniture. It was a hoot to see ol' Oscar again. I stayed connected with him from that time on.

I was in the *Expansion* for about a year. The only reason I got off was because I got a terrible wallop on my head when the rigging let loose and came down on top of me. And that would have killed a mere mortal—they're just lucky it was me! I woke up in the hospital with a fractured skull, but I came out of it pretty good. (You know, you can't keep a good Russian Finn down just by simply hitting him on the head!)

Part VII Full Circle—Back to Kodiak 1953 - 1960

Laura Belle

This is how one alienates friends and influences enemies.
I didn't really steal her from Stan. We just hit it off.
Before I knew it, we were going steady.
~Captain Jack V. Johnson~

After I got out of the hospital I returned to Kodiak. My love life was scarce, but that was about to change. Thelma had divorced me. Flo had left me. Then I met Laura Belle through my best friend, Stan Lee.[86] He was living and working in Kodiak. Stan had a small crab boat, and was working ashore as a carpenter when he wasn't out crabbing.

Stan and Laura Belle was an item. He introduced us. (This is how one alienates friends and influences enemies.) I didn't really steal her from Stan. We just hit it off. Before I knew it, we were going steady. We got married on Armistice Day, November 11, 1954.

My new wife and her two small children moved into my home. (Laura Belle had two children from a previous relationship.) We started living the good life. We soon had had two additional and wonderful daughters, Ola and Teresa, as well as my two wonderful stepchildren, Laurel (who I always refer to as my oldest daughter) and Charlie (who met his demise too early in a motorcycle accident in 1989).

Laura Belle and I had good times and bad times. At times it was downright tumultuous! We separated several times before the candle finally blew out for good. In the beginning, everything was good. I was trying to provide for a new ready-made family. I tried my hand at a lot of things, doing anything and everything I could think of. I applied for and got the wharfinger[87] job on the city dock for the City of Kodiak. I was soon handling all the ships

---

[86] Stan and I had sailed together in several ships, the first time 1941, in Alexandria, Egypt, when I had been left at dock by the *Kanangoora*. We'd met up again on the SS *Morlen*, the *Minnesotan*, and the SS *Mormac Wren*.

[87] Person who takes custody of and is responsible for goods delivered to the wharf and is responsible for day-to-day activities.

Part VII   Full Circle—Back to Kodiak   1953 - 1960

and cargo that came into the town of Kodiak. If you can imagine, I remained with the wharfinger job for five years! That's a long time for a sailor.

I also did pile-bucking or occasionally took a quick trip to Seattle to ship out with the American Mail Line. I went out fishing for halibut and crabbing—for a whopping eight cents a pound! I tried my hand with a salmon troller, and dragged my little family around the coastal regions of Alaska, trying to make a living getting in some of that easy slipper fishing out of Yakutat.

We lived there for a while in the green house on the hill above the dock. Then we tried our luck in Cordova. Cordova is a quaint little town located on the southeastern part of Prince William Sound. It was named by a Spanish explorer after a Spanish admiral Luis de Cordova y Cordova. Copper was its fortune, the Kennecott Copper Mine, and the Copper River salmon. In the 1950's it was acclaimed as the "razor capital of the world." The Good Friday Earthquake in 1964 and over harvest wiped out the clam industry. Traditionally, it was home to the Eyak. Years later, when I returned to Cordova, I met Margie Johnson, and her husband, Dick Boer, who owned the Reluctant Fisherman Inn. Margie became one of my favorite people. She was very influential and political in Alaskan circles. She later became the first woman mayor of Cordova, the first woman president of the Cordova Chamber of Commerce., and instrumental in bringing Cordova together. After the 1989 Exxon Valdez oil spill in the Prince William Sound she devoted her efforts to refocus Cordova's industry. The spill changed everyone. Her efforts were effective and beneficial to buffer Cordova in case of another spill, and getting things back to normal. She was appointed as a delegate to China with Senator Murkowski in the '90s to create a fish market between Cordova and China. Unfortunately, Cordova didn't bring fortune for Laura Belle and me, so it was back to Yakutat. We ended up selling the boat and taking the family back to Kodiak.

In Kodiak, I even tried my hand at cooking and bartending. Often I would pile-buck by day and bartend by night. I became

Part VII Full Circle—Back to Kodiak 1953 - 1960

friends with Alf and Charlie Madsen,[88] who had a Kodiak brown bear guiding operation.[89] Charlie had Guide License One and his son, Alf, had Guide License Two. They were both friends of my family, and said, "Jack, we'll put you to work as a packer and who knows what might happen."

---

[88] Unfortunately, the hunting guide, my friend, Alf Madsen, met a very sad end, September 10, 1960. I was diving out in the inlet building platforms when I got the news. He had a group of hunters at his Chignik Lake camp. He had flown down to Chignik to pick up some supplies and left his assistant guide with the hunters. Staying overnight in Chignik, he got up the next morning, climbed into his plane and didn't get far. He ran right into a mountain. They found he had died of carbon monoxide poisoning! I was very sad.

[89] Kodiak is known for the having the largest brown bear in the world and hunters would come from all over the world to take down a trophy.

Part VII Full Circle—Back to Kodiak   1953 - 1960

Working as a packer, I became known as Jack "Bull Moose" Johnson.

I went to work for them as a packer. I did all the dirty work and camp cooking. They had quite a set up and some beautiful cabins. I was a far cry from my sea physique, going from lean to mean. I was given the name "Bull Johnson," and was hard as nails. One time we were over at Uganik Island, situated west of Kodiak. We took clients by boats to hunting locations. On this occasion they forgot something and asked if I would go back to retrieve it.

To work in the wilds of Alaska, even today, it is best to carry a gun. Alf wouldn't go anywhere without the rifle he received from his father, a 30.06 Springfield, an old relic from WW I. He

Part VII   Full Circle—Back to Kodiak   1953 - 1960

had special ammunition he hand-loaded. Most of our hunters carried rifles like .300 magnums, or .370s. These types of rifles were suited for hunting elk, moose, or deer, but a better bet is a 12–gauge shotgun with a solid slug.

I said, "Sure, but it would be faster if I went over the hill." So I did. All I had was a little .45-70 and a Colt .45 six-shooter. I went up over the hill and came face to face with a *big* Kodiak brown bear. Even worse, a sow! It stood over to my left about 20 feet away. I raised my gun and was getting ready to shoot, when she looked at me and gave out a roar! There came a cub running out of the alders over to my right. The cub ran by me. The sow hit the cub and it rolled down the hill through the alders. Lucky for me, she took off down the hill after the cub. I stood there a little shaken. I sighed with relief and headed to the camp to get a pair of clean underwear, because I nearly had a wreck. There's nothing more dangerous than a sow separated from her cub.

While I was at the Karluk River camp cooking and packing for Alf Madsen, I had the opportunity to meet the King of Nepal, King Tribhuvan Bir Bikram Shah.[90] We were at the camp for several days, but that didn't matter since the King was paying us well. The King wanted to get a bear, and so did his entourage. They did get a bear. In fact, they managed to get three bears. Every evening when we'd get back to camp, we would go down to the Karluk River and he would fly fish. He was delighted to catch some nice steelhead trout. It was my job to cook them for dinner. The King of Nepal and I got along splendidly, and became good friends. After their hunting expedition was over, the King asked me to please come to Nepal to visit!

A year later, I went back to sailing. I was second mate in the American Mail Line ship, the *Oregon Mail*, with Captain Olsen. We were in the port of Calcutta, India. (The port was a military port during WW II.) When you go in, you are locked into a dock. When you open the gate, the Hooley River is rushing by and the

---

[90] King Tribhuvan had escaped to India for asylum, but was restored to improve the social and health conditions of the Nepalese people. Nepal had been a closed, private domain of the Rana Maharajas and for the first time in over 100 years outsiders were invited into the country.

Part VII   Full Circle—Back to Kodiak   1953 - 1960

dock is filled with water. Once they close the gate, you discharge your cargo and back load. We were unaware that when we got into the dock, the stevedores were on strike. We didn't know how long we were going to lay there and the captain was very upset. He didn't want to stay in Calcutta. Calcutta is not a very interesting place to be, and he'd just as soon be heading out.

After a couple of days, I started thinking about Nepal remembering the King's invitation. I talked to the captain and said, "While we are lying here, why don't we do something? What do you think about going to Nepal?"

Captain Olsen looked at me like I was half-crazy and asked, "Why do you want to go to Nepal?"

"I happen to know someone there," I answered. I'm pretty good at persuading people, so it wasn't too long before the captain, one of the engineers, the chief steward, the purser, and I went to Cooks Travel Agency in Calcutta and booked a passage on a flight to Kathmandu, the capital of Nepal. It was an old Douglas DC 3. I swear when we took off they were taking switchbacks to get to the top. We landed and were directed to the hotel. We checked in. It wasn't a very nice hotel, but it wasn't bad. They had a bar for Christians there, so we all ordered our usual Johnnie Walker Red Scotch and sodas. We were sitting there drinking when I said, "I'm going to call and see if I can get a hold of the King. He's the friend of mine that I told you about."

The captain just shook his head in disbelief, "Yah, Yohnson, you go call the King."

I got up and went to the desk. I told the gentlemen at the desk I wanted to talk to the King. The guy looked at me and said, "You can't talk to the King!"

I said, "Well, I'm a friend of the King's and I'd like to talk to him."

He still didn't believe me. Finally, I convinced him to at least make the call. He made the call and handed me the phone. I spoke the chamberlain. I told him I wanted to talk to the King. He told me that was highly irregular. You don't get an audience with His Majesty, the King unless you are some diplomat or stately person visiting.

Part VII   Full Circle—Back to Kodiak   1953 - 1960

I said, "If you tell him who I am, I'm sure he will want to see me."

He said, "I can't do that." After much struggle, I somehow convinced him he should at least tell the King that Jack "Bull Moose" Johnson from Kodiak, Alaska, was here to see him, and that I had been on a bear hunt with him there.

I waited several minutes, then I heard the chamberlain say apologetically, "Mr. Johnson, please forgive me. There will be a transport for you immediately."

I went back to the table and said, "Get ready to go, Captain. We are going to go see the King!"

The captain said, "Yohnson, you are always telling such stories."

Then all of a sudden in the door came these chauffeurs, all decked out in their fancy uniforms. They immediately came to our table. Very politely they said, "We are ready to take you to the palace for an audience with the King."

The captain stood up and looked out the door and there were three beautiful Rolls Royce limousines. I got in the first one, the captain and the engineer got in the second one, and the rest climbed in the third one. Away we went with motorcycle escorts down the cobblestoned street. Throngs of people and livestock quickly got out of the way as we made our way to the palace.

The captain was still wondering what was happening. We were escorted up the stairway with uniformed guards on both sides. There was a red-carpeted hallway that seemed to go on forever. Then down at the end of this red carpet was the King, and he was coming towards us with a couple of other people. We met him about half way, and he came up to me and gave me a great big hug, exclaiming, "Jack 'Bull Moose' Johnson. My friend, it is so good to see you."

The captain just looked at me with his eyes and mouth wide open in disbelief. The King immediately told us we would be staying there at the palace. We got settled in and cleaned up. A car from the hotel arrived with our overnight bags. After we were presentable, we went to a large dining area. We entered the huge austere dining hall. There was a feast "fit for a king."

Part VII   Full Circle—Back to Kodiak   1953 - 1960

There were lamb dishes and several mysterious delicacies. The dancing girls were a delight, as well as all sorts of wonderful things going on. We sat on impressive, straight-backed chairs, and enjoyed every minute of it. The King escorted us around, showing us the palace and the palace yard, as well as special places around Kathmandu. He had a special envoy to take us back to Calcutta. For years, Captain Olsen would talk at the Master Mariners meetings in Seattle about going to Nepal and visiting Jack Johnson's friend, His Majesty, the King of Nepal.

King Tribhuvan Bir Bikram Shah. Ruled Nepal 1913 – 1955.

Life has a way of humbling you. On July 29, 1958, I received the sad news that my mother had passed away. She was 70 years old and a remarkable woman. She had many accomplishments. She was a champion bridge player and her passion was raising chrysanthemums. She even went to Japan for particular seeds. She entered them in flower contests and won with high marks. The funeral was at the Masonic Temple, same as my father's, and as expected, the place was packed. My mother was an exceptional woman, the likes this world may never see again. My life as a sailor is as much her accomplishment as my Father's. And for that, I am eternally grateful.

Part VII   Full Circle—Back to Kodiak   1953 - 1960

Being married with a family, I tried to find employment that would keep me somewhere close to home. It is then I began tending bar. There was a long stint when I often found myself tending bar, more so than out at on the water. It was fast paced, lots of action, and good money. Kodiak nightlife was full of gambling, games, strippers, drinking, brawls, and lots of money. One night I was at the Casino Bar as the fishermen were coming down from Bristol Bay with their pockets full of money, a guy came in and said, "Ring the bell," which meant buying drinks for the entire bar. (It's the same all over the world. Say, "Ring the bell" and everyone in the bar gets a drink.)

This fisherman threw a couple hundred dollars on the bar. I was pouring drinks left and right. He did that about six times. He kept throwing hundred dollar bills to the barmaid and me for tips. Finally he said, "I gotta go."

I called him a cab. He went up to the Breaker's Bar. The bartender, Lou, called me and said, "Hey, I've got this guy here that just came up from your place. He said he left a paper bag down there at your place and it's real important that he gets it back."

I looked around a few minutes, and replied, "No, paper bag here."

About that time, the waitress came up to the bar holding a brown paper bag. She said, "Here's a paper bag I found on the deck." She laid it down on the bar.

I called Lou back and said, "Hey, we got a paper bag here on the bar, what's happening?"

He said, "We're gonna send a guy down to pick it up shortly."

After hanging up the phone, I began thinking that was an odd conversation. I decided to take a gander and look in the bag. I said, "I wonder what's in it?" So we opened it up. It was *full of money*! We carefully counted out $18,000 dollars. Next thing we knew, the cab driver showed up for the paper bag. He took the bag of money to the fisherman at the Breaker's Bar. I bet he kept "ringing the bell!"

I was tending bar at the Montmartre Inn Kodiak, a lively night full of music and strippers. It was halibut season. After

Part VII Full Circle—Back to Kodiak 1953 - 1960

delivering the fish, the crews had a mandatory eight-day layover. To pass the time, they'd have a party. Sven Jurstad, of the big 125' Canadian boat *Linda,* and his 14-man crew were there. They were having a last night in port party with lots of champagne and booze. After closing, a private party continued, and I joined in, along with three exotic dancers moonlighting as strippers for entertainment. There was lots of singing and dancing… and the booze went down like snow in Yuma.

As things were winding down, Sven said, "Jack, my cook didn't come back. I need a cook. Come and cook for me."

I said, "No way!"

He kept after me, telling me it was a short trip, and he had a good crew. I continued to refuse. We were drinking pretty heavy—or at least I was. The last thing I remembered was singing some Russian sailor song. I woke up with the sound of a boat engine and realized I was in a bunk. The next thing I heard was that god-awful voice, "Aye, Cookie, wake up! You gotta get up. Time to feed the boys. We'll be making the first set soon."

I had a Technicolor hangover. *Damn me eyes!* I had been shanghaied! I staggered up over to the washbasin and got cleaned up. Somehow I managed to throw together a fairly respectable breakfast for the boys, the old standby, bacon and eggs. The hot coffee was already made. After they ate, they went up on deck. My job was to hang around the galley until the next shift was scheduled to eat. There were 14 men on that boat. Meal times were at 0600, noon, 1800 and midnight. I thought I was doing a damn good job cooking up a storm. My menu consisted of steaks, chops, roasts, fried chicken, soups—I even got fancy on a few occasions and put out desserts—but no one seemed especially thrilled about the menu. It was the damnedest thing. Up on deck, they had a good catch of cod. We wound up coming in with lots of them. On the fifth day I was still whacking my brain to come up with a meal they liked.

Sven called me up to the wheelhouse and said, "Look, Cookie, there on deck is some nice codfish. Why don't you feed the boys some?" Codfish? What the hell! I went down and picked out a couple of super large ones, bled and dressed them. Nice fish,

Part VII   Full Circle—Back to Kodiak   1953 - 1960

no worms. I had a fine mess of cod ready for the gang at noon. Boiled codfish and potatoes! Olaf, a Norwegian in his 70s, sat down and took one look and loudly exclaimed, "Good god, fish at last!" Everyone enjoyed the meal. After that, the crew began talking to me, "Good morning, Cookie"..."Nice meal, Cookie"...."He's a fine cook, a bit dirty, but a good cook!" The captain greeted me each day, "Good morning, Cookie, some nice fish on deck." We ate codfish and potatoes for the rest of the trip!

The foc'sle was just forward of the galley. I noticed that every time Old Olaf would turn in each evening, he would take a big dip of Copenhagen snoose,[91] and put it in one side of his mouth. Then he'd take another big dip for the other side of his mouth. These were big dips. And then he'd pluck out another pinch of snoose, and sort of bend over, pull his eyelid open, and put this pinch in his eye. Then the other eye! If that weren't enough, he would straighten up, put a pinch up his nose, and make a couple of loud sneezes. He was sound asleep in a matter of seconds! It was the damnedest thing. He did this every time he turned in.

I watched him a few days before my curiosity got the best of me. I was using Copenhagen, but putting it in my eyes? Was there something I was missing? One night, when I had the galley all cleaned up and was ready to turn in, I decided to try the snoose in the eye action. I grabbed a pinch of snoose, just like I'd seen him do time after time. I leaned over and put a pinch in my left eye. Holy, moly! It burned! I hope to smile...! I rinsed my eye out with water for a long time, but it took days before my eye began to feel normal. That Olaf! *Damn me eyes!* How could he do it? I could hardly see to cook the rest of the day and never told anybody on board my foolish attempt at putting snoose in my eyes.

In the halibut boat, I often did double duty. As common with smaller salmon or halibut crews, you'd have two jobs. I would get up in the middle of the night and drag myself to the bait tent to bait up, and then to the galley to cook. One time during a storm in the Bering Sea, the crew came down to the galley to eat. I had a pot of soup on, as usual. It was piping hot, too hot to touch. As the

---

[91] Snuff or sniff tobacco.

Part VII   Full Circle—Back to Kodiak   1953 - 1960

boat pitched and rolled in the wild seas, the soup in the pot would come up in a perfect cylinder. It would go up and down, but it didn't lose a drop! It would seem to come out of the pot with each wave, then go right back in. It was the damnedest thing. It never lost a drop. And the mates never missed a meal. The captain was sad to see me go!

Part VIII   1960 - 1964

Mischievous Ways

He turned to me and said, "Jack, I tell you now. If you went to the moon, there would be people there that would know you!" That statement would follow me everywhere.
~Captain Jack V. Johnson~

Laura Belle and I had just broken up for the umpteenth time. They were still in our home in Kodiak. I was living elsewhere and tending bar at the Showcase. Mary Nester (my new love) was a naval nurse at the Naval Station in Kodiak. She was a full Lieutenant. The head nurse at the Kodiak Naval station was a Commander, a three-striper. Mary Nester and couple of Lieutenant JG nurses would come in the afternoons and sit at the corner of the bar. She would always bring me a little jar of Benzedrine pills; bennies were popular among the bartenders. They always made me feel better.

One evening, Mary, three other nurses, and four Naval officers came in. They sat at the big table. I nodded at them when they came in, yelling over, "I'll be there in a minute." Mary came over and gave me a big hug and a kiss. I followed her over to the table and got their order. That particular shift I didn't have a barmaid, so I played both barmaid and bartender. I went back to the bar, poured the booze, brought it back over on a tray, and started counting, "Let's see, that's eight drinks, fourteen, sixteen, oh, hell, I tell you what, I'll give you a hell of a break! Twelve dollars for the whole works."

The naval officers looked at each other, and one said, "I bought you that drink at the O Club last night."

Then the other guy said, "Yeah, okay, I bought those two drinks the other evening at the O Club."

Part VIII   My Mischievous Ways   1960 - 1964

This went on for a little while. I was looking at them and beginning to wonder who was going to pay for the drinks. The four nurses kept sitting quiet, looking a bit chagrined. Then the head nurse broke the silence. She was a tough lady. She said, "Just a minute. Just a god-damn minute. What did we come here for? Did we come here to have a drink or to keep fucking books?" Then she threw a 20 at me and said, "Here, Jackson, keep the change!"

I ran into Mary a few years later when I was crabbing out at Adak in the *Pacific Fisher* with Merrill Hennington. I was part owner. He was the captain, and I was the mate. Crabbing was very good. You could make up to $60,000 in less than three weeks in a good season. The processor was lying in Finger Bay, the old submarine station the Navy used during WW II. The only thing left was the dock where the processer was tied up.

We were loaded down with crab. Fish and Game had restrictions, mandating a four-day wait after you unloaded and sold your crab. We were waiting to deliver ours to the processor. I went ashore and, walking down dock, saw three people coming up the dock with parkas over their heads. I figured it was some local people coming down to visit. Lo and behold, there was Mary Nester and another nurse, along with the Lieutenant Commander who was working as the security officer for the Naval Station in Adak. Mary was now a Lt. Commander. We gave each other a big hug and a kiss, and Mary introduced me to the others. We didn't have anything to drink on my boat, because Merrill Hennington wouldn't allow booze on board. Ronstad was there in the *Foremost*, and I knew he would have something to drink. I climbed down and asked if it was okay to bring three naval people aboard, two of them nurses.

"Come on down." He reached under the bench in the galley and brought out a couple of bottles of Canadian Club whisky. He said, "Bring 'em down." They came down, and he poured some generous drinks. We were sitting and talking. He turned to me and said, "Jack, I tell you now. If you went to the moon, there would be people there that would know you!" That statement would follow me everywhere.

Part VIII   My Mischievous Ways   1960 - 1964

Kodiak was a rough place. Fishing was good, and it attracted a lot of people, both good and bad. An odd thing was happening around town. Quite a few dogs were dying. Someone had been feeding them ground glass. I had a beautiful dog, a Weimaraner. His name was Hans Froleich Von Kodiak—Happy Hans of Kodiak. I called him Hans. My friend, Bob Waage, had a beautiful chocolate Chesapeake Bay retriever. The two dogs would run and play together. One day, both of them were in serious condition. When we got to them, they were bleeding from the mouth and dying. We took them to the vet, and ground glass was found in their stomachs. Bob and I were outraged. We vowed to track down the person responsible.

We rounded up a couple of other guys to help. It wasn't long before we caught the suspect. We took him over to the garage at Bab Waage's place, tied him up to a chair, and forced his mouth open. Then we put in a light bulb. Then with a crushing upper cut, we smashed the bulb in his mouth, showing him what ground glass tasted like. We did this six times! We untied him and gave him a "blue ticket"[92] out of town—Kodiak style. We made it clear. We didn't want to see him in town again. We beat him up some more, put the boots to him, and kicked his ass out the door so he landed flat on his face. The last we saw of him he was staggering down the road.

Again back at the Casino, a fisherman came in and "rang the bell." He was in pretty bad shape.

I had to have a talk with him. "I'm gonna have to 86 you," I said. "I appreciate your business, but you better go get some rest somewhere."

"Yeah, I guess you're right," he stammered, slurring as he spoke. "Call me a cab!"

I called him a cab. The driver came in and said, "I'm here. Someone called for a cab?"

I motioned him over, tilting my head towards the guy at the end of the bar. "I better help you get him out; he's in bad shape."

---

[92] A blue discharge, also known as a "blue ticket," was a form of administrative military discharge formerly issued by the United States beginning in 1916.

Part VIII   My Mischievous Ways   1960 - 1964

We carried him out, me on one side of the inebriated fellow, and the cab driver on the other. We sat him in the cab.

He said, "Take me to the Casino!"

The cab driver said, "This *is* the Casino."

"No! You drive too fast! I'm not gonna ride with you!" Those fishermen were funny guys. Ring the bell, buy a drink, or go to hell.

Another time, I was on an evening shift at the Montmartre Inn. In walked one of the guys I had worked with as a packer for Alf Madsen. He had two of his clients, the Greene brothers, with him. They owned part of the Golden Nugget Casino in Las Vegas. He introduced us. Later on that evening, one of the Greene brothers spoke to me and said, "Hey, Jack, we like your action. If you ever get to Las Vegas, look us up, and we'll put you to work."

Curiosity got the best of me. I took them up on their offer and two months later went to Las Vegas. They were true to their word and put me to work as a bartender. They paid $14 a shift, but I'd pick up hundreds of dollars in tips. The action was fast. Evidently, the pit boss and head bartender figured that I should spend some of that money back in the casino. I told them I wasn't interested in gambling. Well, that ended my career as a bartender in Las Vegas. No pit boss wants to see the gross of one's earnings walking out the door, even if he is the bartender. It didn't hurt my feelings none, because in truth, I was looking for an excuse to get out of there. I didn't like the action—the Vegas action was too fast for this poor little Alaskan boy.

As I headed back north, I stopped in the bustling town of Tahoe, full of casinos and restaurants. I went to work this time, not as a bartender, but as a chef at the Lake Tahoe Lodge. I worked there six weeks until I made enough cash to drag up and head north again. Once back in Kodiak, I got a job as a bartender again at the Show Case.

One evening, as I was coming on shift, I noticed sitting at the corner of the bar were Milli Markham, the owner of the Montmartre Inn, and the other Milli, married to Blue-eyed Bill. I was pouring drinks up and down the bar. It was a nice evening. A couple had come in, playing the banjo and accordion, hitting some ragtime tunes. Blue-eyed Bill came in the back door. I headed over

Part VIII   My Mischievous Ways   1960 - 1964

to see what he wanted to drink. He stood there and said, "Give the girls a drink, and I'll have my usual," which was a double shot and water behind. I poured the drinks and went about my business up and down the bar.

The next thing I knew, I looked down the bar, and there was Blue-eyed Bill pounding the crap out of his wife. I hopped over the bar, and he glared at me. I said, "What's going on?"

Blue-eyed Bill stopped beating the hell out of Milli. He reached in his pocket and pulled out a gun. He came towards me with the pistol.

I looked him in the eye and asked, "What are you going to do?"

He answered, "I'm gonna kill you."

Thoughts came back to me of my wartime days, and I remembered what to do. I charged towards him, grabbed his gun arm, and hit him in the head with a strong fist. Down he went like a spawned-out dog salmon, flopping around the deck. I took the gun and threw it behind the bar.

Just about that time, in came a cop, Elmer Dean. He asked, "What's going on in here?"

I said, "This guy pulled a gun on me. He was beating up his ol' lady. And there he lies."

Elmer leaned over the guy, turned him over, looked at me, and said, "The guy's dead!"

"He can't be dead," I said, "I only hit him once."

"You must have hit him hard because he is deader than a mackerel," said Elmer. Everyone was kind of upset. Elmer called the ambulance. The ambulance people came and took poor Blue-eyed Bill out the door. Elmer Dean felt bad that he had to arrest me. But all the witnesses showed up the next day and sprung me.

That's pretty much all that came of that except for the nickname that was to follow me around, the name "Death Johnson." Everyone talked about how it only took one punch. "Death Johnson. Look out for Death Johnson."

After I married Iris, she went into a bar in Seward, and when they found out who she was married to, they said, "Oh, you fetched up with Death Johnson! The meanest man in Alaska!"

Part VIII   My Mischievous Ways   1960 - 1964

When I was tending bar in Kodiak at Tony's, the man who owned Kraft's Market, old Ben Kraft—our family is distantly related—would come in for a martini. Ben was one of those martini drinkers with whom one led to two, two led to three, three led to four, and four led to eight. He always wound up with at least four or five martinis under his belt. He came to the bar the same time each evening like clockwork. One of his kids would arrive to drive him home each night. When Ben would get drinking, he became very talkative. With all this talking, he would invariably lose his false teeth. It wasn't unusual for his upper plate to fall out of his mouth onto the bar. Ben would fumble around to put it back in. Everyone always got a kick out of Ben Kraft losing his teeth.

One night he was on his third or fourth martini while talking with everybody. As usual, he lost his teeth. He began blindly reaching around for them. He picked up what he thought was his upper plate. It was actually one of the small ashtrays. He picked up the ashtray loaded down with cigarette butts and stuffed it square in his mouth. He tried to keep talking without skipping a beat as cigarette butts and ashes were falling out of his mouth down his chin. All you could hear was a click, click sound as his lower teeth hit the glass of the ashtray stuck firmly in his upper jaw. Everyone had a big laugh!

Another time I was tending bar at the Mecca, and this guy came wandering in. He was what we called a "barfly." You know the sort, probably homeless, no money, and he'd mooch off everybody. Everybody would feel sorry for him and buy him a beer once in a while. This one time he came in, he put his wallet on the bar, and I could see the corner of a 20-dollar bill sticking out of it. I said, "Yeah, what'll it be there, Donny?"

He said, "Give me a double Seven 7."[93]

I repeated it back at him, "A double Seven 7."

"Put some lemon in it," he said.

"Okay, here's a double Seven 7 with a squeeze of lemon."

---

[93] Seagram's Seven Crown and 7 Up.

Part VIII   My Mischievous Ways   1960 - 1964

"And Jack, get yourself a drink, and get those people down there a drink, too."

"Okay," I got them all a drink. I came back to Donny. I said, "Now that will be $12.50."

"Ain't got any money," he said, downing his drink.

"What do you mean, you 'ain't got any money.' There's a 20-dollar bill sticking out of your wallet." I reached for his wallet and pulled it out, and that's all it was, just a corner of a 20-dollar bill! I laughed out loud, and everyone got a charge out of it. I felt like climbing over the bar and belting the hell out of him, but I was laughing too hard. Instead, I drank the shot I had poured for myself and went down the bar telling what had just taken place.

Here's another story. There was an old fisherman, living on his boat in Kodiak, a real character. We called the little Norwegian a Chinese name, Lars Wang. He had been a highline fisherman all of his life, but he was getting up in years. He gave up fishing. His little vessel was just like a yacht. And a beautiful yacht it was. He had gone to work for the Fish and Wildlife Service supplying the stream watchmen with groceries, coffee, and stuff like that, up and down the peninsula. Lars would also gather their reports and bring them back to Kodiak. For a crew, he would get college kids from the School of Fisheries of the University of Washington.

On one trip, as told to me by one of the college kids, they pulled off into Ivanoff Bay. Ivanoff Bay is a beautiful little place. Today only about 10 or 12 people are living there, but in those days, it was quite a place with a good population with the cannery going full *fhart*. The crew got it in their heads to play a trick on old Lars. They made a replica of the anchor out of wood and bent on the anchor line. As they came into anchor, Lars belted out in his strong Norwegian voice, "Yah boys, throw over the anchor!"

They threw the wooden anchor over the side. Then they shouted, "Lars, Lars, look, the anchor's floating!" as they pointed to the wooden anchor floating on the water.

"Yesus!" Lars yelled back, "Get a pike pole and shove it under before we run aground!"

Here's another one. There was a machine shop in town, and one of the machinists, an old Norwegian guy, worked there. He

Part VIII   My Mischievous Ways   1960 - 1964

had a way about him. No matter what they told him good or bad, he'd always say, "Well, it's never so bad that it couldn't be worse."

The crew got tired of him replying, "it's never so bad that it couldn't be worse" so they decided they would find something that was so bad he couldn't say that. So one morning, the old machinist came in and punched in the time clock. He walked back to the locker room, and one of guys said, "Hey, did you hear about the foreman?" (The foreman was hiding under his desk.)

"No, what's happened to the foreman?" he asked.

"Well, he caught his wife in bed with another guy."

"Umm... You don't say," the old machinist muttered.

"Yeah, he shot and killed his wife and then shot and killed the guy that was in bed with her! Then he committed suicide."

The old Norwegian shook his head in disbelief. "Oh, how terrible! Oh, my god... oh, that's awful," he looked genuinely upset. Then he said shaking his head, "It's never so bad that it couldn't be worse!"

The guys were outraged, "What do you mean it's never so bad that it couldn't be worse?"

The old Norwegian hung his head and admitted sheepishly, "Well, if it had been the night before, it would have been me!"

I've got a million of these stories! Here's another one. Once working as a cook in the power scow *Homer* for Chris Dahl Fisheries, we pulled into Petersburg. We were there for a couple of days picking up some shipments of frozen fish to take south and some cannery machinery that needed to be overhauled. Pulling in, I spied this little Finnlander I had known for years. He usually hung out in Kodiak, but now was in Petersburg. He waved when he saw us, "Yonson, happy to see you!"

I told him I'd be right down.

He said, "We gotta go have a drink."

I agreed and walked down to the dock, shaking hands with a few other people I knew.

As we were walking up the dock, this little kid came skipping along. When he came to us, he stopped and shouted, "Hey, mister, give me 10 cents for ice cream?" This goodhearted Finn put his hand in his pocket, pulled out a handful of change, and

Part VIII   My Mischievous Ways   1960 - 1964

put it into the kid's hand. The little kid looked at it, picked out a dime for ice cream, and threw the rest of the money over the dock. He then ran down the dock for ice cream. The Finn shook his head and said, "Yesus! That kid is sure reckless with my money!"

Part VIII My Mischievous Ways 1960 - 1964

More Hijinks

*I left Oscar in Seattle, and headed back to the Bering Sea
with another Oscar Callow story
of how he kidnapped me from the Marine Hospital.
~Captain Jack V. Johnson~*

In 1962, I was cooking in a fishing boat out in the Aleutians and wound up in a fight with Arnie Flathaug. Arnie was a good fisherman, good sailor, but he had a bad drinking habit and a very short temper. I can't remember what I did, but I pissed him off. He took a swing and belted me one. I hit the floor of the galley, then got up, and grabbed the lifter off the galley range. I hit him with it. Boy, then he belted me one in the eye. The next thing I knew, I was down on the deck, but got up and managed to waylay him. Down he went, and about this time, Captain Merrill Hennington came down and stopped everything by landing me a pretty solid punch. It broke the floor of the orbit—the bony socket—of my eye. I got off the boat and was sent to the Marine Hospital in Seattle. I was on the eighth floor and diagnosed with a broken eye socket; the eye was all haywire and out of place. They didn't know how long I would have to stay there, but it would take some time. I wasn't really hurting bad. I was just stuck there on the eighth floor with the big thrills of the day: breakfast, lunch, and dinner.

In our ward, the guys were in the same shape as I was and nobody was in dire straits. We'd often wind up in the rec room watching television, playing cards, and doing whatever. One bored day, I got the wild idea to track down some of my buddies living in the Seattle area. Not sure how it happened, but I had heard that my buddy, the Major himself, Oscar Callow, was working in Portland, Oregon. He got word I was looking for him, and it just so happened that he was up in Seattle visiting his girlfriend, Dorthea.

He called the hospital and discovered I was stuck on the eighth floor. We talked things over. He and I agreed that, to make things a little easier for the both of us, he could bring me some

Part VIII   My Mischievous Ways   1960 - 1964

Scotch, which we both had a fondness for, of course. The next day he came by with a couple of bottles of Johnnie Walker Red. We had a good time and shared our "spirits" with some of the others on the eighth floor. It wound up being a very pleasant afternoon and on into the evening, though I am not sure how the hospital staff felt about all this. The evening came to an end, and Oscar gave his final "tally ho" and left. He said he'd be back tomorrow before going back home to Portland.

The U.S. Marine Hospital, Seattle, Washington.

Sure enough, Oscar arrived the next day with another bottle of Scotch, and after a few drinks we got the wild idea that I should go with him to Portland. He said, "Jack, you should leave this hospital. There's nothing happening around here. All you're doing is lying around. You're not doing anything! Let's cut out."

I said, "Oscar, there's one small problem, I don't have any clothes; they are all locked up in some locker somewhere."

Oscar replied, "I say, old chap, you do have on a hospital robe. That's some swell gown, with matching pajama bottoms, and cloth slippers to boot." I guess we figured that was enough, because away we went. I walked out of the Marine Hospital in full pajama regalia. No questions asked.

Oscar had a blue DeSoto with fins on the back, which I teased him about being made at the turn of the century. We left Seattle and took off towards Oregon. It's a little fuzzy what provoked the incident, but for some reason Oscar got pulled over for some infraction. The officer came up to the car with me in the passenger

Part VIII   My Mischievous Ways   1960 - 1964

seat decked out in my hospital garb. I had just finished a bottle of Scotch.

The Washington State patrolman started talking with Oscar. Oscar was trying to talk his way through all this mischief and out of a ticket. I looked up and yelled out, "Help! Help! Officer, I'm being kidnapped!"

Oscar had the presence of mind to respond back in his formal British accent, "Don't pay any attention to him. I say, I'm taking this poor chap to Morningside in Portland." Morningside was the mental hospital with many Alaskan residents. Bank then there was a popular joke that there were three sides to Alaska: inside, outside, and Morningside.

The officer, seeing how I was dressed, nodded and said, "Yes, I understand. Carry on."

And away we went. I wasn't impressed. I said, "Hell. I want to get out of these clothes."

We got arguing about Oscar telling the officer he was taking me to Morningside, and it became so heated we pulled over at the nearest gas station and started beating the hell out of each other. Once that was out of our system, Oscar looked at me and shook his head, laughing. "We have got to get some clothes for you."

We pulled up to a tavern still in the state of Washington. This was a place to get a drink. I was still in my robe, pajamas, and slippers. Suddenly, Oscar said, "I have an idea." He began eyeballing the guys in the tavern. He noticed one guy heading for the head.

Oscar followed him in and belted him in the jaw. Down he went colder than a stone. While the poor slob was lying on the deck of the head, we relieved him of his fine-looking clothes, which happened to be a really nice looking suit. Oscar had eyeballed him pretty good, because it fit pretty well. We took everything, even his tie. The poor guy was lying there in his shorts and one of those singlet undershirts. We folded up my robe, cloth slippers, and the funny pajamas and laid them on top of his chest. After all, we were rather decent sorts. We didn't want to leave him completely in distress, making sure he had something to wear when he woke up.

Part VIII   My Mischievous Ways   1960 - 1964

We looked through his billfold. There was quite a bit of money in it. We left the billfold, but helped ourselves to the cash. Then, away we went on down to Portland. When we got to Portland, Oscar had to get back to work. I spent three days lying around his apartment, not doing much of anything but drinking with Oscar when he'd get home. After three days, I wanted to get back to Seattle. We talked it over, and Oscar said, "We'll put you on a bus back to Seattle."

And that's exactly what we did. I was still wearing the guy's clothes, so I wasn't too bad off on the trip back. I got back to Seattle and back to the Marine Hospital. I walked right back in, and the staff said they were wondering where I had been. I told them I had just taken off to visit some friends. All was well, and I checked back in. Oscar came up a couple of more times to visit. He always brought Johnnie Walker Red Label Scotch.

After another couple of weeks, the doctor determined that things were right for the operation on my eye. They went in, straightened my eyeball, and fixed up the floor of orbit. It was quite painful. I wore a cotton patch over my eyes for about a week. I upgraded to a black patch with strict instructions to take it off every two hours until my eye got strong enough. I looked the part of Captain Jack. I left Oscar in Seattle and headed back to the Bering Sea with another Oscar Callow story of how he kidnapped me from the Marine Hospital.

Times were tough. Even though Laura Belle and I had been separated for quite some time, we tried once again to make a go of it. I did what I could to provide for my family. There wasn't much work around Kodiak so I headed off to Seattle and grabbed a quick trip on an American Mail Line ship. I would make one or two trips and then get back to Kodiak in time to go commercial fishing.

It was about that time when the crabbing started in Kodiak. I worked on some of the first king crab vessels out of there. I ended up spending several winters out in the Bering Sea crabbing. That's when I wound up part owner of the *Pacific Fisher* with Merrill Hennington. We had some pretty good seasons, not to mention some hair-raising experiences in the Bering Sea. There's a

Part VIII   My Mischievous Ways   1960 - 1964

television show I catch every now and again called the "Deadliest Catch," narrated by Mike Rowe. I've watched it a few times. I can't say that's exactly the way we did it in the early days, but I can say, "Been there, done that!" I happen to know some of the guys on the "Deadliest Catch"—a good bunch of guys.

These old "halibut heads," as we used to call them, would retire ashore. It wasn't unusual for many of them to start up a boarding house or farming, trying to do something different from all those years out in the Bering Sea and all the hardships that came with fishing.

This one guy, Lars, started a farm and was raising pumpkins. His friend, Ole, drove up one day to visit him. Ole walked up to the porch, and he looked around at all those pumpkins. The pumpkin patch was beautiful, but the pumpkins were all the size of a tennis ball.

Ole says to Lars, "Lars, I'm afraid there's something wrong with your pumpkin patch here. They're all so teeny-weeny."

Lars shook his head looking at the pumpkins, "I don't know; I do everything I can to make the pumpkin patch work, but this is what I got."

Ole scratched his head, trying to suggest a solution, "Are you cultivating them?"

"Cultivating them?" Lars was slightly perturbed. "Yesus Christ, I'm out there digging like a gopher. Yesus, I cultivate! Of course, I cultivate!"

Ole thought some more, not wanting to insult his friend. He began rubbing his chin and said, "Are you fertilizing them?"

"Fertilizing them?" Lars said even more agitated, "Of course. I spread shit so far and wide you can't believe it."

"Well, I don't know," admitted Ole. "Oh, I know, are you irrigating them?"

"Irrigating them?" Now Lars was getting real upset. "Well, of course. I got water going back and forth here like a storm in the Bering Sea. But all I get are these little tiny pumpkins. I don't understand."

Part VIII   My Mischievous Ways   1960 - 1964

Lars broke out the snoose can, and they both took a chew. Nodding their heads, they looked at one another. "Oh," said Ole with a big wad in his lower lip, "are you pollinating them?"

"Pollinating them? What's that?" asked Lars, spitting sluice.

Ole thought maybe they were on to something, "You know pollen. It comes from the flower of the pumpkin. You got the boy pollen and the girl pollen. You introduce them and get together the boy pollen and the girl pollen, and that's what you have to do to make the big pumpkins."

Lars thought a moment and took another pinch of snoose, "I'll cultivate, and I'll fertilize, and I'll irrigate, but, Yesus, I will never be a pimp in a pumpkin patch!"

Part VIII   My Mischievous Ways   1960 - 1964

Fishing, But Catching Bears

*The story went around fast of me plowing into the mayor's bedroom
and backing into Mrs. Hegland's kitchen,
not to mention the head-on collision with a police vehicle.
You've got to hand it to me, if I'm gonna fuck up,
I'm gonna fuck up good!
~Captain Jack V. Johnson~*

Ed Graboski was gathering up a crew to go out salmon fishing. I had never salmon fished with him before, but he called me up and said he needed a cook. "Sure, I'm not doing anything right now. I'll be down there tomorrow." I got there about the time of the opening. We were out fishing and made a great big haul down by Dog Fish Bay. That's when I noticed a couple of other guys out in the bay talking on the radio, using channel 16, which was supposed to be the emergency channel. Here they were admitting to all kinds of stuff. One guy said, "Boy, I don't know what happened. I got my net all fucked up. I'm all fucked up here."

I was listening to the chatter. About that time the Coast Guard came in and responded, "The last transmission, the last transmission. Please identify yourselves."

The next voice you heard said, "I might be fucked up, but I'm not that fucked up!"

Another time, I had a seine boat for a while out of Seldovia on the South shore of Kachemak Bay opposite Homer, for the Port Graham fisheries in Port Graham. The area is known for salmon — chum (dog), humpback (pink), Coho (silver), and even some Dolly Varden (char). With the high tides, the salmon enter the fresh water to spawn (lay their eggs) up stream before making the trip back down to Kachemak Bay to die. A seiner is equipped with a large net (seine net) that hangs in the water with weights along the bottom edge and floats along the top. The long flat nets are used like a fence to encircle the school of fish as the boat circles around, trapping the fish inside. This particular time I was out with my small crew. We had just made a haul and did pretty

Part VIII   My Mischievous Ways   1960 - 1964

good, but competition is the name of the game so we were always cutting corners or taking chances to better our income. I don't know whose idea it was, but we all went along with the plan to sneak up to the head of the bay to rob the creek! Once we arrived, the salmon were running pretty heavy.

We decided "What the hell," and we went a little further up the creek and set out the seine (which was illegal), and within minutes the net was full of fish.

We decided we had better get out of there before the Fish Hawk (Alaska Fish and Game Warden) showed up and busted us for illegal fishing. We started pursing up and said, "Holy shit!" There was a black bear right in the middle of the seine.

We didn't know what to do. It was getting close to the closing period and the Fish Hawk would be showing up. We were in illegal waters, and regulations stated, when the fishing period closed, no one could fish. We needed to be done and get the fish into the boat and run for market as fast as we could. We were caught up with our seine full of fish, too far up river, with closing time breathing down on us, and a mad black bear causing havoc in the net.

We pursed up[94] with the bear in our net, and then we took a knife and cut the seine. The bear fell out. We lost a few fish, but we made a big haul. We got to market in time. There was a tender from Fort Graham lying there. We went and delivered to the tender and were all set for the next fishing period. We used to do some other low-down schemes to better our fishing outcomes. We even painted our boats grey to make it more difficult for the Fish Hawk to see us. We called it "Creek Robbing Grey."

With all my rabble-rousing, carousing, and mischievous behavior, I haven't spent much time in the slammer locked up. I have managed to dodge the bullet many times, like the time I came down the hill in Kodiak after an Elks Convention and made a wrong turn, only to end up in the mayor's bedroom. I had one of the first Volkswagen buses to come out in the '60s. The Elks Convention out at the ol' Beach Comber Bar off Mission Road. It

---

[94] Drew up or bunched up the net.

Part VIII   My Mischievous Ways   1960 - 1964

was unique. The bar was a ship that we had gotten up on the beach and across the highway. They placed sand all around and turned it into a motel. It had a restaurant and bar, as well as a big dance floor. After the convention was over, everyone got involved playing dice games, 4-5-6, and craps. When we called it a night, several of us got into my bus to go downtown. Coming down Mission Road, I made the wrong turn and drove right into the mayor's bedroom.

Everyone in the bus started screaming! "Back up. Back up. Get out of here! Get out of here!"

I was not too familiar with the Volkswagen bus and tried shifting her into reverse. Reverse it was. Then *bam*! Back across the road and right into Mrs. Hegland's kitchen. Glass came crashing in all around us as the side of the building fell over us.

My passengers started screaming again, "Jack, get out of here!" I pulled out and headed up the road only to have a head-on collision with Elmer Dean's police car. I ran smack into him with what was left of my poor Volkswagen bus, which was pretty well beat up by then. He arrested me right then and there, making arrangements for a tow car to take care of my VW. The other guys mysteriously went missing and wandered off somewhere in the night. I went to jail and had my driver's license pulled for 90 days. I appealed, and the magistrate cut it down to 30 days with a stout warning, but I didn't have to do any more jail time, just that one night. The story went around fast of me plowing into the mayor's bedroom and backing into Mrs. Hegland's kitchen, not to mention the head-on collision with a police vehicle. You've got to hand it to me; if I'm gonna fuck up, I'm gonna fuck up good!

After five years, I left my job as the wharfinger for the City of Kodiak and began pile-bucking. Laura Belle and I split up for the last time; the handwriting was on the wall. In 1964 we had an *uncivil* divorce.

I was in Kodiak on a fishing boat, and I decided to wet my whistle. I stopped at a local bar. When I went up to get a drink, these two thugs came out of nowhere. Laura Belle and I had recently divorced, and for some reason, they felt it was their duty to let me have it on my ex-wife's behalf. They took it on

Part VIII   My Mischievous Ways   1960 - 1964

themselves to beat me up. When they were done, I was really beaten up, with two black eyes, and several broken ribs, and my nose out of shape.

A few days after staying aboard the boat and licking my wounds, I said, "The hell with it," and I went out to have a nice steak dinner. I started out the door, but then I went back in and got a pistol just in case anything happened again. I wanted to go to the same place I had been ambushed.

While I was walking up the gangway, the same two guys that had beaten me up were coming down. I took one look at them, drew my pistol, and shot a round between their legs. They threw up their hands and pleaded, "Wait! Don't shoot!"

I felt no pity. I had the both of them leaned up against the FAA boat and shot them both in the kneecaps. That put them on sticks for a while. I went on and ordered my steak. Delicious!

PART IX   1964 - 1972

Connie

Ex-wives may come and go, but shipmates go on forever!
~Captain Jack V. Johnson~

When the '64 earthquake hit, I was in Seattle with Captain Jack Anderson, Sr. I had just gone to work for him and was going to be in one of his many vessels. We were chartered to go to Bristol Bay to "sniff" for oil. The Associated Oil Company wanted to look for oil and eventually would start drilling in Bristol Bay. Captain Anderson had taken the crew for dinner, celebrating the fact that he had made the contract and had things pretty well sewn up. As we were sitting there and the waiter was bringing us drinks and food, the waiter made small talk by stating, "That was a horrible earthquake in Alaska!"

"Yeah, we get earthquakes pretty frequently up there."

"No, this was a terrible one. Anchorage was demolished, and Kodiak was hit with a big tidal wave. It was horrible!"

We all started paying attention by that time. It had also affected Seattle, the water of Lake Union in Seattle, and Crescent City. California had a tsunami that wiped out some of its waterfronts. Our dinner celebration came to a screeching halt. We did everything we could to find out what the real story was, and the only news we got was bad. I still tried to get through to Laura Belle and the kids. I finally got word to them through Pete DeVoe, a famous ham radio operator, who later became mayor of Kodiak and then state senator. I did everything I could to get up to Alaska. No planes were flying. It was Captain Jack Anderson, Jr., who finally got me out on a Navy flight. We arrived to devastation.

In Kodiak, our house had been hit by the tidal wave that hit the waterfront of Kodiak, and it had been pushed six blocks from

Part IX   The Rebuilding   1964 - 1972

where it stood. I found a place to live up on the hill from the schoolhouse. The schoolhouse had been wiped out. The housing was up above the playground. I moved in with my friend and shipmate, Stan Lee. (Ex-wives may come and go, but shipmates go on forever!) Kodiak was wiped out, and rebuilding began immediately. Priorities! The first things to be rebuilt were the bars! And the first to be rebuilt was one of my favorite watering holes, the Mecca Bar. The crews had to have someplace to go after work. Once rebuilt, it was off to the Mecca Bar every evening after work.

Seward, Alaska, earthquake/tsunami damage. 1964.

We rebuilt Kodiak. Then the company got a job to go to Seward to rebuild some of the docks. They asked if any of us wanted to go. Several of us took them up on the offer. We built the big railroad dock. The old dock downtown, the Alaska Steam dock, had been totally wiped out, so we put up a temporary dock out of sheet piling and fender piling, for vessels to tie up as we built the railroad dock. As in Kodiak, we needed a new watering hole, so we'd meet at the Palace Bar. They had us staying in an apartment near the Palace Bar. It was convenient.

The very docks I helped build after the '64 earthquake I would later pilot ships to. Little did I know at the time that I would spend the latter part of my life in Seward, making it my home in 1975.

When the 1964 earthquake came along and changed everything, it was a big chore to rebuild Alaska. I helped rebuild from Kodiak to Seward and on out to Cordova. Being a part of the

Part IX The Rebuilding 1964 - 1972

rebuilding of the state, I found myself rebuilding my own life. Laura Belle and I had divorced after about eight years of marriage.

It wasn't long before I fetched up in Seattle again. That's where I met Connie Gard. She was waitressing in the Scandinavian Seafarers Club. I was enchanted. She was 21 and very pretty. She had the most flashing blue eyes I've ever seen. They were even bluer than Elizabeth Taylor's eyes. She was almost six feet tall, which was a different direction from the pixie-style ladies I usually was attracted to, but something about Connie struck my fancy. When I met her, she said her name was Connie Gard.

I asked, "Any relationship to Earl Gard?"

She said, "Yes, that's my father."[95]

I was intrigued. "I sailed with Earl Gard, and I think I met you when you were a little girl."

I recounted the story to her. I was third mate in the *Mary Luckenbach*. It was in 1950, and we were sailing out of Seattle at the time. The bosun was Earl Gard. I came out of the deckhouse to help the chief mate. We were loading cargo. As I walked forward, this little girl was sitting on a mooring bit by the number three hatch. I said, "Oh, there's a cute little girl. What's your name?"

She replied, "Connie."

I said, "You're the bosun's daughter?"

"Yep."

"He's a nice daddy."

"Nope!"

"He's not a nice daddy?"

"Nope!"

"Do you like ice cream?"

"Yep."

"I'll take you into the officers' mess, and you can have some ice cream."

"Nope"

I said, "Is that all you can say, 'yep' or 'nope'?"

"Yep."

---

[95] Earl Gard was the bosun we gifted with the donkey and monkey.

Part IX   The Rebuilding   1964 - 1972

Connie was impressed with my memory of the occasion, and soon we forged a beautiful relationship. I hate to admit it, but I was 17 years her senior. I was 38, and she was 21. She was a big girl and had a big temper. Connie could hold her own in a fight. It was that mixture of beauty and feistiness that held my interest. I met her on a Tuesday, and we were married that Friday.

After we got married, we took off to Alaska. My friend, Captain Niels P. Thomsen, with the mail boat *Expansion,* helped us out. He had changed it over to a processing vessel for king crab. I shipped out as a cook, and Connie came aboard as a supernumerary working her way north. I was being paid, and she was not, but hell, it was a free ride. The first port of call was Kodiak. Somewhere along the way, I was beginning to have my doubts about Captain Niels P. Thomsen and his processing vessel, but I wasn't letting on. Pay was good, and it looked real promising, but I didn't really appreciate being a cook. Everyone was raving about my cooking except the captain. He used to complain, "Why do you cook so much? Who did you cook for before, the government?"

I said, "I don't know, Cap. I want to make everybody happy." We had quite a crew aboard, the captain, two mates, six sailors, two engineers, two oilers, the processing foreman, four of the processing crew, a second cook, two galley hands, Connie, and me. When we arrived at the fuel dock in Kodiak (I helped build that dock years earlier when I was pile-bucking), there was a pile driver on the inshore side, and it looked like they were driving a dolphin.[96] I went over to look and realized I knew everyone.

They said, "Hey, Jack, we need a front-end man; get down here!"

I said, "I can't. I'm working." Then I got to thinking, "Why not?" I went on board, packed my gear, grabbed Connie, and went to the old man saying, "Pay me off. I'm leaving."

He was out of sorts about it, but he paid me off. He even dropped an extra $300 on me for a bonus, which was rare for Captain Niels P. Thompson.

---

[96] A structure consisting of a number of piles driven into the seabed as marker.

Part IX   The Rebuilding   1964 - 1972

I went to work in construction and pile-bucking. Connie and I settled back in Kodiak. It was quite a time. They were building the small boat harbor so I had plenty of work. We were living up on Signal Hill in one of the trailers they had set up after the quake. It was going along pretty good. Connie was working in the cannery and making good money—for what they paid cannery hands in those days. I was pile-bucking and getting good wages. In the evenings, I was also tending bar. Of course, after thinking about it, bringing a 21-year-old, beautiful bride into my old stomping grounds where I had an ex-wife and kids wasn't the brightest thing I've ever done. So we moved to Anchorage.

I bought Connie a new car, a red 442 Oldsmobile. This was considered a "muscle car" because it had a full size V8 stuffed into a mid-sized car. It was dubbed the 4-4-2 because it had a 4-barrel carburetor, a 4-speed manual transmission, and duel exhausts. We took it for a maiden spin northeast of Anchorage on the Parks Highway to try her out. Connie was driving, and I looked over and noticed a wild look in her eye as she was holding the wheel. I asked, "Connie, what's wrong?"

Clinching the wheel, she said, "I'm doing 110! What should I do?"

I calmly talked her down to a controllable speed, "Take your foot off the gas and just slow down." She sure loved that car.

It was two weeks later and midmorning when some of us pile bucks gathered at the D&D Café for coffee and a shot of booze as we did every morning, waiting to see if any jobs would come up in the Pile Bucks or the Iron Workers Hall. As it happened, Connie was involved in a collision across the street. We all ran out. Connie was screaming at the guy who had collided with her. He tried to get a word in, but she wouldn't have it. She hauled off and hit him! *Pow-bang! Pow-bang!* She laid into him hard and fast, rolling him down the hill over the embankment. Then she got in her car, backed off, and away she went. When the cops showed up, she was long gone, and of course, nobody saw a thing! I didn't dare let them know it was my wife.

Another example of her infamous temper was the night she hit me with a frying pan! She was angry about something. We

Part IX The Rebuilding 1964 - 1972

were out in the galley at our home in Anchorage, off Lake Otis and Laurie Road. I had just gotten back from Israel in '67. She had a mean jealous streak in her, and she was accusing me of trying to make out with our next-door neighbor, whom I admit was a good-looking gal. I claimed I was innocent, which was the truth—at least that time. I never really had designs on her. Connie didn't believe me. She hauled off and took a swing at me. I ducked. Then she reached around and grabbed a cast-iron frying pan that was sitting there, which fortunately was clean and had nothing in it. She hauled off and *kawpow*! She hit me on the head. I made the mistake of coming back up from dodging her first blow. She hit me again so hard it cracked the frying pan! Well, that's the way the story goes. The pan might have had the crack in it all along and just hitting me on the head made it wider, but one could never tell. Just as before, no cops and no witnesses. A little blood loss, but I always figured you got a lot of blood running through you, and it's got to go somewhere. In this case, it went down my forehead and onto the floor.

In Anchorage, work was scarce, and I had been pile-bucking when the little tanker *Alaska Standard* came in to port. The captain Gene Edwards was a good friend of mine. The chief mate was Earl Daly, of the Scroungy Maverick donkey story himself and one of my best mates. I was able to ship in her as AB.

Back in Kodiak, the captain had given us a 24-hour port leave after the cargo had been discharged. We could do anything we wanted for 24 hours. The captain Earl and I were going to town. We hailed a cab, and all got in. It was Big Sandy. She was a bartender and cabdriver. I had known her for many years. She was tougher than nails. When she got a divorce from her husband a few years back, she took a chainsaw and cut their house in two! The captain sat up in the front seat with her. Big Sandy started up the hill, and there was the bosun staggering up the street. He'd been drinking pretty heavy that day.

The captain said, "There's the bosun. Stop. We'll pick 'im up; he probably wants to go up town."

Part IX   The Rebuilding   1964 - 1972

We stopped. The bosun made his way into the back seat behind the Big Sandy. Big Sandy looked back and asked, "Where ya going?"

The bosun mumbled, "To the best damn whorehouse in Kodiak."

Big Sandy turned around and looked him square in the face and said, "You're in it!"

One of the best things to come out of my marriage to Connie was Eirik, my youngest son. His full name is Roald Leif Eiriksson Johnson. He was named after two explorers, Roald Amundsen, a great Norwegian who was known for his Arctic explorations and drifting close to the North Pole, and Leif Eiriksson, a Norse explorer who is considered the first European to land in North America nearly 500 years before Christopher Columbus. We made certain that Roald's name was spelled the Old Norse spelling way as "Eiriksson." Eirik is one heck of a young man. I adopted Connie's oldest son Curtis, and she adopted Ola and Teresa. We had a fine family. Kodiak is a small place even now, but back then it was even smaller. The saying "it's a small world," has been true from me on more than one occasion, and soon even more so.

It was on my birthday, April 12, 1965, that I got quite a surprise. It had been over a year since the '64 earthquake and tsunami wave. Kodiak had these "plywood palaces" that had been built to create makeshift bars. Connie and I were living in Kodiak. I was pile-bucking by day and moonlighting by night tending bar at the Mecca. A lot of our clientele at the Mecca were Navy kids due to the Naval base. You could recognize them by their nice clothes and shiny shoes. Most of them carried themselves quite well. If their dress didn't give them away, invariably you could pick them out by the drink they ordered Rum and Coke, which is a typical Navy drink. On this particular night, in came three young men who bellied up to the bar. The first thing we asked for was an ID to check their age to see if they were 21. After looking at the first two's ID, I looked at the third sailor's identification and noticed it was his birthday. I chuckled, "You're 21 today!" I handed him back his ID and asked, "Okay son, what will it be?" "Rum and Coke," he answered. They all ordered Rum and Coke.

Part IX The Rebuilding 1964 - 1972

"Rum and Coke it is," and I poured him a good one to help his birthday celebration along. I told them it was on the house.

Since it was my birthday too, I picked up a glass and poured me some Canadian Club, announcing, "I'll have one with you; it's my birthday today, too!"

We all raised our glasses, and the birthday boy said, "Here's to you, Pop!"

Just before pressing the glass to my mouth, something clicked! I said, "Son, let me see your ID again."

He handed it to me with a smirk on his face. There, next to his photo and birth date was his name, Geoffrey Patton. He started laughing, waiting to see if I would recognize the name.

I looked at him again, astonished at the discovery, "You're Geoff Patton?"

"Yes, Sir, I am," he said with a smile.

"You're my son?" I kept staring at him in amazement.

He kept smiling and said, "My mother told me to look you up."

I replied, "Damn me eyes! Well, here's to you, lad." That began quite a friendship that has lasted over the years. Geoffrey was an explosive ordnance disposal (EOD) diver in the Navy.

There's a song we used to sing that reminds me of this occasion, *"Drink up and let's have another. Drink up whoever you are. He might be your brother, that guy at the end of the bar."* I'd sing it, *"He might be your son, that guy at the end of the bar."* 'Cause the guy at the end of the bar was my son.

The last time I had seen him he was an infant in Seattle, and now he was 21 drinking in my bar in Kodiak, Alaska. Geoffrey had recently been stationed in Kodiak. His mother, Kathy, kept track of my whereabouts and told him his father, Jack Johnson, was living in Kodiak. She gave him strict orders to look me up when he had a chance.

This was the first chance he had to get around to finding me, and lucky for the both of us, it happened to be on our birthdays. His friends were well aware of what was going on when they came into the bar. All that was left was my part in the scenario, and I didn't disappoint them. We had one hell of a reunion, or at

Part IX The Rebuilding 1964 - 1972

least as wild as a Navy sailor could conjure up without getting into trouble.

I was able to get Geoffrey into the Pile Bucks Union 2520 as a favored son after his hitch in the Navy. He worked alongside me diving, pile-bucking, rigging, or welding—whatever the job asked. Eventually, he got employed with Taylor Divers which relocated him to Louisiana. Geoffrey kept working for them.

At one point, he returned the favor and landed me a job in Louisiana working for this same outfit making saturation dives. Saturation dives are unique. Saturation diving allowed divers to work at great depths for long periods of time. The divers lived in a decompression tank for a week at a time. To avoid getting the bends, saturation divers mastered returning to the surface slowly. Our job involved us getting out of the tank and into a diving bell, which was already compressed to the bottom pressure. They would then drop us down, and we would do our work at 350 feet. When we were finished, they would pull us back up and hook on the chamber. We would live in the chamber until our blood was almost pure nitrogen. We would pull a week at a time doing this. When we dived, we breathed a mixture of gases: nitrogen, oxygen, and helium, and our voice sounded like Donald Duck—like you'd hear if you sucked the air out of a helium balloon.

Briefly, before trying my hand at this saturation diving, I worked as a rack man taking care of the gas. Then Geoffrey pulled a few strings, and soon I was working with him as a diver. Every morning we would get in the diving bell and go down, get to the bottom; and drop out of the bottom to go to work. They would pull us up and then hook us up to the chamber. We'd go in and stay there. We received our food through an air lock. We had all the luxuries of home, you might say, including a toilet and bathing facilities. It was a pretty big chamber. There were always six of us—three on one team and three on another. Geoffrey and I worked on the opposite teams in case something happened.

One time, I was in the bell with the two other divers. Geoffrey was one of the standby divers. As we were going down, the lifting wire parted. The diving bell fell into the mud. We were stuck. There was no way to pull us up. We remained stranded at 350 feet

Part IX   The Rebuilding   1964 - 1972

below the Gulf of Mexico, though we did have communication. It would have been a good place for some missionaries. You know the saying: there are no atheists in foxholes. The same could be said for us. Well, unbeknownst to me, our answer was soon on its way.

Geoffrey did what they called a bounce dive. It required him to get into Kirby Morgan dive gear (still commonly used). Once Geoffrey was suited up, he took the end of another lifting wire and made the bounce dive, 350 feet all by himself. He then hooked us up and bounced back to the surface. As he went up, his tender stopped him at the various spots to decompress. It was pretty warm water, so it wasn't too bad. He was the hero of the day and saved our lives. Needless to say, I quickly retired from the saturation diving crew. That stuff is for the youngsters. I said farewell to my son, thanked him for the opportunity, and headed back to Alaska. Geoffrey stayed and kept on diving.

He now lives in Winslow, Arizona. We still keep in touch, especially on our birthday, April 12. The last I heard, he was driving a truck and trailer rig hauling gas and oil. I never could figure out how somebody could back up one of those rigs. I can handle a 1,000' cruise ship anywhere in the world or vlcc[97] tankers, but I'll be damned if I can back up a semi-truck.

An opportunity came my way to go to work again in Cook Inlet as a diver. This time it was the type of diving I had grown up around, not the saturation kind. The job required moving to Anchorage. So Connie and I packed up our belongings and made the move. We rented a nice home there. The diver's job was for Taylor Divers, the same outfit that Geoffrey had worked with. I worked off Derrick Barge #7. The oil platforms in Cook Inlet were under construction. The job required lots of underwater work. The Inlet water is thick with silt from the run-off from the many glacier streams that empty into it. Underwater visibility is nil. The work was challenging and dangerous. I loved it! I stayed until the job ended. I figured out I did about 750 dives working the Inlet. I was pulling in about $5,000 a week. That was good money back then; hell, who am I kidding, it's good money now.

---

[97] Very large crude carriers.

Part IX   The Rebuilding   1964 - 1972

Fishing Partners

Turning around, she gave me a hug and little peck on the cheek and said, "Thanks for everything." She went out the door, and I never saw her again. She flew out of King Salmon for Anchorage. I guess she had never seen that much money.
~Captain Jack V. Johnson~

When the fishing season would roll around, I would take off drift-netting.[98] There are a lot of interesting people who fish in Alaska waters, lured by the opportunities to make quick money. You could make up to $60,000 a season. The quest for this slimy gold has attracted many who could make the grade, but many couldn't hack it. These little fishing towns that had a population of under 500 year round would soar to 5,000 during the fishing season.

In 1966, I had a drift net permit for Bristol Bay. I ran across a young lady who was looking for a job while drinking at Hadfield's Bar in Naknek one evening before the opening. Dooley was tending bar. He was a good chap and poured me doubles of whatever I was drinking. That evening he asked if I had a boat puller this season. I didn't. I usually worked alone. Sometimes I would hire someone or grab an old friend as a boat puller, but most of the time I would just do it myself. He said, "Big Jack, there's a young lady here who'd like a chance to fish. Do you think you could handle that?" He motioned to the young lady sitting at the table in the corner.

I turned around and looked at her. She seemed pretty green. I said, "Hi!"

She got up and came over to me and introduced herself. She was from northern Minnesota. Her name was Gail Lynstrom.

I asked her, "Where's your gear?"

She said, "It's right over there in the corner."

---

[98] Drift-netting is a fishing technique where nets, called drift nets, float freely at the surface of the water with ropes along the top of the gill net and weights attached to another rope to keep the net vertical in the water.

Part IX   The Rebuilding   1964 - 1972

I thought, okay. "Where are you staying?"

She said, "Oh, Dooley has been putting me up in the back room." She didn't know the first thing about drift-netting, or fishing, for that matter. It was obvious that the cruel Alaska wilderness was both grueling as well as fascinating to her.

I decided to give her a try. Having a few daughters of my own, I know they are pretty capable of handling hard work. I asked her if she wanted to come fish with me. She thought it was a good idea. I took her to the bunkhouse and got her settled in where we were staying. I rigged a curtain divider, stringing blankets across a wire to give her some privacy. The one bedroom now was transformed into two since I was in the company of a young lady.

We got to know each other a little better. I said, "The opening is in the morning. We are going to leave on the tide at 5:00 a.m. and we should make it back on the evening tide. That will end the opening. Then we won't have another opening for two days."

We retired for the evening. The next morning we were up and out of the bunkhouse a little after 4:00 a.m. We got coffee'd up, made some sandwiches, and then out to the grounds. We no sooner got out to the river when I told her we were going to lay out now.

After showing Gail the ropes, we set the net. We ran out three shackles of gear. Once the net was set, we waited for the salmon. We made quite a haul. By golly, she picked it up right away. I showed her just once how to pick fish, and she was picking fish like crazy.

Then I told her, "We're going to go over there by the banana trees. It's my favorite spot."

We made haul after haul. It came time for the fishing period to end, and we had to make for market. We pulled in and unloaded. We sold to a tender, and the tallyman made a good count. We made it in on the tide and put the boat in at the company dock, too late to fuel up. I told her we would have to wait for high water the next morning to fuel up and get ready for the next opening. That seemed fine with her. We walked over to the mess room, had a nice dinner, and then walked back to the

Part IX   The Rebuilding   1964 - 1972

bunkhouse to retire for the evening and start again tomorrow.

It was still pretty early; Gail was too excited to rest and started talking, "Well, how did we do today?"

I said, "Oh, we did pretty good. In fact, we did exceptionally well. It was one of our better days."

She said, "Did we make any money?"

I said, "Don't worry, we did real well! The tallyman will give us the count."

Then she seemed to be fumbling for words and asked meekly, "When do I get the money?"

I said, "You'll get it when the season is over. Or if you need some money, you could always make a draw on what you have coming. When the season is over, of course, we split it, minus grub and fuel and my share and the boat share. You'll end up with your share. It will be a good deal for you."

"Well what did we do today?" she inquired.

"Gee, I don't know, four or five thousand bucks a piece, I guess," wondering where the questions were coming from and, more importantly, where were they headed. I told her we probably would keep going until about the 8th of July.

She continued, pressing, "Well, when can I get that money?"

I said, "Well, I just said when the season is over or, if you need it earlier, we can go there in the morning and take a draw. How soon do you want it?"

"Can I get it now, tonight?" she said in an almost whispered plea.

I said, "I don't know. I guess we can go to the office and find out." I could tell that this was pretty important to her. I conceded. "Come on, we'll go up to the office, and he'll tell us what they can do and how much money you have coming."

She got real excited. When we got to the office, Bill, the office manager, was there. I said, "Bill, can you let us know what we did today and let me know if Gail can get a check for her share?"

He looked us up and said, "Yeah, sure, we have your tally sheet right here. You did real good. It will take me about five minutes to draw a check for her. How much do you want?"

She said, "I want everything."

Part IX   The Rebuilding   1964 - 1972

The guy looked at her. This was highly unorthodox. He looked at me and asked, "How is that, Captain, if I give her everything now, and you can take out her fuel and grub later?"

I said, "Yeah, go ahead. Give her what she wants. Give her everything."

It only took a few minutes, and then he handed her a cheek. It was a little over $5,000 for an afternoon of fishing. We went back to the bunkhouse. She sat there holding the check, just looking at it. When I got into the bunk, she was still holding that check. I asked her, "How much is it?"

She said, "Five thousand, five hundred, and eight dollars!"

I chuckled, "That's better than I expected. Wow, that was a good day."

Then she said, "Wow, all this money. I got all this money."

I said, "Yeah."

The next thing I know, she folded the check up, placed it securely between her breasts, and packed up her gear.

I asked her, "Where are you going?"

She said, "I have to make that last flight out of here!" Turning around, she gave me a hug and little peck on the check and said, "Thanks for everything." She went out the door, and I never saw her again. She flew out of King Salmon for Anchorage. I guess she had never seen that much money. I felt bad for her. She didn't make the connection that the longer you stay, the larger the pay.

I ended up finishing the opening with an old drunken buddy of mine, Oscar Olsen. I had known him for years. Oscar ended up getting the net stuck in the propeller. That was a mess. I had to dive down and take care of it. We finished hauling the gear and started in. I didn't know he had a bottle hidden. The next thing I knew, as we were coming up to the tally scow, Oscar stood up and took a big swig.

I told him, "You'd better tap that light, Oscar." He offered me some, but I declined. Then a big swig! Down the hatch! And he fell overboard! I had to turn around and drag him aboard. He was all shook up that he had lost his bottle. I told him, "Stop that nonsense. I hate to see grown men cry!" I ended up at the last opening with a little over $60,000 for the whole season.

Part IX   The Rebuilding   1964 - 1972

Serving in the Six Day War

*I visited the gravesite of Bill Bernstein,
who had died in the* Exodus *scuffle and a few other places
I was familiar with from my time before in Israel.
I had chosen an auspicious time to be back.
I found myself in the middle of the 1967 Six Day War.
~Captain Jack V. Johnson~*

Work was drying up out in the inlet for jobs like diving and pile-bucking. In May 1967, I headed to Seattle to look for work. Connie and the kids stayed in Alaska. In Seattle, I registered in the Masters, Mates, and Pilots Hall. I was able to find work and got a States Marine Line ship headed to the Mediterranean. She was the new SS *Mary Luckenbach*. I was chief mate. Our run took us to Haifa, Israel. Being in Israel took me back about 20 years earlier when I was there in the *Exodus*.

I had always had an affinity for that country since the *Exodus* experience, so I decided to stay awhile and see how things were. I even had notions of getting Connie and the kids to move to Israel. Much to the surprise of the captain, I paid off. He couldn't figure out why I wanted to leave the ship. Pulling what we sailors call a *"nosedive,"* I claimed to be sick and in need of medical attention. After the ship sailed, I was up out and about exploring hither and yon. I visited the gravesite of Bill Bernstein, who had died in the *Exodus* scuffle and a few other places I was familiar with from my time before in Israel. I had chosen an auspicious time to be back.

It was June 1967. I found myself in the middle of the Six Day War, or as some referred to it, the third Arab-Israeli War.[99] Most of the Palestinian Liberation Organization (PLO) attacks were on Israeli civilians, and the frustration was mounting. With my experiences in warfare, I presented myself to the Israeli Army. I enlisted in the Israeli Defense Force (IDF). I was in the Second Armored Brigade, a tank sergeant. We were up in the Golan

---

[99] It was fought between June 5 and 10, 1967, by Israel and the neighboring states of Egypt (known at the time as the United Arab Republic), Jordan, and Syria.

Part IX   The Rebuilding   1964 - 1972

Heights, which the Syrian army was using to shell Israeli farms, kibbutzes, and villages. The time came for Israel to take the necessary action to hold their ground since the Syrians had sought support from Egypt. The Israelis decided to preempt the expected Arab attack without support from the United States, since President Johnson had already warned, "Israel will not be alone unless it decides to go alone." The announcement from the U.S. State Department was this: "Our position is neutral in thought, word, and deed." So, I joined in the fight, which felt like a modern day David versus Goliath.

Astonishingly enough, the Israeli military commanders had conceived a brilliant war strategy. In less than two hours, some 300 Egyptian aircraft had been destroyed, and it took only three days for the Israeli forces to defeat the Jordanian-Arab legion. On the morning of June 7, 1967, the Israelis formally occupied Jerusalem and their holiest site, the Western Wall.

The surprise decision that shifted the outcome of the war was when Israel chose not to stop fighting on Shabbat. A decision was made to continue through, and the pressure proved to be valuable in the upset of the Syrian forces.

While most of the IDF units were orchestrated to fight the Egyptians and Jordanians, I was part of a small group left to defend the northern border against the Syrians. On June 9, after two days of heavy air bombardment, we succeeded in breaking through the Syrian lines. It came at a high casualty cost: Israel lost 777 soldiers and had 2,586 wounded. When the fighting was over, Israel had captured Sinai, Golan Heights, Gaza Strip, and the West Bank. Again, David slew Goliath.

Part IX   The Rebuilding   1964 - 1972

I was there to witness and take part in the historic event. We did a lot of celebrating, and that was the first time I danced the Hora to Hava Nagila! After it was over, I hung around for a while and was honorably discharged. Although I agreed to remain a reservist until age 55, I didn't get involved in the 1973 Yom Kippur War since I was back living in Alaska at that time.

For a time I thought I was part Norwegian, but found out later that I'm Russian Jew with a little Finn thrown in. As time went by, those ancient roots began to tug somewhere deep down inside. I aligned myself with the Jewish people, since deep down in my being was a connection.

Part IX   The Rebuilding   1964 - 1972

Flying for a Change

*I guess all my running around didn't set too well with Connie.
It wasn't long after I arrived back home that she left me.
Connie found someone who worked as a timber cruiser.
~Captain Jack V. Johnson~*

I returned to Alaska after my trip to Israel and reunited with Connie and the kids. We lived off Lake Otis on Lore Road in Anchorage. I decided to work ashore to make up for the time I had been absent. I pile-bucked, worked iron and took any job I could find. Exhausting most avenues, I decided to take a job working for a branch of Air America out of Chicago in 1969. I didn't want to sail anymore and preferred to stay around home with Connie and the kids, but times were tough all over. I usually liked to keep my feet on the ground, but the money was good. My neighbor, Don, was an air traffic controller at Elmendorf Air Force Base. After dinner one evening, he asked me if I wanted to go to work for Air Mid-America.

I asked my usual questions, "What does it pay, and when do we go?"

Don answered, "You go out for a two-month hitch, and you'll be flying in and around Africa. There are three planes down in Kenai. They are overhauling them right now, getting them ready."

He asked me if I remembered seeing the three big super Connies[100] down in Kenai. I hadn't. The Connies were getting fueled up and geared up for service. I admitted I didn't know anything about flying airplanes.

He said, "No, you don't have to be a pilot. We'd put you on there as a crew chief" (a steward).

I again asked my usual question, "What does it pay?"

He said, "It pays about $800 a week. If you stay the full two months after you get the planes down to Africa, you'll get a bonus."

---

[100] Constellation Starliners or big transport planes affectionately referred to as "Connies".

Part IX   The Rebuilding   1964 - 1972

"Well, that is good money," I thought.

Then he added, "And it's not Air America—it's Air Mid-America. They're headquartered in Chicago. They'll sign you up and take care of all the paperwork. I know all you've done and can vouch for you." He handed me an application to fill out and instructed me to put my résumé on the back. "Fill this out, and we'll see what develops." He left it on the kitchen table.

I looked at Connie and said, "Well, I've done everything else."

Connie thought it over and said, "Maybe you'll make more money than you have before." I filled out the application. Don came over the next day and picked up the completed application. We had a couple of drinks, even though I was trying to be a good Mormon boy in those days, but it wasn't beyond my liberal thinking to have a "heave ahead."

About three days later, I got a phone call. I took the job as a steward. They asked, "Jack, can you be in Kenai the day after tomorrow to meet the plane about 1:30?"

I said, "Yes."

They instructed me, "You need to be ready to go for a long time, but travel light." I knew how to travel light. I packed some gear, a clean boiler suit, a sport jacket, slacks, jeans, hickory shirts, a couple of caps, toothbrush, comb, and toothpaste. I even threw in a bottle of Johnnie Walker Red. I was off to Kenai. I didn't know at that time the CIA secretly owned Air America,[101] as well as off-shoots like Air Mid-America, but to tell you the truth—I didn't care. I wasn't asking any questions. I carefully listened to the instructions on what was required of me to get a paycheck.

Two of the Connies were cleaned up and raring to go with engines running out on the tarmac. Everyone was getting acquainted with the aircraft, and it looked pretty nice. We wouldn't be officially flying out until the next day, Saturday afternoon. Saturday came, and I called home to tell them I was on my way out and I would stay in touch whenever I could. This

---

[101] Air Mid-America and Air America were operated "air proprietary" by the CIA, serving the U.S. and allied intelligence agents in the East under a shroud of secrecy. http://en.wikipedia.org/wiki/Air_America_(airline)

Part IX   The Rebuilding   1964 - 1972

time, I didn't set sail, but took off into the wild, blue yonder. We were off!

The birds with engines were flying. Leaving Kenai, we flew down to McChord Air Force Base near Tacoma and then to McConnell Air Force Base near Wichita, Kansas. From Kansas, we flew to another Air Force base in Texas and from there, down to South America to Belem, Brazil. We refueled and loaded up with a few more things. Refueled and loaded, we crossed the Atlantic, landing in Dakar, the capital city of Senegal. After landing in Dakar, we refueled again and then on down to Salisbury, Rhodesia. (Dakar is now called Zimbabwe, and Salisbury has been renamed Harare.) That was where we were stationed.

Our assignment was in the colonial territories of France, Belgium, and England that were becoming nationalized. There was a great deal of difficulty with greed and fighting among themselves. Those in power and in control were in it for the money, and were determined to exterminate those who tried to take it from them. We rescued people by flying in mercenaries. Our job was to ferret out the bad seed and do whatever we had to do in order to take care of things. We supported anyone we could, trying to make the transition smoother. Mainly, our job was to show a little bit of strength and put down uprisings as necessary. The entire ordeal was very interesting.

It was pretty quiet around Salisbury. I remember it was the first time I ever rode in a British Land Rover. It was assigned to our plane so we would have wheels to get around town. I fell in love with the Land Rover.[102] Out of Salisbury, we flew to many different places, bringing mercenaries in and out, like Air America's motto, *"First in, last out."*

We also transported refugees or people who no longer were able to remain where they were. I was crew chief and kicker. By kicker, I mean my job was to kick out cargo that we dropped down to mercenaries or to those who needed supplies. I would kick it or any paratroopers who were hesitant to go out the door.

---

[102] I wound up buying one, years later for my wife, Iris. I had never forgotten that experience. And after Iris rolled and totaled her Land Rover in Alaska, she never forgot her experience either.

Part IX   The Rebuilding   1964 - 1972

Most of the supplies were strapped to a parachute. Bombs away! Down the supplies would go deep into the jungle. As crew chief, my job was to take care of the people aboard the plane— get them coffee or whatever they wanted, clean the plane, and whatever it took to keeps things going.

We went to one particular area in the Belgian Congo around Leopoldville, where I had been during my sailing days. We would fly into places as far north as Entebbe, Uganda. They had a huge airport. We flew over to Nairobi. For the most part, we were flying in and out of the Congo, which was a terrible, bloody mess. It was a down-right civil war.

The mercenaries were supposed to help establish peace, but it was a fight to maintain any civility. For a little R&R, we would fly from Salisbury to Durban, South Africa, the largest city in KwaZulu-Natal. It had been under English rule and was known for being the largest Asian community in South Africa because of the thousands of indentured Indian servants that had been brought in to work the plantations.

I remembered Durban had an Indian restaurant with the best curry I ever tasted in my life. It wasn't hard to convince the crew into trying what I boasted as the world's best curry. Instead of lamb, they used a local animal called the springbok. It's like a small deer. The springbok curry was just fabulous and *hot*! The sweat would come off your brow when you ate (my mouth waters just thinking about it) *"Damn me eyes!* It was good curry. I can taste it now."

I always made a point, if I was within close proximity, to drop into Durban for some curry. It wasn't long before I had the crew hooked on it, too. Stories about the delicious Durban curry spread around, which meant we would go on curry runs. We made it a weekly thing, sometimes twice weekly. We'd crank up our rig, get her fueled up, and head down to Durban. We'd buy a large amount of curry and bring it back to Salisbury with us, along with a few cases of beer, John Haig Scotch, or whatever we could round up. Back again to Rhodesia, we'd eat on it for a few days before we'd be interrupted by the duty at hand and have to

Part IX The Rebuilding 1964 - 1972

take a flight somewhere. We'd always return to Durban for more curry whenever we could.

A couple of times we went to Fort-Lamy. I had been there before when I was in the French Foreign Legion. It was interesting being back. It was a big, bloody mess. We took a lot of mercenaries in there. When we got there, the mercenaries fell in with the Legionnaires. They did everything they could to calm things down. There was a war going on in all the places as colonies and territories began to fight for dominion.

Many times we were in the middle of the conflict. Our airplane with riddled with bullet holes. Our pilot, Jon Joy, was one hell of a pilot. He was with Alaska Airlines over the years. Jon Joy was a good friend of the famous Captain "Red" Dodge, who was also with Air America when he wasn't flying for Western Airlines. He had quite the reputation for daredevil feats, and one of his endeavors was made into a Hollywood movie *Breakout*, starring Charles Bronson. Red got himself in hot water when one of his missions was to airlift a CIA operative out of a Mexican prison.

My involvement with Air Mid-America wasn't quite that exciting, but there were some hair-raising experiences. One time we rescued a plane full of nuns who were registered nurses, out of Zambezi, a location made famous by Dr. Livingston. On a number of our back hauls, we would load up a bunch of mercenaries and drop them off in the Congo, Uganda, or the French Cameroons. After about two months, our mission was over, and we got ready to fly home.

Other Connies from the Midwest relieved our three planes. We had a little farewell party. We left Salisbury and flew north, stopping at Fort-Lamy. They elected to leave the planes there for the next go-around. I paid off. They paid well. They said—for the extra month, besides our regular pay—we were going to get a bonus. What they called bonuses, I gathered was just pie in the sky. I was proven wrong. One day, about three months later, I received in the mail a check for $10,000! That really was a bonus. We left Fort-Lamy, continued on to Paris, then to London, from London Trans-Atlantic to Gander, Newfoundland, then to

Part IX   The Rebuilding   1964 - 1972

McChord Air Force Base in Washington. In Seattle I caught Pacific Northern Airlines (PNA) home to Connie and the kids.

In 1972, I made a grave mistake. I let my Master's license expire. I had to retake the exam before I could get my license reinstated. I went to school in Seattle and renewed my license. I was registered at the Masters, Mates and Pilots Hall. One thing led to another, and we were back on top. We found ourselves pretty flush financially.

Connie continued to clamor for a home down in Washington, so we bought a place near Port Angeles. Connie moved down there with the children. I followed a little while later. I was still pile-bucking, diving, and doing construction work in Cook Inlet. That was more or less the beginning of the end, because from Port Angeles, we moved down by Shelton. We bought a little place on 20 acres, complete with barns, stalls, and fenced-in pastures. Connie loved Appaloosa horses. We went to Montana, and she bought two mares of foundation stock. She started breeding them on our little farm. She was doing quite well.

I hated the four-legged creatures then and don't fancy the hay feeders to this day. Appaloosas are best known for their link to the Nez Perce Indian tribe. They have a colorful, leopard-spotted pattern on them and often have piercing blue eyes. I found them stubborn and ornery just like their owner, Connie.

As expected, sea legs get to aching if ones been on land too long. I found an opportunity. Captain George Cary (Cal Cary's brother) had the *Korea Mail.* I shipped in her as third mate. I enjoyed working with George, but the job only lasted about three months. I returned to Seattle and joined my family in Washington.

I guess all my running around didn't set too well with Connie. It wasn't long after I arrived back home that she left me. Connie found someone who worked as a timber cruiser. She had fallen in love with this guy named Pat Carney. Our separation was civil enough, meaning she'd let me come and visit the kids. We were on a friendly basis, only Connie wasn't doing anything to move the divorce along, so I decided to help her out. I went and had the papers drawn up and took them to her to sign. Boy, those papers created a big stink.

Part IX   The Rebuilding   1964 - 1972

Once she calmed down and was able to behave cordially again, I was able to assume my visits with the kids. During one visit, I had little Eirik on my knee, and I started teasing Connie, "Are you and Pat going to get married?"

"Yep," in her usually "yep" fashion. She continued, "We're going to get married."

I had set her up for the punch line, "Did you ever think what your name is going to be if you get married?"

She looked at me quizzically, "Of course, Carney."

I couldn't resist, "Carney! So, you'll be Connie Carney. I'm gonna pass the word!" I smiled. I knew I had gotten under her skin. I could see those big blue eyes pierce right through me. Boy, she was angry. A big scowl came over her face. Quickly, her temper—that I had come to know so well—came flaring back at me.

As I was sitting there with the children, Pat Carney drove up in his pickup, unaware of the hurricane that was building inside. Pat whistled up the pathway to the door. Connie got up to meet him. Without any warning, she opened the door and belted him right on the jaw, knocking him flat on his ass. She proceeded to drag him down the pathway, slamming him against the pickup, and punching him out. Pat tried to dodge her blows and get out of her way. He was fending off her punches and yelping, wanting to know what in the hell was going on. She was big enough to throw anybody around. Pat was no exception. Connie continued to swing, yelling, "I'll never be Connie Carney! I'll never be Connie Carney!"

She opened the door to his pickup and threw him in, slamming the door. She came back in and looked pretty defiant, "There, I'm not going to be Connie Carney!"

I didn't breathe a peep about what just went down for fear I might be next. Chuckling under my breath, I thought it was one of the funniest things I had ever witnessed.

Finding myself alone again, divorced and out of work, I ended up back in Seattle. To ease my bruised ego, I did what most sailors tend to do. I went on a couple of good drunks. One night I found myself down at the Sportsman Bar on Westlake. The bar was situated so you had to go downstairs to get to there. It had a piano bar with a little dance floor. Hung on the wall was "The

Part IX   The Rebuilding   1964 - 1972

World's Record King Salmon." I was having a few "heaves ahead" when I noticed there was a crowd gathering at the piano bar.

I moseyed over to join in. A big, dark-haired gal of Middle Eastern descent was rattling on how she hated Jews. She ranted on and on how all the Jews should be killed!

I said. "Doggone it, young lady, I wish you'd be quiet."

She barked back, "What do you mean?"

I replied, "I'm a Jew!" I wasn't expecting what happened next.

She picked up her handbag (that looked as big as a king-sized bed) and belted me across the head with it. It felt like a sack of potatoes had hit me. She swung that handbag again, this time knocking me off the stool.

As soon as I recovered, I picked myself off the deck. This lady was no "lady," so I belted her right in the jaw. She surely didn't expect that. I had a feeling she had pulled stunts like this before. As far as I was concerned, she had it coming. My fist connected with her, *bam*! She flew off her stool, out cold on the deck. The other guys saw me cold-cock her.

They decided to play hero and come to her rescue. Getting up off their barstools, they started punching away at me. I was in my glory then. I've never walked away from a fight and wasn't walking away from this one. I soon had them stacked up like cordwood with my usual Death Johnson blows. One by one, down they went.

The bartender ran for the phone to call the cops. I leaned over and grabbed him. When I shoved him back, I pulled the phone off the wall. Well, the phone call wasn't necessary, because the cavalry was already on the way. Out of the corner of my eye, I saw cops coming down the stairway. I didn't know what to do and had to think fast. These guys, four of them, were all lying out cold. A couple of them were trying to pick themselves up by then. That big, dark-haired gal was still lying there out cold. The cops rushed in and started questioning, "What's going on here?"

Holding my head, I pointed toward the restroom, "The guy's in there!" I said, "He's in the restroom!" They ran past me with hands on their holsters ready to tackle the troublemaker. I scurried upstairs and out the door as fast as I could.

Part X   1972 - 1980

Iris

I wrote her long love letters on yellow legal pads...
I filled them with stories of the sea, dreams, and places I'd take her.
I wanted her to love the sea as much as I did.
~Captain Jack V. Johnson~

I kicked around for a while looking for work. I ran into some people I knew. They asked me if I knew Victor Rossellini. I said, "Yes. He's got a nice restaurant."

That was probably an understatement since Rossellini was acclaimed to have some of the finest restaurants on the West Coast, and he was known as Seattle's premier host. Evidently, he needed a cook. Having a lot of experience cooking, I went up to talk to him about a job. Victor said he didn't need a chef, but he needed someone in the galley as second cook. I took the job. It was a pretty uneventful time as a cook with Rossellini, even though his places were considered a closed society for the most influential and prominent people of the day. One good thing did come of it. I met Iris, my soon-to-be wife.

When I met Iris she was already married. Iris was married to Oscar Callow. Yes, the same Oscar Callow. What a small world. Reacquainting myself with Oscar led to my meeting Iris. Oscar was managing a furniture store in Seattle. I had run into him earlier, a ways back through Dorothy Lewis and when he kidnapped me from the Marine hospital. That was before he met and married Iris.

Iris Beresford had moved to Seattle with her nephew, who was going through some tough times. Iris had just come out of a bad marriage. The only good to come out of the marriage was her faithful companion, a dog named Marduk.

Part X   Lucky in Love, Lucky in Life   1972 - 1980

According to Iris, one fateful Saturday morning in 1966, she came home from the laundromat and walked into her apartment to catch the phone ringing off the hook. It was a friend trying to convince her to come and join him in Lake Union on his new boat.

Iris politely declined because she didn't want to leave Marduk cooped up all day. She replied, "Thanks for the invitation, but I have to decline because of my dog."

"Bring him with you. It will be fun!" came the response. So she and Marduk joined them out on Lake Union for an afternoon of sailing. Soon others arrived, and the party started. They ended up in Bellevue, a ritzy community. The owner of the boat said, "There's a guy who lives just up the hill from this dock, and you guys just have to meet him. He's from England and a real personality. Come on, it will be a hoot! Who wants to go with me?"

A few of them took him up on the offer, including Iris. They walked up the hill to the condominiums. When they arrived, the friend looked around and said, "Damn, it looks like he's not here. That's a shame."

As they turned to head back to the boat, a blue Desoto complete with fins came zooming into the vacant parking lot. "Oh, here comes Oscar now!"

Out of the car came an older gentleman, about six feet tall, broad at the shoulders, narrow at the hips, seeping with aristocratic charisma. The owner of the boat invited Oscar to join them, "Oscar, we came to get you. I got a new boat. Come out sailing! It's a beautiful afternoon."

Oscar agreed. He looked at this cute little pixie and introduced himself in his thick British accent, saying, "Hi, I'm Oscar Callow."

Iris asked, "Oh, like the wine?"

"No," he said, "Callow. *Ca*-double *l-ow*. I'm British, you know."

Iris shot back, "Well, I'm Iris Beresford, which is English, you know!" In England, the Beresfords are all Lords and Ladies. Iris believed it was her status and class that hooked Oscar. She said it was Oscar that sold her on the idea of moving in with him. After all, he was a master salesman. And Oscar has talked me into a thing or two.

Part X   Lucky in Love, Lucky in Life   1972 - 1980

Maybe the timing of their relationship was just trying to make good of a lot of bad misfortune. Evidently, he had just come out of a bad marriage situation, and was devastated. Everyone involved still lived in the Seattle area, and became grounds for contention, especially after he and Iris married.

Iris in Hawaii.

Oscar would tell stories about me to Iris. She thought I was some kind of buffoon. After meeting Iris, I took every opportunity to visit, hoping she would be there. I visited Iris and Oscar several times at different locations as they moved from Seattle to Burien and from Burien to Union Gap, Washington.

Ironically, when I first met Iris, she had already heard stories about me on her second date with Oscar. He had been retelling the escapade of the Gordon Highlanders, and how he had kidnapped me from the Marine hospital, so the stage had been set for her to meet the infamous Jack Johnson, Extraordinaire, or as Oscar referred to me, "Big Jack from Kodiak." When I finally got to meet Iris, it was an opportunity to set the record straight. She was a lot younger than Oscar was and had a real command of the

Part X   Lucky in Love, Lucky in Life   1972 - 1980

English language. She also wasn't afraid to use it. I admit I was smitten with this cute little blonde pixie with great legs. Oscar and I were always extremely competitive. I poured on the charm and was eager to impress Iris. I was sure that Oscar had not painted me with much couth, and I had to convince her I was every bit the gentleman that Oscar portrayed himself.

The universe smiled on me because I was about to be in the right place at the right time. In October of 1972, I was chief mate, along with Tim Christy in *Alaska Husky*, a Foss supply ship. Cal Cary and Dan Claussen were the captains at that time. (Tim is now a pilot with Southwest Alaska Pilots Association, and Cal was a pilot for SeaLand in Anchorage for years.) The *Alaska Husky* was dry-docked in Seattle. I had a lot of time on my hands and decided to visit Oscar and Iris in Union Gap. They had been married for some time, but by the time I entered back in the picture, they were on the verge of splitting up.

Oscar had told Iris he thought she was boring. Well, that was perfect timing for me. Oscar had broken his leg, and Iris was taking care of him. It was obvious they were not getting along. The tension was so thick you could cut it with a knife. I was a welcome distraction for both of them. It was also getting a bit noticeable that Iris and I were attracted to each other. According to Iris, Oscar was emotionally unattached, and she marked it up to his longing for the woman who jilted him and had their child. It was clear Iris had had enough of Oscar's shenanigans. That's when she and I decided to make a go of it. It was Halloween, and we played the most devastating trick. (I should write a book on how one alienates friends and influences enemies.)

We left Oscar high and dry, taking off in Iris' yellow convertible, "Old Yeller," her lambskin coat, a bottle of musk oil, a quart of Scotch whisky, and her dog, Marduk. Marduk is the one that sealed the deal for me. The fact I remembered Marduk's name when I talked with Iris very early in our friendship was a homerun. She later told me that was the first time she was really impressed. It came out of a casual conversation with Oscar. Iris got on the phone, and I asked, "How is Marduk?" My attention to

Part X   Lucky in Love, Lucky in Life   1972 - 1980

detail served me well. Unfortunately, it worked against my good friend, Oscar.

Over the mountains, Iris and I went to Seattle. We've been together ever since. Oscar never forgave me! Iris and he were divorced after seven years of marriage. Connie and I finalized our divorce. Iris and I could officially be a couple. Oscar was a good friend and quite a guy, but it was just one of those things. All is fair in love and war.

An odd occurrence happened several years ago, when Iris was returning from a trip to Manila with her friend, Ellen. When they arrived in Tokyo, Iris took the escalator to connect with her flight. Riding on the escalator, she looked up to view the wall, and lo and behold, there was Oscar Callow, as big as day, portrayed on the wall of the Tokyo airport. The advertisement was for a cruise. Here was Oscar, modeling as a waiter in the cruise ship. (You've got to hand it to Oscar, he had style.)

Oscar Callow pictured here modeling for Unigard Insurance Group Calypso Cruise brochure out of Seattle, Washington in the 1980's.

It was a sad occasion when, in 1986, Oscar died of lung cancer. I got word from Iris about Oscar's demise while I was piloting in the Bering Sea. I had a silent toast of Scotch whisky, a double. It was a farewell salute to my friend, the Major, and one hell of a guy.

Once Iris and I got to Seattle, we checked in with some friends. I had to go back to work because the *Alaska Husky* was out

Part X   Lucky in Love, Lucky in Life   1972 - 1980

of dry dock. Iris decided to go back to Boise, Idaho, and stay with her sister, Karol. Every chance I got, I would go to Seattle and then from Seattle to Boise. Occasionally, Iris would come up to Seattle to meet me. Iris had no trouble with us being a couple, but I had a hard time convincing her to marry me. She had already been married twice and had just come out of a somewhat bad relationship.

She wasn't interested in getting into another long-term commitment. The only long-term commitment she wanted was with her dog, Marduk. She could count on the dog, but she was very gun shy about marriage. I had to turn on the charm, because contrary to the notion that a sailor has a girl in every port, I always had the notion to marry the girl in every port. Maybe subconsciously, I wanted to have someone to come home to. After all, that's what my parents did, and it seemed to work. Iris had experienced just the opposite. Her parents had divorced. She had tried marriage, and it had always ended in divorce. She was disillusioned about the whole marriage deal. Living together was borderline acceptable, but having your own place and going out to have a good time was more acceptable to her. She became my challenge and my muse.

After we had been dating for a while, I arrived in Seattle to meet up with Iris. It was a time of getting reacquainted and partying. On occasion, we stayed at the Moore Hotel at Second and Stewart. Across the street on the northwest corner was the historical Cape St. Regis Hotel. Built in the early 1900s, it was full of elegance with its high ceilinged lobby and a six-foot marble pillar standing at the base of the marble staircase. It had a huge bar. Off to the side was a dance floor with beautiful Italian terrazzo flooring.

I took Iris over to the Cape St. Regis around 5:00 one evening. We stayed until 8:00 p.m., just as the band was coming in. People were beginning to dance. I knew lots of people there. Iris was getting a lot of attention, some because she was with me, some because she was Iris. She might have been pixie in size, but she had great legs. I introduced her to several of my buddies. The room began to fill up. We moved the party to the bar, and the

Part X   Lucky in Love, Lucky in Life   1972 - 1980

drinks and the stories began to flow. I was holding court at the bar, telling sea stories with all eyes and ears tuned in.

I was getting bored with my own stories and announced, "Let's all go down to the Alaska Bar on First Avenue. I know the guy down there. What do you say? Let's get out of here!"

To hear Iris tell the story, the whole bar got up, walked out, and followed us down to the Alaska Bar. You'd think we were leading a parade. I was still in the "impressing Iris" stage, as if my command of all the patrons wasn't enough to get her attention. Out on the sidewalk, I proceeded to leap frog over the parking meters to demonstrate how athletic and agile I was. Men in love do foolish things! I was showing off and in all my glory.

We fetched up at the Alaska Bar and quickly took up all the booths. I ordered champagne for everyone, and it was served in little splits. I was very familiar with this bar. I knew the owner and the people working there, as well as a lot of the patrons who were from Alaska. We stayed and drank a few rounds. I introduced Iris to some more of my Alaskan buddies. With the night still young, I announced a second time, "Hey, let's go to the Marine Room at the Olympic Hotel! It's only a few blocks down the street!" I said to the bartender, "Call some taxis for us!"

Next thing you knew, a bunch of taxis showed up. We exited the bar and stumbled into the lead taxi, heading for the Olympic Hotel. Iris by this time was in shock. I am sure she thought I was rolling in the dough, which, to be truthful, I wasn't. I was paying child support to my ex-wife at that time, but I was going to be damn sure Iris thought I was a high roller! Iris later informed me that the guy (a pharmaceutical salesman) who sat next to her in the taxi as well as at the bar kept putting his hand on her leg. It's a good thing I didn't know that, or there would have been hell to pay—Iris may have witnessed Death Johnson up close.

When we arrived at the Olympic Hotel, I talked to the manager on duty to see if there was a room large enough for all of us. He assured me, "No problem, Mr. Johnson. We have a room for you." We all gathered in a large banquet room. It looked like it was set up for a boardroom meeting. The room was filling up with people. Some I didn't know. A lot of those pharmaceutical

Part X   Lucky in Love, Lucky in Life   1972 - 1980

salesmen had joined us, and had I been aware that the one sitting next to Iris was still having trouble keeping his hands to himself, I would have uninvited him.

Everyone was settled in, and I ordered a round for the house or at least for everyone in the room. Soon platters of food showed up, and I held court, entertaining the crowd with my sea stories once again. I don't recall anyone pitching in to help pay the tab, but I was grateful to have enough in my pocket to bankroll the entire evening. We made it back to the Moore Hotel.

When we went into the bar at the Cape St. Regis the next day, I had to charm my way back in. They blamed me for all their customers walking out of the bar the night before. They had hired a band, which played to an empty room. They were pissed. Somehow I smoothed it over and got back into their good graces. The bartender and barmaids were friends of mine, and they were the most pissed since I had cost them a night's worth of tips. I stayed in touch with the bartender over the years and even ended up going to her wedding. If you heard I helped pay for a large part of it, it is just a wild rumor—or at least that's what I've told Iris.

Being gone a lot, I didn't get a chance to see Iris as much as I'd like, so I wrote her letters, lots of them. Iris still has those letters. I've always been good at corresponding and documenting. I wrote her long love letters on yellow legal pads up to 10, 12 pages. She'd get them once or twice a week. I filled them with stories of the sea, dreams, and places I'd take her. I told her we'd get a yacht and sail around the world. I'd introduce her to the many ports I had been in, not thinking about dodging ex-girlfriends or ex-wives. I promised her I'd take her to walk the Great Wall of China. I wrote about the happenings in the ship. I wanted her to love the sea as much as I did. I told her about Cook Inlet. I described the tides as "too thin to cultivate and too thick to navigate." (They are the third highest tides in the world.) I kept writing to her for almost a year.

Iris has since told me that, beyond the romance, getting those letters was when she really fell in love with me. She teases me often by saying, "There's more to this guy than sex and a terrific

Part X   Lucky in Love, Lucky in Life   1972 - 1980

sense of humor." I had the opportunity to go back over my life and share with her my deepest thoughts. It was very therapeutic.

I finally convinced Iris to move to Anchorage. I moved her from Boise on June 30, 1974, along with her sister, Karol, and, of course, Marduk. Before the end of the year, I had talked her into marriage. When she first arrived, I was so excited and proud to have her with me. I wanted to show her off. We went to the Club Paris on Fifth Avenue—the Eiffel Tower neon sign was one of Anchorage's hot spots. There was a vast array of guys who frequented the joint: the cigar-smoking sort, the martini-drinking sophisticates, and the hard-drinking, risk-taking crewmembers. For many a guy, it became his office and home away from home.

The Club Paris itself was put up in 1936 when Anchorage still had dirt streets. Originally it was a funeral parlor. Word has it that the bar is where the chapel once stood. It became the Club Paris in 1957. The original owner, Tommy, married a French girl, and the Club Paris was a little token of his love for her. There was a little scene up front that looked like a Paris Café with a fake hedge, lamppost, and fabric hanging from the ceiling like an awning to complete the look. The old place has kept its charm to this day and is still known for serving the best prime rib steaks in town. The novelty cash register behind the bar still only rings up to $49.99. I had been a bartender there and knew Frankie Taylor and his brothers. Iris and I walked in and saddled up to the curved bar, sitting on its striped barstools. The bar was full. Sitting next to us was Ray Wilson. He had been a bartender and cook in Kodiak.

We ordered our drinks, and I introduced her to Ray. I told him, "This is Iris, and we are going to get married." Ray looked at Iris and said, "You're going to marry Jack Johnson. Don't you know that Jack Johnson is the meanest man in Alaska?"

Iris got a startled look on her face and said, "No."

Ray went on, "He is! He's the meanest man in Alaska!"

I quickly tried to shut him up and change the subject. I began introducing Iris to others I knew at the bar like Frankie,[103] the

---

[103] In the '70s Frankie met a horrible end. Someone had tied him up to a chair and slit his throat. The cops never found out who it was. But where the cops

Part X   Lucky in Love, Lucky in Life   1972 - 1980

bartender, and his wife Bobbie. Iris asked me when we left the bar why Ray kept insisting I was the meanest man in Alaska. I dodged her questions, spouting something about Ray, and hard times in Kodiak—pile-bucking, working, and bartending. She didn't know about my Death Johnson blow or barroom brawls, and I wasn't about to mess this thing up with her asking a lot of questions. The Club Paris became a regular evening highlight. Later Iris and her sister, Karol, would hostess a couple of the standing card games at the Club Paris.

The stories must not have scared Iris off because we got married in Anchorage on December 30, 1974, by a Justice of the Peace at City Hall. Dave Reynolds was the best man. Karol was the bridesmaid. We have been married for 39 years. (I made sure to marry her before the end of the year to get a tax write-off!)

We flew to Seattle that day and had our honeymoon, while celebrating New Year's Eve. Then back to Anchorage where we set up house at 14th and E Street, near downtown. Our place overlooked Gottstein's home. Barry Gottstein was the largest wholesale grocery distributer in the state at that time and co-owner of Carr's Grocery stores with Larry Carr before Safeway bought them out. Karol lived with us.

failed, some of us knew who it was , and took care of the assailant Kodiak Style. You might say justice was served.

Part X   Lucky in Love, Lucky in Life   1972 - 1980

Shopping for Iris, one of my favorite pastimes.

I hadn't known Karol for very long before she said one day, "Jack, I'm going to run you for governor of Alaska!"

I told her that politics was not for me. We sure had some good times though. I was elated, I had two people to share my stories with. The house on 14th Avenue was roomy, with two full baths, a separate dining room, and a large living room with a floor-to-ceiling stone fireplace. There was a second fireplace in the big recreation room. It was big enough for the three of us including Marduk. Karol got a job as head waitress at the Woodshed Lounge. In 1974, it was one of the nicer steak houses with a cocktail lounge. Experienced restaurant help was hard to find, and she was good at her job. Karol had Iris occasionally bus tables or hostess.

Karol was a very sexy blonde and drew men like a magnet. She started dating one of my pile-buck buddies, and after about a year, they got engaged. After they were married, they built a home in Soldotna, Alaska, about 150 miles south of Anchorage. Around that time, Iris answered an ad for an Avon sales lady in the Anchorage area. She was well qualified, having worked in Avon in the Yakima area. After hearing of her experience, the manager offered Iris two territories. The combination of big money and the shortage of retail products and shopping centers made for big sales in Avon.

Part X   Lucky in Love, Lucky in Life   1972 - 1980

Honeymoon, Alaska Style

*It was still daylight when we boarded the vessel, MV **Roughneck**.*
The small crew with whom I had sailed was all men.
They were tickled to death to have Iris aboard
and whistled their pleasure.
The little pixie was all decked out in her new sailor gear
and was a sight to behold.
~Captain Jack V. Johnson~

At the time we got married, I was chief mate in the supply vessel, *Alaska Husky*, working the oil platforms in Cook Inlet. I put in for vacation time, which I had accrued working seven days a week, for an extended honeymoon. Vacation was granted. I had planned to show Iris around so she could understand why I loved Alaska. I had various romantic trips in mind. First, there was Anchorage. That alone can be pretty impressive to a newcomer. Bordered by the Chugach Mountain Range and the inlet, it is breathtaking. Also, I planned to show her south-central Alaska. We started off the honeymoon with a romantic night. We were excited to start the sightseeing adventures.

The following morning, I lay daydreaming as Iris had her shower. The phone next to the bed rang. I had no idea who it was as I picked up the receiver. It was the office of my employer, Foss Launch and Tug Company. They were in desperate need for a licensed mate in a small vessel due to sail from the Port of Anchorage on the late-tide. The problem was the timing. The vessel was due to sail that night! Cutting into my vacation and honeymoon time was not an option, so I declined. I had plans, and sailing to Valdez was not among them. I voiced my regrets and put the phone down.

All of a sudden, it rang again. This time it was one of the CEOs. "Please, Jack, we have to tow a barge of pipeline materials to Valdez. The material is needed at once. You're our only mate who's not aboard some vessel."

Part X   Lucky in Love, Lucky in Life   1972 - 1980

The pressure was on, but I resisted. I explained that I had been looking forward to this "honeymoon" for a long time and had no intentions of spending the next couple weeks away from Iris. They must have been desperate, because they offered to hire Iris as the ship's cook. I said, "No, she wouldn't like to do that," and hung up the phone.

About that time Iris returned to the bedroom, asking who was on the phone. I laughingly explained that they were trying to get me to return to work that very evening, but I had declined. I made the mistake of telling Iris she could have gone as cook. Well, all hell broke loose. Of course, that command she has for the English language spilled out, and I soon got the picture that she would have loved the chance to work in a real ship. Why had I not called her out of the head? And on and on she hammered me. You have to know Iris. She's pretty forthcoming and usually gets her way. Her tenacity is something I have always loved about her.

She ordered me to call Foss and say we would love to join the ship. I tried to talk her out of the idea, but she started crying, saying how much she wanted the job. Reluctantly, I called the Foss office and said Iris was willing to sail as cook. "Well, we just hired a cook."

Now, I thought, good, I had tried. I was sure I was off the cook hook. Ring! The damn phone rang again. "Okay, Jack, we're desperate. We can't find another mate, so this is what we'll do. We'll hire her as ordinary seaman! We'll prepare a 'Letter of Intent' for her to take to the Coast Guard. How quick can the both of you get here?"

I couldn't believe what I was hearing. This was way out of the ordinary. I had never heard of a woman in Alaska being hired as an ordinary seaman. Only Iris could get such an invitation. The Coast Guard officers who processed Iris' "Z" card[104] confirmed this. Iris was the first Alaskan woman issued a Z card. Needless to say, they were amused. Here's the kicker! They told her she would have to take orders from me. I wondered how well that was going to go over. She was sworn in and received her Z card.

---

[104] Merchant Mariner's document (MMD) as ordinary Seaman (OS.)

Part X   Lucky in Love, Lucky in Life   1972 - 1980

Iris had no idea what to expect as an ordinary seaman. She thought she would wear some old jeans. This time it was me who insisted. If she was going to play the part, I was going to make damn sure she looked the part. She would require proper sailor clothes and gear. I took her to the Northern Commercial Company, the best outfitting store in Anchorage, for bell-bottom pants and turtleneck tops, a sailor's watch cap, rain gear, and rubber boots. Of course a sailor must have a knife, so I got her a buck knife, which was pricey. I was satisfied. Iris couldn't believe I was spending all this money to get her outfitted for this short trip. It was still daylight when we boarded the vessel, MV *Roughneck*. The captain in the vessel was Tom Louis. The small crew with whom I had sailed was all men. They were tickled to death to have Iris aboard and whistled their pleasure. The little pixie was all decked out in her new sailor gear and a sight to behold. I think they just wanted to have something to rib me about later.

When it was time to get to work, I explained to Iris the routine of an ordinary. It would be her job to clean the head daily, dust the wheelhouse, and any time she could not find work, she was to polish the brass in the wheelhouse and elsewhere. I think she was a little startled to find she was more like a maid than a glamorous sailor, but amazingly, she cheerfully set about the chores. Her watch was 12 hours on and 12 off—over eight hours was overtime—and that's where you made the good money. As part of the Inlandboatsmen's Union (IBU), she was to make union wages, as her job fell in that category. Actually, while she was at sea, the union members received a raise, which arrived a couple weeks after we got home, an additional 58 dollars. We sailed with the tide. It was late at night. Time to turn in. Of course, as mate, I took the lower berth. The ship had started to roll from side to side. I rigged some life jackets to keep Iris from rolling out of her bunk and down on to the metal deck. The ship was a modified Landing Ship Medium (LSM) from war surplus. She had a three-second roll. All the rolling had wakened Iris during the night. She was afraid she would be pitched out of the bunk. She could hear water sloshing across the deck. Iris has always been a curious little pixie.

Part X   Lucky in Love, Lucky in Life   1972 - 1980

She slipped out of bed and on to the deck. I, of course, slept like a baby as the ship's rolls rocked me to sleep. Iris opened our cabin door and carefully walked out on to the deck. There was a big moon that night. I think it was then she caught a little bit of the sailing bug. She could understand what attracted me to this lifestyle. As the ship rolled from side to side, the seas came through the scuppers, sloshed across the deck and out the other side and then reverse. Iris was fascinated. Alone in the moonlight, she watched the action. When she told me about it the next day, I was furious she had left the cabin in the middle of the night. What if something had happened to her? Iris just laughed and told me I was silly to worry.

The MV *Roughneck* was towing a loaded barge. Captain Louis was not satisfied with the way our towline had been rigged. It was a "hurry up, half-assed" job, and therefore, he was unable to redo the tow. To make matters worse, it was apparent by morning that we were in a serious storm. There was a real danger of losing the barge we were towing. The only solution was to get out of the weather, which is what we did. We ducked into a cove, Port Dick. We spent three days jogging around in Port Dick, as we waited for a break in the weather. The port was calm. It was a beautiful setting. The water was surrounded by forest. If you watched patiently, from time to time, wildlife could be spotted on the shore as well as in the water. Of course, this was all new to Iris. She suddenly had lots of free time, as Captain Louis got nervous from all the window cleaning and brass polishing. He remedied his worries by telling her she would no longer be taking orders from the mate, but from the captain himself. The first and last order was to stop fussing and get out of the wheelhouse. There would be no more cleaning anywhere, including the heads (toilets). Captain's orders! Iris obeyed with a ready, "Aye, Aye, Captain!"

While in Port Dick, we were out of radio contact with Anchorage. Iris' sister, Karol, tried to call us through the marine operator. When that failed, Karol, who had no ocean experience, assumed the ship had sunk. She phoned the Coast Guard to report her fears. The ship's owner became concerned since they had no idea where we were. After being out of communication for three

Part X Lucky in Love, Lucky in Life   1972 - 1980

days, Captain Louis decided we had no choice but to leave the cove and make a run for Valdez. So the next morning we headed out. The sun was shining brightly, but the waves were rolling high. Iris, who doesn't get seasick, loved watching the sunshine through the towering waves. She commented on how the reflection of the sun turned the waves a translucent green. She couldn't understand why no one had joined her on deck to view such a spectacular sight. That's when she came looking for me. It was around noon when she found me in the wheelhouse with the other crewmembers. My bride popped her head in the door asking, "Jack, are you about ready for lunch? I'm starving!" Well, the mention of food was a shock, as every one of us was seasick!

Iris is not easily deterred so she went down to the galley to see what was for lunch. There she received another surprise. The galley was a mess. The dishwasher door had flown open, and water was rolling around the deck. A big pot of chili had come off the range, even though the stove had a railing about five inches high. The skinny alcoholic cook was perched on the stove rail with his feet pressed against the industrial refrigerator/freezer, trying to hold the door shut. He was less than pleased to see the ordinary, a woman at that, asking how she could help and where was a swab? She invited herself in and started to clean up the mess. Well, the cook had an order for her. "Get the hell out of my galley." It was obvious no one wanted her.

She decided it was their loss, and she went below deck to the berth and retrieved her camera as there was no reason to waste this opportunity on some crusty old sailors. She happily stayed on the open deck clicking a few photos. She was even more elated when she noticed porpoises playing in the spray at the bow of the ship. Leave it up to Iris to scurry herself out to the bow of the ship as it rolled. Lying face down near the bow, she took pictures of the playful porpoises.

We made good time as we were traveling with the wind. By the following evening, we were in Valdez. To Iris, it seemed she had been at sea for a long time. Everyone got cleaned up, ready to go ashore. The cook had one request, "Bring back some cooking

Part X   Lucky in Love, Lucky in Life   1972 - 1980

vodka." He knew we'd have ample opportunity because, like all sailors, once ashore we headed for the first bar.

As we were off the ship, waiting for a cab, one of the longshoremen called to the captain, who was still on board, "Hey, Captain, who's the dame?" cocking his head toward Iris.

Captain Lewis replied, "She's my ordinary. She sleeps with the mate!"

This was at the height of the pipeline construction. The bar was packed. It was a small space shaped like a horseshoe. There were three bartenders, all girls, working steadily behind the bar to keep up with the orders. The cocktail waitresses were serving the booths. The orders for drinks were so constant that the empty liquor bottles were just dropped on the floor, and there were lots already accumulated by the time we arrived. When we arrived, I noticed several of my friends were there. One was "Big Tony," who stood 7'1" tall. We had worked iron together. I introduced him to my bride. He thought Iris was cute. He picked her up and sat her on his shoulder. Her head touched the ceiling. Everyone was gathering around to meet my new bride, including one of my ex-girlfriends. All my friends were happy to see me and congratulated me on my nuptials. They liked the pixie sailor girl. There was an older man sitting at the bar. He asked me, "Who is she?"

I said, "She's a sailor off my ship."

He shoved his drink away, got up, and walked out muttering something about what the world was coming to.

Captain Louis joined us. The crowd consisted of the captain, the engineer and two ABs, Bruce Johnson and Thor Skulstad. They joined us for an evening of bar hopping, drinking, dancing, and telling jokes. The booze went down like snow in Yuma. We got some food along the way, and the festivities lasted long into the night. Someone asked Iris what took us so long to get to Valdez. She replied, "Oh, we were jogging in Port Big Dick!" *Damn me eyes!* Her jogging statement is still told around the bars and waterfronts today. The celebration was good since wasn't I supposed to be on my honeymoon with my bride?

Part X   Lucky in Love, Lucky in Life   1972 - 1980

Settling in Seward

I never did recall what happened to all that Johnnie Walker Scotch. Oh, well, all's well that ends well, I say, and Johnnie Walker Red is a good end to any story.
~Captain Jack V. Johnson~

We remained in Anchorage for over a year. We were quite saddened to have our lease expire on the house on 14th Avenue. It had been our home, and suitable housing was almost impossible to find in Anchorage due to what was being referred to as the "oil boom." The Alaska Pipeline construction was going full fhart. People were pouring in by the droves. There were too many people and a shortage of most everything, except cash. Any bill under one hundred dollars was considered throw-a-way money. It was okay for tipping or buying groceries and little necessities. Pipeline workers carried big rolls of hundred dollar bills when they went out drinking. Large bills littered the bars. Patrons would vie with each other to see who could spend the most money! Iris' sister, Karol, had moved in with her fiancé. So it was just Iris, me, and Marduk seeking living quarters. We were becoming anxious. I was working 7/12s in the supply vessel and had no time to house hunt. Dave Reynolds, best man at my wedding, agreed to sell us a house he owned in Seward. I knew the house. It was at 515 Seventh Avenue. I had helped him remodel it. I took Iris to look at the house to see if she thought she would be happy living in the small town of Seward.

Seward is about 127 miles from Anchorage and located on the Kenai Peninsula. Iris would be a little closer to Karol, who lived about 95 miles away in Soldotna. The little picturesque town of Seward was spellbinding with the Kenai Fjords National Park practically in our backyard and the Chugach National Forest surrounding us, all nestled in Resurrection Bay. Iris loved Seward at first sight. We bought the house and have made Seward our permanent home. The house was on Seventh Avenue, the street next to the Bay. Lots of debris from the '64 earthquake still littered the beach. Iris and Marduk spent many happy hours

Part X   Lucky in Love, Lucky in Life   1972 - 1980

beachcombing. Our house and yard began to take on the look of a waterfront junkyard. Iris dragged home all sorts of items. Many were left from the railroad that was demolished in the quake and tidal waves. Other odds and ends arrived in the tides. Sometime in August of that year, we painted the place a beautiful yellow. Iris christened our little home "Toadstool Nine North." We made the move to Seward in October of 1975. It was a happy time. We lived there until 1985. When we decided our little home was too small, we bought our present home on First Avenue. By the way, the name has stayed the same. We still refer to our current home as "Toadstool Nine North!"

Seward is a nice little town. My first memories go back to the age of five in 1931 when my father, mother, sister Ethel, and I arrived from Seattle in the Alaska Steamship passenger vessel SS *Aleutian*. We got off the ship and onto a train. That was my first train ride, from Seward to Anchorage. Even at the age of five, the waterfront along the coastline mesmerized me. I remember the thick trees that cushioned the mountainside as the train traveled between water and mountains. We arrived in Anchorage, which wasn't much of a town in those days, and stayed overnight. Leaving Anchorage, we continued our travels on an old cannery tender *Minnie B* down Cook Inlet to Seldovia. My father had an interest in herring fisheries with a friend of his, Squeaky Anderson. They did quite well using a large fleet of herring seiners. They were buying the herring, and it was being processed in Seldovia and down in Kodiak.

Off and on over the years, I had the pleasure of being on different vessels in and out of Seward. I always liked the place, wonderful people, and a beautiful location. I watched it become more of a city than a town as the years went on. I spent a lot of time in there when I was in the mail boat *Expansion*. Every month, we would take the mail from Seward up to Seldovia, Kodiak, and different ports down the Alaska Peninsula, and on out to the Aleutians. When we took the last mail in and out of Kanatic on July 14, 1953, there was one last remaining family. They were a fairly young family with a little boy about seven. I got a kick out of him. I could tell he was on his best behavior, but there was a

Part X   Lucky in Love, Lucky in Life   1972 - 1980

glint of mischief in his eyes. I was second mate in the *Expansion* in charge of the grocery store. We had quite a grocery store onboard and sold hard-to-come-by items like fresh groceries and fruit. I went into the store, got a banana, and brought it out to the little fellow, and said, "Here, you'll like this."

He looked it over suspiciously and asked, "What is this?"

I chuckled, "It's a banana. You can eat it."

Well, that's what he did. Only he bit into the yellow peel on the side. He made a horrible face, shook his head, and handed the banana back to me, "I don't like that."

Trying to hold back my laughter, I helped him out, "No, you've got to peel it." I peeled it for him and coaxed him, saying, "You can bite it now. Right here," pointing to the soft white part.

He looked at me, then looked at the banana, then looked at me and back at the banana, and very slowly he took a bite. His face lit up, his eyes got real big, and he crammed another bite in his mouth. I guess he liked it because he ate it all and wanted more, and more, and more. I think I gave him six bananas in about as many minutes. He really enjoyed them. I still see him around. He's in his seventies and still likes bananas!

We'd hit 19 ports out and 18 ports back in the *Expansion* from as far west as Dutch Harbor and then out to a farthest little village, Nikolski, in the Aleutians. We dropped our last mail there and then on the way back, we'd hit 18 ports, from Nikolski to Seldovia, from Seldovia to Seward. Once we returned to Seward, we'd tie up and wait for the next mail to get in from Seattle the next month. It usually wasn't a long wait, but during that time, we'd head for the beach and get to know all the bartenders. At that time, I think there were 14 bars in Seward, some which still exist today. I have spent many happy hours in each and every one.

If you have bars, then you've probably got houses of ill repute. There was a famous brothel in Seward. I first became acquainted with the brothel in January of 1943. I was with the Army Transport service, and we were pulling into Seward in the troop ship USS *General W. C. Gorgas*. It was one of the two times I sailed below, working in the black gang as a coal passer. My job was to take "an Irish baby buggy" and push it out to the bunkers,

Part X   Lucky in Love, Lucky in Life   1972 - 1980

fill it up with coal, bring it out, and dump it on the deck for the firemen to stoke the fires in order to make steam. I never cared for sailing below. Once we docked, we quickly headed for the bars and anything else we could find.

There was a joke that said the ladies of the evening were in mourning just because they saw us coming. This particular evening, I went back aboard ship so I could be up at 3:30 a.m. to stand my watch in the stoke hole. Some of the crew had stayed ashore. We got news that the whorehouse had burnt down, and unfortunately, our fireman and a few ladies died that evening. I was promoted to fireman.

The Seward Highway was well traveled, even though up to the early '50s, the 127 miles were gravel. Moose Pass, just outside of Seward, was part of the original Iditarod Trail at mile 23, going up through Johnson Pass. Even today, it is one of the last communities before Seward. When you reached Moose Pass, you were almost there. And of course, Seward was the end of the line, road wise, unless you were catching a vessel. Working and living there, Moose Pass became our last stop going into Seward, and our first stop coming out. For us, it was the location where we mugged up with a couple of "heaves ahead" as we headed for Seward and then, when we were leaving and driving up the gravel road to Anchorage, we'd stop and get a couple of "heaves ahead." It became a tradition to stop in Moose Pass on our way to and from Seward, especially in those early years after traveling two or three hours on a gravel road. Then we'd stop again at the Bird's Nest before getting into Anchorage. I used to date a girl who had lived in Kodiak and had moved to Seward. It was quite the trip to visit her on the gravel roads.

Before moving to Seward, I had worked in the *Alaska Husky* for a while, but left to take up pile-bucking again. I worked off and on, switching jobs during my time off. I had two gold claims outside of Seward on Canyon Creek. Moose Pass had been settled as a gold mining town. (*There's a lot of gold in them thar hills.*) I got pretty good color out of them, but I never had the time to pursue it. I ended up giving them to my godson. His father, Jimmy Foster,

Part X   Lucky in Love, Lucky in Life   1972 - 1980

was a pile-bucking buddy of mine. The son went off to Vietnam, and when he came back, he was in pretty bad shape.

Once I found out how he was doing, I offered him the claims for a split. I'd take 25%, and he would take 75%. By golly, he took it right up. He had done a little bit of prospecting before, so he had a portable dredge and scuba gear. The first season he came out with a $12,000 clean up. He is still working the claims and even has his son working them with him. We stopped our split after about 15 years. I hear he's still making good on the gold. He works out of IUOE Union 302 as an operating engineer with his journeyman son. He would stop in every once in a while and say hello to me at the "boars' nest" in Anchorage.

The MV *Tustumena*.

I love the Aleutian Islands; they are full of wonder and beauty. I had the good fortune to discover a species of Aleutian Canada Goose, *Branta Canadensis leucopareia*, thought to be extinct on the treeless volcanic Buldir Island.

One of my favorite pastimes in Seward was swimming with my dogs. Iris and I had a couple of Newfoundlands and they loved the water as much as I did. I would suit up in my survival suit and take the pups out for a good swim.[105] Jon Stetson commented one time, "Jack's daily ritual was to don his survival suit at the water's edge and go for a good long swim with his Newfies. Suited up, he looked even bigger than the giant man he was, especially flanked by two massive dogs, and the sight of the three of them making way in a perfect formation into three-foot seas sometimes drew a crowd."

---

[105] Alaska Marine Highway – 50th Anniversary – Jack V. Johnson, Legendary *Tustumena* Chief Mate by Captain Bill Hopkins, AMHS Retired.

Part X   Lucky in Love, Lucky in Life   1972 - 1980

While living in Seward in 1976, an avalanche took out the bridge at Snow River, and it cut off all the traffic going into the town. I was chief mate in the *Tustumena* and had gone to Anchorage to pick up Iris' new car. I was given a rare privilege to drive Iris' Christmas present that year, a brand new top-of-the-line Ford Granada. It was to be her favorite color blue (when I called her from the dealership, she said it could be any color *but* blue. But blue it was)! Me and a few of the guys from off the ship were headed back to Seward, and as good Sewardites, we stopped in Moose Pass for a "heave ahead." And you know the count—one led to two, two led to four, four led to eight. Before you knew it, we were on our 16th "heaves ahead." While in Moose Pass, we met up with Bobby Norton, one of my relatives from Kodiak. Along with traditional Moose Pass heaving, now there was another reason to celebrate—a happy family reunion.

Finally it was time to continue on to Seward and home to Iris. We started along our happy way, only to be stopped because the bridge was out at Snow River. We had to cross Snow River to get to Seward. It was a predicament. How were we going to get to Seward? Well, being sailors, we decided our best bet was by sea. We put our brains together and thought, if we could get our hands on a canoe or boat of some kind, we could cross the river. There wasn't anything on the river, so we backed the car up and went down to Kenai Lake where we could cross the lake over to a little gold mining place, Primrose Mine, and continue on our way down to Seward. Of course with every good plan, there should be some good drinking to go along with it. We stopped for a few more nips. I was drinking Black Russians at the time. We located a skiff from a lady friend of mine. She was more than happy to help. The skiff had a nice kicker, and we cut across Kenai Lake to Primrose Creek. I had called Iris to meet us. She did. As we staggered ashore, the first question she asked was, "Where is my new car?"

"Car?" I retorted. "Hell, we're lucky to be alive! Your car is fine. There was an avalanche!"

All my excuses didn't seem to satisfy her since all my rebuttals were overshadowed by the fact I was holding a sundry

Part X   Lucky in Love, Lucky in Life   1972 - 1980

of bottles of booze in my arms, mainly Johnnie Walker Red Label Scotch. Still trying to find our land legs, we all piled into Iris' old car. She drove us into Seward and down to the ship where the two guys got out and went aboard. She drove me home so I could sleep soundly and drown out her complaints about not having her new car. Being the chief mate meant I was on days so I didn't have to be in for work until the next day. I remember getting home and getting the booze in, but it's a little blurry after that. I must have slept like a baby. Iris' new car would have to wait.

I went aboard the *Tustumena* the next day, ready to set sail that Friday evening. I have always hated sailing on Fridays. Sailors are a pretty superstitious bunch, and sailing on Friday was bad mojo. In fact, some sailors take this very seriously. In 1850, the British Navy went out of its way to prove this superstition untrue. The Admiralty was getting fed up with ships not wanting to sail on Friday and crews not doing anything on Friday. Friday was considered a bad luck day. The British Navy decided to eliminate this hogwash once and for all. Its plan of action was to build a ship completely around Friday. They laid the keel on Friday and did all the major construction like stepping the masts and riggering her up on Friday. Everything of any major importance was done on Friday. They christened her on Friday and launched the ship on Friday. They even named her the HMS *Friday*. The Admiralty shipped her on Friday. She sailed on Friday. *And…*they were never heard of again! That didn't stop the *Tustumena*. I was only the chief mate, and no matter how hard I screamed like a gut-shot cougar about sailing on Friday, nobody paid any attention. We managed to sail without incident. What about Iris' car? Oh, it remained at my friend's house. After the avalanche was cleared away and a temporary bridge was erected, I was able to get the skiff and kicker back to my friend's house and drive Iris' new blue Ford Granada back to Seward—not before partaking of the Moose Pass tradition, mind you. I never did recall what happened to all that Johnnie Walker Scotch. Oh, well, all's well that ends well, I say, and Johnnie Walker Red is a good end to any story.

Part X   Lucky in Love, Lucky in Life   1972 - 1980

The Hanging Judge of Seward

*My wife became "The Hanging Judge of Seward,
the Law south of Moose Pass!"
We made quite the pair—the captain and the judge.
~Captain Jack V. Johnson~*

When we moved to Seward, Iris continued with her Avon for a while. She loved meeting the local people and won several prizes for high sales. Then the Magistrate, Genevieve Schaefermeyer, asked Iris to join the Alaska Court System as an Acting Magistrate. Genevieve had been a U.S. Commissioner before statehood and had been magistrate 18 years before drafting Iris. Iris hesitated to accept, but I kind of liked the idea of having a judge for my wife. God knows she always had a strong opinion about things and an excellent command of the English language. She was second-guessing her decision, but I encouraged her to think it over. My wife became *"The Hanging Judge of Seward, the Law south of Moose Pass!"* We made quite the pair—the captain and the judge. Iris was with the court for about five years and became very well known in our community. She was a magistrate from 1976 to 1981.

Everyone knew Iris. I may have a good sense of humor, but Iris is very quick witted. She's always the first one with a pun or a twist and has stolen the room from me on many occasions. Not everyone catches on to her humor, but I liked the jib for jab and had to stay on my toes to have a quick comeback for her. I have always appreciated her intelligence and wit. If it was looking like she would outshine me, I'd just shrug my shoulders, roll my eyes, and sing out, "Why me? Why me?" Worked every time!

On one occasion I was sent to face the "hanging judge" herself. The ladies in Moose Pass had just about had enough of people driving straight through Moose Pass and *not* slowing down to 35 mph as the posted highway signs indicated. They got together and purchased a brand new radar gun for the local law enforcement officers at Moose Pass. It was locked, stocked, loaded, and itching to be used. I was driving Iris' car back from

Part X   Lucky in Love, Lucky in Life   1972 - 1980

Anchorage one day. I got to Moose Pass, and with behavior very unlike me, I elected *not* to stop for the traditional Moose Pass "heave ahead." I drove right straight through to Seward.

The problem was I didn't slow down going through Moose Pass and was hauled over by Trooper Wreath. He clocked me doing 60 knots through a 35 mph zone with that radar gun. According to him, I was the first person ever caught on the radar gun, and to make matters worse, Iris was the magistrate! I was going to have to appear before *"The Hanging Judge of Seward, the Law south of Moose Pass!"* I humbly paid my fine so I didn't have to face the judge, but I couldn't shake my new reputation as word soon spread that Captain Jack was caught speeding by the new radar gun and Iris as the magistrate! The town got a pretty good kick out of it.

Iris, "The Hanging Judge," holding court on her birthday.

Part X   Lucky in Love, Lucky in Life   1972 - 1980

There was a lady, Clara, in the late '70s who had a carnival that traveled throughout Alaska. The carnival rides, Ferris wheels, and such traveled around via the ferry to the coastal areas. I had the good fortune of having her aboard my ship. She came to the *Tustumena* with all her gear in a big semi-truck heading for Kodiak. She insisted on special handling of a trailer rig. I was chief mate. She looked at me, put her hands on her hips, and asked, "Are you the fucking mate?"

Somewhat taken back, I confirmed, "Yes, ma'am, I am."

"Well, I want this loaded. I want the damn trucks down in a certain way so I can look at them," she demanded. "Can you do that?"

I assured her, "Yes, ma'am, they will be loaded better than perfect just for you."

She was a very interesting lady. I got to know her quite well. She had a very lovely daughter, who was constantly apologizing for the way her mother treated people. I wouldn't have changed her for the world. I kind of liked watching her operate. She was a woman who knew how to get things done exactly in the way she wanted them done.

In July 1978, we had a group of gypsies come aboard the *Tustumena* as passengers. They were trying to escape from someone in Michigan for some crime. Before long, the cops came aboard, asking the captain and me if we knew where the gypsies were. We did. They proceeded to gather them all up and take them off to jail in Seward. One of the girls was still trying to peddle me fake Rolex watches as they were hauling her away. Iris was the judge. The gypsies were in her court the next day.

One of the responsibilities of Iris' job as acting magistrate was to take over in the magistrate's absence. Iris stepped in while the magistrate, Genevieve Schaefermeyer, who hired Iris, took a three-week trip to the Philippines. When she returned, Iris kept remarking how amazing Genevieve looked. She looked younger and raved at how wonderful the trip had been. Genevieve had been having some health issues, and it appeared that all was well upon her return.

Part X   Lucky in Love, Lucky in Life   1972 - 1980

Genevieve's son, Darrell, talked about the surgical operation the spiritual healers or psychic surgeons had done with their bare hands. There are no instruments involved, and yet they can make incisions, remove the disease or infected tissue, and close the incision without anesthesia and without a scar.

As Darrell described what had happened, Iris asked, "How can that be?" and he answered, "It's like they are in another dimension."

Iris was fascinated. Iris talked me into going, as well as a co-worker, Ellen. Iris set it up through a tour guide in Anchorage for a two-week stay. I wasn't against the idea and had heard stories about the healers in my travels, so I thought, "What the heck. I could use a little R&R." So off we went. I ended up going to the Philippines twice to see healers about certain ailments.

As was described, the healers don't use any instruments, just their fingers. It's kind of spooky. On our first trip there in 1977, we went to Baguio City, a city in northern Luzon up in the mountains and pines. It was also the location of the summer palace in the Philippines because of the cool temperatures. At this time, I had some physical problems that were quite acute. I had something wrong with my lung. The healers managed to clear that up in just a matter of minutes. Iris didn't have any health issues, but she wanted that aura and energy her co-worker had returning from her trip.

We took an entire entourage of people with us from Alaska. We met in Anchorage at the airport and flew an international flight to Tokyo. The next morning we got on a Philippines Airline plane to fly into Baguio City. They booked us in an old hotel called The Diplomat. It was on a peak. It had been a monastery before it was a hotel. The landscaping was beautiful, and it was very clean. It was my understanding that the healers were part of the hotel staff. For the package deal we had rooms, food, swimming pools, a nightclub, all the conveniences, and, of course, the healing rooms. Each hotel room had a staff of people who served only us.

There were people everywhere doing odd tasks, like sweeping the lawn or other tasks. It was very luxurious. Each day

Part X   Lucky in Love, Lucky in Life   1972 - 1980

started with breakfast, and then you could either go on side trips to the South China Sea or the Zigzag Road, as well as spend time with the healers. When you went into the healing rooms, there were small waiting rooms. Then they would come and greet you. There were two tables, similar to chiropractic tables, in an open area. One healer and a student healer or apprentice treated you.

Like I said, I had an issue with my lungs. I had had pneumonia a few months before and developed a slight cough and often complained about having trouble breathing. You didn't tell the healers any of this. They just took you in and did their thing. Iris was running late when I was to start and wasn't there at the beginning of my procedure. I was told to remove my shirt and lay on the table. The healer informed me I would feel no pain or discomfort. They didn't ask what was wrong with me or what I wanted them to work on. The healers started moving their hands up and down my body until they identified a problem. Once Iris arrived, she said the lady standing over me appeared to be in some sort of a trance. Iris observed everything they were doing and was allowed to take pictures. The healer's fingers disappeared within my flesh. The flesh was opened. Iris noticed that other substances emerged similar to seeing a layer of fat. Whatever was wrong was discovered and pulled out. Blood came out immediately with what looked like blood clots in her hands over the lung area. Iris described that, once the hand was removed, and the opening closed up, some blood was still visible on the skin.

When Iris came over to observe, the healer looked at Iris and said, "I clean his lungs."

She went around to the garbage can and threw the clots away. Immediately afterwards, the incision was closed, and they cleaned me up. I got up off the table, fumbling with my robe, turned to Iris, and said, "Pix, I can breathe! I can breathe!"

Once they were finished, you were through for the day to rest or go sightseeing. What an amazing experience. You might say this whole healing thing is a bunch of hogwash, but I was and am a believer. I have never had any trouble in my lungs since. Iris also experienced some remarkable occurrences. We both left believers. Each of us came back to the healers on other occasions.

Part X   Lucky in Love, Lucky in Life   1972 - 1980

We had had a lot of fun with the group we were traveling with as well as our Filipino companions. On our way back, we stayed overnight in Manila at the Peninsula Hotel. The Peninsula Manila was a five-star hotel in the Philippines. It was referred to as the "Jewel in the Capital's Crown." It was known for its spectacular location, rich history, and timeless design. It was truly a beautiful, luxurious hotel.

Dancing at a Baguio City night club, The Pines.

While we were dining, someone in our group mentioned to our Filipino friends that I had been to Manila in the 1950s. This seemed to please them, and they encouraged me to take part in the traditional dancing on stage. Soon with enough persuasion and enough alcohol, I was inclined to go up and dance with the lovely dancers. We did the tingaling, which is one of the most popular traditional dances. The dance has two people beating and tapping while sliding bamboo poles on the ground and against each other in coordination with one or more dancers, who step over and in between the poles in dance. It takes five steps. The dancers must be quick enough to hop in and hop out and not to get their feet caught or crushed, especially as the dance rhythm goes faster and faster—all this while the bamboo sticks are being banged louder and louder.

I had learned the dance when I lived in the Philippines for a year in 1950. I managed to be very coordinated and got through the dance with all feet attached. That was enough for them to

Part X   Lucky in Love, Lucky in Life   1972 - 1980

applaud loudly. I stayed up on stage for another little shaky dance. Afterwards, I hopped off stage and sat next to Iris. A few minutes later, I felt a tap on my shoulder. I looked up, and there stood the biggest damn Filipino I had ever seen.

He leaned down and whispered in my ear, "Please join me," and tilted his head over to the left. I didn't want any trouble and didn't know what to expect, so I followed the big guy.

Dancing in the Philippines, February 1979.

When I arrived at the table, I found a beautifully fashionable lady in great company. She motioned for me to take the seat next to her. I sat down. She placed her hands on my arm and elbow and said, "You dance our traditional dances very well. You must have spent some time here? Do you like to dance?"

I explained I had danced a little bit and told her about the Russian Cossack dance and the Viennese Waltz. Then her eyes lit up, and she said, "Oh!" She motioned over to the big Filipino, and before I knew it, he was leaving our table and approaching the band. They stopped the song they were playing and began playing a Viennese Waltz.

Part X   Lucky in Love, Lucky in Life   1972 - 1980

I knew this was my cue, so I stood up and extended my hand to her as we waltzed around the dance floor. I can always say I danced a Viennese Waltz with Imelda Marcos. She held political office then after the death of her husband, President Ferdinand Marcos. She was an exquisite dancer. I finished the dance and kissed her hand. She nodded to me and said, "Until we meet again."

Imelda Marcos.

I went back over to my seat and told Iris what was going on. She just kept shaking her head, saying, "You never cease to amaze me!"

PART XI   1980 - 1992

Tustumena

It's rather awesome when you feel a strong, almost electric feeling in the air. The sea keeps getting higher and higher. The screaming of the wind has often lent me to lift up a small prayer, "Oh, God, your sea is so large and my vessel so small."
~Captain Jack V. Johnson~

I had the opportunity to work for the Alaska Marine Highway System (AMHS) in 1974.[106] The AMHS is operated by the state of Alaska and travels along the south-central coast of the state, as well as the eastern Aleutian Islands, the Inside Passage of Alaska, and British Columbia, Canada. A large advantage of the ferry system is you can travel from Alaska to Washington without going through Canada to the rest of the contiguous United States. People from all walks of life came aboard the ship. By day it was a pleasant sea excursion; by night, it was wall-to-wall sleeping bags as patrons found a spot on the floor to hunker down.

The *Tustumena* is the only mainline ferry in south-central Alaska and the Aleutian Chain. The *Tustumena* runs from Seward to Kodiak, Seldovia, Port Lions, and Homer. Once in Homer, you can connect to the road system. My favorite change in the schedule was in the summer when she made the voyage out to the Aleutian Chain eight times each year. In 1979, I was responsible for talking the powers that be into expanding the Alaska Marine Lines service. Since the charts in some of the areas were incomplete, I'd use the old charts from the mail boats. I would use the old courses from the trips with my uncle, Heinie Berger, when

---

[106] Most of Alaska is not accessible by roads. Ferries connect towns, villages, people with transportation, and supplies. AMHS 3,500 miles of routes go as far south as Bellingham, Washington, and as far west as Unalaska/Dutch Harbor.

Part XI   *Tustumena* to Southwest Pilots   1980 - 1992

we would run mail between Seattle and the Aleutians. This helped open up the ferry transportation system to Cold Bay.

I have to give Captain Andy D. Santos and Captain Hofstad credit for opening up the Westward route, as our combined knowledge of the mail boat routes provided the charting used today to make the Westward Run. We kept pushing through until 1993, when the Alaska Marine Highway expanded from Kodiak, to Chignik, Cold Bay, False Pass, King Cove, Sand Point, Akutan, and eventually to Unalaska/Dutch Harbor, making it the most intriguing route. We couldn't make the voyage in the winter because the conditions and weather become too dangerous.

I love the Aleutian Islands; they are full of wonder and beauty. I had the good fortune to discover a species of Aleutian Canada Goose, *Branta Canadensis leucopareia*, thought to be extinct on the treeless volcanic Buldir Island.

Iris and I loved the seaside ports and coastal regions, which is why our home in Seward fits us like a glove. Living in Seward, We also picked up some property and a house in Sequim, Washington, to toggle back and forth between Alaska and the "lower 48." We initially planned on living there six months out of the year. I was going to work six months on and six months off, but life seems to happen without asking about our plans, and it took us in another direction. We loved the Sequim area. It is also picturesque like Seward, lying in the center of the Sequim-Dungeness Valley with mountains bordering the small town. The Olympic National Forrest covers the area with lush trees. The lavender farms that surround the area fill the air with a hint of lavender. The Olympic Peninsula is complete with historic lighthouses located at the end of the largest natural spit[107] in the world, beckoning to sailors from all over..

Down at the Dungeness spit was a wonderful oyster plant, and on another spit was the world-famous Three Crabs

---

[107] A sand spit is a small point or low tongue of land made of sand or gravel, attached at one end to the mainland and having the other end in open water (usually a bay). This finger-like extension of the beach is deposited by the process of littoral drift, in which particles of sand are pushed by currents and onshore winds that move in the same direction. www.answers.com.

Part XI *Tustumena* to Southwest Pilots   1980 - 1992

Restaurant located right on the beach in Dungeness, Washington. It was a pretty hopping spot and catered to many influential visitors and residents. Some of the local color included Walt Disney. The Walt Disney Studio used the Olympic Game Farm there for years, filming on the farm and other parts of the Olympic Peninsula. You might recall movies like *Charlie the Lonesome Cougar*, *The Incredible Journey*, and the television series *Grizzly Adams*. Disney Studios used the location and the animal actors to create Disney's signature animal shows.

But the patron the town boasts most proudly of is the actor John Wayne, who had an affinity with the sea. John Wayne frequented Sequim in his family yacht *The Wild Goose* and owned property in the area. He envisioned a marina in the small community. After his death, his family donated 22 acres to bring the John Wayne Marina into being. It's featured as the "Best in the West."

The weather was always better in Washington, but the magnetic pull of the Northern Lights and the Bore tides in Alaska kept us grounded. Weather is a huge factor on the sea as well—in fact, it is critical. I have been accused of watching the weather channel like most guys read *Playboy*. Even today, I check it several times a day, a habit of being a sailor. I have always been impressed with the weather, especially when it's flat and calm on a beautiful sunshiny day with birds singing—there is nothing prettier. But when the winds are blowing at a steady 45 knots, with gusts to 70, sometimes 120 knots, it can be a bitch. Having spent a lot of time in the Aleutians, I can testify that there is a reason they are known as the birthplace of the wind because of the parade of low-pressure systems that issue forth from there.

In 1990, I was featured in *The Quarterly Alaska Geographic*[108] on Alaska's weather. I was with Southwest Alaska Marine Pilots at the time. Having fished, crabbed, served on mail boats in the Aleutian Islands, and piloted state ferries and ships in and out of Alaska's deep-water harbors, I have extensive first-hand experience on the critical conditions the weather can play in a

---

[108] *Alaska Geographic: Alaska's Weather*; The Quarterly/ Volume 18, Number 1. Editor Penny Rennick; pgs. 73 – 74.

Part XI *Tustumena* to Southwest Pilots   1980 - 1992

sailor's voyage. I have been in almost every type of marine weather imaginable.

This would include hurricane-force winds, freezing temperatures where the ocean spray freezes on deck, or fog so thick you could cut it with a knife. It's rather awesome when you have a strong, almost electric feeling in the air. The sea keeps getting higher and higher. The screaming of the wind has often lent me to lift up a small prayer, "Oh, God, your sea is so large and my vessel so small."

Iris and me at home in Seward, Alaska.

It is most difficult when you are trying to bring to dock a ship the size of about two and half football fields. Conditions have to be just right to safely bring in a ship that size. The direction of the wind has a lot to do with it. If you are experiencing a steady 40-45 knot wind, it can push the ship toward the dock, and in the worst

Part XI   *Tustumena* to Southwest Pilots   1980 - 1992

of situations, it could hit the dock. If winds alone weren't bad enough, combine them with the icy frigid temperatures of the Alaskan winters, and you have another ballgame altogether. The winds whip the waves overboard, sending sheets of water over the deck and pilothouse. The water and spray instantly freeze, coating everything on deck in thick ice layers. This makes the ship top-heavy. It is these circumstances that make fishing or crabbing in Alaska's waters one of the most dangerous occupations in the nation.

In 1955, I was out in the mail boat *Expansion* during a particularly harsh winter. We were bound for Port Graham out of Kodiak. The boat iced up and began listing. By the time we reached shelter in the Barren Islands, the boat was laid over some 30 degrees. We chipped ice all night. It's during these most excruciating times that one begins to think it would be easier to drown than break the ice off. It can get a little hairy. I have been nervous a few times due to bad weather, but when it's in your blood, you can't keep an old Alaskan-Finn down. In 1988, I was a pilot for an international cruise ship sailing around the northern coast of Alaska through the Northwest Passage. We got stranded for five days in the ice pack of the Beaufort Sea. A dozen polar bears gathered around the stern, licking their lips, while the crew worked to free the ship before the ice crushed it.

There are other experiences out at sea that are absolutely incredible and stay with you a lifetime. In 1985, while I was on that same Northwest Passage route, I witnessed an unusual sight. I saw a vivid occurrence of a meteorological phenomenon called "the green flash." The "green flash" has been a mythical experience sailors chase all their lives and seldom see. Captain Back of HMS *Terror* first mentioned it in his writings in 1837, while exploring the Arctic. Up in the Arctic there is no pollution in the air. The clear, unobstructed horizon gives way to perfect conditions. A green flash is easiest to see on a cold, clear day as the sun is setting. The atmospheric layers of lights work like a prism to bend the colors until, under certain conditions, green is the only color visible. Often this is only for a split second, but that summer eve, it lasted for about 15 minutes. I have been fortunate enough to see the "green flash" many times at sea, but none as

Part XI *Tustumena* to Southwest Pilots   1980 - 1992

exceptional as this sighting. The captain and I logged it. It was a once in a lifetime—once in several lifetimes—sighting. Working with the Alaska Marine ferries, weather can turn a pleasant trip into a white-knuckle excursion. Even though we stay in coastal waters, the rough seas can create havoc for the passengers. It is not uncommon to see passengers laying belly down on the deck to try and calm the bowels and stomachs as the ship bounces readily up and down. Those who could afford the berths weren't any better off. Lying on the deck is still the best remedy for seasickness.

Part XI *Tustumena* to Southwest Pilots   1980 - 1992

**In Florence, Oregon, all decked out for a photo shoot
held for a maritime publication. 1995.**

I remained with the *Tustumena* until early 1980. I had just gone Master when the opportunity came to join the Southwest Alaska Pilots Association. I had remained with the Alaska Marine Highway System for about five years, just enough to get vested and scrape out a small retirement from the state. They sent me a small check for a couple of thousand. Any other retirement plans after that would be entirely up to me.

Part XI *Tustumena* to Southwest Pilots   1980 - 1992

Pilot for Southwest

Iris said she never questioned the "sea stories" again, because every time she did, someone would come along— validating each unbelievable tale.
~Captain Jack V. Johnson~

When I started with the Southwest Alaska Marine Pilots Association, their strategy was different. You are considered your own entity.[109] You retire when you retire. Their routes consisted primarily of the south-central Alaska ports like Icy Bay, Prince William Sound, Resurrection Bay, Cook Inlet, and Kodiak. They would bring the ships in and out of Alaskan ports from Cape Spencer. Today, they go from Yakutat to the 156th meridian just west of Kodiak.

When I joined, we were covering all the waters around south-central Alaskan ports and out to the end of the Aleutian Chain, through the Bering Sea, around Barrow, and all the way over to Demarcation Point. In the time I was with the Southwest Alaska Marine Pilots, I piloted eight ships through the Northwest Passage (my favorite area). The first one was with Don Oldow. He was the Senior Pilot for Southwest Alaska Marine Pilots. I was just riding along as an observer, breaking in as a pilot and getting ready for my Northwest Passage trips. We were going east to west in 1982. I joined her in Resolute, high in the Arctic Circle, in the *Lindblad Explorer*. The *Lindblad* later became the *Society Explorer*. I would pilot her also. Other times I would pilot tankers or whatever ship needed a pilot. I remained with the Southwest Alaska Marine Pilots Association for 27 years.

Being out at sea has some down time, and I would often pass the time by doodling word plays. For instance, several of my fellow Pilots were avid golfers, but I never did fancy golf. I expressed my frustration with the game by this morsel.

---

[109] The Southwest Alaska Pilot Association accumulated pilot fees and employed bookkeepers, dispatchers, and pilot boat skippers. Each of us owned a share of our pilot boats. The jobs would come through the dispatcher.

Part XI   *Tustumena* to Southwest Pilots   1980 - 1992

GOLF: a frustrating endeavor attempting to impel a diminutive spheroid into an exiguous aperture, indicated by a numerable roseate banner, while utilizing inadequate instruments and constantly maintaining an ambling gait spanning a verdant landscape in the eternal pursuit of the aforementioned diminutive spheroid...I'd much rather write about the game than play it.

Taken at the Alitak Cannery. 1999.

Part XI   *Tustumena* to Southwest Pilots   1980 - 1992

Around the mid-80s, Iris was hired by Alaska Maritime Agencies as their ship agent for vessels arriving and departing Resurrection Bay. Seward is a Port of Entry for foreign vessels. Therefore, ships arriving from many countries come to Seward for official permission to enter the United States' waters. Iris did the actual work of boarding the ships and examining the ships' documents. She had many duties; in fact, most everything the captain or the ship personnel required while in port was her responsibility. Cruise ships had started coming to Seward, and there were lots of Japanese trampers (refrigerated cargo carriers) coming to Prince William Sound and Resurrection Bay to load frozen seafood. Iris loved the challenges of the many duties of a ship agent. She earned her title of "Super-Agent."

As Iris and I traveled, I would introduce her to all my friends and acquaintances, especially when we visited Seattle. On one occasion, I introduced Iris to my friend, Dorothy Lewis. Dorothy, as you recall, had been my conduit to finding Oscar Callow after all those years, which eventually led me to meet Iris. When Iris met Dorothy, she was the vice-president of one of the banks in Seattle. Dorothy and Iris hit it off and became fast friends. Sometime later, Iris and her friend, Sue Kaanta, made plans to vacation in Spain with Iris using the air miles I accumulated.

Sue had friends in Minorca, an island off of Barcelona, and it seemed like a good idea. They were going to be in Minorca for 10 days, but Sue had to get back. I encouraged Iris to stay on and take a longer vacation. I suggested she get hold of Dorothy Lewis. Iris did and talked her into coming to Spain to finish out the vacation. The two of them toured Spain and Portugal together for almost a month. They rented a BMW and made the European trip in style. Iris had always thought my stories were just what she called "sea stories," something like mermaids, I guess. Having Dorothy on vacation with her gave her the perfect opportunity to set the record straight.

Iris told Dorothy she had never quite believed the story of how Oscar and I were reacquainted, so she wanted to hear it from her. Dorothy went on to relay the story of how she had met me on a blind date set up by her friend. She had people waiting for her

Part XI *Tustumena* to Southwest Pilots   1980 - 1992

back at her home, so she talked me into coming to her house to meet the people waiting there, as we walked toward the house, I heard a laugh, and said, "I know that laugh. That's Oscar Callow!" Iris said she never questioned the "sea stories" again because, every time she did, someone would come along validating each unbelievable tale.

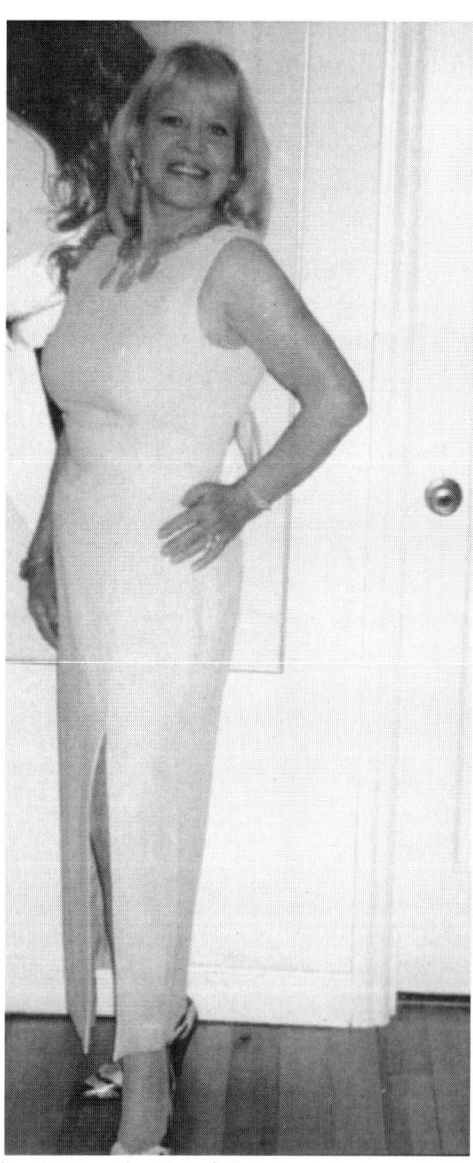

Iris in Seattle at Dorothy Lewis' apartment—going to the opera.
Lucky in love, all right.

Part XI   *Tustumena* to Southwest Pilots   1980 - 1992

In 1982, I took a ship-handling course in Grenoble, France. This was required course training by the Southwest Alaska Pilots. Grenoble was beautiful and known as the "capital of the Alps." It is no wonder the 1968 "X" Olympic Winter Games were held there. They had a big lake where we took the schooling. We'd get into the man-model ships, which were scaled down from big container ships and super tankers. We went through all the courses, taking them into the Suez Canal and docking, undocking, anchoring, and tying up to a mooring buoy.

When the course was over, I made a phone call; I contacted Luigi and Maria Gambozzi, the couple who had adopted my daughter, Giannina. I told them I was in Grenoble, France, and would like to come to Basel, Switzerland, to visit them. They assured me it would be easier if they came down to Grenoble where I was staying. They thought it was marvelous we could meet. Luigi, however, didn't come down, but Maria and my daughter Giannina came. This was the first time I saw Giannina Maria after 33 years. I was taken back. Oh, how I was taken back. It was very emotional seeing her again—a lot of tears and a lot of laughter. She was beautiful. I saw so much of her mother in her. She had Margherita's raven-black, naturally curly hair and eyes of blue, standing about 5'4". If I would have to choose a feature that looked like me, I'd have to say, "She has my nose."

They stayed a couple of days. We didn't have many memories to recall, but we shared a lot of laughter and a lot of tears. I told her a little about my life and how I was living in Alaska with my wife, Iris. She shared about her life. My daughter had grown to become a renowned harpist, who can play any string instrument and is very musical. She married a petroleum engineer, who worked for a Swiss company all over the world. When she and her husband were in Jakarta, they fell in love with the people. They adopted two Indonesian children. Iris and I hear from them, usually at Christmas.

After my visit with Giannina, I went over to Scotland to a small lodge on the river. I thoroughly enjoyed myself with the beautiful Scotland scenery and lots of fly-fishing. I can always say I caught a brown trout in Scotland. I took a tour and found myself

Part XI   *Tustumena* to Southwest Pilots   1980 - 1992

on the Island of Islay at the Laphroaig Distillery, which produces some of the world's finest single malt whisky.[110] Laphroaig is a favorite of Prince Charles. They even have their own label.

When I had my first taste of the "water of life," I was 10 years old, recuperating from polio. I used to sit in a bay window we had, looking out at the world when I was supposed to be resting. As most boys my age, my rest didn't last long. I began inventing games. On one occasion, I realized the seat I had been sitting on all this time had a wonderful secret. Underneath it was a way to climb down on the outside ledge and enter my father's den. My father had an enormous den that included his office, bookcases, and to my delight, Scotch whisky, as well as other stashes of alcohol. I can still remember the 25-year-old Double "O" Scotch and Laphroaig. I pinched a few bottles. My dog, Nero, was not fond of Scotch, but was more inclined to drink apricot brandy!

While on the Island of Islay, I went sampling the Laphroaig wares and found myself quite delighted with the aging whisky. I made a deal and bought five barrels of the Scotch with the business arrangement that, when they bottled it, I'd make a hefty profit. After my nice visit and sampling of all the Scotch, I arranged for a car and driver to get me to the ferry and on to London. As I was leaving, I turned to look at those five wonderful barrels of whisky. I said, "If you can't sell it, send it." They all got a big kick out of that.

The Johnsons have a reputation in Seward for throwing one hell of a party! People gathered at our home "Toadstool Nine North" for many occasions. Our home is big enough to host large gatherings. We have a nautical motif with numerous artifacts and knickknacks. Our walls are covered with pictures of large sailing ships, many of which I had been in at some point in my sailing career. Some of the pictures were given as gifts, signed by various captains as I left their service. Others were homage to the four-masted ships, such as the *Passat* or the *Pamir, the likes of which the seas will never see again.* (Both the *Pamir* and the *Passat* are four-

---

[110] Scotland is known for Scotch whisky. Imported by a Catholic priest from Ireland in the 15th century, the earliest record of whisky was found in 1495. It was referred to as the "water for life."

Part XI *Tustumena* to Southwest Pilots 1980 - 1992

masted barques, 3,700 gross tons, and length about 356 feet on deck.) Prominent artists have been commissioned for several paintings. One painting Iris had commissioned was by Lola Theresa. It is mounted in regal honor over the fireplace and above our handcrafted mantel. It is a 3' by 4' portrait of me dressed as Captain Jack. I was at that time captain of the *Tustumena*. The portrait has me in formal dress with four stripes indicating my status as a captain. In the background is the Flying P-liner sailing ship with the *Pamir* over my left shoulder, from a photograph taken by a captain of the tug that towed us out of Vancouver in rough windy seas.

My portrait, *The Long Voyage Home*, by Lola Theresa.

I have fond memories of the *Pamir*. She sailed under the New Zealand flag. Over my right shoulder is the barque *Passat*, depicted from a painting by a famous artist that has her location

Part XI *Tustumena* to Southwest Pilots   1980 - 1992

in the North Sea sailing home to the Aland Islands of Finland.[111] In the upper left-hand corner is a lighthouse—a guiding light bringing me home. Below the lighthouse is Iris, shown as a whimsical pixie sitting on top of the bluffs beckoning me like a siren on the banks of the Rhine River and luring me to my fate. Down on the beach is an anchor. That's where you put the anchor when you "swallow the hook" or "ring down finished with engines."[112]

To finish off the mantle is a framed picture of me at the wheel of the ship crossing the equator. The picture was taken April 12, 1940. I was ordinary seaman in the MS *Mirrabooka*, a Swedish American-Line vessel. Too young to sail in American ships, I sailed out in the MS *Mirrabooka* at the age of 13 and crossed the equator on my 14th birthday. Iris is also an artist, and her work is displayed throughout our home. Other conversation pieces adorn our humble abode, but the most cherished are the memories we have with family and friends.

Our family dinners are always a huge success and are usually not limited to family members, but also friends and acquaintances. If there were local or national celebrities in town, they usually found their way to our home. I like to cook and often would "man the grill." Iris is one hell of a cook, as well as a hostess, so she could whip together a banquet fit for a king with short notice. We have a pleasant little barroom off our living room that opens out to our wraparound deck. The bar is always well stocked. Each dinner usually entailed entertainment, and I recited my favorite poems, like Rudyard Kipling's *Gunga Din*:

> *You may talk o' gin and beer*
> *When you're quartered safe out 'ere,*
> *An' you're sent to penny-fights an' Aldershot it;*
> *But if it comes to slaughter*
> *You will do your work on water,*
> *An' you'll lick the bloomin' boots of 'im that's got it.*

---

[111] The most beautiful archipelago of Scandinavia is called the Åland Islands.

[112] In 1978, the artist entered the portrait in an art competition. The "Long Voyage Home," oil on canvas, was selected to hang at the Anchorage Museum. It was highlighted with special lighting on a wall of suitable size.

Part XI *Tustumena* to Southwest Pilots   1980 - 1992

I was always one for drama and flare and enjoyed cleverly enunciating every word with exact accuracy in emphasis and rhyme. It was more entertaining while wearing "me Scottish kilt and beret," barking commands in rhythm.

My "harem" Iris and me "Sheik of Arabia" at Halloween!

Part XI *Tustumena* to Southwest Pilots   1980 - 1992

While I was piloting, each year on my birthday, April 12th, we'd have a birthday party. All the pilots were invited and all our many friends. People would come from all over Alaska as well as the lower 48, even some from far across the seas. We started referring to our annual April 12th party as "The Spring Fling."

Another occasion for grand parties at our little home was Halloween. Iris has a flare for the dramatic, so masquerade parties at Halloween were a fun event. Iris would decorate the place with black and orange streamers and other decorations.

It got more difficult each year to come up with just the right costume. One year I was a Sheik of Arabia, and Iris was part of the "harem," dressed as a hooker. We went down to the Breeze Inn in Seward and took first prize!

I was a pirate one year, and Iris was Diamond Lil.[113] She even got a little diamond stuck on her tooth to carry off the authenticity of the character. Other outfits included French Foreign Legion costumes from Hollywood Wardrobe.

The most famous Halloween costume was when I came dressed as a Russian Cossack, in full regimentals, with the Cossack hat and full uniform. The party started out at a bonfire over at our friend Penny's home. Somebody had sense enough to have some vodka handy. That started things off. I was speaking Russian and singing Russian songs, and I led the Cossack dance. We wound up at our house as the party continued. Evidently, everyone was wondering who that strange person was? Nobody realized it was me, their beloved Captain Jack! Iris came as Marilyn Monroe and pulled off a striking resemblance herself.

With Iris as the Alaska Maritime ship agent for vessels arriving and departing Resurrection Bay and me as a ship's pilot, we were known for having some good times. On one occasion, the three-masted barque *Cuauhtémoc*, the Mexican Navy Sail Training Ship, came into port. They were on a goodwill mission, coming from Dutch Harbor to Seward then to ports on down the West Coast. Captain R. Gomez was the captain. His crew consisted of 10

---

[113] Diamond Lil (1928), a play by Mae West.

Part XI *Tustumena* to Southwest Pilots   1980 - 1992

officers, 27 sailors, and about 200 cadets. They were traveling with a public relations person from San Francisco.

Reliving my Legionnaire days!

Part XI   *Tustumena* to Southwest Pilots   1980 - 1992

Iris was responsible for honoring the Mexican Navy under the name of Sail Pacific. They were cruising the Pacific Rim from Mexico, down around Australia, across to New Zealand, through Tonga, Tahiti, Taiwan, Manila, Japan, Alaska, and back to Mexico. We were their last Alaskan stop. They arrived in the Port of Seward on June 6, 2005. I was the pilot taking her in and out on departure. When she arrived in port, Iris was on shore taking pictures. As we approached the dock and just off our home, the crew "manned the yards," which is a courtesy to everyone.[114] This meant that all the crew not required on deck to handle the ship go aloft, and spread out along the yards. It symbolizes a salute to the United States, particularly to the Port of Seward. The crew of the *Cuauhtémoc* is famous for manning its yards with its crew standing on the yards themselves, rather than in footropes. All the crew was up on the yardarms[115] standing shoulder-to-shoulder or yardarm to yardarm, as we would say.

When we got to the dock and tied up, Iris came aboard at the captain's invitation as a courtesy to me. We were invited down to Captain Gomez's big saloon. We were all drinking tequila, toasting the United States and Mexico. Captain Gomez was very gracious. It was around that time Iris extended an invitation and invited the captain and officers. Captain Gomez asked in very good English, "Would it be okay to bring a few crewmembers?"

"By all means," said Iris. "We have room for 10 to 20 people." The captain, some officers, and a few crewmembers showed up at our door. Not one or two, or three or four, or eight or nine, *but all of them*, plus the captain and officers. The captain, officers, and cadets, as well as the public relations representative and many of our friends, joined the festivities. We had quite a party.

Iris' only response to this story is that, fortunately, it was summer and we could accommodate a lot of people out on the expansive deck. I knew a little Spanish, but my Italian is better.

---

[114] It is a common practice among the modern square-riggers. It displays the whole crew to the harbor authorities and the other ships present to assure them her intentions were peaceful.

[115] The yardarms on a sailing ship are the horizontal timbers or spars mounted on the masts, from which the square sails are hung.

Part XI   *Tustumena* to Southwest Pilots   1980 - 1992

Put them together, and I get by pretty good. Iris knew a little Spanish, but we thought it would be helpful to have someone who spoke it fluently. We invited our neighbors, who spoke Spanish, to join us in the celebration to help us with the translations.

The party started with musicians singing and dancing, with four guitars, one violin, two mandolins, and one accordion! I joined in the Mexican hat dance. Captain Gomez was holding court. As far as we were concerned, everything was going fine. Being June in Alaska meant that it was pretty much daylight 24 hours, so there was no indication that the party was stopping anytime soon.

ARM *Cuauhtémoc*, the three-masted barque and Mexican Navy Sail Training Ship, Captain R. Lopez, officers and crew and cadets, arriving Port of Seward, Alaska, June 6, 2005.
Yards are manned for courtesy and salute to the U.S.A.
I was the pilot taking her in and out on departure.

Part XI *Tustumena* to Southwest Pilots 1980 - 1992

Driving our suburban, some of the crew made a trip back to the ship to get more booze—not just one or two bottles, but armloads and armloads of tequila and eight cases of beer. (In fact, I still think we have a few bottles of that tequila left.) Everyone was drinking. With the party being indoors and out on the deck, the noise traveled, and before we knew it, here came the cops. I answered the door with Iris right behind me. She graciously invited the officers in. They came in and nodded to Iris. They all knew her, Iris having been a magistrate and judge. They informed us they had had some complaints and that we were making too much noise and disturbing the peace. Iris, with her usual charm, invited them in for a drink. They had to decline. One of the officers, Joe, smiled and said, "Sorry, Iris, you know we can't join you. We're on duty."

Iris understood and teased, "Maybe later?" They laughed and told her we needed to quiet down. As they were turning to leave, Joe turned and said, "Iris, this is all going down in history."

The crew settled down a little bit after that, but the evening remained pretty lively. I thought it lasted a couple of days, but Iris said it only lasted until morning. As they began to stagger down to the ship, the captain began thanking us for the party and the hospitality.

Captain Gomez spoke his parting words with a grin, "In Mexico, we don't consider a fiesta a success unless the *policia* come." He nodded to Iris, and off he went.

Seward is small enough so they could get to the ship by themselves, which was a good thing since no one was in any condition to drive. We enjoyed their company once again when we went aboard for lunch the next day. Iris kept in touch with them for a couple of years through e-mail and exchanging gifts, t-shirts, and Mexican calendars.

Ships of all flags and destinations have docked in Seward, even submarines. Over the 1987 Independence Day celebration, I piloted the nuclear-powered strategic missile submarine USS *Alaska* and tied her up alongside the submarine tender *McKee*. I had piloted *McKee* in before the USS *Alaska*. I had been in grade school with the guy they named the *McKee* after—William W.

Part XI *Tustumena* to Southwest Pilots 1980 - 1992

McKee. He wound up being a full admiral in the Navy. The commanding officer didn't like that I referred to submarine as ships. They are called boats. The crew was not submariners (sub-mar'-in-ers); they were submariners (sub-ma-reen'-ers). I made sure to get that right.

The Commanding Officer took Iris and me on a tour in the USS *Alaska* when we were all fast alongside the tender. Iris was the agent. They invited both of us to lunch. It was pretty interesting. They had big missile silos which had the crews' quarters in between each silo. They were set up a little different from when the Germans lived aboard their U-boats. The USS *Alaska* was a bit more sophisticated. I got to go through a U-boat after the war when I was in Germany, years ago. What those U-boats might have lacked in sophistication, they made up in guts; they torpedoed me four times, didn't they?

Often I worked out westward, what we pilots referred to as Unalaska Dutch Harbor. We took care of all the ships going out to the Bering Sea up the Alaska coast and around to the Northwest Passage. I enjoyed working in the Aleutians, and the Northwest Passage was one of my favorite areas. One trip through the Northwest Passage in 1988, we stopped at Gamble in St. Lawrence Island. We had a lecturer on board, who was fluent in Russian. Somehow the conversation steered towards us going to Provideniya, Russia.[116] The lady lecturer contacted the Mayor of Provideniya and asked if we could go over for a visit. He said, "Wonderful! Please come!"

Captain Aye, the captain of the expedition cruise ship, *Society Explorer*, was delighted. I sailed with Captain Aye on several occasions, and we became fast friends. Upon entering Soviet waters, we picked up a Russian pilot, who took us into Bukhta, the port for Provideniya. It has a natural coastal port with good shelter. Alongside the dock, we were greeted with a great welcome. I went ashore. The ability to speak and understand Russian again proved to be very useful. I used it to go shopping.

---

[116] Provideniya is 100 miles above the Arctic Circle, the most eastern Russian Port in the Arctic.

Part XI *Tustumena* to Southwest Pilots   1980 - 1992

In Provideniya was a prison. The prison was part of the GULAG.[117] This was where prisoners and German POWs mined coal. The buildings across the bay were the prison.

Bringing in the USS *Alaska*.

The warden of the prison came aboard the ship to welcome us. I fell in with the warden, a lady, tough but very pretty. She drove me around and gave me a tour. I recall one vast field, a mass graveyard, where the German prisoners of war ended up. At one time there many thousands of prisoners held there, but on the

---

[117] The term "GULAG" is an acronym for the Soviet bureaucratic institution, *Glavnoe Upravlenie ispravitel'no-trudovykh LAGerei* (Main Administration of Corrective Labor Camps), that operated the Soviet system of forced labor camps in the Stalin era. Wiki.

Part XI *Tustumena* to Southwest Pilots   1980 - 1992

day we were there, only about 3,000 remained. We went back to town, and she invited me to her apartment. She wanted to give me a drink of vodka, but I turned it down. She couldn't understand why a sailor would refuse a drink. I had gone on the wagon by then and wasn't drinking, but it was quite a visit. One I'll never forget! Never!

Captain Aye was pretty proud to be the first cruise ship into Provideniya. However, the U.S. officials were none too pleased. On his return to Alaska, Captain Aye had a lot of explaining to do! He had neglected to get clearance from the U.S. Coast Guard to depart United States' waters. We left Provideniya and headed back towards the Northwest Passage, and that's when the real trouble began.

Just past Cape Horn bound east to the Falklands, thence on to Antarctica in 42' ketch *Mahina Tiara*.
February 7, 1995.

Captain Aye had to explain himself to the U.S. officials in Barrow about leaving U.S. waters without clearance and returning without entrance permission. The ship was fined $5,000. We continued on our way through the Northwest Passage, on to

Part XI *Tustumena* to Southwest Pilots   1980 - 1992

Greenland, and back to Canada. Back in Anchorage, I was met with TV cameras that wanted a first-hand story on the incident. I was happy to oblige. Well, someone had to do it, and I for one have never been camera shy!

It's a funny thing about people; if you let them, they can remain friends for life. I met people in Provideniya with whom I have continued to be friends. We still keep in touch. In fact, they have come to Anchorage and visited us in Seward. I have gone back to Provideniya, Magadan, even as far down as Habrusk on the China border to visit friends as well.

Part XI   *Tustumena* to Southwest Pilots   1980 - 1992

The *Exxon Valdez* Oil Spill

Just prior to the **Exxon Valdez** *running aground,
I was in the tanker* **Chevron Mississippi** *as an observer pilot
in Prince William Sound. This would have been one of the trips to
qualify me as a* **Valdez tanker pilot**.
We came out ahead of the **Exxon Valdez** *by a couple of hours.*
~Captain Jack V. Johnson~

I love Alaska. I have seen her through some of her best days and some of her most challenging days. On March 24, 1989, I witnessed the *Exxon Valdez* oil spill, first hand. The *Exxon Valdez* ran aground, and 11 million gallons of Alaska crude oil went out into the water throughout Prince William Sound, along the north coast of the Gulf of Alaska and on down towards the peninsula. Captain Hazelwood was the captain of the *Exxon Valdez*.

I was piloting tankers in Valdez at that time. You had stints, two weeks on and two weeks off. Just prior to the *Exxon Valdez* running aground, I was in the tanker *Chevron Mississippi* as an observer pilot in Prince William Sound. This would have been one of the trips to qualify me as a Valdez tanker pilot. We came out ahead of the *Exxon Valdez* by a couple of hours. I had gotten off the *Chevron Mississippi* and was aboard the *Emerald Island* (the station keeper) relaxing. The pilot boat brought Ed Murphy aboard, and we were both enjoying a cup of coffee when we got the news. I knew the captain fairly well, and the AB was my ex-brother-in-law, Larry Gard, Connie's brother. Just before getting ready to turn in, I was waiting for the next inbound tanker. That's when I got word of the tragic incident that changed our lives. The *Exxon Valdez* had gone aground.

She was a new vessel of the Exxon Shipping Company's 20-tanker fleet. No one had expected much trouble after leaving the Alyeska Pipeline Terminal at 9:12 p.m., Alaska Standard Time on March 23, 1989. It was routine as usual, like the other 8,700 times over the last 12 years of vessels safely departing Prince William Sound.

Part XI *Tustumena* to Southwest Pilots   1980 - 1992

According to State of Alaska documentation, the *Exxon Valdez* had reached the Alyeska Marine Terminal at 11:30 p.m. on March 22 to take on cargo. The crew included Captain Joseph Hazelwood and 19 crewmembers. The third mate was Gregory Cousins. At 5:00 a.m. on the 23rd, terminal crews began loading the crude oil onto the vessel. When it was loaded full and down, they left Valdez around 9:00 p.m. William "Ed" Murphy was the Marine pilot who had piloted her in earlier the night before and would pilot her back through the Valdez Narrows. The passage through the Valdez Narrows was uneventful. Captain Hazelwood did go below for a while, as Murphy had the con, piloting her through the Narrows. The captain going below was in violation of the Exxon Company policy, which required two ship's officers on the bridge during the transit of Valdez Narrows.

Murphy finished the passage, and when Hazelwood came up on deck at 11:10 p.m., Murphy disembarked at 11:24 p.m. He got off at the Pilot Station, which at that time was Rocky Point. He said goodbye to the captain and left the vessel. Ed Murphy would later testify that in no way did Captain Hazelwood have alcohol on his breath nor did he detect any odor. Captain Hazelwood got very poor press. There were false allegations that he was drinking, along with others to explain why the *Exxon Valdez* ran aground.

The more accurate account goes like this. The vessel was going out in the southbound lane. There was a traffic control system for an inbound lane and an outbound lane that were controlled by the traffic control station Coast Guard in Valdez. Captain Hazelwood preceded south. There were reports of ice coming out of Glacier Bay. He could see the ice ahead. He called the Coast Guard and reported the ice. In order to avoid the ice, he again called the Coast Guard and asked to change from the southbound lane to the northbound lane since there was no incoming traffic. This was about 11:30 p.m. The Coast Guard agreed and granted him permission.

The captain ordered a course change to cross the half-mile wide separation zone, fetching up in the northbound lane. After crossing and steadying her on course, he brought her up to speed.

Part XI *Tustumena* to Southwest Pilots   1980 - 1992

Captain Hazelwood turned to Mr. Cousins and explained all that needed to be done. He said, "It is all yours. I'm going below. I have some paperwork to do. Call me if you need me." Then Captain Hazelwood left the bridge.

As pilot on the bridge of the small cruise ship *World Discoverer* in Northwest Passage. 1997.

This is the only thing we sailors could find to fault him on: he left the bridge. It was that plain and simple. We are convinced with 99.99% certainty that the spill would not have happened if Captain Hazelwood had not left the bridge that night. Cousins

Part XI *Tustumena* to Southwest Pilots   1980 - 1992

was supposed to call the second mate, but hesitated because he knew that the officer to relieve him had worked over his shift, so he gave him a few minutes more of sleep. This was also in violation of policy, since there were not two officers on the bridge. The third mate was busy with something at the chart table. The lookout was on the starboard wing of the bridge and reported a flashing red light on the starboard bow. The third mate came in, looked out, and exclaimed, "Oh, shit!" He saw the buoy marking Bligh Reef.

At that instance, they ran aground. Captain Hazelwood, of course, returned immediately to the bridge. He assessed the situation and contacted the Coast Guard that they were aground and looked like they were spilling oil. Captain Hazelwood, according to the actual recording, did everything in textbook style regarding the grounding. He definitely was not drunk, as was reported by the press. He had, unfortunately, left the bridge. The rest is history. The spill extended south out of Prince William Sound and along the coast into bays and channels, up into lower Cook Inlet and around Kodiak, down Shelikof Strait, and west!

Part XI *Tustumena* to Southwest Pilots   1980 - 1992

The KGB

Word came that a KGB agent was coming on board to "monitor things." The morale of the crew went from cheerfulness down to gloom. The captain even said, "I didn't order anybody." The KGB agent who came aboard was named Vladimir Vladimirovich Putin—the same Putin who would become the President of Russia and the Russian Prime Minister.
~Captain Jack V. Johnson~

They called in help from all around the world to contain the oil spill. The government of the Soviet Union volunteered the use of one of their vessels, the MV *Vaydaghubsky*. She was a multi-purpose vessel: a harbor dredge, a small capacity tanker, and a skimmer. She had skimmers aboard that she could deploy on each side and skim up the oil. She was famous all around the world and had been used in other oil spills. I ended up being the pilot in her because of my knowledge of the Russian language.

The MV *Vaydaghubsky*.

Part XI *Tustumena* to Southwest Pilots 1980 - 1992

We kept the *Vaydaghubsky* just off the coast, trying to stay ahead of the spill. We concentrated down towards Kodiak and the peninsula skimming up the oil and working our way back. Everything was going fine. Captain Sergey Rekin was a really great guy. He was from the Russian Far East. His home at that time was in the Sakalin Islands, and that was where the *Vaydaghubsky* was based. The ship had a Russian interpreter, even though Captain Rekin spoke very good English. There was also a man from the Anchorage Russian community, who was born and raised in the Ukraine. His language skills were helpful. Then there was me, as the pilot. Iris was the Alaska Maritime shipping agent for Seward. That made Iris the agent working *Vaydaghubsky* on behalf of the ship's owners.

Iris was privy to the first conversations of the *Exxon Valdez* representative who came aboard to assess the situation with Captain Rekin. The *Exxon Valdez* man portrayed a totally different version of the account to the press and media than Iris had knowledge of as an Alaska Maritime agent. I later had an opportunity to set the record straight. I tried to be as vocal as possible. I was interviewed for several national spots, but when there are two narratives of the same account, it is hard to have your voice heard. As pilot in the *Vaydaghubsky*, we laid out a plan as to what was going to happen and proceeded along as planned. By this time the oil had reached Resurrection Bay near Seward. We started our skimming at the western entrance of Prince William Sound. As we moved along, it was a pretty happy ship. Everyone seemed to get along with each other. The cooks treated us as though we were royalty. Wonderful food! It was a good job.

The *Vaydaghubsky* was a multi-purpose vessel. She was a small tanker, a harbor dredge, and a skimmer. Her dredging apparatus were big arms that they would lower down and suck along the bottom and fill the central part of the ship with what was brought up. The skimmers on the *Vaydaghubsky* were Norwegian oil skimmers and weren't adapted as well as they should have been for the conditions we were under. We were doing a fair job, but they weren't doing as well as expected because of the heaviness of Alaska's black crude. I was on the

Part XI   *Tustumena* to Southwest Pilots   1980 - 1992

bridge with the captain and the chief engineer and mentioned, "These aren't working," pointing to the skimmers.

They agreed, "These Norwegian skimmers are not adapted to pick up this heavy oil."

I said, "Now, you're a suction dredge. I see these big dredging arms with the suction heads. Could you lower the suction dredges over the side and down to the water so they could suck up the oil?"

He thought it over and decided to try my idea. Boy, we really started to suck up the oil. It was working better than it had been, but still not as well as we'd like to see. Even though we were doing a pretty good job skimming, the oil was so heavy that the suction dredges weren't working as they were designed to work.

I pondered the situation and asked the captain and the chief engineer, "Could you lower them down in the water and tip the suction part 180 degrees and have it turned up and then go along with that in the water sucking up the oil?"

He thought it over and said, "Damn, that's a pretty good idea; it just might work."

So that's what we did, and man, we were really sucking up oil! We had made the adjustment. We were in business. We continued skimming and went down the coast from Prince William Sound, keeping up with the spill as far as Sutwik Island, which is southwest of Kodiak. That was the extent of the spill.

I was approached by the media to appear on the nightly news, after the ship had been skimming and doing so well. I conducted the interview from aboard the ship, telling of our success much to the chagrin of the Army Corps of Engineers. But as stated before, the message didn't seem to go far. They didn't want to hear that the Russian *Vaydaghubsky* was doing so well. The others were doing a fair job with their dredges, but not as good as our ship. They began casting doubt to the *Vaydaghubsky's* job performance and her necessity, saying she wasn't really needed, even though the *Exxon* engineer and I tried countering their allegations. So much misinformation was going out on the airways with conflicting stories about the Russian involvement. Even while I was airing my account of the positive

Part XI   *Tustumena* to Southwest Pilots   1980 - 1992

accomplishments of the Russian ship, the opposing channels were airing broadcasts of negative reports—of how the Russians were of no help and shouldn't be there. I was glad to offer a more accurate account of the whole ordeal.

Off Wide Bay on our way back with a full load of skimmed oil, word came that a KGB[118] agent was coming on board to *"monitor things."* (That was the term they used: *"monitor things."*) The morale of the crew went from cheerfulness down to gloom. The captain even said, "I didn't order anybody."

No one seemed to smile after hearing this guy was coming aboard. Sure enough, a small plane flew over and landed. The water was very calm. They sent a boat to pick him up. The KGB agent who came aboard was named Vladimir Vladimirovich Putin—the same Putin who would become the head of the KGB and then the President of Russia and the Prime Minister of Russia.[119] When Putin came aboard, he introduced himself to the captain, the engineer, and me. I introduced myself in Russian, but he spoke very good English, so it wasn't difficult to carry on a conversation with him. We got along famously, but the crew never did recover its cheerfulness.

The crew avoided Putin and anything he was doing, keeping close to themselves and minding their own business. They'd go around whispering instead of really talking. Putin took to hanging out on the bridge, talking to me; Jerry, the Russian businessman from Anchorage; the captain; and the mates. Everything seemed to be going nicely. I talked with him a lot, and we compared notes. I told him about my days in the 13th Tank Army 2nd Regiment B Company and about Major Serge Panamariov and Marshall Konev. Putin thought that it was outstanding I was in their Great Patriotic War.

We got orders to go back to Seward to discharge what we had and then stand by. As pilot, of course, I had the duty of taking the *Vaydaghubsky* back to Seward. Iris was the Alaska Maritime agent

---

[118] KGB is an acronym for the national security agency for the former USSR.

[119] In Russia, executive power is split between the President and the Prime Minister, who is Russia's Head of State.

Part XI *Tustumena* to Southwest Pilots 1980 - 1992

for Seward and the agent for our ship. She was standing by as we came in. I put the ship alongside the dock. The oil had gelled, making it somewhat difficult to discharge. Steam pipes and heating devices were brought in to get the oil moving.

KGB Agent Vladimir Vladimirovich Putin.

After all the paperwork was done, Iris thought it would be a good idea to have a crew party at our house. She told Captain Rekin that everybody in the crew was invited to our home for a party, including Putin. They thought it was a grand idea. It wasn't long before the crew finished everything for the evening and was in route to our house for a little relaxation. In the meantime, I had gone to the liquor store and got what I figured was enough booze: five cases of vodka, 12 cases of Budweiser beer, and a sundry mixture of brandy and gin—all the things sailors like to drink. Russian sailors are no different from any others, though they tend to favor vodka.

We were having a good time. The Russian ship's crew included four very attractive women. They were the cooks. When

Part XI *Tustumena* to Southwest Pilots   1980 - 1992

the women showed up at our little shindig, they were dressed to the nines. They wore lots of makeup, glitter on their eyelids, net stockings, high heels, and their nails done. They fell in love with our Newfoundland dogs. We have pictures of these beautifully dressed Russian women hugging our Newfoundland dogs. Those women were an exotic touch! Iris had invited a few of her local friends: her sister, Karol; a lady houseguest, Joan Skogan, who writes books for children; and a Japanese man from one of Iris' other ships. We had a full banquet spread with several Russian dishes like salmon roe and rice, as well as Russian dishes that I remembered from my childhood days in Kodiak.

The party was in full swing. The drinks were going down like snow in Yuma! Before long, the rug was rolled back, and a couple of Russian guests performed the Cossack dance for us. I joined in Cossack dancing and even surprised everyone by singing a couple of Russian folk songs that I had learned from my grandmother. Putin was among the celebrators. Iris noted that Putin had charisma, and Iris' sister, Karol, told her that Putin had the most "sex appeal" of all the men at the party. He had a presence about him.

Iris was the perfect hostess, as always. During some part of the evening, Iris starting reading palms. She did this from time to time, as one of her party favorites, and it is always a big hit. Everyone lined up to get his or her palm read, and to everyone's surprise, so did Putin. Iris read his palm. When she looked at his hand with the creases and crisscrossing of lines, she pronounced, "You are going to advance to high places."

He kept saying, "More, tell me more!" (And as the world knows, he did indeed advance to high places.)

The crew remained around for several days, trying to get the oil out of the dredge. Putin left shortly after the party, but we were able to see the captain and crew during the rest of their stay in Seward. I always look back with great remembrance at the tropical trees painted on our little barroom wall and recall how the soon-to-be Russian President shared a drink and got his palm read in our humble abode!

Part XI   *Tustumena* to Southwest Pilots   1980 - 1992

KGB Agent Vladimir Vladimirovich Putin on right, enjoying the party for the crew of the *Vaydaghubsky*.

As one can guess, I am fond of my Russian comrades and neighbors. Over the years, I have had several opportunities to use my language skills, often to the Russian's surprise and my advantage.

I was the pilot in a Russian vessel, the *Sulak*, out in the Bering Sea. I took the ship into Dutch Harbor. The captain was a Russian woman. The agent had asked me to stay aboard while they were getting clearance before returning to the Bering Sea. I was the designated pilot. I was waiting on the bridge after anchoring up, when one of the mates came up and told me that the captain would like me to join them in the saloon where they were having a meeting with the agent, customs, immigration, and agriculture people. I went down and everyone was having a drink. The captain turned to me and asked, "Would you like a drink?"

I declined, saying, "No, thank you. I'd better not; I am working."

She said, "Oh, well, never mind that. Here!" and she reached for a bottle whose label was in Russian. It said "Spirits."

Being able to read Russian, I immediately understood it was a bottle of 190 proof grain alcohol. She poured a big glass for me.

Part XI   *Tustumena* to Southwest Pilots   1980 - 1992

Everybody lifted their glasses and made a toast to the United States of America and down the hatch. I could barely breathe after swallowing my drink. She tried to pour me another, and I shook it off, insisting, "No more. No more!"

She said, "You don't want to toast the Soviet Union?"

I knew I had better not refuse *that* toast, so I reluctantly said, "Okay." But this time I grabbed the bottle of Stoli vodka instead of the 190 proof grain alcohol. I then told her in Russian, "I will drink this. I know what that is!" pointing to the "Spirits" bottle.

"Ohhhh!" She was taken aback and squirmed a little sheepishly, realizing I could read and understand Russian. She had a little egg on her face. Everyone got a big kick out of it.

The Alaska State Ferry dock used to be at the end of Fourth Avenue in Seward. This was before the building of the Alaska Sea Life Center. It was a nice dock. Once I had a ship come in on a beautiful summer day to the Alaska State Ferry dock, but another vessel was using the dock. Iris was the Alaska Maritime agent for the ship, and she contacted me to pilot the ship over to a dock on the other side of the bay. It was a tight fit, but I managed to squeeze the vessel along the little makeshift dock. Iris got the Coast Guard documents and all necessary papers ready for the ship. The captain was getting ready to have dinner, and as Iris was getting ready to get off the ship, he turned to her and asked, "Is there any place for my crew to get a drink?"

She answered, "No, it's five miles to the nearest bar, but I'm going to move the ship tomorrow, and you will be able to get off and go to a bar just up the street."

She didn't think much about it and left it at that. When Iris returned the next day to get the ship moved, the captain had a humorous story to relay to her. The sailors were told that there were no bars around for five miles and that they would have to wait until the ship was moved. They were not happy. Then they happened to see some bright lights a short distance away. They decided to hike over to the bright lights to get themselves a drink. They got quite a surprise when they arrived at the location of the bright lights. It was the well-lit Spring Creek Correctional Center, one of Alaska's two maximum-security prisons, complete with

Part XI *Tustumena* to Southwest Pilots   1980 - 1992

barbwire and armed guards. They had a bit of explaining to do to get out of that situation. Needless to say, no drinks were dispensed that night.

The next day the ship was shifted to the Ferry dock. Iris later told me that the captain went AWOL. Some members of a small Russian community, the True Believers, invited the captain to accompany them to their village, which is over 100 miles from Seward. While the captain was off on the visit, his crew went out of control with everyone, including the interpreter, getting drunk. When Iris made her courtesy call at the ship after a couple days, she sensed something was amiss when she saw several sailors loafing on deck, holding beer cans and cigarettes and ignoring her arrival. The tide was out, making the deck of the ship 15 feet below the dock.

The captain and crew were responsible for the safety of the ship's agent. Ordinarily, two or more crewmembers would have been right there to make sure she got down the ladder safely. Iris boarded and discovered everyone was drinking. It seemed the Russians had returned to the ship from their outing with the captain, as well as several women. Iris asked to see the captain. They started to take her to the captain, but they were so drunk they kept getting sidetracked and losing their concentration. The purser, who was also the translator, lured Iris into his cabin and wanted her to drink with him. Iris managed to get out of his cabin and demanded to see the captain.

Then someone ran up to her and in broken English announced, "We have a sick man. We have a sick man. He won't go to his cabin. You have to do something."

Iris saw the man lying on a bench, sweating and not able to speak. People were hovered around him. The ship's doctor showed up about that time. He referred to a doctor's book written in Russian and tried to translate what Iris needed to do. He thought the man was having a heart attack. Iris tried to get to the ship's radio to call 911 police dispatch in Seward to get an ambulance to the ship. Finally, Iris found the ship's radio operator and ordered an ambulance. Obviously, she never did see the captain.

Part XI *Tustumena* to Southwest Pilots   1980 - 1992

Her dealings with the Russians were not always this horrendous, though she did have ordeals of mates jumping ship and defecting. A while later, Iris got a phone call one evening at our home from a man who identified himself as an agent of the FBI in San Francisco. He asked for details regarding three Russians who had slipped away the previous night while their ship was at the dock. She was a little miffed and alarmed, thinking she was in trouble as the agent for the ship. After some discussion, the FBI agent finally said, "I hope they get away and start a new life in the United States. Thanks for your cooperation."

One year we had some big Polish fishing vessels called trawlers working in the Gulf of Alaska. Sometimes as pilot, I would bring in as many as four or five to the dock. The crew was always jumping ship. In fact, a lot of the Polish sailors who jumped ship are still living in Anchorage and Seward.

I remember one Polish trawler, where the captain said, "Well, I'm very happy to tell you, Pilot, nobody on my ship leaves. Everybody stays aboard."

I said, "I'm very happy to hear that, Captain," backing the ship out dead slow astern.

Suddenly three guys in the foc'sle head jumped off and onto the dock. I looked at the captain, "Looks like three of them just left."

The captain just shook his head, shrugged his shoulders, and said, "Oh, well..."

The Polish defectors were quite successful with the Polish communities throughout Alaska. Even the Russian Orthodox Church had a network set up to assist them in their defection. This, of course, was entirely against the law at the time because of the political asylum issues associated with Poland.

Part XII   Hard Sailing, Easy Life   1992-2006

Part XII   1992 - 2006

Telling Stories to Michener

*Never in all my dreams did I think
I would one day be entertaining James Michener
with my sea stories.
It was the greatest compliment!
~Captain Jack V. Johnson~*

August 16, 1993, I was climbing up a ladder to board a Japanese processing ship in Akutan. I got on deck when a boom came down and hit me, knocking me head first into and through a closed door! I hurt a bit—to say the least—but seemed okay. About two weeks later, I fetched up in Anchorage. I told Iris my neck felt funny. She told me to see Dr. Wickman, the well-known orthopedic surgeon in Anchorage. I dealt with the pain for a while longer until it got too bad and I decided she was right. I made an appointment. He listened to my concerns, and then ordered x-rays. He didn't seem too concerned and said to go have some coffee in the cafeteria while they processed the x-rays.

I had just sat down to enjoy a pleasant cup of coffee and a piece of pie when a voice over the intercom said, "Captain Johnson, wherever you are, *do not move!*"

Evidently, I had gone around those few weeks with a broken neck! To make matters worse, I had to wear that big cast around my neck and head for six weeks. But after four weeks, the cast came off, and I was back piloting.

The route through the Arctic Ocean and along the north Alaskan shoreline via waterways passes through the Canadian islands is exceptionally beautiful. It connects the Atlantic Ocean with the Pacific Ocean. I really enjoyed piloting cruise ships

Part XII   Hard Sailing, Easy Life   1992-2006

through the Northwest Passage.[120] Only recently has the Northwest Passage been open to regular shipping, because the ice pack that usually prevents it has broken up. Passage through the Northwest Passage is economical since the 4,300-mile route is shorter than the current shipping route through the Panama Canal. I was fortunate enough to make it through the Northwest Passage eight times!

Piloting cruise ships in Alaska enables you to meet a lot of people—some famous, some not so famous, but each trip I made new friends. I mentioned earlier that I had met the U-boat 123 commander Reinhard Hardegen, who led me to the Commander of U-boat 861, Captain Jürgen Oesten, who had sunk our ship SS *William Gaston* in 1943.

The smaller cruise ships were pretty laid back with 150 to 200 passengers. There was always some celebrity movie star or singing artist, political big shot, or well-known author on those cruise ships. Erma Bombeck, the comedic newspaper columnist, sailed once. I also have a postcard signed by Pamela Anderson when she was filming for the *Love Boat* television series.

In 1985, the author James A. Michener was with us through the Northwest Passage. James A. Michener was quite a guy. I liked him. I met Mr. Michener when I got a call from the dispatcher to fly out of Anchorage to Attu and meet a ship coming from the Orient to Nome. I was told James A. Michener was going to be flying with me to board this same ship. Knowing Iris was a fan, I asked if she would like to join me in Anchorage to meet Mr. Michener. She was delighted. I called my stepdaughter, Laurel, who was living in Anchorage, and had her pick up a couple of Michener's books for Iris to take to the meet and greet, hoping to get his autograph. Iris and I met at a small private Anchorage airport. I handed Iris the books.

When we walked into the room where everyone was gathering before boarding, Mr. Michener was already seated. He was a complete gentleman and stood up when Iris came into the

---

[120] Norwegian Roald Amundsen took three years to go through the passage in 1903. There wouldn't be a commercial ship to cross the passage until 1969 when oil was discovered in northern Alaska.

Part XII   Hard Sailing, Easy Life   1992-2006

room. Gathered round us were the pilot of the plane, the co-pilot, Customs, and other officials. We took a seat against the wall. I sat next to Iris. Iris positioned herself next to James Michener. Introductions were made, and of course, Iris got her autographs. Mr. Michener was dressed very casually and ordinary. Iris shared later that she liked him instantly, especially when she noticed lint on his dark socks. She thought, "This is a regular guy."

Michener asked the pilot who we were. It wasn't long before they zeroed in on me and began asking me questions. I took the opportunity and began holding court. The 45-minute wait flew by swiftly until it was time to board the plane for Attu. Iris remained in Anchorage with her novels, now personally autographed: "To Iris, James Michener." I wrote Iris from Barrow telling her more about Michener.

It just doesn't get much better than this.
Pilot on starboard wing of bridge of small cruise ship MS *World Discoverer* in Icy Bay, Alaska. Behind me is Mt. St. Elias. July 1993.

We arrived at Attu, where we joined the *World Discoverer*, a very luxurious ship. The cruise had originated in Japan. I was pleasantly surprised that Michener's wife, Mari Yoriko Sabusawa, was already in the ship waiting to join him. She was a beautiful Japanese American woman. As we proceeded along the coast

Part XII   Hard Sailing, Easy Life   1992-2006

towards the top of the world, it became routine to have Michener's request to "pass the word to the bridge: send the pilot down!"

The pilot, of course, was me. I always dressed sharp; after all this was a cruise with passengers who had a lot of money and were used to the finer things in life. I would be in fitted dress slacks, an expensive blazer, white shirt, and necktie. It wasn't hard to oblige Michener and respond quickly to the request. I would go down and meet with him at his cocktail party or at his table, whichever would be the case. As the pilot, I couldn't drink, though everyone else was partaking of martinis and the like. He'd have me tell sea stories. He was always taking notes. I guess I helped reference one of his passages in his book, *Alaska*.[121]

Never in all my dreams did I think I would one day be entertaining James Michener with *my* sea stories. It was the greatest compliment! The cruise ships were filled with passengers from all walks of life and professions, and the smaller size of cruise ships allowed us to get to know the passengers more intimately. We would always have something going on to entertain the guests going across the Arctic Circle. Once, the crew talked me into playing along and dressed me up as King Neptune. Here I was stripped to the waist wearing a crown. I have a picture with me on the throne and Mrs. Michener standing next to me with her hand on my shoulder.

Somehow my reputation preceded me wherever I went. It didn't matter where we'd end up, I would run into someone I knew. To illustrate this, I was pilot in the cruise ship the *Society Explorer* that flew the German flag destined to go through the Northwest Passage. The crew and Captain Aye were German. This was a very expensive cruise and carried a couple of hundred elite, wealthy, high-paying guests. We were hitting the villages along the way, the little hidey-holes up the coast from the Alaskan Peninsula.

In every small town we'd stopped in, along the way, I knew somebody from Dutch Harbor on north. We stopped over at Little Diomede Island out in the Bering Sea where you'd cross the

---

[121] A historical novel of Alaska written by James Michener, 1988.

Part XII   Hard Sailing, Easy Life   1992-2006

International Dateline—the place on earth where your bow could be in Monday while your stern was still in Sunday! The captain with several others of us went ashore and gathered in the schoolhouse. I was holding court when in walked Old Jake, the Village Chief.

He said, "Hello," to the captain, nodded his head to the others, and then made a beeline for me. Jake embraced me with a big hug along with all the other Eskimos, who were happy to see Captain Jack.

Captain Aye was beside himself. They were supposed to make a fuss over him. He looked at me and shook his head, "If we went to the moon, you'd know someone!"

I heard that statement, almost in those exact words, over and over again throughout my life. It sure didn't help the German captain's bruised ego. This went on all the way up the Alaskan coastline from Nome on north up to Point Barrow. It really rang true when some of my relatives came aboard with the City Mayor and Magistrate and made a big to-do over seeing me. The same thing happened; they came aboard, just nodded at the captain, and made this huge fuss over me.

I was pilot on bridge of cruise ship MS *Regent Star*.
Our vessel was on fire. SS *Rotter Dam* in background was taking
our 850 passengers and 400 +/- crewmembers aboard.
Captain, deck crew, some engine crew, and pilots stayed aboard.
Ship was towed to Whittier and later to Seattle. July 22, 1995.

Part XII   Hard Sailing, Easy Life   1992-2006

Another time, going into Aklavik on the Mackenzie River in Canada, the same thing happened. This is a difficult passage, and very few ships ever go there! I had been there two times and knew how to get in and out. We maneuvered the ship, tied her up to the dock, and were greeted by the Royal Canadian Mounted Police (RCMP). They warmly welcomed us. We went ashore, walked around the village, and fetched up in the schoolhouse. Soon the schoolhouse was filling up with Eskimos. And you guessed it. They all knew me. While refreshments were being served, Captain Aye mingled, admiring the uniqueness of this village and the remoteness of its location and beauty. He commented on it being like the "ends of the earth" and yet here were all these people. Then he looked at me and laughed, "Pilot, if you went to the moon, there'd be someone who knew you!" (Little did we know that he'd have a chance to verify this claim a few years later when I met up with him while on an excursion on the opposite ends of the earth in Antarctica.)

The same thing happened to me while I was fishing with Merrill Hennington out in the Aleutians. One day we pulled into Attu Island. No sooner had we tied up at dock, than a group of natives came running down the gangway waving and shouting, "Jack, Jack!"

Merrill looked at me and shook his head, swearing under his breath. He said, "Jack, you would know somebody even if it's on the moon."

One of my favorite stories involves a new Southwest Alaska pilot, Bob Baker, who had joined our association. He was a good pilot and one hell of a sailor, too. For some reason or another, Bob went to Russia. The way he tells the story, when he got off the plane, he had on one of our Southwest Alaska Pilots Association caps. He walked into the terminal at the airport in Russia where someone came up to him, looked at his cap, and said, "Southwest Alaska Pilots! Do you know Jack Johnson?"

Bob came back with that story and said, "I'm a son-of-a-bitch! Everywhere we'd go, somebody knew you." He continued, "And they didn't just know you there, but further on as well. I don't know how it happens, but everybody knows you, Jack!"

Part XII   Hard Sailing, Easy Life   1992-2006

Boarding log ship in Danger Bay, Kodiak, Alaska. 2000.

Part XII   Hard Sailing, Easy Life   1992-2006

It got to be a running joke that, no matter where we went, whatever godforsaken island or port we'd arrive at, someone would recognize me, and I'd meet up with an old friend. I have had several people sum it up in an old story about the Pope in St. Peter's Square. You see the story goes like this…

One day there were thousands of people crowded around to listen to the Pope. A couple of guys were passing through and stopped to see what all the commotion was about. Straining to get a glimpse, one of the guys leaned over and said to the other guy, "Who is that guy in the purple robe?"

"You mean the one wearing the purple robe and beanie?"

"Yeah."

"Well, I don't know who that guy is, but the guy standing next to him is Jack Johnson!"

Part XII   Hard Sailing, Easy Life   1992-2006

Around Cape Horn—Again

*It was very solemn to stand at this memorial,
which is a large sculpture featuring the silhouette of an albatross.
The dangers of sailing around the Cape
have made it an infamous sailors' graveyard.*
~Captain Jack V. Johnson~

In 1997, I had the opportunity to sail again around Cape Horn again. It had been decades since I had been to South America. The last time was in 1949 when I was in the *Passat*. Sailing around the Cape felt a little like coming home. It was happenstance working in my favor. One day, perusing the *Anchorage Daily News* newspaper, I came upon an advertisement for a yacht excursion around Cape Horn and south to the Antarctic. I told Iris I'd really like to make that trip. I'm not sure she has forgiven me yet for not taking her along.

I booked the excursion. It is quite a feat getting to Puerto Williams, Chile, where I met the *Mahina Tiara* and her captain and crew. First, I flew from Anchorage down to Florida and then to South America, landing in Santiago, Chile. Santiago is Chile's largest city. I spent a few days there before flying down to Punta Arenas in the Strait of Magellan.[122] From Punta Arenas, I took a little island hopper, DAP Airlines' small bush plane, to Puerto Williams.[123] It was a bumpy ride flying through the cloudbanks, playing peek-a-boo with the Darwin Cordillera Mountains, glaciers, and narrow fjords.

I met Captain John Neal, the owner of the *Mahina Tiare*, and his mate, Amanda Swan, in Puerto Williams. John said he was born on the banks of the Sudan's Blue Nile River. He sailed most of his life—logging over 257,000 miles at sea. He began his

---

[122] Strait of Magellan is named after the famous Portuguese navigator, Ferdinand Magellan, who discovered the area for Spain while looking for a passage to the East Indies.

[123] Puerto Williams is considered the world's most southern town. It is located on tiny mountainous Isla Navarino. A nearby island, Tierra del Fuego, was created by the strait and is divided in half between Chile and Argentina.

Part XII   Hard Sailing, Easy Life   1992-2006

passion by conducting sail-training expeditions. This allowed him to share his knowledge of sailing and his love of the sea. The voyages took place between Patagonia, Antarctica, Atlantic, Scandinavia, and the Arctic. I felt a real camaraderie with John. He was a guy who spoke my language.

Amanda, his shipmate, was also a remarkable woman. She took up sailing in New Zealand. Amanda competed in the first all-women Whitbread vessel, the *Maiden*, as a rigger in the Around the World Race. She held a New Zealand Commercial Launch Master and Ocean Yacht Master license. She joined the *Mahina Tiare* in 1994. She and John married shortly after our excursion.

The yacht we sailed in was a beauty. Her name was *Mahina Tiare*. She was a magnificent vessel designed for ocean sailing. The *Mahina Tiare* had started from Ushuaia, Argentina, on January 4, 1997. I joined the 47-foot sailboat and crew in Puerto Williams on the 8th of February. The entire expedition took five weeks. My time with them would be about 14 days. My portion of the route started at Puerto Williams, Chile, then on towards Cape Horn.

I remember going down one passage in particular. It was my job to watch for kelp and anything else that would hinder our passage. I told John, "Looks like we've got some williwaws out there."[124]

They are common in that part of the world. We were in the middle of one when John said, "Looks like we'll make it." But he spoke too soon. It laid us right over flat in the water. We managed to get her upright. We turned around and anchored, waiting out a cold front with the 60-knot winds to pass. The next day was a little better. We were standing seven cables off Cape Horn. This was the sixth time the *Mahina Tiare* rounded Cape Horn and my third time.

The *Mahina Tiare* went around to a little cove on the east side of the Cape, where a big mooring buoy was anchored. We tied on to it. It was magnificent. Cape Horn is the southern tip of the southernmost island and considered the headland of the Tierra

---

[124] Williwaw is an Alaska term for a sudden blast of wind. We saw lots of those in the Aleutian Islands and the coastal fjords of the Alaskan Panhandle and Peninsula.

Part XII   Hard Sailing, Easy Life   1992-2006

del Fuego archipelago of southern Chile. It's the most southerly point of the South American continent. Sailing the waters around the island are risky, with high winds, large waves, and strong currents. Only a skilled sailor can maneuver through the obstacles and dodge the icebergs found in this region.

The Chilean Navy keeps a station there, complete with a residence, utility building, chapel, and lighthouse. We went ashore and climbed the 182 steps up to the lighthouse, which is manned by six Chilean Naval Ratings. We visited with them for a while. I took a short hike to a memorial honoring the sailors who died while attempting to "round the Horn."

The Unknown Seaman's Memorial at Cape Horn.

It was very solemn to stand at this memorial, which is a large sculpture featuring the silhouette of an albatross. The dangers of sailing around the Cape have made it an infamous sailors' graveyard. After we visited there all afternoon, we continued on our voyage towards Antarctica.

We continued eastward to the Falkland Islands, stopping in Port Stanley, the capital and only true city in the Falklands. It is known for its whalebone arch, a totem pole, and several war memorials, as well as shipwrecks. We stayed a couple of days before heading south to Antarctica. That was some passage. With a force-8 westerly blowing, the seas were 30-40 feet high. Soon we arrived at our destination, the Palmer Peninsula. This was the

Part XII   Hard Sailing, Easy Life   1992-2006

second time I was in Antarctica, but there was no Johnnie Walker Red Label Scotch this time—John didn't allow alcohol on board.

Antarctica is the fifth-largest and the earth's southern-most continent. It covers the South Pole. It is known for being the coldest, driest, and windiest place on earth. This is probably due to having the highest average elevation of all the continents. It is considered a desert, even though it is covered by ice. It was a little difficult managing the elements while we were anchored there. We had to fend off icebergs, using a 14-foot "bergy pole" of carbon fiber with stainless spikes at the end of it.

Massive icebergs blocked us when we tried to sail through the Lemaire Channel. We had to make several attempts. Not much survives there other than seals and penguins. Ashore, penguins surrounded us. Penguins would literally walk up close to the boat as if to see what was going on. At sea, the seals and orca whales were very entertaining. It was exquisite. The southern region of the world flips its season, so since it was February, it was summer in Antarctica. We enjoyed the balmy 20 to 40 degree weather. You had to dress for comfort and practicality. Goggles were a necessity due to the snow and ice. The right gear was essential, especially when the high winds came. The secret to keeping warm in cold climates is layering. Even the gloves consisted of at least three layers. Similar to summer in Alaska, we experienced almost 24 hours of daylight, averaging about four hours of twilight. Did I mention the sunsets? They were spectacular!

On shore we visited with some scientists and support personnel at the British research station.[125] We assisted in the restoration of an old historic hut in Port Lockroy. It had been taken over by Gentoo penguins. There was penguin crap everywhere. I've shoveled my share of crap, but penguin crap is unique. Two of the Brits' crew boarded the *Mahina Tiare,* and we sailed over to Dorian Bay to check out another hut that had been built there 20 years earlier by Richard Atkinson. A film crew was there from ESPN filming an upcoming special.

---

[125] There were research stations from Argentina, Britain, Russia, Chile, and the U.S.A.

Part XII   Hard Sailing, Easy Life   1992-2006

In Antarctica waters, weather and ice are the greatest challenges. When reversing our voyage and returning to South America, we hit adverse weather. After leaving Palmer Station, we were blocked by ice and faced 40-knot winds in the Lemaire Straits. The GPS and radar helped us maneuver safely through the treacherous waters. We made stops in the Antarctic Peninsula and the group of islands known as the South Shetlands. The one stop we made on the mainland was at Faraday Station. While we were there, the MS *World Discoverer* was in the area. Captain Karl-Ulrich Lampe was surprised to see me. I didn't go aboard, just chatted with them for a spell.

Leaving Antarctica, we traveled back across Drake Passage to the Port of Ushuaia, the capital of the Argentine province of Tierra del Fuego. That's where we all paid off and had a farewell party — with Johnnie Walker Red, of course. After no booze on board ship, the Johnnie Walker went down like snow in Yuma. I spent a few days there. Ushuaia was unique. It had a prison for repeat offenders and serious criminals. An escape from Ushuaia had perilous consequences because of its location and terrain. It would be similar to Britain's Tasmania and the France's Devil's Island.

The *Society Explorer* was docked there, captained by my old friend, Captain Aye. I was really taken aback to see the *Society Explorer*. I met the chief mate Tilo in a bar, and after a few drinks, he wouldn't hear of anything other than my coming aboard. I went aboard and greeted the rest of the crew, most of whom I knew from Alaska. We went up into the bridge and out came Captain Aye. He took one look at me and did a double take. Then said, "Jackson Jackson, Pilot."

I corrected him, "Jack Johnson, Sir."

"Ah, yes," replied Captain Aye. "What are you doing here?"

I told him of my excursion to Antarctica. He acknowledged it was good to see me again and reiterated those words he had said several years back, "Ah, Pilot, if you went to the moon, you'd know somebody! Is it any wonder that we are here at the end of the earth, and I run into my ol' friend, Pilot Jack Johnson?" We all laughed.

Part XII   Hard Sailing, Easy Life   1992-2006

Then he quickly added, "You'll have to go to Antarctica with us!" I had to beg off since I had just come from there, but he grabbed my arm and motioned me back to a deluxe room and said, "This is where you will stay when we go to Antarctica."

I managed to dissuade him. It was a hoot to see all those familiar faces. I stayed aboard for a while and had dinner with them before returning to my hotel in Ushuaia.

In Ushuaia, I was doing a little souvenir shopping in a local establishment when I met a lady who raised Alaskan Husky sled dogs. She had overheard me say something about Alaska, and she introduced herself. Her connection with Alaska was her Alaskan Huskies. She and her husband raised sheep on their ranch just east of Ushuaia. She insisted I come and see their ranch and her sled dogs. I spent all day and ended up staying overnight at the ranch. They raised the huskies for dog sled races in the wintertime. They had gone to Alaska and picked up a breeding stock of Malamutes and Siberian huskies. She was inter-breeding the Siberians with the Malamutes to create her own specific breed of sled dog. She said she almost always placed in the winner's circle with her fine Alaskan Huskies. I have kept in touch with her and her husband over the years, sharing letters and pictures.

When I got back to Ushuaia, I ran into an airline stewardess whom I had met on the plane from Santiago to Punta Arenas. Her name was Inez Rodriguez. She was off for a month and traveling around on vacation. We ended up having lunch together. We flew together from Ushuaia to Punta Arenas where I had first met her. I have heard from Inez over the years.

From there, I went to Puerto Montt. I kicked around a while in Puerto Montt. I thought about buying some property in that area. Going over to an island, I looked at a parcel of beach property that was for sale, thinking Iris and I could have a place in South America. I never did make the purchase.

When I returned to Puerto Montt, there was a Japanese ship I had piloted in Alaska. It was a reefer ship (tramper) loading salmon. It seems to never fail: get me close to a port, and I am bound to run into a ship or people I know.

Part XII   Hard Sailing, Easy Life   1992-2006

My South American vacation was drawing to a close. I got in the plane and began the long haul of about 16 hours home to Alaska.

The *Alexander Von Humboldt*, three-masted barque.

Part XII   Hard Sailing, Easy Life   1992-2006

In 1998, I had the opportunity to sail in the three-masted barque *Alexander Von Humboldt*.[126] It sailed under the German flag. Ships like the *Alexander Von Humboldt* were wind-powered with tall masts in the "golden age of sail."

The ships are classified according to their rig, which is the number of masts and configuration of the sails. The *Alexander* was classified as a barque.[127] This was a common rig. She was a three-masted vessel with the fore and main masts square-rigged and the mizzen fore and aft.

Hearing about this ship, I got hold of them around November and was informed they started their cruises around the Canary Islands. The Sail Training Association of Germany (STAG) provided the crew and cadets. This was a group formed in 1984, modeled after the Britain Sail Training Organization to give opportunity for German youth, adults, ship owners, or sea lovers alike to taste and appreciate the finery of various masted ships at sea.

I was fortunate enough to sail in the *Alexander Von Humboldt*. They welcomed me aboard for a two-week sail around the Canary Islands. We were in the capable hands of Captain Rudolf Wittenhagen and Hein Behn. It was fun to watch the kids—the cadets—learning the rigging and out on the yards. It brought back a lot of memories.

She was fantastic, a beautiful little ship. After we made our way around the Canary Islands, it was off to the mainland at Agadir, Morocco. The crew went ashore, taking the opportunity to taste the Moroccan cuisine and have a few beers. The young people were very therapeutic for me. Even though I loved my job with the Southwest Alaskan Pilots Association, being in this three-masted barque tickled my fancy.

---

[126] Built in 1906 by a German shipyard. Originally named *Reserve Sonderburg*, after the scientist who used her for his scientific studies. In 1986, she was converted to a three-masted barque by the German shipyard Motorwerke Bremerhaven and re-launched as *Alexander Von Humbolt* in 1988.

[127] They required small crews and were great for coastal and off-shore sailing. Ships with this kind of rig could get more velocity from the wind current by pointing higher into the wind. This was extremely helpful when maneuvering in areas where changing winds like those surrounding a coastline were prevalent.

Part XII   Hard Sailing, Easy Life   1992-2006

August 1995.

I rejoined them the next year for the same cruise, but this time I did three cruises with them. The beauty of the area and warmth of the sun provided a much-needed contrast to the Alaska weather during the fall months. I soaked in all I could before returning. I never did return after that second time, even though I'd hear from them when they'd update me on their sailing dates.

Part XII   Hard Sailing, Easy Life   1992-2006

They even went as far as to call and try to get me to rejoin the STAG. It put a smile on this old sailor's face. Life has a way of moving past you. I had no way of knowing that my life was getting ready to face one of its hardest chapters yet to come.[128]

What I'd give now for another cruise in the *Alexander Von Humboldt*...

---

[128] *We Alaskans, stories of people who helped build the Great Land;* compiled and edited by Sharon Bushell, copyright July 2002; pgs. 80 – 86.

Part XII   Hard Sailing, Easy Life   1992-2006

Hard Sailing at 75

*My choices were either fight or flight. I chose to fight.
After all, I had never backed down from a good fight in my life.
~Captain Jack V. Johnson~*

In 2001 I sailed through my own personal terror. The doctors discovered a big cyst on my liver and a cyst wrapped around my heart. I spent 31 days in the Alaska Regional Hospital. After much testing and procedures, I was lying in the bed, helpless—which is not Jack Johnson style—when my wife, Iris; my sons, Eirik and Curtis; and daughters, Ola and Teresa came to see me. They arrived in time for more of the prognosis.

The doctor walked in with his usual non-bedside manner, announcing, "Well, you got cancer!" Later, it was explained in more details. I had cancer in the esophagus. My matter-of-fact doctor stated, "That's about the worse kind of cancer a man can get!"

After several consultations with doctors and specialists, they gave me four options: chemotherapy, radiation, surgery, or just go home and die. My choices were either fight or flight. I chose to fight. After all, I had never backed down from a good fight in my life, so why should I start now? I decided against chemotherapy for personal reasons—chalk it up to vanity—but I didn't want to lose my beard or my hair. I didn't want radiation—the idea of being cooked with radiation didn't set well with me. So I said, "Cut me open. Take it out."

On October 31, 2001, Dr. Richard Peters over at Providence Hospital in Anchorage did the surgery. He took out my esophagus, stretched my stomach out and up into the new esophagus, and took out my gall bladder and the cysts. I was in the operating room for nine hours. I have 67 stitches from one incision and 47 from another to add to my collection of tattoos. And that would have killed a mere mortal—they're just lucky it was me! I spent 17 more days in Providence Hospital. Finally, they turned me loose, and I spent another month on a day bed at the "boars' nest."

Part XII   Hard Sailing, Easy Life   1992-2006

I have never been one to lie around. It was one of my hardest battles to remain still while I was fighting to regain my health. Iris was by my side. The nurse visited daily to make sure the tubes were in position and to check my vitals. The physical therapist visited to help me begin the long process of regaining my strength. It wasn't the most restful period, with my days filled with visitors and family, all giving me warm wishes for a speedy recovery, but their visits helped to pass the time. Finally, it came time to remove the tubes. I was advised to stay close to the medical facilities in Anchorage. That meant I would have to make the "boars' nest" my home for a while, and Iris would be responsible for our home and pets in Seward.

There is a saying, "Physician, heal thyself." Well, I became my physician, changing my eating habits, working out religiously, and being my own health advocate. I even took up belly dancing. My doctor said it was good for the digestion.

As soon as I could, I went back to work with the Alaska Marine Pilots. I always have enjoyed learning and experiencing different facets of sailing. In February of 2003, I attended a manned model ship handling school at Port Ash, Australia. With its scale-model vessels and tugboats and a mini port, the Australian Ship Handling Centre at Port Ash outside Raymond Terrace looks like a fun park. But this is serious business. The facility is one of only four in the world. It provides training in ship handling for masters, ship officers, and pilots. They specialize in the practical aspects of ship handling and the control of ships at low speeds in confined and shallow waters with and without tug assistance. It was pilots training pilots and very hands on.

I took in a whale watchers' outing in Nelson Bay while I was there. On board, I tried to play the didgeridoo. It was a little different than playing the baritone horn of my youth.

Part XIII   2006 - 2010

Captain Ike & Me

I would actually be able to meet with my captain of the **Exodus** —
Captain Yitzhak Aharonovitch — Captain Ike.
Never in my wildest dreams did I imagine such a thing.
~Captain Jack V. Johnson~

Over the years I have contributed to many organizations and causes. Due to my passion for Israel and identification with the Jewish people, when I had the opportunity to attend a Jewish Gala event in Anchorage, I took it! The annual Jewish Gala raises money for the Alaska Jewish Museum. This particular year's fundraiser was to benefit the Alaska Jewish Museum and was held in November of 2006.

Our friends, the Siegels, bought a table and invited us to join them. I had worked with Richard in the Tustumena, and Iris was friends with his wife, Vicky. It was a dress-up affair, which always appealed to Iris. The evening was lovely with everything that suits my fancy: a delicious elegant dinner, wine, fresh challah bread, dancing, speakers, and to our delight, a silent and live auction. The silent auction was downstairs. Iris did her best to bid on several items. I pointed out the things I was interested in, like a menorah and other Jewish items. Then we fetched upstairs to join Richard and Vicky at their table.

It was time for the auction's live main event, a round trip for two to Israel with a guided tour by Rabbi Yosef Greenberg. How could I resist? I showed the brochure to Iris and said, "Pix, I'd like to bid on this."

She answered, "Jack, why do you want to do that?" She knew I was pro-Israel, but hadn't registered my connection through the *Exodus* except it was just another ship in another place.

I asked her, "Pix, how much can I bid?"

Part XIII   My Captain & Me   2006 - 2010

She answered, "How much is it worth to you? Why is this trip so important?"

I told her, "I want to return one last time to visit the graves of an old shipmate, Bill Bernstein, and Captain Ike. I want to see their graves and pay my respects before I die."

Iris and me at the Jewish Gala.

Iris looked at me, still confused, and now pondering how much time this spry 80-year-old had left. Then she handed me the credit card and said, "Go for it. Bid what it's worth to you."

The bidding was fast in the beginning, but slowed down until it was apparent there were just two of us—me and another

Part XIII   My Captain & Me   2006 - 2010

guy sitting in the back of the auditorium. The room was dark, and ushers with spotlights would shine down on the bidders to enhance the dramatic tension. The drummers brought the music up as the bidding got up in the high teens. The suspense worked up to the last bidder bidding $18,000. My bid of $18,500 took home the golden opportunity. I was elated. Iris was stunned—realizing I just spent $18,500 on a trip to Israel.

The ushers surrounded our table, and the hoopla continued. Everyone was clapping and congratulating us. Then came Rabbi Greenberg, whom I had not met before. This well dressed, articulate, Russian-born and Israeli-raised Jewish Orthodox Rabbi came up to our table and introduced himself. I responded likewise. As we began to talk and acquaint ourselves with one another, he asked me, "What prompted you to bid so much money for this trip? Surely you could have gone to Israel for a whole lot less?"

I mentioned that in 1947 I had shipped in the *Exodus*, but it was a failed mission to get refugees into Palestine, and that I would like to go and visit the grave of a fallen shipmate, Bill Bernstein, as well as pay my respects to Captain Ike's grave. (I had no idea he was still alive!)

The Rabbi became quite excited and said, "You were in the *Exodus*?" After that, our trip took a different focus. Rabbi Greenberg, who is well connected, made several phone calls, and the whirlwind began. I had always wanted to go back, and this time it was even more rewarding to have Iris by my side.

The celebration continued with lots of dancing and merrymaking, and I was up for it all, still elated over my newest opportunity.

February 14, 2007, we departed for our trip to Israel. The trip was arranged that we would fly to London, overnight and then on to Israel. It was a long trip. We left on a Friday, but being Shabbat, the Rabbi didn't join us until a couple of days later. When we landed, we were met by our guide and were taken directly to the Dead Sea. Our Israeli tour had begun. The driver had instructions to take us to a resort at the Dead Sea for the night. The resort gave suits to go into the Dead Sea and float. Iris' luggage didn't make it

Part XIII   My Captain & Me   2006 - 2010

when we landed in Israel. She was trying hard not to panic. We did a little sightseeing, ate at the buffet, and remained there until the end of Shabbat. The next morning, the driver showed up with Iris' luggage. She was relieved. After breakfast, he took us to Masada.[129] We left Masada and went to a few more tourist sites, taking most of the day. One of the highlights, according to Iris, was feeding the camels. I had had my share of the pesky creatures and wasn't too impressed, but she was delighted.

Dancing the Hora.

We did some shopping. I bought Iris a bracelet set with Dead Sea stones. We headed to Jerusalem and were pampered at the kosher hotel. Rabbi Greenberg arrived the next day and accompanied us to the "Wailing Wall" or "Western Wall," as others refer to it. We didn't actually go to the Wall, because Iris was with us, and they keep the men and women separate, but we could see where all the Jewish men were praying. We were privileged to be able to enter into areas that were restricted to most tourists.

While we were there, we were instructed to write prayers to stick into the crevices and cracks. It is believed that the Shekhinah (divine presence) resides there, so it is like making a local call to

---

[129] Masada was built by Herod, the Great between 37 and 31 BCE. According to the historian, Josephus, almost 1,000 men, women, and children burned the city and took their own lives rather than surrender to the Romans during the Great Jewish Rebellion.

Part XIII My Captain & Me 2006 - 2010

the Almighty. Iris and I both wrote down our prayer requests. Iris later told me that she wrote, "Dear Jehovah, please bless our family."

I wrote, "I hope I can come back again."

Rabbi Greenberg with Iris and me at the Western Wall in Israel.

An unexpected turn in our trip was when the tour guide announced he knew Captain Ike's daughter and told us that the captain was still alive. Amazing! Rabbi Greenberg quickly got on the phone and arranged a meeting. I would actually be able to meet with my captain of the *Exodus*—Captain Yitzhak Aharonovitch—Captain Ike. Never in my wildest dreams did I imagine such a thing. It was both humbling and honoring after all these years. We changed locations and stayed in Haifa. Haifa is one of Israel's largest cities.

Our hotel was just above the Russian district. I could read the signs and spoke to many of the local Russian residents. The next morning, we went to Captain Ike's in Haifa. Captain Ike had, like me, spent his years at sea. He even built his house in Zichron Ya'akov in the shape of a ship. When we arrived at the captain's home, there was already a gathering. The Israeli media had been tipped off. Cameramen and Orthodox reporters with untrimmed beards and pe'ot (side curls) were busy documenting the event.

Part XIII   My Captain & Me   2006 - 2010

Captain Ike and me on the cover of the *Israeli Post*. 2007.

The reporters kept questioning me as I walked up to the captain's home. I answered, "I decided that, if my captain was still alive, I had to meet him."

First seeing Captain Ike, I was taken aback at the sight of this vibrant, white haired, elderly gentleman in front of me. How did we both get to be so old?

"Yes, Ike, it's you – my Captain. You were a great captain," were the words I spoke to him with tears in my eyes. I joked with him, "Your hair isn't the same?"

And Captain Ike replied jovially, "Yes, I dye it!" At first, Captain Ike didn't recognize me after 60 years. It was understandable since he was 23 years of age and I was 21 at the time. He commented, "I really don't remember you. Are you sure that you were in the ship? We only had one non-Jew on ship."

Despite Captain Ike's confusion, I kept describing the events in the *Exodus* and the parts I played. It still wasn't clear to him. Captain Ike chain-smoked as I recounted how we left the port of Sète in France. I then began listing the members of the crew. He seemed to get excited since I had a good command of the details. He replied with a twinkle in his eyes, "You apparently were there, but I still don't remember, I'm sorry – but tell me more."

Part XIII My Captain & Me 2006 - 2010

I couldn't keep from crying. It was so rewarding to spend time with my revered captain. I said, "My entire body is excited to see you. I just don't believe that I'm meeting my captain once again. Even today you act as you did then, like a true captain."

I recalled, "I wanted to dive underwater and release the stern line that got fouled in the propeller, but you and Bill Bernstein, who was killed in the attack of the British, insisted on doing it yourselves, telling me that I was new and should move aside."

It was when I reminded him about my Second Mate's license that he seemed to remember. We talked for several hours recalling memories, moments of fear and courage. Captain Ike brought out his *Exodus* album, and we recalled the difficult battle and talked about how surprised we were that the British attacked in the open sea, and how the passengers threw potatoes and canned goods at the charging British. We remembered with pride tossing the brazen British overboard.

My Captain and me. 2007.

At the end of our visit, Captain Ike hugged me and said, "Thank you, thank you for doing this!"

Part XIII   My Captain & Me   2006 - 2010

The *Israeli Post* printed our reunion on the front page! Captain Ike and me were the headlines of the day and we were pictured on the deck of his home in Haifa.[130]

On the deck of Captain Ike's home
with Rabbi Yosef Greenberg and our guide. 2007.

As far as I was concerned, I was content and only needed to see Bill Bernstein's grave and go home. But that wasn't the case. We went back to Jerusalem and stayed. The VIP treatment continued when Iris and I were escorted to a meeting with Israeli dignitaries, including the former Prime Minister Benjamin Netanyahu. (Someone told me that they delayed a meeting with Condoleezza Rice in order to meet with me.) When we arrived at the Knesset, the Rabbi took us into a huge dining hall. There were many dignitaries grabbing a bite to eat. We had a prominent table. There was a lot of attention given to the Prime Minister's table and another gentleman that we later realized was the son of a war hero. The Rabbi seemed to know them. The Prime Minister came over to us and introduced himself, allowing us to take pictures.

---

[130] In December of 2009, Yitzhak "Ike" Ahronovitch, the captain of the *Exodus* ship died at the age of 86.

Part XIII My Captain & Me 2006 - 2010

**Iris, Benjamin Netanyahu, me, and Rabbi Yosef Greenberg.
February 19, 2007.**

    He took us to President Moshe Katsav's office. The President gave me an Israeli flag pin, which I wore on my lapel throughout the remainder of my visit (and proudly wear often). From there, we were taken into a large auditorium flanked with security. A Palestinian speaker, President of the Palestinian National Authority, Mahmoud Abbas, was holding court. From our location up on the balcony, we could see Condoleezza Rice seated below us. I surmised Condoleezza was miffed I was receiving so much attention.

    We meandered our way down to the floor of the great hall. Iris hadn't felt well directly after our visit to the dining room. Her nose had begun to run, and she tried to go get her purse to retrieve a tissue. Her big, black Neiman Marcus purse had been taken from her when we were checked through security. She needed the tissues she had tucked away in the side pocket. Trying not to be conspicuous, she pussyfooted her way over to the purse. But unbeknownst to her, I noticed several security guards following her. When she started to reach for the purse, a swift hand immediately stopped her. She didn't attempt again.

Part XIII   My Captain & Me   2006 - 2010

After the visit to the Knesset and being recognized officially by the Prime Minister, we continued on our tour. I went with the tour guide, while Iris spent the rest of the day in our hotel room, recovering.

I went sightseeing to Nazareth and the Sea of Galilee (the largest fresh water lake in Israel). Close to the Sea of Galilee, I could see the Golan Heights where I fought when I had enlisted in the Israeli army, the Israeli Defense Force (IDF), and exchanged fire during the 1967 Six Day War. As Iris was trying to rest, reporters started calling, asking for information and how they could get in touch with me. Iris told them I was out sightseeing and told them to call back later. One of the reporters did call back. She was making a documentary and wanted me in it.

I was taken to the National Maritime Museum in Haifa. A newspaper reporter showed up and vetted me. I guess she wanted to find out if I was legit. She pulled no punches and pressed me for details. I then became part of the National Maritime Museum chronicles. What an honor! Professor Gutenberg from the Hebrew University arrived at the museum and wanted to meet with me. He had been a youngster in the *Exodus.* The Professor was glad to talk to someone who had been there. I remembered him.

We talked about the voyage and the hardships, particularly about the latrines backing up and the wretched stench. I distinctly remembered him because Gutenberg wanted desperately to get out of the hold and up on the deck. I had roused up some paint and canvas and gave it to him, instructing him to paint the famous sign "Haganah Ship *Exodus* 1947." Gutenberg came out of the latrines and onto the pages of history.

He told me that the Israelis considered the *Exodus* a crucial point in securing United Nations' support for Israel. The Holocaust survivors may not have made it to Israel that day, but their voices were heard because of it. He continued, "Now you are a national hero of Israel, and we are going to strike a coin for you." The video of the meeting showed later on the television — but nothing ever came of the coin.

Iris had recovered and joined Rabbi Green and me. Our driver took us back to Haifa to pay our respects to Bill Bernstein.

Part XIII   My Captain & Me   2006 - 2010

We had arranged to meet Captain Ike there. The drive from Jerusalem to Haifa was an experience. The cab rides were something else. The driver drove very fast. He had at least two cell phones, and the Rabbi had three. They would talk simultaneously with people on each of the phones. It appeared that one was designated for English and one for Hebrew, and the Rabbi's third phone conversation was in Russian. I could understand bits of the Russian conversation. Iris thoroughly enjoyed watching them interact with their phone conversations, thinking it was hilarious!

Placing flowers on Bill Bernstein's grave.

Just before we made it to our destination, Iris suggested our guide stop and purchase flowers for the grave to show our respect. We arrived at Martyrs' Row cemetery in Haifa. The last time I was at that site was in 1947 when I helped wrap Bill's body in an American flag and bury him after his death in the *Exodus*. It

Part XIII   My Captain & Me   2006 - 2010

was hard to grasp that 60 years had passed since that fatal day. Iris took pictures, and I placed the flowers on the grave and said a prayer.

A short time later, Captain Ike and others arrived at the resting place. We paid our respects to Bill Bernstein, as well as to the two other young men, Hirsch Yakubovich and Mordecai Baumstein, who had died in the *Exodus* struggle. Their gravesites were two down from Bernstein's gravesite. A reporter Iris had talked to earlier met all of us there for pictures for the documentary she was filming. We continued on our tour for a few more days. The 10-day trip came to a close. We returned home, staying overnight in England once again, and enjoying a fine dinner and a nice glass of wine. It was a lot to absorb.

The front page of the *Anchorage Daily News*, April 2, 2007.

Returning to Anchorage, the circus continued. The media picked up on the story, running it on the front page of the *Anchorage Daily News*, April 2, 2007. The news stations interviewed us in the Rabbi's study downstairs in the Synagogue. I was interviewed for a Canadian online reporter. I received a lot of attention for what I had determined was the least productive part of my life's voyage. It was still baffling that a mission I had deemed a failure, was perceived a success by others.

Rabbi Greenberg summed it up when he said, "We thought it would be a wonderful trip to Israel, but it turned into the whole *Exodus* story! It was just unbelievable."

Part XIII My Captain & Me 2006 - 2010

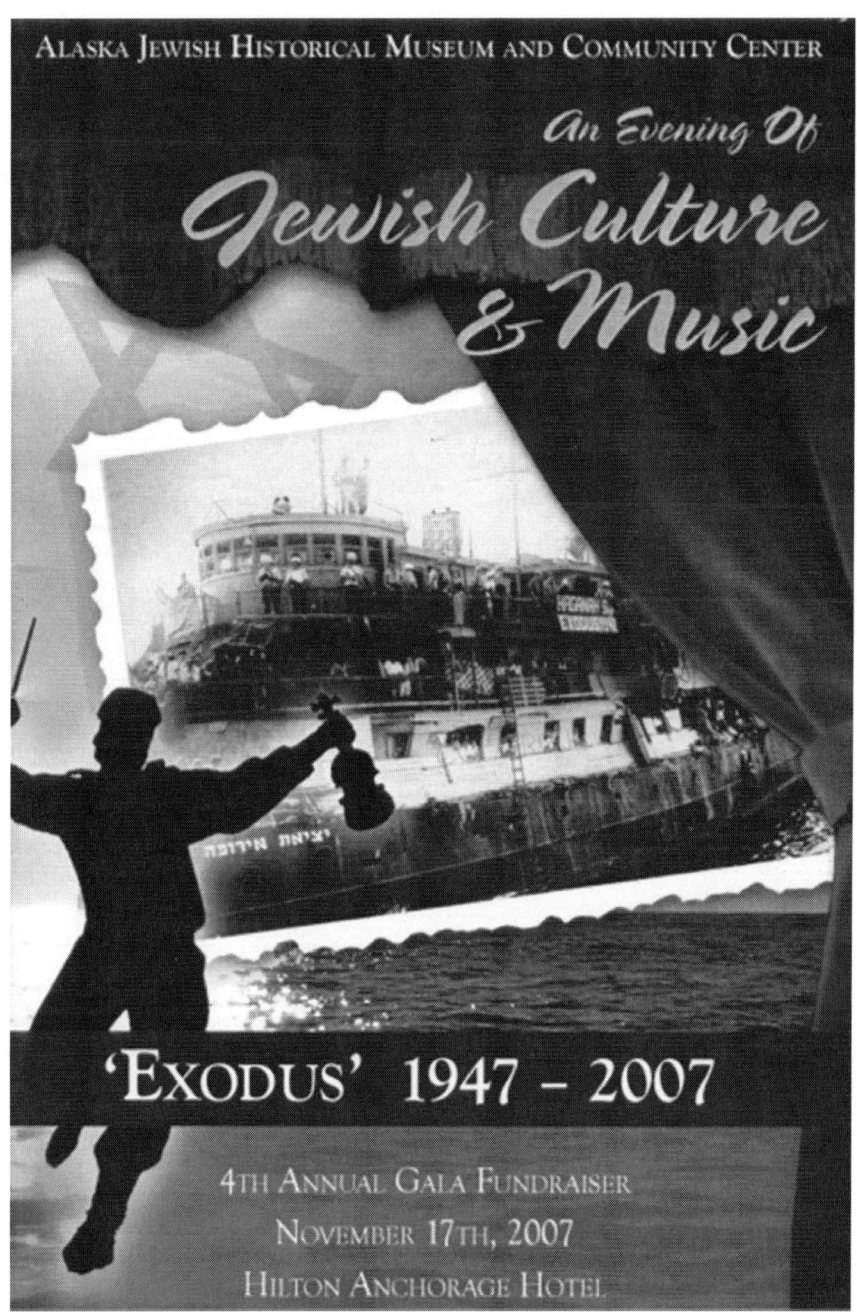

The evening's program.

Rabbi Greenberg went on to say, concerning our Exodus/Israeli connection, "To me, it's an unbelievable act of dedication and selflessness. In Jewish tradition we have a term for

Part XIII   My Captain & Me   2006 - 2010

it, which is called a very kind person—*hacidamato*—a very kind person of the nations of the world who really felt for the Jewish people."

I would have been happy to be just a donor for the Alaska Jewish Museum that was set to break ground in the spring. Now, I was going to be featured in one of their exhibits! The photos from our trip and my part in the *Exodus* were to be displayed when their museum was established.

Iris and me at the Jewish Gala.

February 2009, I accompanied Rabbi Greenberg, Perry Green, and Alaska State Representative, John Harris, to New York to be a part of Ruth Gruber's celebration on her contributions to Alaska. They dubbed it "The Night the 'Jewskimos' Came to New York to Honor Ruth Gruber." I was privileged to be part of the assemblage since Ruth's book, "Exodus, *the Ship that Launched a Nation,"* was part of her contribution. I was now a part of the story.

Part XIII My Captain & Me 2006 - 2010

In April 2009, three producers, Ruthann Crosby-Cleeves, Deborah Stone, and Pamela Doerr—hoping to make a documentary about the 1949 Alaska Airlines Yemen Rescue story, Operation Magic Carpet, were scheduled to make an appearance at the Alaska Jewish Museum board meeting. I was on the board, and that's when Pamela introduced herself. Her business partner, Ruthann, (who is also a Jewish Chaplain,) had arranged the meeting with the board and Rabbi Greenberg. Ruthann had been telling Pamela about my speaking engagement at "A Night to Honor Israel" city-wide event in 2008, and my involvement with the *Exodus* story. While they were waiting for the Rabbi to accompany them to Alaska Airlines' corporate office, my life took another turn, and like a lucky penny, it was heads up!

Rabbi Yosef Greenberg of Anchorage, left, and Jack Johnson of Seward recently visited Israel 60 years after Johnson was on the crew of the Haganah ship Exodus, which attempted to bring 4,500 Jews from Europe to British-controlled Palestine in 1947 after World War II. The British Royal Navy boarded the ship off the coast of Palestine, killing three people and removing the passengers in Haifa port for deportation to France. Johnson was reunited with the ship's captain, and both were featured in a photo in the tabloid newspaper Yediot Acharonot.

EXODUS: *Israelis give crewman hero's welcome*

Rabbi Greenburg and me.

They filmed an impromptu interview, and Pamela began asking questions about my experience in the Exodus. After that interview, she approached me about writing my life story. (Dana Stabenow, an Alaska mystery novelist, was the first to encourage

Part XIII   My Captain & Me   2006 - 2010

me.) Days later, I had my first meeting with Pamela and Ruthann. Pamela began meeting regularly with me, as she recorded and documented my stories. She would fly into Anchorage from Montana, or we'd meet via the telephone. In November, she and Ruthann, arranged to have me speak at the Alaska Jewish Museum. It was part of the museums open house.

Iris and I attended the Jewish Gala once again in November of 2009. Iris and I bought a table and invited Pamela, her mother, Barbara Carr, to join us, along with my daughter, Ola, and friends. That year the gala's special tribute was paid to the "Women of Valor." The guests of honor included my friend, Dr. Ruth Gruber, the acclaimed author, journalist, influential humanitarian, government advisor, advocate for holocaust refugees, and Friend of Israel, with also, Rosemary Schindler, the great niece of the legendary Oscar Schindler. I ate challah, drank good wine, danced the Hora, and felt like a kid again. Iris bid on several auction items, and we had even donated a few.

Part XIII My Captain & Me 2006 - 2010

Program for the Alaska Jewish Museum Event

Pamela and Ruthann arranged for me to speak on the following Monday evening at the Jewish Museum. It was part of the museums open house. Deborah Stone was credited for contacting Rosemary Schindler. She came and was featured in 2009 Jewish Gala. Pamela had made the arrangements for her flight and stay in Anchorage. Ruthann had arranged for her to speak at the museum. I think we made a pretty good pair.

Part XIII   My Captain & Me   2006 - 2010

Two beautiful women, on my right is my daughter, Ola. And on my left is Rosemary Schindler. And of course, the handsome guy in the middle is yours truly.

I always enjoy telling my story. My favorite audiences are students. Iris has been in attendance on various occasions when I would be asked to speak a few words at some engagement, and after a few minutes I would be holding court. She has commented that I held even the youngest participants' interest for well over an hour. In 2010, Pamela corresponded with Alex Bortnick, an East High School teacher, and arranged to have me address his U.S. History classes in Anchorage about my WW II experience in the Russian Army. The talks were originally scheduled to be in his classroom, but interest exploded, and on April 12th, I found myself in a large auditorium, holding court. The event was open to the student body, and the students filmed the entire session. They also honored me with a birthday cake since it was my 87th birthday.

Pamela and Alex arranged for a sequel. I went back the following year, again on April 12th, and the students again surprised me with a birthday celebration. Each time, I got to speak and have my cake, too! I was also surprised and honored to

Part XIII   My Captain & Me   2006 - 2010

receive a plaque from the student body signifying my accomplishments.

Guest Speaker at the Jewish Museum 2009

In the fall of 2010, the Gala came back around. Iris and I bought a table and again we had the good fortune of having family and friends gathered around us. Pamela joined us from Montana, along with her husband, Mitch and Barbara. The next year, thanks to Ruthann, Iris and I attended the Gala. This would be my last appearance. That's more than I can say for Nicolas Cage and John Cusack, who were scheduled to appear at the 12th Jewish Gala, but that didn't happen. I missed 2012's celebration

Part XIII   My Captain & Me   2006 - 2010

due to illness. Iris attended, however, and enjoyed herself immensely. She danced with Ruth Gruber's daughter and granddaughter who were there for the Anchorage Museum's "Ruth Gruber Photojournalist" exhibit, celebrating her life and accomplishments. Ruth turned 101 and was unable to attend.[131]

As we began to record my voyages, I have been honored to work with local celebrities in the Alaska community. Dave Stroh, who anchored the local KTVA CBS evening news and is "Super Dave" the radio DJ, lent his talents for a couple of days and interviewed me on a video segment, produced by Ruthann and Pamela. Several talented cameramen (including Ruthann's husband, Scott,) and computer techs worked to get the segment ready for viewing. Rumor had it that we stole Mr. Stroh away from Ted Danson, who was in Alaska on a movie shoot filming *Big Miracle*.

---

[131] http://www.tabletmag.com/category/podcasts/page/16/audio Captain Jack
http://www.press.feedmebubbe.com/press/?tag=newspapers-magazines
The Canadian Jewish News August 23rd, 2007 — Newspapers / Magazines
And we meet "Captain Jack" Johnson and find out how he "contributed to Jewish statehood" when he signed on as a Second Mate in the ship Exodus in 1947. [tinyurl.com/323ytg]
http://forward.com/articles/103392/alaska-honors-ruth-gruber/
http://northjew.blogspot.com/2007_04_01_archive.html

Part XIV   2006 - 2013

Poor Old Retired Pilot

*I came into this life on a promise and a fight,
and I intend on going out the same way, kicking and screaming.
Giving it the old Death Johnson punch!
Not out of fear of the unknown, but out of zest for life itself.
It has been exhilarating and a hell of a ride!
Reflecting back, it surely has been a long voyage home.
~Captain Jack V. Johnson~*

My saddest date was December 31, 2006. That's the date I retired after being with the Alaska Marine Pilots for 27 years. I have hated every minute of retirement. On the day I retired, they threw one hell of a retirement party. The big celebration was held in the Sheraton Ballroom in Anchorage to honor Captain Robert "Bob" Hendricks and me, as both of us were retiring that year. Everyone was dressed to the hilt. There were white cloth-covered tables, a fancy dinner, and an open bar. Most of us sailors appreciated the open bar the most. There were dignitaries about, like Senator Lisa Murkowski and others. The event had a slide show presentation. Iris had secretly gathered up several photographs of my escapades throughout the years. They presented them on PowerPoint up on a big screen in the ballroom.

Imagine pictures of me as a youth crossing the equator and then a shot of me sitting in a claw-footed bathtub filled to the brim with bubble bath, reading a paperback, tattoos and all! That got the crowd's attention. If the pictures weren't enough to embarrass me, they opened the floor up for *open mic*, so people could come up and comment on either of us.

Ed Murphy got up and said that, of the 23 pilots in our group, "When Jack comes into the room, you know there is a presence there!"

Part XIV   Poor Old Retired Pilot P.O.R.P

Flattering words are a little uncomfortable to digest. I'd have rather had him roast me than toast me! After the toasting, came the real roasting. Everyone had a Captain Jack story. And of course, the familiar phrase I have heard numerous times in my life crept up again in the roasting party, "If Jack went to the moon, somebody would know him."

As much as I like talking about myself, I am not comfortable being talked about, especially when I am present. To quote Iris, "When I first met Jack, I thought all his stories were just BS—then I began to meet his friends, and they told me the same stories. I was astonished—you mean they're all true?"

Iris was asked to sum up her life with me. She stated it matter-of-factly, "Sometimes, I hate him because he can be selfish, bossy, and domineering, and he always wants his way. But most people recognize his presence, that charisma when they first meet Jack. Jack has a trait to attract people from various walks of life, regardless of status, economics, or lifestyle. He knows people wherever he goes, and people don't forget him. Also, Jack doesn't let people go. He keeps them in his sphere. That includes girlfriends, would-be girlfriends, ex-wives, and even the offspring and grandkids of ex-wives. So what are you going to do with the son-of-a-bitch? Love him? Admire him? But unlike the other women in Jack's life, I was the one! I married the meanest man in Alaska, but that's just one side of the Jack Johnson coin. The other side is that I love him dearly! He is a remarkable man who lived an amazing life."

Hearing those words made me realize why we've stayed married all these years: she's the only one who tells it like it is and doesn't take any of my lip!

Until recently, I had spent most of my days in the "boars' nest"—our condo in Anchorage. The convenient location allowed me to keep busy with projects, lectures, and talks with various audiences. Every few weeks, I'd head home to "Toadstool Nine North," to check in with Iris and the dogs, or often she would come to the big city for a shopping run, doctor appointments, or a Nordstrom fix.

Part XIV Poor Old Retired Pilot P.O.R.P

Now days I'm just a P.O.R.P.—Poor Old Retired Pilot! Old pilots often refer to their jobs as 90% boredom and 10% sheer terror. Well, compared to my life before, I still have the 90% boredom—but I'd take the 10% sheer terror any day of the week.

Holding court with my favorite audience—students—at St. George Island, the Pribilofs, Alaska. Talking to the kids and showing them my tattoos! I had just piloted the first ship into the new harbor. 1989.

In 2012, Iris and I sold the "boars' nest" and moved anchor from Anchorage to Seward due to my increasing health issues. I just recently celebrated my 87th birthday. Friends and family gathered in our home in Seward all day long, and I had a captive audience, which delighted my soul. I had phone calls from my children and friends. I even received two phone calls from two prominent diplomats. The first call came from Vladimir Putin, the President of Russia. He has called me on several birthdays, but this was a highlight of my day. The next call that was unexpected

Part XIV   Poor Old Retired Pilot P.O.R.P

came from "Bibi" Benjamin Netanyahu, the Prime Minister of Israel. He wanted to know if I was ready to move to Israel. I replied I was ready and willing, just not quite able at the moment.

Today, I am in the hardest and longest battle of my life—my battle with my health. As with most things in my life, I take them on one day at a time. I have a picturesque view of Resurrection Bay and the majestic Kenai Mountains every day when I open my eyes. I can see the ships coming in and out of the bay. Eagles frequently soar past me as if to say hello. Hummingbirds gather outside on the deck. I have family and good friends surrounding me.

Part XIV Poor Old Retired Pilot P.O.R.P

Taking it easy, a long ways from salt water...
in *"me tropic kit"* at my villa in Sedona, Arizona. 1999.

Part XIV   Poor Old Retired Pilot P.O.R.P

And, of course, there is Iris, sweet Iris, at my beck and call. I know there are days she'd wish I'd call a little less, but she brings me joy just to see her face. During the healing prayers of a good friend, I have felt whisked away, transported to far away shores by the wave of a hand and familiar chanting. In a vision I saw monks surround me. They comforted me, and I nodded, but not yet—not yet.

I came into this life on a promise and a fight, and I intend on going out the same way, kicking and screaming all the way—giving it the old Death Johnson punch! Not out of fear of the unknown, but out of zest for life itself. It has been exhilarating and a hell of a ride! I am grateful to have shared my adventures with you. In fact, I have loved every minute of it. I wish you well, and may the winds of good fortune forever fill your sails. As always, smooth sailing. "As you sail through life whatever be your goal, keep your eye upon the donut, and not upon the hole."

As, I bid adieu, "I leave you with these parting words, "I don't know who the guy is wearing the beanie, but the guy standing next to him is Jack Johnson!"

Yep. This is me, before all my stitches.
I was showing off a few of my bits of skin art
while pilot in *World Discoverer*. Summer 1998.

PART XV Appendices

Brother Bucko Tramps at Sea

Oh, I signed aboard one Sunday
A salty guy.
When the sea looked green on Monday
So did I.
When we hit that storm on Tuesday
You could hear the captain shout.
If there's anything inside of man
The sea will bring it out.

Ship ahoy! Do you know where you're going?
Tramp ahoy. Do you care where you're going?
You're a cock-eyed hobo, with a cock-eyed soul,
And your cock-eyed soul is free.
You and I are brother bucko tramps at sea.

Went ashore down in New Guinea
To be tattooed.
When I got tattooed by Minny
I stayed tattooed.
She had an awful history,
But a swell geography.
When I left my fat tattooer,
She had designs on me.

Ship ahoy! Do you know where you're going?
Tramp ahoy. Do you care where you're going?
You're a cock-eyed hobo, with a cock-eyed soul,
And your cock-eyed soul is free.
You and I are brother bucko tramps at sea.

Part XV   Appendices

Scourge of the Bering Sea

By Ed McElroy, Chief Mate
RV *Acona*, Bering Sea Cruise, Fall of 1976

You can talk about your Blackbeards
And your Captain Blighs,
Old nutty Captain Ahab,
And all those other guys;
But there is one you may have missed
In perusing nautical history.
He's known from Dutch Harbor to Barrow
As "The Scourge of the Bering Sea!"

They say he hails from Seward
And his given name is Jack.
When they labeled him "The Scourge"
That seems to date way back.
But he differed from the pirates
In how he won his fame…
'Twas a driving lust for seafood
That gave "The Scourge" his name.

Aye, seafood was his weakness,
It was the devil's curse!
Each passing of the midnight sun
Just made it worse and worse.
He was attacked some years ago, they say,
By a school of giant herring.
So he vowed right then and there that he
Would eat up all the critters in the Bering.

The innards of a killer whale
Would never make "The Scourge" a meal.
So for dessert some jellyfish
And perhaps a Northern eel.

Part XV   Appendices

Davey Jones was his grocery boy.
He kept "Scourge" in supply
Of crab and fish of every sort
And giant octopi.
The Eskimos and Aleuts,
You could see them by the score,
Running to hide their kemuk and muktuk,[132]
When "The Scourge" came near their shore.
And all the mermaids would dive below
From the stormbound rocks on high,
For if "The Scourge" were 'ere to catch them
They could kiss their tails goodbye.

And all you fisherman, too, take warning,
For "The Scourge" is still around.
You may find him west of Adak
Or up Norton Sound.
He may raid your gear and crab pots
Of most anything you've caught,
Open up your hatches and eat
The whole damn lot.

And landlubbers also listen!
From Kodiak to Nome,
For you're not even safe in
The confines of your home.
He will pillage all your freezers
Of halibut, salmon, and sole,
And when "The Scourge" takes his leave
Better check your goldfish bowl….

---

[132] Whale cheek and whale blubber that is eaten.

Part XV   Appendices

In full uniform in Scotland, while visiting an old friend
from the Gordon Highlanders. 1982.

Part XV   Appendices

Affidavit from Oscar G. Callow

County of King } ss.

OSCAR G. CALLOW, being first duly sworn on oath, deposes and says: I have known Jack Virgil Johnson, now of 7506 Zurich Street, Anchorage, Alaska, 99502, since on or about April 29, 1942.

He had just survived a bombing raid aboard the British Merchant Ship "Empire City", and landed west of Alexandria, Egypt, north of El Alemein.

At that time I was Staff Sargent serving in "D" Company, Gordon Highlanders, 51st Highland Division, British 8th Army.

Johnson attached himself to my unit. Subsequently he enlisted in the field on May 4, 1942.

He served with me in "D" Company until August 2, 1942, when he volunteered with me to join the unique unit "Popski's Private Army. This was a long range desert reconaissance unit whose purpose was to turn (i.e. go behind) the enemy lines and/or infiltrate and commit sabotage against their rear supply points such as petrol, water, munitions etc. By this time I had been promoted in the field to Lieutenant and Johnson to Lance Corporal.

Johnson soldiered well, serving with considerable valour and upon being discharged, when his correct age was discovered was awarded the Military Medal and the Africa Star at a parade held for that purpose at base headquarters, Cairo, Egypt. This was on November 23, 1942.

I personally served through North Africa and all of Italy into Austria, being demobilized in February 1946 with the rank of Major.

I further state that over the years I have known Jack Virgil Johnson, he has proven to be industrious, honourable and of absolute integrity.

Oscar Callow O.B.E, M.F.

SUBSCRIBED AND SWORN to before me this 4th day of May, 1971.

William M. Christie
Notary Public in and for the State
of Washington, residing at Seattle.

DELBRIDGE, CHRISTIE
& THOMPSON
ATTORNEYS AT LAW
SEATTLE, WASHINGTON 98106
CH 4-4200

Part XV   Appendices

Foc'sle Chatter

by Les Kerton

Black Jack Johnson was quite a guy!
You never knew if he was telling the truth or a colorful lie.
He claimed to have been Bosun on the Barkentine *Ko Ko Head*,
Besides bragging about the ladies he had taken to bed.

It was said he could drink whisky by the barrel,
Yet, hold a tune and sing all the works to the Christmas carols.
If a fellow shipmate happened to pass away,
He could say a few parting words,
before sending him out to a watery grave.

He claimed to have sailed
in the German Barque *Pamir* in the nitrate trade,
Here it took top-notch sailors to make the grade.
We tried to catch him in a little white lie.
We never could no matter how hard we tried.

Johnson made the sea watches go fast,
With his great yarns and rhymes of the past.
As time went by we heard he got a mate's berth.
No doubt, filling the officer's mess
with his special brand of mirth!

Part XV   Appendices

While on a whale watchers' outing in Nelson Bay in Australia,
I tried to play the didgeridoo.
February, 2003.

Part XV   Appendices

Sailed Under 18 Different Flags

American (U.S.)
1939   *Charles R. Wilson* – three-masted schooner
1939   *C.S. Holmes* – four-masted schooner
         Various S.S. companies from OS to Master
         19 Liberty Ships
         Several T-2 Tankers and many others

Swedish
1940   MS *Mirrabooka* - First offshore ship
1941   MS *Kangangoora*

Norwegian
1946   MS *Thor Isle II*
1950   MS *Hindanger*

British
1942   SS *Empire City*
1944   SS *Sam Suva*
1949   SS *Adrastus* – Blue Funnel Liner

New Zealand
1946   *Pamir* – four-masted barque

Finland
         Passat – four-masted barque

Israel
1947   *Exodus* - Haganah Ship

Italian
1948   *Maria* – two-masted schooner

Swiss
1949   *Santa Maria* - small two-hatch freighter

Part XV   Appendices

French
  Le Ami Trois - The Three Friends - Our own tops'l schooner

Greek
  Ioannis Goulandris - modified Liberty Ship

Panama
  Transship *Alaska* - Chief Mate, then Master

Honduras
  Ex-Navy Y.O. Tanker - Carried Nitroglycerin

Russian
1988   *Sulak* - Ice pilot and pilot

Dutch
  Sunda - An American 8500 Victory Ship out of Batavia

Japan
1952   *Miho Marv* - Master

Liberia
1989   MS *World Discoverer* – Ice pilot in Northwest Passage, three times – West to East

German
1998   *Alexander Von Humboldt* - Barque – 2nd Mate and instructor to cadets

Part XV   Appendices

About the Author

Calling Alaska home, Pamela L. Doerr alternates hanging her hat between the Land of the Midnight Sun and Montana's Big Sky Country. Married for over 30 years and the mother of five children, she has scheduled most of her life around their events. She started her college education at Eastern Montana College in Billings, Montana, but by 2011 when she returned to continue, it had become Montana State University, Billings. She refers to her writing style as "eclectic" and has written magazine and local newspaper articles, as well as community productions. She works as a wellness and fitness coach, teaching clients to observe a healthy lifestyle, with a strong emphasis on balancing life's demands.

Being raised in the heart of the Matanuska Valley, she resonates with the pioneer spirit. Pamela has followed her Alaskan State Trooper husband all over the 49th state, moving their family from village to village.

Currently, she is the program director and host of a weekly radio program with her son, David. She is still closely involved with her family as they range from Pennsylvania, to Montana, to Alaska. Late in life she discovered running, and has run half marathons from coast-to-coast—Anchorage, Santa Cruz, Pasadena, Philadelphia, and Billings.

She met Captain Jack Johnson through the Alaska Jewish Museum. Intrigued by Captain Jack's stories and charismatic personality, she knew this was a story that had to be told. This is Pamela's first book.